The Marquess of ~~London~~derry

N. C. Fleming is Lecturer in Modern History at the Queen's University of Belfast. He was awarded a PhD by Queen's University in 2002 and called to the Bar of England and Wales in 2003. He is co-editor of *The Longman Handbook to Modern Irish History since 1800* (2005).

The Marquess of ~~Londo~~nderry

Aristocracy, Power and Politics in Britain and Ireland

N. C. FLEMING

Tauris Academic Studies

LONDON • NEW YORK

Published in 2005 by Tauris Academic Studies, an imprint of I.B. Tauris & Co Ltd
6 Salem Road, London W2 4BU
175 Fifth Avenue, New York NY 10010
www.ibtauris.com

In the United States of America and Canada distributed by St Martins Press, 175 Fifth Avenue, New York NY 10010

ISBN: 1 85043 726 2
EAN: 978 1 85043 726 0

A full CIP record for this book is available from the British Library
A full CIP record for this book is available from the Library of Congress

Library of Congress catalog card: available

Printed and bound in Great Britain by MPG Books Ltd, Bodmin, Cornwall Cornwall, from a camera-ready copy formatted by Catherine McColgan, Belfast.

Contents

Acknowledgements

A studentship and research fellowship at the Queen's University of Belfast enabled me to write this book and the doctoral thesis from which it is drawn. I have also received assistance from the trustees of the T. W. Moody Award at Trinity College, Dublin, and the Eoin O'Mahony Bursary, awarded by the Royal Irish Academy.

I would like to thank Lady Mairi Bury for access to the papers of her father, the seventh Marquess of Londonderry. I owe a similar debt of thanks to the Ulster Unionist Council, the Hertfordshire Record Office, and Mr Israel Shachter.

During the course of my research I benefited from the help of staff at the Public Record Office of Northern Ireland; the National Archive, London; the House of Lords Record Office; the Manuscript Collection, Trinity College, Dublin; the Department of Manuscripts, Cambridge University Library; Durham County Record Office; John Rylands University Library, Manchester; the British Library, London; Belfast Central Library Newspaper Collection; the Main Library, and the Institute of Irish Studies, Queen's University, Belfast; the Institute of Historical Research, University of London; and the Library of the *Irish News*.

I am grateful that so many people gave me encouragement and assistance throughout the course of this project, in particular Brian Walker, Gillian McIntosh, Alan O'Day and Bronach Kane. I also owe a debt of gratitude to Stuart Ball, Catherine Boone, Tim Bowman, George Boyce, David Cannadine, Fionnuala Carson Williams, Lester Crook, Peter Denis, Sheridan Gilley, Ben Goldsmith, David Hayton, Alvin Jackson, Steven Jaffe, Sir Ian Kershaw, the Marquess of Londonderry, Catherine McColgan, William Maguire, Patrick Maume, Roland Quinault, Nick Topping, and Charles Villiers. Last but far from least, I thank my family and friends whose support I could never have done without. To my mother and father I dedicate this work.

Introduction

Viewed in its entirety the political life of the seventh Marquess of Londonderry was unique. Although not one of the great men of history, he played an active part in events that shaped the destinies of Great Britain, Ireland and arguably, through his work at the League of Nations, the world. No other delegate to the Irish Convention at Dublin would subsequently sit at the Geneva Disarmament Conference determining the future of aerial bombing. No other mourner at the funeral of John Redmond, leader of the Irish Parliamentary Party, would later discuss international relations with the head of German National Socialism, Adolf Hitler. No other member of the first government of Northern Ireland had been driven through the streets of late-Victorian Dublin amid the pomp and splendour of a Viceregal parade. These contrasting aspects of Londonderry's career have led to contradictory assessments of his impact on British and Irish politics. Therefore, the founder of non-sectarian education in Northern Ireland is remembered by many for bigotry, particularly anti-Semitism. Although a consistent defender of the existence of the Royal Air Force, he has been found guilty of undermining the strength of the Luftwaffe. And while the Labour party labelled him a warmonger for his performance at Geneva, many more recall him as an arch appeaser of Nazism.

It was Londonderry's aristocratic background that bound together and gave coherence to much of his career. Rather than being motivated by a sense of national identity or political philosophy, Londonderry was by instinct, method and temperament, an aristocrat. In 1908 the political correspondent of *The Sunday Chronicle* described him as 'an aristocrat to the very tips of his fingers.'[1] The Countess of Oxford and Asquith noted that he was one of seven aristocrats who 'had the finest manners of any men that I have ever known.'[2] For Sir Horace Plunkett he 'belonged a little more to the later nineteenth century and early twentieth century than either of his parents.'[3] To Harold Nicolson he 'looked more like Lord Londonderry than any Lord Londonderry had looked before.'[4] For the socialite and diarist Sir Henry 'Chips' Channon:

> He was a good friend and grand seigneur of the old school; even
> his appearance was almost theatrically 18th century. Slim, with an
> elegant figure and pointed features he was red in the face and
> dressed with distinction. He was always gay and amiable and
> completely sure of himself.[5]

In her recent autobiography, Annabel Goldsmith, nee Vane-Tempest-
Stewart, recalled that her grandfather:

> was tall, thin and very bony, with an oddly high forehead ... I
> remember particularly his long blue fingers, which we used to
> imitate, rigid as they hit the piano keys. I wondered if he was ever
> able to unbend and I now find it difficult to understand how this
> stiff, formal man was able to justify his reputation as a great
> lover.[6]

If Londonderry was generally well regarded then why was his political
career replete with misunderstandings and disagreements with colleagues
and observers? The short answer is that he was too individualistic.
Londonderry never became an acolyte of the leading men and yet depended on their patronage, nor did he attempt to develop, or join, a group of
like-minded politicians. With leading society figures attending receptions
at Londonderry House, he had the opportunity and ability to ingratiate
himself, but the very existence of these functions, especially in the 1930s,
often had the opposite effect. Even when he periodically modified his
views to remain in tune with the leadership, Londonderry always displayed
an independence of mind that could make him unpopular with colleagues,
a strain that was particularly acute on the eve of a general election.

Often supporting unwelcome opinions, and lacking charisma and a
strong power base in the Conservative party, it is unsurprising that
Londonderry's career was not as successful as that of other contemporary aristocrat-politicians such as his cousin, Winston Churchill, or the
third Viscount Halifax. Nevertheless, this begs the question of why
Londonderry was able to succeed in achieving government appointments
throughout the 1920s and 1930s, when many had written off both the
man and his social order? The answer, rather surprisingly, is that
Londonderry, helped by his formidable wife and their immense wealth,
consistently acted as if aristocratic status, and the attendant influence it
carried, was an appropriate and effective means of obtaining political
office. Indeed, it was this attitude that made Londonderry such an indi-

vidualistic politician, one reluctant to give up the traits that defined his very existence. That this approach succeeded, at least in securing political appointments for the seventh Marquess, highlights that even in a period of declining fortunes for the aristocracy, the adaptation of aristocrat-politicians to this trend could vary considerably.

Aristocratic decline was undoubtedly a feature of British and Irish politics from the 1880s, but the effect of this can be exaggerated. It is probably more instructive to regard the period between the 1880s and the 1940s as one of transition, when traditional authority did not so much collapse, but instead gave way to the unstoppable march of legal-rational authority, culminating in the 1945 election victory of the Labour party. Even in the interwar period, noble rank, to say nothing of the untitled gentry, still proved a useful entrée to the House of Commons: at the general election of 1935 the peerage returned thirty of its sons to the lower house.[7] And although the House of Lords had its powers blunted by the 1911 Parliament Act, peers continued to be a conspicuous presence in the Conservative cabinets of Andrew Bonar Law and Stanley Baldwin. Many of Londonderry's appointments, successes and failures, were either because of, or facilitated by his aristocratic background. The influence of his father, a former cabinet minister, was instrumental in Londonderry's selection as the MP for Maidstone in 1906. After years of obscurity on the backbenches, Londonderry's patrician performance at the Irish Convention of 1917 to 1918 led Churchill and Walter Long to insist that he receive junior ministerial office in the post-war Coalition government. His aristocratic aloofness from populist Ulster unionism made Londonderry a credible Minister of Education in the troubled first government of Northern Ireland. The General Strike and miners' strikes of 1926 should have ended any hopes Londonderry might have had for a political career in Britain. Instead, he called for sacrifice on all sides, echoing the One Nation rhetoric of the Conservative leader Stanley Baldwin, and was rewarded in 1928 when Baldwin appointed him First Commissioner of Works. When the National Government was formed in 1931 Londonderry had already achieved a significant political profile. And yet his appointment to that government, and soon after the cabinet, was and continues to be widely attributed to Lady Londonderry's controversial friendship with the Labour leader and man-of-the-hour, J. Ramsay MacDonald.

Despite, or perhaps because of Londonderry's wide-ranging involvement in the high politics of Britain and Ireland, there has been no attempt, until now, to map out and critically analyse his 'political life'. When each of his political roles is considered separately, as they often are, and only then in a few sentences, the longevity and variety of Londonderry's career is overlooked. This is not to say, however, that his life has not been considered at all.[8]

In his *The Londonderrys: A Family Portrait* (1979), H. Montgomery Hyde charted the history of the Londonderry dynasty and devoted a considerable portion of the book to the seventh Marquess and his wife. Hyde's talent as a popular historian was certainly evident in his survey of the earlier marquesses and marchionesses of Londonderry, but his account of the seventh Marquess and his wife lacks systematic analysis and verges on hagiography. This is partly a reflection of Hyde's intimacy with the Londonderrys, one that brought both privileged access and the restrictions of friendship. Indeed, it is hard not to regard Hyde's book as an apologia, for it ignores uncontroversial yet relevant aspects of Londonderry's political career, preferring instead to focus on the contentious areas and adhering uncritically to the Londonderrys' viewpoint. Moreover, as it is argued in chapter 7, Hyde was a silent collaborator in Londonderry's short book on appeasement, *Ourselves and Germany* (1938), and may also have assisted him with his memoirs, *Wings of Destiny* (1943). Together they constitute much of the source material for Hyde's own book, not to mention the many other accounts that have had cause to make reference to the controversial career of the seventh Marquess.

If Londonderry has until recently suffered from a degree of neglect, then the same cannot be said of his famous wife. As a formidable political hostess, Edith, Lady Londonderry, has received the attention of both populist writers, such as Anne de Courcy, and scholars of women's history, in particular Diane Urquhart and Susan Williams.[9] The source material for much of this work is Edith's autobiography, *Retrospect* (1938), and her private papers at the Public Record Office of Northern Ireland.[10] The centrality of Lady Londonderry to the career of her husband is something that these writers are keen to stress and this study in no way challenges. That Edith continued the tradition of salon politics into the 1930s is a major theme of this study, for such activities were seen by many as outmoded, and yet they remained popular with the great and good until 1936, when Lord and Lady Londonderry began their association with Nazi Germany. Moreover, as this analysis will confirm, the role of family, past, present and future, is vital to any understanding the aristocracy in general, and the Londonderrys' political ambitions in particular.

Given the scholarly neglect of Londonderry's political life it is useful to outline some explanations of why this might be the case, and what benefits there are from a critical examination of his career.[11] As has already been mentioned, Londonderry was not a great man of history, but this study does not claim that he was or that he should be regarded as such. Indeed, it would be a victory for the critics of biographical analysis if such studies were restricted to the famous or infamous.[12] If not a great man, Londonderry has remained a shadowy but definite presence in the interwar high-politics of Britain and Ireland. It is known that he played a part in some of the great controversies of that period, but little has been said on what that role involved. Perhaps the explanation lies, in part, on the reluctance of historians to consult the Londonderry papers at the Public Record Office of Northern Ireland. Those who do mention Londonderry in their work prefer instead to rely on *Ourselves and Germany* and *Wings of Destiny*. As is evident from this study, any reliance on these two books will present a distorted picture that borders on literary interpretation. For it is only through a detailed and rigorous use of the vast archive that constitutes the Londonderry papers that the actions and significance of Londonderry's career can be fully understood. Londonderry was aware that *Ourselves and Germany* had implicated him as an arch appeaser of Nazism, and that the government restrictions imposed upon his memoirs had curtailed his efforts at vindication. Given this, Londonderry hoped that his private papers would exonerate him.[13] This study does not seek to fulfil his wishes, but it is important, at the outset, to acknowledge the subject's opinion that such a study would rescue his reputation. Should it do so, it will be by default, for it is not the purpose of this critical analysis. That purpose is twofold, to remove the shadow that has obscured what is a remarkably revealing career, and to explore aristocracy in Britain and Ireland at a time when it was under siege and considered outmoded. These are overlapping aims, for Londonderry, while not representative of the aristocracy per se, did represent in his career the diminishing continuation of traditional authority at a time when the public sphere was more legal-rational than ever before. Moreover, as a case study it affirms the observation of Jonathan Powis about the historiography of aristocracy:

> Rapid growth in the study of social history has made the sheer
> fact of aristocratic power (and its tenacity down the centuries)

increasingly visible. That tenacious hold requires analysis: and so
far as possible analysis which discards anachronistic assumptions
about the inevitability of decline.[14]

I

Why should the Londonderry family, and the seventh Marquess in particular, have felt that it was worth expending so much time and effort in the
pursuit of a political career, especially at a time when such influence was
in decline? To answer this it is necessary to appreciate the centrality of
power to the history of aristocracy. However, given the inherent difficulty of defining the nature of power, even aristocratic power, themes relevant to this topic will be examined through an outline history of the
Londonderry dynasty.

In his survey of constitutions, Aristotle defined *aristokratia*, or aristocracy, to mean rule by the best, and although this included oligarchies, the
definition was not restricted to them.[15] However, by the eighteenth century the term 'aristocracy' was being applied to a stratum of society that,
to varying degrees, inherited wealth, political privilege and rank: a class of
people who were literally born to rule. In the localities in which aristocratic families owned land, their authority was significant, although this
often depended on the proximity and size of rival landowners. For this
authority to translate into a prominent role on the national stage, aristocratic families generally needed to possess greater wealth, rank or input
into the state, through either inheritance or a will to power.

John Stewart was one of many Presbyterian Scottish settlers who
occupied land in Ulster granted by James I in the early sixteenth century.
Stewart's property was relatively small and his pedigree questionable, so
when his great-great grandson, Alexander Stewart (1700–1781), sought
to extend the family's resources, he had to venture into business and
commerce, first in Belfast, and later in London.[16] Alexander Stewart's
fortunes were improved when he served a term as MP for Londonderry
City in the Irish House of Commons, an assembly dominated by the sons
and agents of Ireland's landed elite. However, Stewart's real success was
in marrying his cousin, Mary Cowan, the daughter of Sir Robert Cowan,
onetime Governor of Bombay. The marriage helped to consolidate and
extend the resources of both families, Mary having inherited the fortune
her father had amassed during his time in India.[17] Their combined wealth
allowed the Stewarts to purchase in 1744 the adjoining manors of

Newtownards and Comber, both in County Down. The family then moved from their original home at Ballylawn, near Moville in County Donegal, to a demesne near Newtownards, originally called Mount Pleasant, but later renamed Mount Stewart. The onward march of Alexander Stewart was soon halted however when he failed to secure the local political interest, it being retained within the family of the former owner of the property. Nor was he successful in being elected an MP for Belfast due to disagreements with the first Marquess of Donegall.

If Alexander's progress was halted then his son Robert (1739–1821) took the family to new heights. Robert successfully sought the hand of Lady Sarah Seymour-Conway, the daughter of the Marquess of Hertford, a wealthy landowner in County Down who in 1765 was appointed Lord Lieutenant or Viceroy of Ireland. Hertford, not surprisingly, was keen to look after his son-in-law and solicited him a peerage, but Stewart preferred instead to represent County Down for the independent, or non-Tory, interest in the Irish House of Commons. In this he succeeded, and five years after Sarah's death in 1770, Robert married Lady Frances Pratt, daughter of the first Earl Camden, Lord Chancellor of Great Britain. Just as Hertford had helped Robert, so too with Camden. Robert's sons were sent to Eton and Cambridge, and after Robert had lost his seat in the Irish House of Commons, Camden secured him an Irish peerage in 1789 as Baron Londonderry, with a seat in the House of Lords at Dublin. In 1795 the second Earl of Camden, as Lord Lieutenant of Ireland, had Londonderry raised in the peerage as Viscount Castlereagh. The following year he was raised yet again, to Earl of Londonderry, enabling his son Robert to be styled Viscount Castlereagh (1769–1822). It was for Castlereagh's services to the state that Londonderry's title was raised finally in 1816 from an earldom to a marquessate.

The famous political career of Viscount Castlereagh—he was only Marquess of Londonderry from 1821 until his death the following year—is not dealt with here. However, it is important to acknowledge that he was the first of his family to hold a truly significant place at the centre of the state. It was to Castlereagh that future generations of the family would look back with pride, although this legacy was not altogether positive, for Castlereagh's suicide only fuelled gossip that the family shared his mental instability. Nor were Castlereagh's great political legacies, the Irish Act of Union (1800) and the Congress of Vienna (1815), beyond controversy, although many at the time and ever since hailed them as great successes. Alongside the accumulation of political capital,

Castlereagh married Lady Amelia Anne Hobart, daughter of the second Earl of Buckinghamshire and heiress to her mother's fortune. Impressive as this match was, it was as nothing compared to that engineered by Castlereagh's half-brother and successor as third Marquess of Londonderry.

The third Marquess (1778–1854) had served in the army with some distinction before settling down, with the help of Castlereagh, to a diplomatic career in Berlin and Vienna. For these services he was in 1814 created Baron Stewart of Stewart's Court and Ballylawn in the United Kingdom peerage. Six years after the death of his first wife—Lady Catherine Bligh, daughter of the third Earl of Darnley—in 1812, Lord Stewart married Frances Anne, daughter of the Countess of Antrim and her first husband, Sir Henry Vane-Tempest. Frances Anne was the heiress of vast estates and an immense coal mining fortune amassed by the Vane-Tempests of County Durham. The couple moved to Wyndham Park in County Durham and soon after purchased property at the coastal town of Seaham. By the time Stewart inherited his half-brother's titles in 1822, Castlereagh having died without issue, the new Marquess had two large properties on either side of the Irish sea totalling around fifty thousand acres. Also in 1822, the family purchased a large London property, Holdernesse House, on the corner of Park Lane and Hertford Street. This building, later known as Londonderry House, was intended to impress and secure the place of the now immensely wealthy Londonderrys at the heart of London society. Upon becoming the third Marquess, Londonderry resigned his ambassadorship and insisted that the government satisfy his claims to advancement in the United Kingdom peerage, a generous pension, and government office. The Tory Prime Minister, the second Earl of Liverpool, only assented to the first of these, creating him Earl Vane and Viscount Seaham. It was not uncommon for holders of Irish peerages to seek 'advancement' to the British peerage, it being deemed to confer more status on the holder than Irish titles. From the government's standpoint, it allowed them to add fresh members to the House of Lords, and in Londonderry's case it also acted to satisfy a claim to further honours without bringing him into the government.[18] Londonderry therefore did not enjoy the political career that the second Marquess had achieved, in part, because his own odd behaviour was attributed by gossips to the same madness that had ruined his half-brother. But it was his implacable opposition to parliamentary reform that ultimately ruined Londonderry's political reputation, ensuring that the first Duke of Wellington—with whom he had served in the Peninsular War—did not appoint him to the government. However, the third Marquess could take some comfort from his appointment in 1842 as Lord Lieutenant of County Durham, for this official recognition of the family's local importance confirmed their place at the heart of Durham conservatism, a position they retained until the 1920s.

The most significant success of the third Marquess was his marriage to Frances Anne. Despite her husband's failings in obtaining government office, Frances Anne was successful in using the rituals of society to court highly placed politicians like the young Benjamin Disraeli, and secure the marriage of one of her daughters to the Marquess of Blandford, later seventh Duke of Marlborough. The offspring of this marriage included Lord Randolph Churchill, father of the future Prime Minister, Winston. Frances Anne's efforts at salon politics were similarly rewarded when Disraeli assisted the political careers of her sons and stepsons.[19]

Following the death of her husband in 1854, Frances Anne took a part in managing the Londonderry coal mines, including new pits sunk at Seaham. In doing so she not only broke with traditional expectations regarding the role of women, but also the presumption that aristocratic owners of industry should leave the day-to-day running of such matters to others. Ownership of the mines protected the Londonderry family from economic and political decline; unlike landowners that depended on agricultural holdings, those with mineral deposits or urban land were not adversely effected by the growth of industry and commerce. This ensured that by the 1880s, far from being in decline financially, the Londonderrys were among the top-twenty wealthiest families in the United Kingdom, with a gross landed income of around £110,000.[20]

Like their forebears, the fourth and fifth marquesses of Londonderry were expected to pursue a career in politics. As we have seen, Frances Anne did her best to promote the interests of her stepson, Frederick (1805–1872), who became the fourth Marquess of Londonderry in 1854, and her own son, Viscount Seaham, who inherited his father's United Kingdom peerage to become the second Earl Vane. The fourth Marquess had been one of two MPs for County Down since 1822, and briefly held government offices under Wellington, as Lord of the Admiralty, and Robert Peel, as a Tory Whip in the House of Lords. If he was an able politician, the collapse of these two ministries—in 1829 and 1834 respectively, both not long after his appointment—gave him little opportunity to demonstrate it. Like his father he had to settle instead for a lord lieutenancy, this time in County Down, although he was also made a Knight of St Patrick, the highest order of chivalry in Ireland. The fourth Marquess spent the last decade of his life suffering from mental illness. He died in 1872 and was buried at Newtownards.

As the fourth Marquess left no heirs, his half-brother, Lord Vane, became the fifth Marquess of Londonderry (1821–1884). Like Frederick, the fifth Marquess had served as a Conservative MP, in his case for County Durham, before succeeding to the earldom. And like his father and brother, the political career of the fifth Marquess was also unremarkable. Although Disraeli ensured that he received the honours then due to a man of his rank—the Order of St Patrick in 1874 and the lord lieutenancy of County Durham in 1880—he was not judged suitable for government office. This hiatus in the political fortunes of the Londonderry family was by no means unusual in the aristocracy, but the situation might have been different had the wives of the fourth and fifth marquesses possessed the political determination of Frances Anne. As Diane Urquhart has outlined, such influence could be crucial in aiding the careers of their family.[21] But the energies of Frederick's wife were devoted to religion, she having converted to Roman Catholicism in 1855. And far from the fifth Marquess consolidating and extending his local power base, he preferred instead to live at Plâs Machynlleth, his wife's estate in Wales. Nevertheless, if the political careers of the third, fourth and fifth marquesses are judged as failures, then it was because they were unable to take advantage of their inheritance. The family, however, had retained its substantial wealth and status, and it was this that the sixth Marquess and his wife utilized successfully to gain office, albeit under fortuitous circumstances.

The sixth Marquess of Londonderry (1852–1915) was educated at Eton—where he was Arthur Balfour's fag—the National University of Ireland, and Christ Church, Oxford, during which time he was known as Viscount Seaham.[22] Following his father's succession as fifth Marquess in 1872, Seaham's courtesy title changed to Castlereagh, and it was as Viscount Castlereagh that in 1875 he married Lady Theresa Chetwynd Talbot, eldest daughter of the nineteenth Earl of Shrewsbury. Emotionally, the marriage was not happy due in part to Theresa's passionate indiscretions—satirized by Vita Sackville-West in *The Edwardians*—a trait her eldest son would inherit.[23] Politically however, Theresa's passion for politics and her unceasing quest to advance the family would prove highly important in returning the Londonderrys to government.

Castlereagh followed tradition and sat in the House of Commons from 1879 until his father's death in 1884. It is significant that he represented County Down and not County Durham, for his association with Irish affairs was to leave a deep mark on his political career. When the third Marquess of Salisbury formed his second government in July 1886, he invited Londonderry to become Lord Lieutenant of Ireland. The posting was significant for several reasons. When he sat for County Down, Londonderry was one of many grandees in Ulster who met the challenge of nationalism by enhancing alliances with other pro-Union groups in the region. This involved joining the largely proletarian and petit-bourgeois Orange Order, and acquiescing in the development of an independently minded group of Irish Conservative MPs at Westminster. Even with the defeat of W. E. Gladstone's first Home Rule bill in 1886 and the return of a Conservative ministry, tensions remained in Ulster where many Unionists feared not only Irish nationalism, but also the 'Unionist' government's attempts to kill nationalism through ameliorative legislation. Londonderry therefore occupied an uneasy position, conscious of his status as a leading light for Irish Unionists, but also the member of a Unionist government concerned to ensure party unity and survival. Nevertheless, the posting itself did not demand too much from the holder except immense wealth—it being the most expensive viceroyalty outside India—for the political work was largely in the hands of Arthur Balfour, Londonderry's Chief Secretary at Dublin Castle.

Londonderry's appointment was also significant in that it came at a time when the politically active peerage had responded to franchise reforms and a more critical public sphere by making the House of Lords work effectively. Salisbury was crucial to this process, balancing the need for the upper house to appear constructive and pragmatic, while also ensuring that peers occupied around half the number of executive offices. Andrew Adonis has demonstrated how adaptability and professionalism on the part of these peers allowed traditional authority to survive at the heart of government until the Liberal victory at the 1906 general election.[24]

Londonderry was not only useful for his Irish connections, but also for his political and financial position in County Durham. The more practical concern of financing politics nationally was also a factor, for contributions by Tory peers to central funds increased after 1885, amounting to less than half of all monies raised. So it is little wonder that following his posting to Dublin, Londonderry served as Postmaster-General from 1900 to 1902, and thereafter in Arthur Balfour's government as President of the Board of Education. From October 1903 he also served as Lord President of the Council.

This phase of what might be called constructive aristocracy had from 1902 begun to unravel. This was in part due to internal Unionist divisions on the question of tariff reform, although it was exacerbated by their being out of office from 1906, replaced by a Liberal government intent on significant reforms, culminating in the 1909 Budget Crisis. It was a period when the Londonderrys could have lost the political capital they had gained under Salisbury and Balfour. But circumstances would ensure that this was not the case, in particular the crisis of 1912 to 1914 that surrounded the third Home Rule bill. For the Irish question not only returned the sixth Marquess to national prominence, it also paved the way for his son to begin a career in politics that would last until the 1940s.

II

Charles Stewart Henry Vane-Tempest-Stewart was born on 13 May 1879 at 76 Eaton Place, London, the second child and first son of Lord and Lady Castlereagh. The early life of the future seventh Marquess of Londonderry was one of seemingly unruffled financial, social and political privilege. Charles, or Viscount Castlereagh as he was known from 1884, was fourteen years old when he first attended Eton, having spent the previous few years at the preparatory Mortimer Vicarage School at Reading. He later acknowledged that he failed to distinguish himself at school either academically or physically.[25] So instead of university, he chose to enrol as a cadet at Sandhurst Royal Military College, the army being 'the aristocratic profession par excellence'. If Castlereagh's academic abilities continued to let him down at Sandhurst, then his pedigree would ensure he achieved a prestigious posting following his passing out in June 1897: the Royal Horse Guards or 'the Blues'. Cavalry regiments were 'the most glamorous and exclusive element in the army', thus making Castlereagh's appointment as adjutant of the regiment at the age of 22 all the more notable.[26]

Alongside his military duties, Castlereagh played an active role in society and court. In this social scene he met Edith Chaplin, daughter of an MP and former Conservative cabinet minister, Henry Chaplin, and Lady

Florence Leveson-Gower, eldest daughter of the third Duke of Sutherland. Only months after they first met, the couple were married on 28 November 1899, at St Peter's, Eaton Square, London. Edith would be an enormous asset to her husband, for like Frances Anne and Theresa, Edith possessed a passion for politics and a determination that the family use whatever advantages they had to aid the political career of her husband.

As the son of a marquess and cabinet minister, Castlereagh grew up in a world of privilege, politics, government and royalty. His mother pressed upon him the importance of a political career, telling him stories about his great ancestor and namesake. His father introduced him to the various institutions he would one day inherit, the mining business, the social role of Londonderry House, and the family's prominent position in the local affairs of both Ulster and County Durham. The sixth Marquess also ensured that his son became acquainted with political proceedings, from parliament through to routine party meetings. Nor was the young Castlereagh allowed to watch from a distance. He was eight years old when his parents entered Dublin in state in 1886. As he sat in the coach with the Viceroy and Vicereine, Castlereagh—following instructions given to him by his mother—tipped his hat to the cheering crowds that lined the streets.[27] It would be the first of many ceremonial functions he would be obliged to perform by virtue of his rank. Such displays promoted the image of a governing class, but the spectacle bellied the reality of an aristocracy tenuously holding on to its stake in the government.

So determined were the Londonderrys that Castlereagh make a mark in politics that they forbade him from seeing action in the South African War of 1899 to 1902. Castlereagh was, after all, their only surviving son, his younger brother Reginald having died in 1899. This restriction was met with great resentment, all the more because Castlereagh enjoyed the soldiering life and did not look forward with any joy to a career in politics.[28] While his brother officers were serving their empire, Castlereagh remained at home, living the life of a gentleman—the hunt, polo, horse racing and society functions—and performing the ceremonial duties he had been born to fulfil. Indeed, the only time Castlereagh's military career and the Boer conflict converged was in 1900 when he commanded Queen Victoria's escort in a parade to celebrate the relief of Ladysmith. The elderly Queen was impressed by her escort and asked that the Castlereaghs visit her at Windsor Castle.[29] Her death in 1901 provided

Castlereagh with another opportunity at ornamental soldiering when he was appointed aide de camp to Lord Wolseley. Edward VII had assigned his Field Marshal the task of formally announcing the succession to other monarchs, so Wolseley and Castlereagh toured the courts of Europe and beyond, visiting the masters of a world that was to vanish during the First World War.[30]

A similar fate would await the aristocratic character of government in the United Kingdom, one presided over by an aristocratic sovereign. However, before the era of popular monarchy, the Saxe-Coburgs were happy to flaunt their friendship with the higher aristocracy, including the Londonderrys. In 1902 King Edward sponsored the Christening of the Castlereagh's first son, Robert. The following year witnessed visits by the King to both Mount Stewart and Wynyard. Not only was the latter to mark Londonderry's appointment as Lord President, but it involved convening the Privy Council at Londonderry's house, reputedly the first time this had been performed at such a location since 1625.[31]

Castlereagh's final years outside parliament, from 1903 to 1905, were taken up touring the empire, an Edwardian version of the European grand tour that had characterized earlier aristocratic travel. Accompanied by his wife, whose illness had prompted the trip, Castlereagh sailed to Bombay on the same vessel as the Viceroy of India, Lord Curzon. They spent Christmas 1903 with Curzon near Calcutta, and during their subsequent tour of the subcontinent the Castlereaghs met and stayed with Indian princes and British provincial governors. India would feature in Castlereagh's future career, for the visit made him an immediate supporter of limited plans for Indian self-government, and his first visit to the Northwest Frontier would be repeated three decades later, on that occasion as Secretary of State for Air.[32] Before returning to Britain in the second half of 1905, the Castlereaghs travelled through Singapore, Hong Kong, Japan, Canada and New York.

Towards the end of 1905 it was clear that a general election loomed in the New Year. From 1903 the Conservative and Unionist government of Arthur Balfour had been compromised by divisions on the question of tariff reform. It resigned on 4 December to be replaced by a Liberal administration under Sir Henry Campbell-Bannerman. Although Londonderry was determined that the moment was right for his 26 year old son to take a seat in the House of Commons, Castlereagh did not want to leave the army. However, a sense of duty, not to mention the threatened loss of financial help from his parents, ensured that his father's will was obeyed. Castlereagh later admitted: 'my father was very anxious that I should stand for Parliament ... He even thought I was wasting my time, enjoying myself with my soldiering. All during that autumn he was constantly urging me to find a seat somewhere.'[33] Lady Castlereagh later recorded that it was with 'a heavy heart my husband agreed ... and I cannot think that I was any help to him in this decision. I much preferred the easy going soldiering life, but the fiat had gone forth.'[34]

With many of the safer Unionist constituency-nominations already allocated, including the family palatines of Down and Durham, Castlereagh haunted Conservative Central Office in search of a constituency near London. He failed to get anywhere when he attended interviews at Unionist associations in Chatham, Shrewsbury and in the capital. It was only when Londonderry sought the help of a former cabinet colleague and fellow free trader, Aretas Akers-Douglas, that Castlereagh became a viable candidate for the constituency of Maidstone in Kent, where Akers-Douglas was a prominent landowner.[35]

Tariff reform dominated the 1906 general election, although home rule for Ireland and the education reforms piloted through parliament by Londonderry also featured prominently.[36] As tariff reform was such a divisive issue within the Unionist party, Castlereagh preferred to address the Maidstone association on his opposition to home rule. It was a strategy recommended to him by the prominent Irish Unionist Sir Edward Carson, for it was an issue in which Castlereagh could claim a family interest and one on which Unionists were resolutely united. Carson attended Castlereagh's first meeting to help him gain the nomination and reported back to his confidant, Lady Londonderry:

> it was very full and many could not get in. Castlereagh was very well received and made a sensible short speech, not touching on fiscals and leaving the bulk of the evening for me. I was quite delighted with the way he met people, and he was affable and jolly with them.[37]

Castlereagh's speech also sought to associate himself with his father's recent education reforms, a topic that like Ireland was used to promote Tory unity. However, if Castlereagh sought to inherit his father's mantle, then he was also wary of their inescapable association.[38] For it was Londonderry who had sparked off the most recent dispute between

Joseph Chamberlain and Balfour on tariff reform. On 1 November 1905 at Sunderland, Londonderry urged caution publicly on the question of tariff reform and warned his audience that Chamberlain's policy might split the Unionist party.[39] Chamberlain's immediate response was to attack Londonderry, but it was soon clear that his real target was Balfour.[40]

On Christmas Eve 1905, staying at his house, Springfield, at Rutland, Castlereagh informed Lady Londonderry that his adoption for Maidstone would be a 'very near thing', that 'there was a good chance, I think, as they like a lord.'[41] It was therefore from the very outset of his political career that Castlereagh was convinced that his background was not a barrier to office, that it could even be played up in order to help his chances. And if he was complacent or even arrogant in thinking this, especially at a time when many aristocrats were loosing their confidence about remaining a force in government, then the Maidstone constituency association clearly agreed with him. Having been adopted as their candidate, Castlereagh chose to carry on with the style of politicking that aided him thus far. This, he hoped, would help him overcome the serious obstacles that stood in his way of winning the constituency. These not only included his recent arrival to the area and his lack of experience, but also the more serious difficulty of winning the seat from a sitting Liberal, the businessman Sir Francis Evans. Given that both men were free traders, the central issue at the election would invariably centre on the background of either candidate. Unable and unwilling to deny his high birth, or even compensate for it, Castlereagh played to the gallery, encouraging his mother to help and give 'the Maidstone people a show' by making an appearance in the family carriage.[42] She did not fail him and combined regal tours in her coach with speeches and canvassing.

Castlereagh's return was very much a family affair, from his father's intervention in finding a constituency to the assistance of his wife and mother on the stump. This was typical of a style of electioneering that was fast dying out, but Castlereagh's success in achieving the nomination, and afterwards the seat, did little to shake his confidence in the old order. However, Castlereagh found even this distasteful to his finer sensibilities, informing his mother that: 'I shall be heartily sick of this vote cadging in a very short time'.[43]

After polling day on 12 January, Castlereagh received news of his slender victory over Evans by 132 votes. Given the Liberal landslide that had decimated Unionist representation throughout Britain, 367 seats to 157, it is unsurprising that elements of the press viewed Castlereagh's victory as remarkable.[44] Nor did the election heal Unionist divisions over tariff reform; indeed, the party ranks were divided between 109 tariff reformers, 11 'Free Fooders', 32 supporters of Balfour, and five undecided. The subsequent period would be an immensely difficult time for the Unionist party and the aristocracy in particular; the latter becoming the party's only parliamentary bulwark against a reforming House of Commons and the target of much Liberal invective. As if to underscore how much had been lost, the hopes of some aristocrats that the organic society championed by Edmund Burke might resurface, if suitably cultivated, were dashed brutally by the return of 53 MPs for Labour, alongside the now inevitable encampment of 83 Irish nationalists.

More immediately, Castlereagh found his return challenged a fortnight after polling. Maidstone's reputation for electoral corruption, the national swing against unionism, and the narrow margin of Castlereagh's victory may all have influenced Evans' decision to contest the result.[45] Other than that, it is hard to discern if his claims of bribery had any validity, but we do know that at least one of Castlereagh's local activists was sure that there had been 'elaborate care taken to prevent anything of the sort.'[46] Evans' election petition contained 'ninety-seven allegations, comprising specific and general bribery by money, treating in public houses, distribution of free meat, illegal voting, and unlawful payments to voters for travelling expenses.'[47] From reports in the local press, it would appear that Castlereagh treated the challenge with a light heart. On the sixth day of the hearing in May 1906, the 26 year-old MP was 'cheered on his arrival at the Court House, while Sir Francis Evans was greeted with hisses'. Castlereagh is reported as having given 'a witty defence under cross examination', but he may have went too far when he fell asleep during the hearing, sitting as he was at the front of the courtroom at the side of the judge's bench. Matters became more serious when the MP endured a grilling from Evans' barrister, but within a week the petition was dismissed.[48] With Castlereagh now secure in the House of Commons the Londonderry dynasty appeared safe for another generation.

The Londonderrys had determined that their son would carry on the family tradition of parliamentary representation, but they also cultivated in him a sense of duty that would sustain him in politics long after their deaths. At his son's delayed coming of age celebrations at Mount Stewart in 1899, the Marquess hoped that the assembled tenants 'would not deny that Lady Londonderry and he had done their best from his birth to bring up their son in the way he should go, and to realise the great responsibilities that in the future must be his. They had attempted to bring him up the way an Irish landlord should go.'[49] Their tutelage had a profound impact on Castlereagh, for he not only accepted their charge, but he adopted the methods of constructive aristocracy that had been so successful during his father's period in the Salisbury government. There is no indication that he ever doubted his right to have a leading role in the political sphere, a consequence of his parents' influence no doubt, but also an intellect that was too reliant on assumptions. He was born to rule, no matter what others said, for his parents had instilled this in him.

1

Politics and War, 1905–1918

The years from Viscount Castlereagh's election to the House of Commons in 1906 to the First World War can be interpreted in a variety of ways. For George Dangerfield, it was the period when highly placed Unionists like the Londonderrys presided over the death of liberal England, a process that is said to have transformed Britain from a rational parliamentary system to one of irrational street politics.[1] On the other hand, there is the view, expressed by Stanley Baldwin, that the future seventh Marquess of Londonderry had 'failed to make an impression, particularly when Home Rule became a vital issue, and for not speaking at a time when Conservative and Unionist opposition was so depleted.'[2] And yet both statements are in part correct, for the Londonderrys did position themselves to maintain a high profile role in national affairs at a time of socio-political transition, and Castlereagh did not succeed in making a mark in the Edwardian Unionist party. But it would be incorrect to suggest that the Londonderrys were engaged recklessly in the demise of parliamentary democracy, or that Castlereagh's lacklustre performance on the opposition benches was wholly attributable to personal failings. On the contrary, the picture that emerges from a detailed analysis of the role of the Londonderry family during this period is far more nuanced, and demonstrates both the tenacity of the aristocracy and the limits of its influence.

On 21 February 1906, three days after he first took his seat in the House of Commons, a nervous Castlereagh used his maiden speech to address the Irish question. He began this short oration by declaring a 'hereditary interest' in the matter, and indicated that he 'expressed sympathy with the claim that Ireland should be ruled according to Irish ideas, but insisted that they should be consistent with the unity of the Empire. He very much doubted whether Nationalist views would stand that test.'[3]

If Castlereagh sought to associate himself with an issue that could unite Unionists, then the numerical weakness and bitter divisions of the party ensured that it was a seed sewn on stony ground. For although Ireland remained the *raison d'etre* of the Conservative and Unionist party, it was not the foremost issue in post-1906 Unionist politics until the passing of the Parliament Act in 1911. In the meantime, the divisions over tariff reform that had propelled the party into opposition continued to divide it, with the majority of its depleted rows of MPs in favour of some measure of fiscal reform and a minority against such a move. In a period when few rose through the ranks of the party, it is notable that those of the new intake who did were in some form or other in favour of tariff reform, men like Andrew Bonar Law, F. E. Smith and Stanley Baldwin. With this wing of unionism working tirelessly against Arthur Balfour's equivocal stance on fiscal policy, it is therefore unsurprising that newly elected Balfourites like Castlereagh were unable to make similar progress.

It is in this context that Baldwin's much later recollection must be judged. It was after all a period when accusations of absence were made frequently by Unionists about other Unionists.[4] Indeed, it was not uncommon for the opposition benches to be largely empty at this time, with many Unionists of all hues disenchanted by their loss of power and endless internal wrangling. For his part Castlereagh quickly found the Commons tiresome, but he did nevertheless regularly attend debates, especially when they touched on issues about which he took a personal interest.[5] Shunned politically by the majority of his fellow Unionist MPs, Castlereagh formed political alliances with free traders and Balfourites like his cousin Lord Helmsley, Lord Hugh Cecil, and Charles Mills.[6] Contemporary impressions of Castlereagh's years in the House of Commons also challenge Baldwin's later recollection. Reporting on the Maidstone MP's first performance in parliament, the Asquithian *Westminster Gazette* referred to him as a 'fresh talent'.[7] And two years later the Tory free-trade Manchester *Sunday Chronicle* described him as 'a keen politician, and a first rate speaker ... never gets excited, and never speaks except on subjects he knows something about ... There is no dash or splash about his speaking; he argues quietly, cogently, clearly.'[8] It even concluded by predicting that Castlereagh would be elevated to the front bench in the next Unionist government.

Castlereagh's parliamentary speeches in defence of laissez-faire were directed at both Unionist tariff reformers and the Liberal government. He championed the status quo against those in both parties who sought to change established practice. In delivery, however, his speeches were nearly always directed at the Liberals—on one occasion he mocked their steady abandonment of a laissez-faire economy by accusing them of going against the free trade beliefs of their 'patron saint' Richard Cobden.[9] But he was all too aware that many in his own party also sought a scheme that challenged the principles of a laissez-faire economy; tariff reform being their alternative to the radicalism of David Lloyd George. Similarly, although Castlereagh's stance on issues such as changes to the army, the regulation of coal mining, alcohol prohibition, and Ireland were outwardly partisan, they also railed against a cross-party trend that saw social legislation as the solution to many of the country's ills. What therefore emerges in Castlereagh's speeches is not only an ongoing critique of the Liberals, but also an attitude that cared little about shifting opinions in his own party.[10]

I

With a background in the cavalry it is unsurprising that one of the first issues Castlereagh took up in parliament was that of army reform. Early in 1907 the Secretary of State for War, Richard Haldane, sought to make savings and deal with the threat of a continental war by introducing a bill to amalgamate all voluntary military organizations into one territorial force. This was not a simple party issue, although aristocrats were among the leading opponents of what became the Territorial and Reserve Forces Act 1907. For his part Castlereagh only opposed sections of the bill, regretting the need to end the tradition of local volunteers, militia and yeomanry. He suggested instead that the threat of continental war could only be met by universal military service.[11] There is little doubt that Castlereagh had logistical concerns, but his opposition to this particular reform also reflected his attitude to Liberal reform in general. The aristocracy had close associations with local voluntary militias, and although legislation in the nineteenth century curtailed this link, the measures outlined in the 1907 bill proposed to end this emanation of local status completely. Like other aristocrats opposed to the bill, Castlereagh therefore resented this infringement on a culture that was felt to be under attack in the widest sense.[12]

More revealing is the reference in his speech to conscription, exhibiting as it does a strain of authoritarianism that Castlereagh would never loose. This however needs to be qualified. He did not intend to propose conscription, rather, he suggested that it would be more effective in raising a new reserve force than the measures proposed in Haldane's bill. This is not to say however that Castlereagh would have opposed a scheme of conscription. He would not have seen conscription as a breech of laissez-faire, the military being regarded by many of a similar view as protectors of free trade and British interests.[13] In any case, only a minority of MPs spoke in favour of emulating continental style universal military service before the First World War, and Castlereagh was not among them.[14]

His parliamentary interventions were more frequent and unequivocal when it came to the series of coal mining reforms that the Liberal government hoped would appease an increasingly restless labour movement. Castlereagh began one of his speeches on these reforms by remarking, somewhat impertinently, 'that if it were not regarded as an absolute crime to be connected with a coalowner, I should like to advance some reasons against this [Eight Hours] bill.'[15] Mining magnates were still reeling from the Trade Disputes Act 1906 that prevented them obtaining damages from trade unions for peaceful picketing. Speaking on the Eight Hours bill in April 1907, Castlereagh avoided his obvious reason for objecting to the measure—further interference in the profits and management of mining—by tailoring his objections to what he viewed as the concerns of his employees and consumers. He argued that the Eight Hours bill restricted the freedom of miners to work as many hours as they chose, adding that modern ventilation had reduced the risk of damage to their health. When he addressed the financial difficulties involved, he pointed out that the inevitable rise in the price of coal would effect those who depended on cheap supplies, namely the working class and the struggling industrial sector.[16] Faced by an onslaught of Unionist amendments, the bill was delayed for over a year by a cautious government. On 9 December 1908 Castlereagh, having become a leading opponent of the bill, broadened the scope of his attack:

> He was opposed to the measure because it was the first attempt made in this country to curtail the hours of adult labour, it was not called for by the people, and because it established uniform legislation to meet wholly different local conditions. It was quite obvious that if the principle of the Bill was once admitted it must extend to other industries and eventually control the whole of industrial life of the country.[17]

Despite such objections the bill was successful in the House of Commons, and like similar legislation, was allowed safe passage in the House of Lords. The Unionist dominated upper house was wary about taking a stand against the Commons on an issue concerning labour, for if a stand had to made, it needed to be one that would command wide sympathy. For his part, Castlereagh behaved more like a partisan MP than a Unionist lord, and even objected to bills that his party was in broad agreement with, such as the 1909 Coal Mines (Clock Weighers) Act. And yet it is noticeable that he avoided criticism of his employees, the very people whose representatives sought reforms to the industry. Instead, he preferred to think of the workers as individuals who exercised a choice, although this sat uneasily with his contention that their best interests were in placing the success of the industry above their own concerns. For example, commenting on an attempt to introduce wage boards he argued that: 'No wages board could fix a rate which would at once give the workers adequate wages and ensure plenty of work for the factory'.[18]

If Liberal reforms were intended to appease the labour movement then they were a spectacular failure. Strikes had been a relatively rare occurrence during Balfour's premiership, but in 1907 it was recorded that three million working days were lost through industrial action. And despite or perhaps because of government movement on reform, this figure rocketed to 41 million in 1912.[19] Towards the end of 1911 the government attempted to offset the risk of a major miners' strike by introducing the Coal Mines (Regulations) bill. Given that the bill was designed to increase pit safety, Castlereagh's objections were reduced to defensive claims that he was not solely motivated by profit, that safety was a concern of owners, and that regulations would recognize local conditions better than an act of parliament. Rather than blaming the miners, he chose instead to dismiss the activities of trade unionists and accuse the government of constantly violating the law of contract.[20]

Nevertheless, legislation continued to lag behind union demands, in particular their call for a minimum wage. Following a breakdown in negotiations the Miners' Federation of Great Britain called a strike in March 1912. Unlike the three-month strike in 1910—which only hit the Durham and Northumberland coalfields—the 1912 stoppage had a crippling effect on the mining industry generally. It was therefore difficult for Castlereagh to maintain his rather naïve impression of miners' interests in the face of such action, although he did attribute the rising number of strikes to greater government interference. What emerged as the Coal

Mines (Minimum Wages) Act 1912 bore little resemblance to the disaster
Castlereagh had predicted it would herald.[21] Just as he rejected national
pay agreements in favour of local agreements, so the Act established district conferences at which miners, owners and government representatives would negotiate a local deal.[22] Coming as it did in the wake of the
Parliament Act 1911, and during the period of the Ulster Crisis of 1912
to 1914, it is notable that unlike earlier mining legislation, Castlereagh
adhered rigidly to the policy of his leaders, objecting to the bill only during its second reading.[23]

The Liberal government's preoccupation with regulating the alcohol
trade was another area of politics in which Castlereagh cast himself as a
defender of laissez-faire and the working man. The Liberals, influenced
by the nonconformist lobby within their ranks, took a paternalistic line,
arguing that too much money was being spent on alcohol. Although
Castlereagh was typical of many Tories in his defence of the alcohol
industry, he met Liberal paternalism with his own, claiming on 4
November 1908 that the closing of workmen's clubs would 'do a great
deal of harm to the lives of working men.'[24] When the issue of alcohol
control had arisen the year before, it then focussed on the question of
'local option' in Scotland, where a harsher regime of public-house open-
ing-hours existed than in England.[25] Castlereagh argued that prohibition
would not be successful and cited the failure of similar schemes in the
United States. He claimed that it would:

> spread the habit of secret drinking and the consumption of bad
> liquor, which were so detrimental to the mental and physical
> conditions of all classes of the community ... pointing out that
> one area might be entirely a prohibited area, and another in close
> proximity might be doing a roaring trade.[26]

Like many Unionists, Castlereagh regarded these Liberal measures as
'class legislation' intended to harm the natural constituency of the
Unionist party, in this case the breweries and distilleries. And like his
defence of the mining industry, such objections could be camouflaged in
a Tory paternalism that was inevitably more welcome among drinkers
than miners. Therefore, unlike labour reforms, the Unionist dominated
House of Lords was able to successfully hold off the various schemes of
prohibition put forward by the Liberals, at least until the First World War
when regulation was deemed necessary for strategic reasons.[27]

Until the general elections of 1910, Ireland was not the central issue it would become in the wake these polls. However, Castlereagh often spoke in parliament on what he viewed as a partisan Irish policy that was motivated more by political than economic concerns. In particular he rounded on the Evicted Tenants (Ireland) bill, supporting what he viewed as the more practical provisions, but ultimately opposing the whole bill as being motivated by the government's need to appease the United Irish League.[28] Such attacks were echoed in the House of Lords where the bill was amended so as to be less harmful to Irish landowners. Despite Castlereagh's attempt to make his views on Ireland appear motivated by economic concerns, he was, like most Unionists, especially those with Irish connections, motivated by deeper passions. For example, in February 1909, during a Commons debate on crime in Ireland, Castlereagh accused the Irish Chief Secretary of being 'heart and soul' with the criminals and that he allowed Irish people to feel that crimes had been committed with his 'sanction and connivance'.[29]

II

In the closing months of 1909 a constitutional crisis emerged that dominated the political agenda until 1911, and created the conditions thereafter for the Ulster Crisis of 1912 to 1914. In an effort to rejuvenate flagging support for the government, the Chancellor of the Exchequer, David Lloyd George, introduced the 'Peoples Budget'. This attempt to raise and invent new taxes in order to pay for social reform was to be borne most by the rich. It included a rise in income tax and death duties, a new super-tax on the wealthy and a duty of 20 per cent on the unearned increment of land value. Landowners felt particularly aggrieved with the bill, although City bankers, merchants and businessmen were also opposed to it.[30] But as David Cannadine has argued, the bill 'was not just a budget designed to raise money from the rich: it was the landed rich who were its principal target and victim.'[31] Whatever Lloyd George's original intentions, his dislike of the landed elite was well known and manifested itself in a bitter exchange with Castlereagh in March 1914. This row erupted when the Chancellor accused the dukes of Sutherland—the family of Lady Castlereagh—of land clearances on their Scottish estates, comparing the treatment of tenants then with policies recently pursued by his own government in the areas concerned. In what became known as the

'Sutherland Case', Castlereagh responded angrily to Lloyd George in *The Times*, accusing him of 'endeavouring wilfully to mislead the public.'[32]

Nevertheless, in the clamour of Unionist voices rushing to oppose and attack Lloyd George's budget, Castlereagh's is striking for its relative moderation. Like all landlord-parliamentarians, he believed that the budget was intended as a punitive measure. But unlike the majority of his party, even those who had previously stood in the free trade camp, Castlereagh was wary of undermining a budget that Unionists sought to counter with tariff reform. Therefore, rather than attacking the principle of taxing the wealthy, he instead focussed on questioning the proposed level of taxation.[33] He was therefore out of step with his own party leader, Balfour, whose belated willingness to embrace tariff reform as his party's alternative was matched by his resolution that the House of Lords would veto the bill and thus break a centuries old precedent.[34] Faced with this stand-off, Herbert Asquith—who replaced Campbell-Bannerman as Prime Minister in April 1908—dissolved parliament and went to the country to get a mandate for both the budget and reform to the House of Lords.

The indecisive result of the January 1910 general election ensured that a resolution to the crisis would not be arrived at quickly. A small swing to the Unionists meant that they now held 273 seats to the government's 275; but the Liberals were supported by votes from 82 Irish nationalists and 40 Labour MPs. For his part Castlereagh retained Maidstone with a moderately increased majority of 247.[35] Such a victory could only add to the confusion of the Unionist party, for the election result had left them divided over whether tariff reform had helped or hindered their performance. Further divisions were evident over how they should react to Asquith's Parliament bill, a measure that proposed to end the vetoing powers of the upper chamber. Castlereagh's response to the crisis year of 1910 was to lay the blame firmly with the Liberals and John Redmond's Irish nationalist party: 'the conduct of the Government deserved the deepest censure … [Unionists] saw the whole fortunes of this country thrown into the melting-pot and prostituted before Mr. Redmond.'[36] It was a common claim among Unionists, but it did little to solve the divisions still afflicting their own ranks.

The death of King Edward VII on 7 May led to a truce of sorts during which an inter-party conference was arranged to discuss constitutional reform.[37] In the meantime Castlereagh had found another issue on which to attack the government and delay the passage of legislation concerning the House of Lords—women's suffrage.[38] On this issue he was strongly influenced by his wife, Edith, a leading light of the constitutional suffragists in Britain and Ulster.[39] In April 1910 Castlereagh pressed the government to make time for the discussion of women's suffrage and attempted an amendment to stop them from conducting any more business until a bill was discussed.[40] And on 18 November 1910, against the backdrop of militant suffragette riots, Castlereagh attacked Asquith's opposition to suffrage reform and again demanded movement on the issue.[41] Given this odd reversal of roles, it is easy to mistake the Castlereaghs' support for Millicent Fawcett's National Union of Women's Suffrage Societies as being at odds with the Unionist party, or just a purely tactical device, especially as some suffragists regarded the movement as being more Liberal than Tory.[42] However, suffrage was not a simple party issue, as is evident from the position of Asquith, and peoples views 'were often deeply rooted in individual psychology and so transcended the usual categories of ideology and class.'[43] Therefore, whereas Lady Castlereagh was actively in favour of suffrage, her mother-in-law, Lady Londonderry, and father, Henry Chaplin, were both very much opposed.

Following the tense breakdown of the constitutional conference on 10 November 1910, another general election was arranged for the following month.[44] Once again Unionists debated the merits of advocating tariff reform, a pressing issue given the obvious unpopularity of food taxes. Castlereagh had nailed his colours to the mast the previous July when he opposed a scheme for imperial preference on the basis that it would tax the poor.[45] Even tariff reformers like Andrew Bonar Law were not immune from the realization that food taxes could create difficulties for the party at the December election. Balfour took advantage of this situation by proposing that the party promise a referendum on tariff reform in place of their existing policy to implement it if in government.

Despite the pains taken by Unionists to formulate an acceptable fiscal policy, the future of the House of Lords was undoubtedly the main issue.[46] However, the indecisive result of the second general election of 1910 left no one the better informed. The Unionists made only a small advance, winning 271 seats to the Liberals 272. But this was not enough to scupper the government's plans, especially given their promise of a third Home Rule bill in return for the continued support of the Irish nationalists. Nor did it help Unionist divisions, each wing of the party arguing that the other had been the cause of their failure to win a majority. For his part, Castlereagh was returned again for Maidstone, only this time with a majority of 70, a drop of 177 votes.[47]

In contrast to the government's continued determination to implement the Parliament bill, Unionist divisions extended to how they would react to the measure in the House of Lords. Castlereagh's attitude fluctuated between pragmatism and frustration. Speaking in March 1911 he highlighted a perennial problem for those who sought to reform the upper house in the name of democracy:

> the hereditary element—which was condemned on all sides—tended to maintain in the House of Lords a Second Chamber which would not attempt to compete with the House of Commons, but would be subordinate to it, in the management of public affairs. The only solution of the question was one arrived at by compromise.[48]

If this expressed a hope for further negotiations, then he was equally frustrated with the government's handling of the issue. The following month he revealed how he 'felt in a hopeless position because the Government had taken up an absolutely uncompromising attitude towards amendments, and orders had been issued to their followers to adopt a negative line.'[49] The following month he accused them of abusing their majority to the detriment of others the House of Commons: 'For the purpose of maintaining the coalition upon which the Government rested Ministers were abusing the mandate they had obtained to alter the legislative machinery of the nation.'[50] By July 1911 his argument was more dramatic, not only objecting to the 'unscrupulous and increasingly rigid application of the 'guillotine'', but also threatening to use unspecified measures to stop what he regarded as a 'revolution'.[51]

The last outburst was in the wake of news that George V had agreed to create enough Liberal peers to pass the bill in the House of Lords should that chamber reject it. If Castlereagh had sounded over the top in his denunciation of the government's tactics, then he did not join the ranks of the substantial minority of Unionist peers who fell into the 'ditcher' camp. This was no doubt due to the continued support given by his father, Lord Londonderry, to the beleaguered Balfour, who felt that the upper house should allow the Parliament bill to pass. For although much of the opposition to the bill was on the basis that it would pave the way for home rule, many peers felt that such a stand would be futile. Indeed, many in the upper house had been increasingly sceptical of their effectiveness for sometime, but especially since the return of the Liberals in 1906. With their confidence sapped, and overly cautious about using their veto, the Parliament bill offered a solution by giving them a statutory power to delay bills for two years.[52] When the House of Lords finally divided on 10 August 1910, the bill was allowed passage by 131 votes to 114. Having laid the issue to rest, the Unionists squared up to the most pressing consequence of the Parliament Act, a third attempt at home rule, and did so with a new leader, the compromise choice of Andrew Bonar Law.

In his history of the decline of the aristocracy, Cannadine argues that the Parliament Act was something of tremendous significance:

> they might, in some cases, retain great individual wealth, political influence, or personal prestige. But the belief in their innate superiority, in their collective political wisdom, in their unique position as the responsible and hereditary custodians of the national interest, was gone forever.[53]

This was certainly true for many aristocrats for whom the political sphere was no longer theirs by right. But Castlereagh continued to believe in his innate right to play a role in national affairs. And this feeling only increased when he inherited his father's title and position in 1915.

III

The political turmoil surrounding the third Home Rule bill dominated British politics from 1912 until the outbreak of the First World War in August 1914. It was an issue that allowed Unionists to unite and attack the Liberals without fear of internal dissension, although even this did not entirely overshadow the question of tariff reform. In March 1912 the only members of Law's shadow cabinet to oppose the retention of food taxes were the seventeenth Earl of Derby and Lord Londonderry; aristocrats with strong connections to industries that relied on free trade. This was to change however, and by December 1912 a compromise had been reached that allowed the party to focus on the Irish question and avoid another electoral failure. It was a blow for tariff reformers, for Law not only limited the number of proposed food taxes, but also shifted 'the whole onus on to the Dominions by suggesting that the proposed duties would only be imposed if the Dominions regarded them as essential to Imperial Preference.'[54] In January 1913 Castlereagh publicly stated his support for Law's compromise position. Addressing the Ulster Women's

Unionist Council—of which his mother was vice-president, then from 1913, president—Castlereagh claimed that he 'believed in tariff reform', but, in a sideswipe at the Chamberlainites, that imperialism to him meant not imperial preference but the union of Britain and Ireland.[55] This was no Pauline conversion for Castlereagh—this would have to wait until the 1929 Wall Street Crash—but rather an attempt, along with many other Unionists, to unite the party for the more pressing struggle against home rule.

The third Home Rule bill was introduced to the House of Commons on 11 April 1912. Sir Edward Carson, leader of the Irish Unionists from 21 February 1910, and James Craig, the leading figure of unionism in Ulster, led the opposition attack. Following Craig, Castlereagh delivered a measured speech that argued that the bill would 'postpone indefinitely the great settlement to which the country was rapidly coming ... Only by the hearty co-operation of the different sections, races, and creeds in the island could real Irish prosperity be reached.'[56] Like some others in the Unionist party, including Carson, Castlereagh was sympathetic to a federal arrangement for the whole of the United Kingdom that might accommodate Irish nationalist aspirations within a larger scheme of home rule. It was not, however, an approach that had any significant effect on the home rule debate.[57] His speech also emphasized the Londonderrys' ancestral and familial obligations to the union. This was particularly important for Irish aristocrats with close connections to the Unionist leadership, for the Irish Unionist movement was, by 1904, a bourgeois-led and regionally focussed organization, wary of both British supporters and local landlords.[58]

In June 1912 Thomas Agar-Robartes, a backbench Liberal MP, proposed to reconcile Ulster Unionist objections with Irish nationalist aspirations by proposing that the four northeastern counties of Ireland be excluded from a home rule settlement. Following a conference on the matter at Londonderry House, Unionist MPs decided to back Agar-Robartes' amendment, not through any desire for partition, but so that they could not be accused of avoiding a compromise. Nevertheless, in a speech to the House of Commons on 18 June, Castlereagh reflected this development by taking on a more sectional and defensive tone than he had previously:

> The men of Ulster were not anxious to go into the Union, they were forced into it; but since they went in they had realised that

the Union made for their prosperity and interest. Having pros-
pered they wanted to remain as they were ... The hon. member
for East Mayo [John Dillon] was going about saying that the
Protestants of Ireland would not be satisfied with anything less
than a position of ascendancy. They had never asked for that and
did not want it. All they desired was to be left alone.[59]

Although this reading of Irish history was far from uncommon, especially among Unionists, the speech also reflects how the Ulster question
touched a deep resonance for aristocrats with connections to the
region.[60] Although the Belfast bourgeoisie remained firmly in control of
the Ulster Unionist Council—formed in 1904 to replace weaker landlord
dominated structures—they continued to encourage the participation of
the provincial landed elite. As such, while Carson was leader of the parliamentary party, Londonderry was chairman of the UUC. Moreover, the
landed elite, particularly titled grandees with seats in the House of Lords,
added respectability to a campaign that would become increasingly
unconstitutional. Nor was this all one-way, for the aristocracy of indus-
trializing Britain and Ulster had been courting the bourgeoisie throughout much of the nineteenth century, a process that F. M. L. Thompson
has referred to as 'aristocratic embrace', thus ensuring some consensus
among the various political and economic elites of the United
Kingdom.[61]

Aristocratic embrace was particularly evident in the political salon of
Lady Londonderry. She had befriended Carson in the 1880s when her
husband was Viceroy of Ireland and Carson a promising young Dublin
lawyer.[62] If this was fortuitous, then her role as hostess for the widower
Law was more opportunistic, especially given her initial disdain for this
socially inferior successor to the House of Cecil.[63] In time, Carson and
Law came to depend on Theresa personally as much as she and her husband depended on them politically. With the firm coalescing of British
Unionist and Ulster Unionist interests from 1912, the Londonderrys
were in an ideal position to continue their prominent role in political
affairs. But this should not be overstated. For although Lord Londonderry
often graced platforms with Carson, and was counted among the most
senior of leaders in Ulster, he is notable only for his calming patrician
influence and significant financial help, while the practical input of his son
could be likened to that of a sympathetic English MP.[64]

A series of great demonstrations were arranged throughout 1912 to
impress upon a seemingly indifferent Liberal government the resolve of

Unionists to oppose the third Home Rule bill. At all of them Londonderry took his place beside Carson, both men a somewhat deceptive frontage for a movement that was primarily Ulster based and bourgeois led.[65] But such display was the main function of these great rallies, at Balmoral, near Belfast, on Easter Tuesday, and several months later in July at Blenheim Palace, near Oxford. It was only at the grandest of these rallies, on 28 September 1912 at Belfast, that Castlereagh played a prominent part, albeit purely ornamental. This was the occasion of the mass signing of the Ulster Solemn League and Covenant, a defiant pledge of contractual loyalty to the crown that rejected the Home Rule bill proposed by the King's ministers.

Castlereagh resented not being among the inner circle of Ulster Unionists, and he found it galling to watch as leading English MPs like F. E. Smith and Lord Hugh Cecil took a more prominent role in the campaign than he. His experience of being shunned politically by the tariff-reform wing of the party, men like Smith and Law, only added to his sense of bitterness, which was made worse yet again by his mother's aristocratic embrace of the two politicians. He wrote to his wife from the campaign in Ulster:

> It is damnable here and I am bored to tears, nothing in the world to do; I am simply loafing about; as yet I have done nothing; tomorrow evening a meeting and the same on Thursday and I sign on Saturday. I wish I had just come over for the signing; for all the good I have done or will do I might have been at Timbuctoo. I hate swelling the train of Carson and F. E. [Smith]; there are so many anxious to do it. I have no news, I am bored here. I played golf this morning and I do the same this afternoon.[66]

As part of the attempt to drum up excitement for the impending 'Ulster Day' Castlereagh addressed a meeting at Crumlin, County Antrim, accompanied by other speakers including Colonel Hercules Arthur Pakenham, the fourth Viscount Templetown and Charles Craig, brother of James Craig. Like Templetown, Castlereagh made reference to his local ancestry. More ominously, he warned the government—with a vagueness characteristic of such threats—that violence could result if their demonstrations were ignored.[67] After Crumlin, Castlereagh was summoned by his father to meet Law at Wynyard, a trip he resented, for it was one thing for Castlereagh to toe the line for Law, but quite another for him to attend the court of a man whose leadership he resented.[68] Following his return to Belfast, on the day before the signing, Castlereagh's frustration boiled over: 'This blasted week has put me all wrong. Never again do I undertake a week like this unless I am the central figure, and I fear that it interests me less and less. The cast and the humbug of the whole thing is really sickening.'[69] On 28 September 1912 at Belfast City Hall, in what was a deliberately theatrical performance, Carson applied his name to the Covenant, followed by Londonderry, and then the leaders of six protestant denominations. Castlereagh was next to apply his name, no doubt in recognition of his famous name, for it reflected no promotion within the ranks of the party.[70] In total, 471,414 signatures were collected throughout Ulster and elsewhere.

Debate in the House of Commons took on a more heated tone following the spectacular of Ulster Day. Asquith, however, continued to exude a cool temper and maintain his policy of wait and see. Like many Unionist MPs, Castlereagh was exasperated with this muted reaction to recent events. Speaking in parliament on 14 October, he 'attributed the docile attitude of the Government's supporters to the fact, among other things, that the Government had bribed the House of Commons.' This prompted one MP, in a reference to the Irish Act of Union of 1800, to exclaim: 'Castlereagh on bribery!' The interruption was ignored: 'As long as the Government's supporters obeyed the party Whips their £400 a year was safe; if not, they came under the ban of the caucus and out they went.'[71]

It is undoubtedly the case that Unionist MPs sought to delay the passage of the third Home Rule bill with procedural devices and delaying tactics, although these were often checked by the government's use of the guillotine. Nevertheless, it is noticeable that Castlereagh's attempted amendments tacitly accepted that the bill would be passed. It may be that he too, like the government, doubted the resolve of Ulster Unionists to oppose home rule come what may. In June 1912 he sought an amendment to ensure that the proposed Dublin parliament would be subservient to Westminster.[72] In October, after all the excitement of Ulster Day, he proposed that the Home Rule bill codify concerns that he feared might be left to an Irish nationalist dominated parliament. These included the enshrining of 'rigid' safeguards for Irish Unionists and reforms to the congested district boards.[73] On 24 October Castlereagh, supported by James Craig, proposed that under home rule the position of Viceroy of Ireland be replaced with that of a secretary of state on the basis that this would make the head of the Irish executive more accountable to London. In doing so he also championed the harmonization of Irish government with that in the rest of the United Kingdom:

> The Lord Lieutenant in these times was a complete anachronism, and retaining this appointment served to accentuate the fact that England had been separated from Ireland. If the federal scheme of the First Lord of the Admiralty [Winston Churchill] were to be attempted, would there be a Viceroy for England, another for Lancashire, another for Scotland, and another for Wales?[74]

The Liberal policy of wait and see was frustrating for Unionists, and that frustration could turn more threatening when goaded. This happened in mid-October when the President of the Board of Agriculture, Walter Runciman, mockingly compared the fervour of feeling in Ulster with the business-like way Unionists behaved at Westminster. Echoing his earlier warnings of heightened militancy, Castlereagh hit back on 28 October in the House of Commons:

> Did the Government think it was all bluff and brag? ... The people of Ulster were a minority and felt they were being treated tyrannically. When people felt like that there was no limit to what they would do in defence of their liberty ... If the Government were endeavouring to goad the people of Ulster into a frenzy (Ministerial laughter) by the irritating suggestions responsible Ministers were making in various parts of the country, then their blood be upon their own head.[75]

The dramatic end of the first reading of the bill illustrated how wrong Runciman had been about well-behaved Unionists. Not only did Unionists call and win a snap division on the bill in November 1912, 228 votes to 206, but the House of Commons was also the scene of some violence when a book was thrown at the Treasury front bench following Asquith's refusal to recognize the division.[76]

The third Home Rule bill was sent to the House of Lords in January 1913 where, predictably, it was rejected. The Parliament Act 1911 ensured that this meant the bill would be delayed until the autumn of 1914. It did not, of course, signal the end of the bill, and so the hitherto purely parliamentary struggle now extended to the drilling fields of Ireland. This did not mean that the political process had ended, rather, it now ran parallel to a more militant mobilization in Ulster. In January 1913 the UUC sanctioned the creation of the Ulster Volunteer Force and began to make plans for a provisional government in the event of a parliament at Dublin being established. The continued support of British Unionists for these developments ensured that the landed elite of Ulster was united in its support for, and participation in, the UVF and the provisional government. Indeed, they not only added respectability to these barely legal organizations, but military experience and the ownership of substantial land ensured they were particularly prominent in the UVF. It has been claimed that Carson attempted to dissuade Londonderry from involving his family in this militant phase of Ulster Unionist opposition: 'They can do little to me ... But you have great possessions, a great title, friendships at court, a seat in the House of Lords. You have to consider also the future of your son Charley.' With tears in his eyes, Londonderry is reputed to have replied: 'My dear Edward, if I was to loose everything in the world, I will go with you to the end.'[77]

The exact involvement of the Londonderrys is not easy to discern, although it is clear that their participation was quintessentially aristocratic, that is, highly placed, fund raising, and ornamental. Therefore, Londonderry, already chairman of the UUC, was appointed to the proposed provisional government. And like other prominent businessmen in the region and beyond, he contributed to a £10,000 indemnity fund for the volunteer force.[78] As for Castlereagh's involvement in the UVF, the picture is more confusing. Ronald McNeill, a contemporary of Castlereagh, names him as an officer.[79] A document among the Londonderry papers names him as 'commanding officer' of the North Belfast Regiment.[80] However, A. T. Q. Stewart claims that a 'Captain Malone' took command of North Belfast.[81] Stewart's evidence, taken from the UUC papers, may be more reliable, especially as the Londonderry papers contain only one reference to the self-styled 'Regiment'.[82] To confuse matters, the Mount Stewart estate had its own UVF company; in January 1914 this combined with others in the area to form the second battalion, North Down Regiment.[83] One of Carson's official biographers, Ian Colvin, recounts how, on one occasion, Castlereagh accompanied the Ulster Unionist leader as his aide de camp on a visit to the army commander in Ireland, General Sir Nevil Macready.[84] It may be that the confusing picture of Castlereagh's involvement in the UVF is attributable to a deliberate attempt to obscure it, or that his father refused to allow him any position that might risk any serious danger to his life. He had, after all, prevented his son from attending the South African War for the sake of dynastic survival. What is certain is that the Londonderrys filled that social and political niche they had so assiduously carved for themselves, for example, by housing the commander of the UVF, General Sir George Richardson, at Mount Stewart from 1913 to 1919.[85] The Londonderrys' involvement was therefore important for its financial and symbolic value, crucial factors to a potentially dangerous and unconstitutional venture, and was celebrated in 1915 when a wing of the UVF Hospital at Belfast was named after the family.[86]

Whatever activity Castlereagh was involved in, it was at the expense of his parliamentary appearances. A regular speaker in the House of Commons during 1912, his attendance dipped the following year when he spoke on only eight separate occasions.[87] In 1914 this record improved only slightly, albeit doubling the previous year's activity.[88] The few speeches Castlereagh did make in 1913 dealt in the main with army matters and not Ireland, while his speeches in 1914 protested against the possible use of the army in Ulster, and complained about extravagant spending on the Palace of Westminster. This lack of parliamentary performance would tend to confirm Stanley Baldwin's later criticism that Castlereagh did not make a mark on the home rule issue.[89] However, Castlereagh was hampered by his years of isolation in the free trade wing of the Unionist party, and more latterly by the purely symbolic role expected of him by the Ulster Unionist leadership. And yet he occupied a political space in 1912 that he might have made his own had he possessed the charisma to do so. But Castlereagh was not a creature of twentieth century mass politics. As if to confirm this, he announced in March 1913 that at the next general election he would be standing as the Unionist candidate for the affluent constituency of Kensington.[90] As one of the safest Unionist seats in the country, Kensington amplified Castlereagh's place at the heart of London society; constituency work here would better suit the lifestyle of an aristocrat-politician whose career was drifting towards backbench obscurity.

The momentous events of 1914 do not need to be rehearsed here, especially as Castlereagh, like many Unionists, was not party to the decisions taken by his leaders. Like the country at large, he had to wait and see what the consequences of gunrunning at Larne in April would be, and a similar pause of breath was adopted when it came to the inter-party conference at Buckingham Palace in July. Carson and Redmond's failure to agree on the area to be excluded—the former favouring the exclusion of all of Ulster and the latter feeling unable to deliver it—meant the conference ended in deadlock. This failure only helped to increase fears of what might happen in Ireland. That the First World War would temporarily freeze the Irish question is well known, what is less appreciated is the dramatic change it would have on the political career of Castlereagh.

IV

On 4 August 1914 the United Kingdom declared war on Germany. The inconclusive results of the inter-party conference meant that when the Home Rule bill was given royal assent on 18 September, it contained no special treatment for Ulster. However, the wartime emergency served to ensure that the Act would not come into force until after the war had been concluded. This equivocal outcome allowed both Carson and Redmond to encourage their respective supporters to enlist in the armed forces, albeit with some initial hesitation on the part of both men. Their sanction, however, was not necessary for all Irishmen, or even those who occupied a prominent position in the Ulster Unionist movement. Like many in the aristocracy of Britain and Ireland Castlereagh rejoiced at the opportunity to return to the army and fulfil one of the few remaining aristocratic duties of real practical value. According to Paul Fussell, the war 'took place in what was, compared with ours, a static world, where the values appeared stable and where the meanings of abstractions seemed permanent and reliable. Everyone knew what Glory was, and what Honour meant.'[91] Re-enlisting held out the hope for Castlereagh that he could return to such a static world, one free of the tensions and defeats of almost a decade of Liberal government. Nor was it merely a matter of reaction, according to Cannadine:

> By tradition, by training, and by temperament, the aristocracy was the warrior class. They rode horses, hunted foxes, fired shotguns. They knew how to lead, how to command, and how to look after the men in their charge. Here, then, was their chance - to demonstrate conclusively that they were not the redundant reactionaries of radical propaganda, but the patriotic class of knightly crusaders and chivalric heroes, who would defend the national honour and the national interest in the hour of its greatest trial.[92]

Despite Castlereagh's wish to revert to his former career, he was not to find the glorious role he desired. Indeed, with little opportunity to engage the enemy, it encouraged uncomfortable memories of his first spell in the army. And his hope that previous military experience would lead to a command had the opposite effect. Not only had the 35 year-old spent over eight years out of the army, he had also missed the South African War, an essential training ground for aspiring commanders in the First World War. Castlereagh was not unaware of the obstacles his ambition faced:

> How much better I should have done if I had remained in the Army, and done the staff college instead of stagnating for eight years in the House of Commons. It is very irritating to see people in important positions, no better than me, and to feel that I am a sort of mixture of footman and a clerk and this I shall remain as I see no prospect of doing anything else.[93]

If the interference of Castlereagh's parents in 1899 was detrimental to his long-term military aspirations, then the meddling of his wife in his posting to the Western Front was more immediately harmful. Lord and Lady Londonderry had not lost their concern for the bodily welfare of their only son, and Lady Castlereagh took advantage of this by asking her friend, General William Pulteney, commander of Third Corps, to appoint her husband as his aide de camp. Captain Castlereagh reluctantly accepted and arrived in France with Pulteney at the end of August 1914. Removed from the front line, and lacking a command, it was not long before he grew to despise both his job and Pulteney.

Castlereagh's frequent correspondence with his wife is notable for its revealing detail, a feature facilitated by the King's Messenger system. He provided her with information on morale, troop movements, and battles involving himself and the army generally. Aware of the potential danger of such information, he warned his wife early on not to reveal the content of any of his letters.[94] Shadowing Pulteney, Castlereagh was privy to the strategy of allied commanders but not party to its formulation, an unfortunate echo of his ornamental role in Ulster. In letters to his wife he criticized Sir John French's top-heavy administration and the occasional visits of government ministers: '[John] Seely told me Winston [Churchill] was at Dunkirk ... He sent me a message. Winston I suppose came over to get a medal; he is entitled to one if he sets foot on French soil I believe.'[95] By December 1914 he was more barbed about the First Lord of the Admiralty: 'Winston arrived here this morning looking very old and very flabby. I do not know what excuses he makes to come here, mere joyriding, and he has a destroyer to take him back again.'[96]

Some of the controversial opinions Castlereagh expressed in the 1930s as Secretary of State for Air had germinated during his time at the Western Front. His dislike of the French, for example, was apparent early on: 'The French I fancy are useless. I do not believe they ever put up a fight. The thing is they really don't care.'[97] Conversely, he was one of many British soldiers at the front to admire the German army, but Castlereagh's early reference to it is somewhat striking given his later views on appeasement. Writing to his wife in November 1914, he stated that he did not 'know how you defeat a nation which has prepared in every detail for years'.[98] Less controversially, he noted his first encounter with military aeroplanes: 'The thing that has most impressed me here has been the aeroplane service. A splendid lot of boys who really don't know what fear is.'[99] And like many officers with little experience of mixing with those who constituted the ranks, Castlereagh wrote in glowing terms of a rare visit to the trenches, made after his first flight in an aeroplane:

> I only spent a few hours in the trenches … and got tight on rum. There was no shelling only sniping. I only flew for about ten minutes, a delightful sensation. I seldom enjoyed anything more. I was rewarded for going to the trenches, the Irish Fusiliers. I never saw people so pleased; they say the staff never go there and don't realise what they have to go through. There were 15 inches of water in the fire trenches.[100]

Although not ready for the Battle of Mons, the troops under Pulteney's command did make it on time for the German retreat from the Marne and the Battle of Ypres, the latter lasting from mid-October to November 1914.[101] Being near decision-making and not part of it, Castlereagh's correspondence grew increasingly angry about what he regarded as the mismanagement of the war. He wrote of the great strain the troops were under and expressed pity for the Belgian refugees who were victims of the constant shelling. Castlereagh's ten months with Pulteney were frustrating, a situation made worse by the general's reluctance to let him transfer to his old cavalry regiment. This, and so much else, would change following the unexpected death of the sixth Marquess of Londonderry on 8 February 1915.

The seventh Marquess of Londonderry took leave from the army to attend the funeral, and to return his father's Garter insignia to the King.[102] Despite his close involvement with Irish affairs, the sixth Marquess, unlike his son in 1949, was buried at Long Newton Parish

Church in County Durham and not at Mount Stewart. At the end of the month Londonderry returned to the front with a promotion to major.[103] Edith, now Lady Londonderry, pressured Pulteney to recommend her husband for a military honour, but the influence of the Londonderry family on Pulteney had ended with the death of the sixth Marquess.[104] The seventh Marquess was thus able to resign as the general's ADC and rejoin his cavalry regiment, albeit without the medal his wife had requested. However, far from satisfying his determination to serve at the front, the War Office placed him in command of the reserves stationed at Regent's Park, London.[105] Although he was far from happy with this placement, it proved useful for spending more time with his wife and four children.[106] It also allowed him to begin the ornamental duties that his new status demanded of him.

The new Marquess's earliest acts of noblesse oblige and campaigning were very much war related. Not atypically for the owners of large properties during the war, the Londonderrys had overseen the conversion of Londonderry House and a property at Seaham into soldiers' hospitals. Lord Londonderry spoke at a small ceremony at the opening of the latter in October 1915, prompting his mother to observe that he emulated his father, although she claimed that her son spoke more slowly.[107] In June 1915, in what was perhaps a bout of over enthusiasm, the new owner of the Londonderry Collieries attempted to press upon the government the idea of converting his mines into munitions factories.[108] The state may have been desperate for shells, but it was determined to ensure that the equally vital mining industry was running to full capacity. Therefore, Londonderry's suggestion was not only ignored, but in 1917 the government extended an earlier scheme to control mines in south Wales to cover all of Britain.

Much more significant was Londonderry's political contribution to the war. It introduced him to a sincere and increasingly personal involvement in Irish affairs. In the summer of 1915 he joined the Central Council for the Organization of Recruiting in Ireland.[109] Wartime recruitment was a divisive issue in Ireland and became more so after 1916, when the threat of conscription increased support for Sinn Féin at the expense of Redmond's constitutional nationalists. Like many Unionists Londonderry failed to appreciate the differences between Redmond's party and the more militant Sinn Féin.[110] He therefore had few qualms about advocating conscription for Ireland in 1917 on the basis of equality with Britain, adding that without large scale recruitment, Ireland would suffer a national dishonour.[111]

It is ironic that Londonderry's association with the Ulster Unionist movement was significantly enhanced by his government appointment to the lord lieutenancy of County Down in August 1915.[112] He was not the first choice of the Ulster Unionists, but his appointment strengthened his own weak links with the region and recast his involvement with the bourgeois-led movement. This may have been what the new coalition government of Liberals and Unionists intended. The candidate recommended by Richard Dawson Bates, secretary of the UUC, was Colonel Sharman Crawford, a member of the county gentry with close connections to the UUC. Bates had written to Law on the matter only days after the death of the sixth Marquess. But Londonderry was appointed, although there is nothing to suggest that he lobbied hard for the post. Indeed, Law, now a coalition minister, may have felt some sense of loyalty to the Londonderry family, or he may have viewed Londonderry as more acceptable to his Liberal allies, for Londonderry was appointed despite the hopes of Bates.[113]

Once a powerful position in local government, the role of lord lieutenant had evolved during the nineteenth century to become almost purely ornamental, although they still retained some limited powers of local patronage. Not long after his appointment, Londonderry found himself involved in a sectarian row over the appointment of his deputy lieutenants. The Liberal Viceroy of Ireland, the second Baron Wimborne, determined that Londonderry would appoint at least two Roman Catholics as deputy lieutenants.[114] Sharman Crawford, one of Londonderry's existing deputies, objected strongly to one such candidate, and without mentioning his denominational background, argued that he was out of the question because he was a publican. In case Londonderry did not take his objection seriously, Crawford reminded him that his election to the exclusive Kildare Street Club at Dublin was still pending.[115] Objections were also received by Londonderry about another nationalist candidate, and again they focussed on his social deficiencies, specifically that his promotion to the directorship of a company had been achieved through marriage and not inheritance, and that his 'origins and surroundings' made him unable to fit into the county set.[116] In the end neither candidate was appointed. There is nothing to indicate how Londonderry viewed this episode at the time, but he did inform Lloyd George in June 1916 that Wimborne was an 'abject slave of Redmond' and that all appointments were 'invariably' given to nationalists.[117] It is worth noting, however, that when Londonderry was a member of the first government of Northern Ireland in the 1920s, he would revisit these arguments, and find himself advocating the appointment of Catholics. In any event, even if Londonderry had backed Crawford's concerns in 1915, Wimborne ensured that the candidates the Ulster Unionists had favoured were not appointed either.[118]

In spite his new roles in Ireland and the safety of commanding cavalry reserves in London, Major Londonderry was keen to see action and return to the front. By the winter of 1915 he felt increasingly stuck in a rut, the War Office refusing to consider a return to the theatre of war until early 1916.[119] Londonderry claimed some two years after his service in London that he had then refused an offer of command from General Sir Douglas Haig. It was a bizarre claim that was used promote his campaign for a good military placement in 1918, for there is nothing otherwise to indicate that Haig ever made such an offer.[120] Indeed, had Londonderry received such an offer it would have been accepted without hesitation. As the dowager Marchioness of Londonderry noted in December 1915: 'Charley threatens in every letter that he is going to the front after Christmas.'[121] She knew she could not dissuade him given his new status, but also because of the family row in 1899 over 'the South African affair'.[122] 'I wish he would be content to stay in one of the reserve regiments in Regent Park [sic], but it is impossible that any child of mine could be content with doing nothing.'[123]

In the third week of January 1916 Londonderry was allowed to serve with the Blues at the front and was promoted to second-in-command under Colonel Lord Tweedmouth. Although once again a subordinate, Londonderry felt closer to the action and no doubt hoped this would eradicate his lack of front-line experience. His new posting coincided with the determination of British strategists to launch a major offensive; it was thought that the cavalry would play their traditional part by following the infantry on horseback to capture the enemy's position. The carnage wrought on the first day of the Battle of the Somme, 1 July 1916, proved how utterly outmoded this orthodox strategy actually was. Writing to his friend Colonel Cyril Hankey a fortnight into the Somme offensive, Londonderry complained about the recent attachment of cavalrymen to infantry units, arguing that they could be better used as a unit, and backed this up with some logistical analysis. But his feelings on the matter also touched a deeper chord, for like so much else he had keenly felt the demise of, the traditional functions of the cavalry could not meet the challenge wrought by the First World War.[124]

In September 1916 Londonderry was temporarily transferred to another cavalry battalion as its second-in-command, and soon made a lieutenant colonel following the departure of its commanding officer. It was however a thoroughly boring post for Londonderry as the troops under his command were behind the lines and non-combative.[125] This mundane command was broken with leave to England in September and December.[126] The latter visit coincided with the formation of a second coalition government, this time under Lloyd George. It was a government Londonderry had no hope or expectation of joining, at least not until he had proved his worth in Irish affairs.

Londonderry returned to his old regiment in early 1917. In April the Blues participated in the Battle of Arras. During the battle Londonderry temporarily took command following the death of his commanding officer, General Bulkeley Johnson.[127] But his military superiors did not think him suitable for such a post and had a replacement appointed soon afterwards.[128] This was in stark contrast to the attitude of the leadership of the UUC which, around the same time, was discussing the nomination of Londonderry as one of its delegates to the proposed Irish Convention. On top of this came speculation that Londonderry might be appointed British ambassador to Paris, a highly unlikely scenario, but one that satisfied Londonderry's overestimation of his own worth.[129] His involvement with the Irish Convention is examined in the next chapter, but it is instructive to note here that Londonderry viewed that assignment as only a temporary one, and continued to lobby for a position in the military that he felt would suit him best. Even in July 1917, when the Convention had barely started its proceedings, Londonderry made efforts to join the tank corps. However, General Capper was not impressed by the peer's credentials and refused to 'hold out any prospects', adding somewhat dramatically that the only scenario in which Londonderry could join would involve a decimation of existing officers.[130] A few months later Londonderry was pressuring the Secretary of State for War, Lord Derby, to allow him to join the Royal Flying Corps; the future Secretary of State for Air was advised to not pursue the matter.[131]

Londonderry's lobbying was not to seek a way out of the Convention, but to achieve either a promotion to command or a placement in a highly technical unit such as the tank corps or the flying corps. When it looked as though he might be recalled to his post as *second*-in-command of the Blues in early December 1917, Londonderry protested that he was too busy with his duties in Ireland.[132] Only a week later however he informed his wife of rumours about a vacancy for the command of the Blues.[133] His failure to obtain that command, and his fulfilling role at the Irish Convention, made him realise with some reluctance that his ambitions had to be confined to the political sphere. Following the breakdown of the Convention in April 1918, Londonderry asked for Derby's advice on whether he should remain in politics, the War Secretary replied unequivocally:

> You have done your bit and I think people will quite understand your taking up politics … I am quite certain of one thing: there is nothing worse for the army than that a man should be one thing one day and one thing another. He must either be a politician or a soldier.[134]

With that Londonderry remained in politics and out of the army. His subsequent political career was indelibly marked by his time in the House of Commons and return to the army in 1914, particularly the constant failures he endured. Never the cleverest of politicians, by the end of the war Londonderry was nevertheless astute enough to realise that he needed to be more adaptable and less complacent about his right to rule. And yet he could not leave behind the expectation that he was born to fulfil a great role, the product of an aristocratic upbringing that filled him with confidence, but not the ability necessary to match those ambitions. Nevertheless, from being a political anachronism, Londonderry was able take advantage of his landed background to remould himself as a credible politician, and did so, paradoxically, in Irish politics, an arena more used to being the graveyard of aristocratic ambition.

2

Ireland, 1916–1918

It is somewhat ironic that Lord Londonderry was rescued from political oblivion at a time of profound change in British and Irish politics. Before this, Londonderry's political career was marked by frustration and failure. But the rapidly changing situation brought about by the First World War created a political environment in which he found a new role, one useful to both the government and Ulster Unionists. This change of political fortunes was greatly influenced by his succession to the Londonderry title and economic interests in February 1915. It was a position of some potential significance, for his mother and father's efforts at aristocratic embrace had reaped a series of appointments to the cabinet and a prominent place in the Ulster Crisis of 1912 to 1914. Their role in the latter owed much to the coalescing interests of the Ulster Unionist Council (UUC) and the British Conservative and Unionist party. This had allowed Ulster aristocrats with close connections to the Unionist front bench to avoid the tensions that had previously marked their relationship with the provincial and bourgeois-led UUC.

Like previous marquesses of Londonderry, the seventh Marquess could claim an office in the gift of the state by virtue of his immense wealth and title; this having long been used to confirm the family's senior position in County Down, County Durham, and at Westminster. When the owner of this status and wealth was viewed as a political asset, as in the case of the second and sixth marquesses, a place in the government had been forthcoming. In the case of the third, fourth and fifth marquesses, it secured more ornamental rewards such as a lord lieutenancy, a rise in the peerage, or membership of the orders of the Garter or St Patrick. The seventh Marquess, at least until he inherited his father's title, was far from being a major asset to the Unionist front bench. But he was nevertheless, from 1915, a grandee magnate at a time when that still

counted for much, and as Lord Lieutenant of County Down, a potentially useful check on the militant and increasingly self-reliant leadership of
Ulster unionism. In all probably however, very little would have been
expected of Londonderry as a lord lieutenant in what was a mainly ornamental office. What could not have been anticipated was that the fluidic
political situation in Ireland would unfold in such as way as to give
Londonderry considerable prominence; out of tune with many Ulster
Unionists, but very much in tune with their considerably more influential
British allies. As a result, Londonderry not only obtained the Garter, but
also a government post at the Ministry of Air.

The Easter Rising of 1916 dramatically returned the Irish question to
the forefront of British political concerns. Up until this point,
Londonderry had adhered to the Unionist policy of supporting the coalition government headed by H. H. Asquith, despite his unhappiness about
increasing state interference. But the Rising led Londonderry to break his
silence in a letter to *The Times* about the Liberal government's Irish policy. He began by criticising the willingness of coalition Unionists to shoul-
der responsibility for the Rising, and the 'understanding that any suggestion of controversy must be avoided':

> Ten years of Radical rule in Ireland has culminated in the tragedy
> of a fortnight ago. Peace and prosperity have given place to
> rebellion and martial law. The feelings of the relatives of those
> killed in the performance of their duty have not received due
> consideration. The minds of those who cry the loudest for sym-
> pathy with the rebels seem somewhat out of focus in face of the
> facts and figures. Hundreds of soldiers and civilians have been
> murdered by men openly in league with the King's enemies, yet,
> when these men have to face the consequences of their crime,
> there is a chorus of compassion from certain sections of the
> Press and public. Surely the innocent rather than the guilty
> deserve our sympathy.[1]

The letter made no immediate impact, aside from Londonderry receiving
support from other people critical of the government's Irish policy, but
it did mark him out as a potential critic of Edward Carson at a time when
Irish unionism and the coalition itself looked as if they might fall apart.[2]

This tense situation had developed out of David Lloyd George's post-
Rising meetings with Carson and Redmond, and his belief that he had
been empowered to reach a settlement with them concerning the imme-

diate implementation of home rule. Lloyd George was remarkably quick in reaching an agreement with both leaders, although controversy surrounds what each man knew or desired to know about provisions for excluding the six north-eastern counties.[3] Carson and Redmond both managed the difficult task of securing party majorities in favour of the scheme. For his part, Londonderry played a small but strategically important role at the two UUC meetings summoned on 6 and 12 June to decide on the proposals, his authority in the movement having been enhanced by his inheritance and lord lieutenancy.[4] Speaking in favour of Carson's negotiations with Lloyd George, Londonderry aligned himself with the Belfast bourgeoisie and Andrew Bonar Law. It meant rejecting the concerns of southern Unionists, many of whom were fellow landlords, and Unionists in the three outlying counties of Ulster. Londonderry wrote to his mother the following day:

> It was a very sad day for us all but there was nothing else to be done and I think our action was tactically right. The offer we got is a better offer than we have ever had before or are ever likely to get again and if there is a Bill to establish a clean cut, that places us in an impregnable position. It remains now to see what the Nationalists are going to do. I cannot believe that they will accept the situation and in that case we get all the credit for having taken the patriotic line and of having made a real sacrifice.[5]

Southern Irish Unionists were hostile to the immediate implementation of home rule, a view also shared by their allies in the cabinet, Walter Long and the fifth Marquess of Lansdowne.[6] Long made his objections known to Lloyd George on the 29 and 30 May, after which he was said to be happy with developments. However, after almost a fortnight of public silence on the issue, Long launched a blistering series of attacks on Lloyd George and Carson in an attempt to ruin the deal and even challenge the Unionist leadership.[7] On 1 June he wrote to Edith, Lady Londonderry, probably under the impression that her husband's recent letter to *The Times* placed the couple against Carson and Lloyd George. Long sought Lady Londonderry's help to oppose the settlement and reorganize the Unionist party:

> We must form a real Conservative Party. We have been betrayed. We shall save the state now but we must be prepared for the

future and I want you to join the 'salon'. It is a great opportunity and we want you. I am writing Charlie. He must come out as
the great Irish Gentleman.[8]

Although Lady Londonderry supported Long's argument, her husband, who had been serving at the front, was not so persuaded, and
chose instead to support Carson at the UUC on 2 and 12 June. On 14
June Londonderry drafted a letter to Lloyd George in which he expressed
his hope that the stand he took alongside Carson at UUC would help the
government at a time of crisis, although he also admitted to having 'mis-
givings' about immediate home rule for the south and west of Ireland.[9]
On 15 June, after almost two weeks of public silence, Long criticized the
settlement in a memoranda to his cabinet colleagues, the main thrust of
which was that Lloyd George had not been given cabinet authority to
make the deal he had with Carson and Redmond. Londonderry had
returned to the front by this stage and was therefore away from
Westminster just as divisions deepened between cabinet Unionists, with
Arthur Balfour and Law on one side, and Long, Lansdowne and the second Earl of Selborne on the other. With Selborne's resignation on 26
June, and an angry encounter between Long and Carson three days later,
the future of the Unionist party and coalition appeared uncertain.
Despite her husband's support for Carson at the UUC, Lady
Londonderry remained convinced of Long's critique of the settlement,
and this in turn led to her own charged encounter with the Carson-loyal-
ist Ronald McNeill. In the combative correspondence that arose from
this, Lady Londonderry gave particular emphasis to Long's argument that
it was inappropriate to alter the constitution at a time of war.[10] McNeill
took the opposite view, that war made a settlement necessary, and that by
agreeing to this the Ulster Unionist leadership were making a legitimate
and practical sacrifice.[11]

Long wrote to Lord Londonderry at the front on 2 July, the day after
the opening of the Somme offensive.[12] It is clear from a letter
Londonderry subsequently drafted that he was confused about recent
events, and that he felt duped by Lloyd George. Nevertheless, he erred
on the side of Carson and advised his wife to do likewise:

I know that everyone like myself who is out here does not count.
I am not saying this with any bitterness, because it is obvious that
unless one can make one's voice heard that one is bound to be
ignored. It is very tiresome for me, but while the war lasts, I must

be here taking a very small part here [sic] as you know and letting
all my own interests and duties at home slide ... In Ireland my
position is just an interested one. Before I succeeded I established no position in Ulster at all but I feel that the inherited position carries a certain responsibility with it. I wish you could see
E. C. [Carson] and find out exactly the position from him. I have
every confidence in him and I am sure that he can explain to you
what seems so obscure now. I was in full agreement with him in
Ireland. I was persuaded by him that we should support that proposal ... that Home Rule should come into operation at once for
the 3 provinces and that there should be a permanent clean cut
of the six counties. I did not like the arrangement and I said so
but my objections were removed by two very important things. I
understood that the United Cabinet had come to the conclusion
... I did not agree but it appeared to me that as the whole Cabinet
considered that the American situation was so dangerous that it
was a necessity for the winning of the war that I did not feel justified in my doing anything else but follow E. C's lead and do my
best to bring delegates to see the pressing importance of acquiescing in this arrangement ... You can judge my astonishment
when I heard that the Cabinet had never considered the matter
and that the proposal put forward by E. C. was not the same proposal as Redmond put before his followers.

There may be other good reasons for urging the Ulstermen
to accept the present policy which I gather is nearer the proposal put forward by Redmond, but the reasons which persuaded me
were those which E. C. put forward at the Conference and these
I understand were based on an absolute misunderstanding. L. G.
[Lloyd George] has employed very ordinary tactics. He told
everyone that everyone else had agreed and as no one met; everyone thought they were in a minority of one. I may be very stupid
and of course it is very difficult out here to keep in touch but I
think it is a pity that there should be any split in our old Unionist
party and it seems to me that must be avoided, but it won't be
avoided if there is any bitterness and I do see great bitterness...[13]

In an attempt to assuage the concerns of Long and Lansdowne, and
growing discontent among Unionist backbenchers, a cabinet committee
was established to look at increasing the safeguards for Unionists under
a home rule settlement. The changes this committee recommended
proved, not surprisingly, too much for Redmond, and his rejection on 22
July of the altered settlement effectively killed the enterprise. If this

episode was crucial to the unravelling of the broad Unionist alliance, then Lord Londonderry was an unintended beneficiary of this process from the outset. He may have been a relatively unimportant, if still prestigious, member of the UUC, but his support for Carson and Law ensured that he would have a political future within both mainstream conservatism and Ulster unionism. An alliance with Long and the southern-Irish landed elite may have been tempting, but he was never as close to them as he was to Carson, Law and Balfour, however strained and seemingly unrewarding his relations with them had been during his years on the backbenches.

I

Even if the Irish question was temporarily put on the backburner after July 1916, the demands of the world's first total war ensured that addressing it was of increasing strategic importance. Nor indeed could British politics escape from the demands of war. In December 1916 a second coalition was formed with Lloyd George as Prime Minister, Asquith having been judged unfit for the post by Unionists and Lloyd George-Liberals. This new alliance, dominated numerically by the Unionists, marked an end to the pre-war era of party factionalism and ushered in a new phase of consensus that endured until 1922.[14] Post-1916 developments in Irish politics provided Londonderry with the opportunity and position to demonstrate a consensual approach, thereby bringing him favourable government attention and patronage.

High-level discussions on how the Irish question might be resolved occurred throughout the winter of 1916 to 1917, but the entry into the war of the USA made this more urgent for 'appearances as well as for ends'.[15] Therefore, on 16 May 1917, Lloyd George offered the Irish party leaders a choice between the alternatives of immediate home rule, excluding the six north-eastern counties, or an Irish Convention, to debate a way out of the political impasse. All sides, for differing reasons, agreed to the latter; Unionists having ensured that Convention conclusions would be non-binding, and nationalists having been satisfied that parliament would enact any substantial agreement reached.[16] The government hoped that this assembly of Irishmen on Irish soil discussing Irish affairs might foster good relations between Britain and the USA, the latter containing a politically significant 'Irish-American' lobby.

Membership of the Irish Convention was, and still is, a matter of some controversy.[17] In particular, the absence of any Sinn Féin delegates undermined the Convention's claim to be representative. However, among the hundred or so delegates who did attend the Convention were representatives of labour, the churches and government appointees, alongside sizeable delegations representing nationalism, the UUC, and southern unionism. That Londonderry would be swept up in this large assembly is not that remarkable. What is of note is that although he was selected for not being a leading Unionist, his actions at the Convention served to enhance his authority on both sides of the Irish Sea.

It may be that Londonderry sought to make a pragmatic contribution to the Convention from the outset, for he was slow to accept his nomination as a delegate of the UUC; he may have instead sought nomination as an Irish peer, or as one of the government-appointed delegates. On 15 June the ninth Viscount Midleton, leader of the southern Unionists, informed Londonderry that he would not be one of the two delegates the Irish peers were entitled nominate to the Convention, but that 'the Government have it in mind to make you one of their representatives. It is quite clear you ought to have a seat on the Convention'.[18] However, on 22 June and again on 17 July, Downing Street notified Londonderry that he had failed to reply to the Prime Minister's confirmation of his nomination as a delegate of the 'Ulster Party'.[19] If the government and Irish peers were reluctant to appoint Londonderry as an independent delegate, then that might be explained by a notably Ulster Unionist speech he made to the House of Lords on 21 May 1917:

> I have watched with great surprise and sorrow the speeches of politicians … and the attitude of those newspapers which have urged Irish loyalists to give up principles in which they believed and to adopt some entirely new attitude to the Irish question because of the exceptional circumstances of the moment. We in Ulster have always believed that our prosperity and of the position which we occupy in the world is due to the union betwixt England and Ireland. We believe in the connexion, and sincerely we hope that no steps which will be taken by the British Parliament will endanger that policy … I would like to think that there was a possibility of uniting the Irish nation. But there is a dividing line. We are of a different race, a different creed, and we believe that the best government of these two different races is under the British Crown.[20]

He did however allude to his desire for a federal solution: '...there were bound to be great extensions of government and great changes in the future, and [Ulster Unionists] were willing to go forward with Great Britain in those great extensions.'[21] If Londonderry had typecast himself as an Ulster Unionist before the Convention, then his subsequent advocacy of federalism not only questioned this assumption, but also placed him, at last, within mainstream opinion in the House of Commons.

That Londonderry should represent the UUC at the Convention was not due to any rapid rise to the top of the movement, but the very opposite. Ulster Unionist leaders were wary of the Convention from the outset and sent a delegation not of leading men, but of party lieutenants. This allowed the leadership to distance itself from any potentially unpopular conclusions reached by the Convention. The leader of the UUC delegation was therefore not Carson or James Craig, but the Scotsman Hugh Thom Barrie, MP for North Londonderry. Lord Londonderry, nominally honorary secretary of the delegation, was effectively the deputy leader, and at 39 he was also one of the youngest delegates at the Convention. The other UUC delegates included Sir George Clark, a Belfast linen baron and a former MP, Colonel Robert Wallace, Grand Master of the Orange Order, and Michael Knight, a solicitor and leading Unionist from County Monaghan. Although not officially nominated by the UUC, other Ulster Unionists and their supporters met with the UUC delegation, including Hugh Pollock of the Belfast Chamber of Commerce; Sir Alexander McDowell, a Belfast solicitor; and the heads of the Anglican and Presbyterian churches. The secretary of the UUC, Richard Dawson Bates, also a solicitor, acted as secretary for the delegation.[22] More ominously, an External Advisory Committee was established to ensure that the UUC's team did not stray too far from party dogma.[23]

The Irish Convention first met on 25 July at Trinity College, Dublin, and continued to meet until its undignified demise on 5 April 1918. After some deliberation at its first meeting, the Convention elected Sir Horace Plunkett—a former Unionist now in favour of home rule—as its chairman, and Sir Francis Hopwood—subsequently created Lord Southborough—as the secretary.[24] The delegations outlined their positions at the opening meeting. Londonderry spoke first for the UUC and according to Plunkett was 'listened to with the closest attention, there being, naturally, much anxiety as to the line the Ulster Unionist groups would take.' Londonderry was keen to demonstrate that Ulster Unionists were not intransigent, stating that they had come to the Convention in 'friendliness' and with an 'open mind' to reach 'some general kind of agreement of what is the best for the government of this country.' He took pains to explain how Ulster Unionists believed that their economic prosperity was attributable to the union and the empire, and how they viewed the British Isles as a common unity, and not as colonizer and colonized. Plunkett recorded that:

> The speech produced the best possible impression ... It was delivered with an obvious lack of platform practice, which he explained by three years spent in discharging the duties of a soldier in France, but its tone and temper were perfect. As I listened to him I felt that he had all the charm of his father and a good measure of his mother's brains. He seemed to belong a little more to the later nineteenth and early twentieth century than either of his parents.[25]

As a fellow aristocrat, it is not surprising that Plunkett should have welcomed Londonderry's presence. It is also noteworthy that despite the above notes being included in Plunkett's 'confidential report' to the government, they were widely circulated among delegates, including Londonderry.[26]

Barrie and Pollock also spoke for the Ulster Unionists at the opening meeting, and again stressed economic arguments against home rule, but like Londonderry they failed to put forward a firm proposal of their own.[27] This is not entirely surprising given that they were not at the Convention to make proposals but to safeguard six-county exclusion. Yet Londonderry believed from the outset that his delegation could reach an agreement if that proved possible. This is evident from an exchange between the advanced nationalist George Russell and Londonderry on the first day of the Convention. In his 'Thoughts for a Convention', published in May 1917, Russell had rejected Unionist claims that economic success in Ulster depended on the union and empire.[28] It was his reiteration of this argument at the Convention that prompted Londonderry to reply that 'Unionists can be won if they can be persuaded that self-government is better than the Union'.[29] Given Londonderry's later conduct at the Convention, it is clear that this was no idle gesture on his part, but a sincere belief that seemed to ignore the restrictions that had been placed upon his delegation. Plunkett's policy of allowing all the delegates to air their views meant that the Convention did not get down to any serious negotiations until after the summer. In September 1917 the

Convention met at Belfast and then at Cork. When it met in the north-east, Londonderry emulated what other landed aristocrats had done and invited some delegates to Mount Stewart. It was an act that Plunkett hoped would have a more political function:

> The entertainments in Belfast and Cork were part of the active and var-ied social life which developed round the convention and which, it was hoped, would break down the isolation of the Irish political groups and promote acquaintanceships and understanding. The dinner and garden party were expected to prove useful accessories to the technique of nego-tiation.[30]

For Londonderry, it seemed as if a more successful and personally sat-isfying career in Irish politics was opening up before him. On 1 September 1917 he wrote to his confidant Lady Desborough:

> The Convention so far has passed a normal course … my ambi-tions in another sphere having failed this does satisfy a desire to be someone and to be really filling a place somewhere which car-ries responsibility with it … Last night I had a private confabula-tion with Labour, which was very interesting. The working man here does not look with such suspicion on a lord as his confrere in England does.
>
> I am enjoying being in Ireland very much. I really like it infi-nitely better than England, and I get on better with the people.
>
> I entered the Royal circle at the Viceregal Lodge and met rank and beauty in dazzling profusion. Another night I dined with the Lord Chief Justice (Sir James Campbell) and met old [Professor J.P.] Mahaffy and Tim Healy which was most interesting and we sat talking for a very long time, Tim being in his best form; the softer side was represented by the amusing daughter of my host, a wild-eyed Celt and an acquaintance (no more than that) of Countess Markievicz. I played bridge too, so beauty, politics and cards passed a delightful evening for me.[31]

If Londonderry was enjoying the social whirl of Dublin high society, then he was privately frustrated by the restrictions the Ulster Unionist delegation found placed upon them by the leadership at Belfast. Londonderry wanted to make the Convention work, and despaired at the lack of common ground among the delegates. In the first week of September he complained to the Secretary of State for War, Lord Derby, that the government had little concern for the lack of constructive progress made at the Convention.[32] But he was also frustrated by the UUC, and little wonder given how far he was prepared to go in negotiations. Writing to his mother on 23 September:

> We could govern Ireland from Belfast but I am not sure the stalwarts want to do that; they would much prefer to remain behind a six county [border] and make faces at the rest of Ireland. They have the whole thing in their own hands and I expect the verdict in a fortnight or so.[33]

II

A fortnight or so later and the cumbersome size of the Convention was addressed by the formation of a sub-committee of nine. This cross-party rebellion against Plunkett's plodding chairmanship included nine senior delegates from the main parties, but excluded the hapless chairman. Barrie, Londonderry and Pollock represented Ulster unionism on the sub-committee, which also included Midleton for the southern Unionists. The increasingly fragmented range of nationalism was represented by Redmond, Joseph Devlin, Bishop Patrick O'Donnell, George Russell and William Murphy.[34] The participation of the Ulster Unionists on this sub-committee was eased by O'Donnell's assurances that its deliberations would be non-binding, thus paving the way for all to discuss the powers and composition of a hypothetical parliament for the whole island.

Unionists were keen to ensure that their minority status was addressed by this hypothetical parliament. After some debate, the sub-committee agreed that the proposed senate would be a distinctly ascendancy chamber, appointed and not elected, with representatives from the churches, the peerage, the Privy Council, and organized commerce.[35] Such agreement was less forthcoming when it came to the lower house. However, Londonderry assured Midleton that the more 'satisfactory' representation was for Unionists the more liberal they could be about the powers of the parliament.[36] In the end Barrie settled at 40 per cent, having originally demanded 50 per cent, and the nationalists also conceded continued representation at Westminster.[37]

Having settled the question of composition, the sub-committee turned its attention to what powers a hypothetical parliament would possess. In contrast to the preceding consensus, a combination of economic fears and political intransigence led to deadlock on the amount of fiscal independence Ireland should have from Britain. O'Donnell proposed that Dublin should have control over customs and excise, but Ulster Unionists feared that this was too much of a concession. Plunkett intervened to suggest that each side write down their fears and objections about the economic policy their opponents were proposing. The Unionist sub-committee members felt that too much financial independence for Ireland would harm industry and commerce in the northeast, they therefore rejected nationalist offers to offset this with an imperial contribution from the Irish parliament, and for the retention of a British Isles free trade area.[38] Plunkett suggested that the nationalists send their economic concerns to the Unionists first. But unknown to him, they did so with a covering note that revealed how their economic policy was determined by considerations of nationhood and self-determination. In reply, the Unionists similarly mixed economic concerns with more political considerations, claming that an Irish parliament would evade contributing to the United Kingdom national debt and defence spending, and that fiscal autonomy would so separate an Irish parliament from Britain that it would achieve the goals of Sinn Féin.[39]

The ensuing deadlock created a mood of gloom. The sub-committee met on 15 November to prepare a negative report for the Convention's 'Grand Committee', scheduled to meet a week later. With all seeming lost Londonderry suddenly, and without warning, offered a glimmer of hope. It became known that he was going to table a motion for a federal scheme at the last meeting of the sub-committee, scheduled for 21 November.[40] The idea of a federal United Kingdom, with Ireland as a constituent part or parts, was not new to the Convention or Londonderry. However, there is little to indicate what he might have envisaged by a federal scheme, although he was in contact with other advocates of federalism, including Carson, the fourth Earl of Dunraven, and the former Liberal Foreign Secretary, the first Viscount Grey.[41] And given that federalism's leading exponents, Frederick Scott Oliver and the second Earl of Selborne, influenced these men, it is possible that Londonderry also shared their vision of national assemblies with wide powers.[42]

If it is uncertain what Londonderry meant by federalism, or how the nationalists might have reacted to it, the intention to offer it as a solution revealed his determination to make the Convention work. As Plunkett noted: 'Now an Ulster leader suddenly announces his intention of not only making, on behalf of his party, a constructive proposal, but of offering at any rate a certain measure of self-government, presumably for the whole of Ireland.'[43] But the UUC had not intended their noble delegate to preserve an assembly whose business they regarded with deep suspicion and fear. The UUC's advisory committee, which had been set up to shadow their delegation at the Convention, now stepped in to gently but decisively dissuade Londonderry from making his proposal. On 16 November a letter was written to him from Adam Duffin, a Belfast linen baron and member of the advisory committee:

> I am fully impressed by the view held by you and Mr. Barrie on the desirability of the Ulster Unionists on the convention showing readiness to consider if not to initiate some alternative constructive policy while breaking with the Nationalists on the demand for fiscal autonomy. I gather that you think this should take the shape of a federal scheme which would fit it with a wider one likely to be adopted before long for the United Kingdom … I am sure you will see the necessity of confining any such suggestions to the most general terms. I feel that you may be launched upon a sea of fresh controversy if they are even tentatively accepted as a basis for discussion by the other side, especially as you would have to make large reservations for Ulster, including probably education and judiciary.
>
> I am more than ever convinced that it should be frankly confessed that the Convention cannot come to any agreed settlement at the present time and that its deliberations should be suspended until such times as they may be renewed at the request of the Government.
>
> This is no time to succeed in framing a constitution for Ireland…[44]

Somewhat remarkably there is no minute of any meeting between the Ulster Unionist delegates, or their advisors, in the week following Londonderry's offer.[45] But pressure had been applied, and on 21 November, at the last meeting of the sub-committee of nine, Barrie announced that Londonderry would not propose a federal scheme as the Ulster Unionists 'did not think that such a course would ease the situation.' As Plunkett noted in response to Barrie's announcement: 'There was nothing for it but to take Lord Londonderry's will for somebody else's deed'.[46] When the grand committee met the next day, Barrie blamed the failure of the sub-committee on the distance between Unionists and nationalists on the fiscal question.

Londonderry, however, remained open to attempts at reaching a settlement, and regarded federalism as a solution in waiting, even if not one for the Irish Convention. Five days after the last meeting of the sub-committee, Londonderry outlined his views in a long letter to the nationalist Countess of Fingall, with whom he had clashed after the two had met at the Theatre Royal:

> There would be nothing easier than to rise in the Convention and by means of a few phrases to gain thunderous applause from a number of very ignorant men. Suppose I had reason to suddenly change my views, what purpose would I serve, because if that is what you intended to suggest please let me say at once that if the principles which I hold are so flimsy that Sinn Fein pressure can completely change them, those amongst whom I live are of totally different material. And after all, what is the gist of your argument, that we are so stupid or so avaricious that we will not subscribe to the Sinn Fein programme? Let me say that there is no difference between the loyal Nationalist programme and the Sinn Fein programme, the distinction lies in the attitudes of these two sections towards the Empire as explained by their leaders. Redmond so far as he expresses a definite view at all, claims that the feelings of benevolence which he undoubtedly entertains towards England and the Empire will ensure that separation will not be the result of the policy. Sinn Fein frankly states that the policy is intended to lead to complete separation ... I am absolutely convinced of one thing and that is that so long as the British Empire exists Ireland must remain politically within the circle of the United Kingdom and whatever path is chosen, long or short, or through whatever intermediary stages man in his wisdom or his folly may ordain she shall pass, that Ireland will be politically governed in exactly the same manner as England or Scotland or Wales. My plan is a Federal one...
>
> The demand to which you and others with varying degrees of invective ask me to agree is to give powers to Ireland, in a word "to keep her quiet", powers, which a Federal Government are bound to take away ... If I was certainly lacking in principle, which I hope I am not, I could propose two courses which might serve the needs of the moment. One would be to surrender to all Sinn Fein demands, knowing that this step would entail a bloody revolution at the end of two years. This surrender might just serve the purpose of temporarily strengthening the position of the Empire, in that this tiresome problem would be in

abeyance while patriots were fashioning a machine of Irish Government. It would not gain one single additional recruit for the Army, so in the surrender even this advantage would not be gained. But this position of admitted independence cannot stand under a Federal system ... I am not thinking of the moment in my work in the Convention, I am thinking of the future and the road along which lies the solution to the problem. You and your southern compatriots are idealists, you have always thought that the acquisition of what was in your minds at the moment meant satisfaction and living subsequently and for ever in peace and goodwill and happiness. Your friends have averred this during every great Irish controversy and the only result is that differences are more acute now than they have ever been before and the demands formulated more exorbitant and more impossible.

The second course I might pursue were I still totally lacking in principle is to back the Separatist demands. This would result in Great Britain applying coercion forthwith to the whole of Ireland and perhaps conscription as well ... There is no truth or object in denying that Ireland can prosper under the Union. There is Belfast a monument of industrial success and there is agriculture in all parts of Ireland manifestly in a prosperous condition, and it is obvious that had Irish Nationalists flung themselves into the task of local patriotic endeavour instead of always standing aloof and encouraging agitation and the hopeless pursuit of romantic and sentimental ideals, you would see a very different state of affairs in the political life of the country. There is no limit to local self-government which the evolution of modern government may not reach and to this movement I am a willing subscriber, but I repeat that this must limit Irish aspirations so long as the British Empire exists and if it does not exist God help Ireland ... I will say at once that while I am willing to proceed on the lines of Federation, I am convinced that it is folly to choose this moment to establish so far-reaching a change and so far as I can judge the only reason you desire a change which you never have defined if I may say so, is because Sinn Fein will in your opinion break out in open revolt. Do you imagine you are going to restore Redmond? Never have I had an illusion so shattered as regards Redmond; an Irish Leader with the gift of superb eloquence, but without a plan of any kind, and this is your prospective Prime Minister ... [Do] not ... quote me as saying that Ulster was the cause of the war. This I repudiate absolutely. One of the many causes controllable by human agency was the criminal folly of the Irish-Radical-Socialist

> alliance which seduced our Army, wrecked our Constitution and for wholly immoral reasons unconnected with that issue endeavoured to force on a free community a measure of Home Rule which, mark you, is now repudiated by everyone.[47]

Fingall responded positively to Londonderry's long letter, suggesting that he seek the assistance of George Bernard Shaw to promote federalism.[48] If this was a little fanciful, then she was not alone in regarding Londonderry as the possible broker of an agreement. It was a view shared by others, most notably by Professor W. G. S. Adams of the cabinet secretariat, and also the secretary and chairman of the Convention, Southborough and Plunkett.[49] Despite their hopes, Londonderry would not be prepared to break with the UUC, although this did not prevent him making his frustrations known to them.

On 18 December, at the last meeting of the Convention before it adjourned for Christmas, Midleton proposed a new scheme that he hoped would command wide support. The central thrust of his proposal was that Ireland should have a parliament with powers over all Irish affairs; this would be mitigated by the retention of customs at Westminster, and by safeguards for Unionists throughout Ireland. The Ulster Unionists—having resolved at a meeting beforehand that their role at the Convention would be to safeguard 'the interests of Ulster'—were now faced with another test of their ability to toe the UUC line.[50]

III

The Convention reconvened on 2 January 1918 with Midleton pressing for his scheme to be adopted. Given the recent high-level speculation about Londonderry, it was hoped that he might give some northern support to Midleton's proposals. As General Bryan Mahon, commander of the 10th (Irish) Division, informed Londonderry the previous month: 'I believe you are the only hope of any settlement being arrived at, both parties trust you'.[51] This may not have been entirely accurate, but it is notable that Londonderry remained on reasonably good terms with southern unionism from the start of the Convention, even though the divisions between Ulster Unionists and southern Unionists were wider than ever before.[52] In an attempt to attract Londonderry to the Midleton scheme, a southern Unionist, the third Baron Oranmore and Browne, suggested that it might form part of a federal plan. According to

Professor Mahaffy, Londonderry was not impressed by Oranmore's 'too recent' conversion.[53] It is more likely however that Londonderry's reaction reflected a meeting held the day before between the Ulster Unionist delegates and their advisory committee. This was convened to ensure that the delegation rejected the Midleton scheme and propose instead a settlement that excluded the six north-eastern counties.[54]

In pursuance of this 'advice', Barrie outlined the Ulster Unionist position to the Convention on 3 January:

> the Northern Unionists had come to the Convention to find a compromise between the Act of 1914, which had been accepted as a final settlement of the Nationalists demand, and the partition proposals of 1916. Now the Nationalists, only three years later, 'entirely owing to outside influences,' had enlarged their demand and submitted proposals which 'headed for separation and nothing else'.[55]

But it is clear from what Barrie said next that he personally was not entirely closed to the prospect of a deal. After the above denunciation of outside influences, he 'hoped that it was not even now too late to find a mean between the two extremes of the Home Rule Act on the one hand and the partition of Ireland on the other'; adding that an Irish parliament could demonstrate its worthiness to Ulster Unionists.[56] The following day the stakes were raised when Redmond gave his approval to the Midleton scheme on the proviso that the government legislate for it immediately, adding caustically that it was the Ulster Unionist delegates and not the nationalists who were 'pledge-bound to consult an outside body'.[57]

R. B. McDowell has argued that 'goodwill was in the air' in the first few days of January, a large majority of Unionists and nationalists seeming to back the Midleton scheme, leaving only the die-hards of either side at the periphery.[58] Not surprisingly, Londonderry regarded the scheme as a 'great opportunity', and Barrie is reputed to have assured Midleton on 3 January that he could rely on the Ulster Unionist delegates not to oppose him.[59] However, the momentum gathered in these first few days of 1918 was soon lost following the decision of Plunkett to adjourn this debate in favour of a debate on the land question; although he claimed this was also to allow parliamentarians to attend Westminster. Londonderry was also removed from the Convention at this time due to ill health, a victim of the notorious influenza epidemic that was the cause of many deaths during the winter of 1917 to 1918.[60]

With the major backers of Midleton's scheme absent, the main opponents of the proposals were able to consolidate their positions. Still determined to secure full fiscal autonomy for Ireland, Bishop O'Donnell received the backing of the Catholic hierarchy and a number of prominent nationalists. Redmond was therefore compelled to withdraw his support for Midleton when he returned to the Convention on 15 January.[61] With this the parties returned to their entrenched positions. Londonderry feared that instead of grasping something positive, the UUC had allowed themselves to be blamed for the Convention's failure:

> The Leadership of Ulster is not altogether a comfortable position and a great deal will depend on what comes out of the next few weeks. I think the Ulster men have a great opportunity but I do not think they are going to take it and it certainly looks as if they would come out of the Convention as being quite *non-possumus*.[62]

A fortnight later he informed his wife that someone had:

> suggested that the Ulster Division should mutiny or words to that effect ... not even to win the war is a single concession going to be made ... the rest of Ireland can go to blazes ... Belfast always disheartens me ... and the hatred of Ireland is a thing I really resent.[63]

In the wake of this latest crisis to afflict the Convention, the Prime Minister intervened by offering to receive a delegation of Convention representatives in order to hear their views and encourage progress towards a settlement. It was, however, an admission of defeat, for the hope that Irishmen could resolve their differences on Irish soil was shown to be wishful thinking. Informal discussions preceded the actual meetings with the premier. At these preliminary meetings Barrie considered a vetoing Ulster committee in the Dublin parliament, and Carson mulled over the idea of an Irish parliament containing two lower houses, one representing the north and the other representing the south.[64] Lloyd George exchanged these ideas with other parties until he finally met the whole Convention delegation on 13 February.

Lloyd George's hopes of creating a working consensus proved too ambitious; and his insistence on the fiscal question being left until the end of the war, and his view that partition was a barrier to a settlement, could only offend the die-hards on either side. Having been influenced by F. S. Oliver's most recent pamphlet on federalism, Carson wrote to Lloyd George on 14 February urging him to propose a settlement on federal lines.[65] But Carson was hemmed in by the demands of the UUC, and therefore compelled to insist on six-county exclusion, but he did try to suggest that Ulster could be part of a federal scheme.[66] Barrie expressed his frustration to Londonderry on 16 February:

> You will recall … the Chief's letter which I received yesterday … Reading it over carefully it means an absolute refusal of the P.M's suggestions, and no doubt this is a correct interpretation of the feeling of most of our delegates. I had rather hoped that we should have arrived at the same end by allowing the Bishops and their friends to veto these proposals, but we must be guided by our Chief and loyally obey his instructions.
>
> In view of this communication I seen [sic] no purpose in having the intended meeting of our Advisory Committee, and it will be sufficient that we have the usual meeting of our delegates on Monday evening week 25 inst. at 9 p.m., at the Shelbourne [Hotel, Dublin].[67]

On 21 February Lloyd George wrote to Barrie putting forward a compromise position. The plan included home rule, a delay in the fiscal question until the end of the war, greater representation for Ulster in the Irish parliament, and an 'Ulster Committee' with the power to veto relevant legislation. The Prime Minister suggested that the Ulster Unionists should consider his proposals favourably for the sake of the war effort and to appease critics in the USA.[68] Londonderry was concerned that Ulster Unionists would reject the scheme and drafted a letter to Carson on the same day:

> I never was in your confidence before my Father died and I certainly am not in it now. I believe your view is more or less the same as mine, namely that the war must take precedence of every other problem great and small and that even a temporary arrangement of our prejudices and difficulties ought to be come to if it can possibly be done.
>
> I believe also that you are satisfied that the offers suggested to be made to Ulster now eliminate those dangers which induced us in 1914 to take up arms in our own defence. But even holding these views … you feel that because Ulster opinion appears to be

so strong, we should not even make an effort to induce our con-
stituents not only to consider the desperate position of the
Empire, but also to realise that from the tactical point of view we
can brand the R.C. Church as really opponents to a settlement of
the question.

If this is so I feel very unhappy about it. You are the only man
who has any real over-riding influence in Ulster – we do not
count and I especially do not count, for reasons which I need not
go into and as your determination seems to throw your weight
into the scale of the strongest opposition to any settlement; then
all I can say is that I wish that instead of procrastinating because
we have done nothing else, we had left the Convention some
months ago.[69]

Four days later, on 25 February, the Ulster Unionist delegates met with
their advisory committee at Belfast.[70] Londonderry's fears that the Ulster
Unionists would reject the premier's scheme were confirmed. One of the
advisors, Hugh de Fellenberg Montgomery, a landlord who had reluctantly accepted the 1916 Lloyd George settlement, took the precaution of
contacting Londonderry the following day on the matter of why he had
taken issue with him at the meeting:

It may have appeared unnecessary and perhaps offensive to insist
so strongly on your bringing L[loyd] G[eorge]'s proposal before
us again before giving any sort of consent to it, but what I felt
was that your statement was to the effect that Lloyd George had
asked you to bring the suggestion before us, and that you had
done so, therefore, merely to give you a free hand, [sic] would
have implied that you were at liberty to consent to this proposal
if you liked, which I was sure the Advisory Committee or the
majority of them were not prepared to do. L.G's reasons for urging you virtually to come to some agreement, [sic] with the
majority of the Convention seemed to me absolute bunkum.
What is really meant is that Lloyd George has involved himself
in promises to the Home Rulers and possibly to the Americans
and other sentimental sympathisers and finds he cannot deliver
goods, and wants us to enable him to do so, he gives absolutely
no reason for the statement that a settlement would make it easier to get on with the war. Would handing over the administration of a great part of this country to the friends of the enemy
… help to win the war … Having said this much I may add that
I think at the present stage of the Convention it would be quite

useful to represent the upshot of our meeting as a refusal to consider the suggestions in Lloyd George's letter, till they are put in a clearer and more detailed form ... I was never able to see the force of the argument that in the present troubled state of Ireland and in the war going on [sic] we ought to join the Redmondites. It appeared to me that the proper conclusion to draw from the state of things was that the moderate Redmondites ought to join us.[71]

Londonderry blamed Carson for not having the strength to overrule doubters in the UUC; he did not appear to appreciate the constraints Carson faced, or even consider the potential electoral difficulties that might face a more pragmatic Ulster Unionist leadership. It would be a character trait he would exhibit throughout his career. On 27 February he wrote to his mother: 'I think Carson is quite impossible and he thinks that he can come and go as he likes; back one day, disappear the next'.[72] In a fit of pique not too dissimilar to the frustration he felt in September 1912, Londonderry concluded his letter by refusing to return to Ulster politics until the rebelliousness of Ulster Unionists had waned. In response, the dowager Marchioness engaged in that long practised art of pressuring the Tory leadership to have her son appointed to the government.[73]

Rather than uniting the Convention, Lloyd George's intervention sealed the divisions that had been fermenting from July 1917. Having repeatedly been dressed down by their advisory committee, the Ulster Unionist delegation could do little else other than to offer the Convention their original exclusion proposal. And although Londonderry once again touched on the possibility of a federal solution, an idea that now commanded a wide spectrum of support at Westminster, Ulster Unionists were fully aware that it was unlikely to attract much support from the nationalists.[74] In the meantime—in contrast to the forced unity of the Ulster Unionist delegation—the southern Unionists began to split on the question of immediate home rule, and O'Donnell demanded a greater amount of self-determination in the face of Ulster Unionist unwillingness to drop exclusion.

On 6 March the Convention adjourned to mark the passing of John Redmond, his death seeming to symbolize the demise of the old nationalist party. Londonderry was the only leading Ulster Unionist to attend the funeral at Westminster Cathedral. On 16 March he wrote to Ethel Desborough:

> The Irish Convention is doomed and the sooner it is wound up the better ... [Lord Midleton] oscillates now between bearding the R.C. bishops and shaking his fist at my colleagues; but he is still good enough to retain his regard for me although the fact I have maintained my virtue has diminished his respect ... I then processed behind Redmond's remains for 2¼ hours ... The stout Protestants of the north with whom I am associated look on this [referring to a riding injury] as a direct visitation for associating myself with Papistry. Perhaps there is something in it ... Ireland has always been a tragedy and I am at a loss to know what to do now. It is such a pity that Ireland cannot be pushed a little further out into the Atlantic ... I am planless now. I do not know what place to drop into.[75]

When the Convention reconvened on 12 March it began a process of voting on an extensive list of proposals. As a bloc, the Ulster Unionists voted against anything that did not make provisions for exclusion, and proposed that a secretary of state be appointed for the excluded area.[76] O'Donnell and his supporters also voted against many of the proposals. Nevertheless, a combined majority of southern Unionists and Redmondite nationalists voted in favour of the schemes put forward, but their political weight outside the Convention was not nearly so strong. A final report was considered in early April and passed by a majority of 44 to 29. The Ulster Unionists and O'Donnell-nationalists compiled their own minority reports, reciting their positions respectively on exclusion and fiscal autonomy. Plunkett sent all the reports to Lloyd George and wrote a covering letter citing the chief difficulties as being Ulster and customs.[77]

IV

The Convention's failure coincided with an increasing demand for manpower at the front. Ireland—which had been spared the enforcement of conscription but not the constant rumour of it—was an obvious but by now largely unwilling recruiting ground. From the end of March 1918 the cabinet had begun to discuss the possibility of simultaneously implementing conscription and home rule. Concerns were raised in cabinet about the reaction of Ulster Unionists to home rule, and of the effect conscription might have in increasing support for Sinn Féin, but even Law and the first Viscount Milner leaned in favour of this solution.[78]

But the government faced a problem. The Convention was still draft-ing its final reports in the first week of April, so the home rule scheme could not be immediately adopted, whereas the army's request for more manpower needed to be addressed as a matter of urgency. On 9 April the Prime Minister announced to the House of Commons that legislation allowing for conscription in Ireland would be drafted. In his memoirs Lloyd George records that Londonderry did not support the application of the Military Service Act to Ireland.[79] Yet the evidence suggests other-wise, not least Londonderry's speech to the House of Lords on 17 April, the day before royal assent was granted, in which he 'urged the conscrip-tion of Ireland as an Irishman who was jealous of the good name and honour of Ireland.'[80] Indeed, on 20 June 1918 he demanded that con-scription be implemented in Ireland on the basis of equality with the rest of the United Kingdom and again called for a federal scheme to be adopted by the cabinet committee then considering the implementation of home rule for Ireland. This latter speech was part of a more damning critique of the coalition government and its Irish policy, and was made not long after Londonderry had refused a very junior position in that government:

> Members of such a Government were inclined to lose their indi-viduality, and to accept doctrines to which in pre-war times they were opposed. They had seen a policy pursued which those under whom he had served had always condemned—Ireland cajoled at one moment and dragooned at another.[81]

Londonderry went on in his speech to welcome the recent appoint-ment of the first Viscount French as the Viceroy of Ireland, hoping that the accompanying restructuring of Irish government would allow French to govern without interference from London. Londonderry was referring to a new departure at Dublin Castle whereby the Viceroy took charge of Irish policy with the assistance of a fully subordinate Chief Secretary. French's home rule sympathies and tough stance on law and order meant that he initially had a 'unique crossparty appeal' in Ireland.[82] Nevertheless, Londonderry was not convinced that the government's simultaneous policy of delaying conscription until the autumn would be effective in raising the hoped for 50,000 volunteers.[83]

Londonderry would soon find himself part of the new pro-consular arrangements at Dublin Castle, but not before he rejected an offer to join the government itself. With the demise of the Convention on 5 April

1918, Londonderry was considering a return to the army, but his friend Lord Derby, the War Secretary, encouraged him instead to continue in politics. The dowager Marchioness had meanwhile been busy lobbying the Tory leadership to find a post for her son.[84] On 28 February Arthur Balfour reported to Law:

> The Dowager Lady Londonderry has written me an impassioned appeal to get Office for her son ... I have not answered her letter, but when I see her I shall tell her that this is no affair of mine, and that I never thrust in my advice on such matters. I shall also add that I have communicated with you! Londonderry, who is a very good fellow, really appears to have done very well in the Irish Convention, and to have won golden opinions from all Parties.[85]

Law replied:

> I think myself that Londonderry is well entitled to get an appointment and if he had not gone to the House of Lords I am sure he would have got it long ago. As it is we are all anxious to find something for him and the first vacancy there is of any kind for which a Peer is suitable will, I hope, be of such a kind as to make it possible to offer it to him.[86]

The increasing slippage of government posts from the House of Lords to the House of Commons was not new in 1918—Londonderry even addressed the upper house on this matter in July 1918—so the first suitable vacancy to arise came out of a vastly diminished pool.[87] In early June Londonderry was offered the post of Whip. Whips in the Unionist dominated Lords had more powers than their equivalents in the Commons, particularly in the management of government business; but Londonderry, with the support of Derby, felt that this was not enough to 'muzzle' him on the Irish question.[88] It was in the wake of this rejection that he went on to launch his stinging public attack on the coalition.

If Londonderry had previously enjoyed an uneasy relationship with fellow Ulster Unionists, then his refusal to join the government certainly went down well among those such as his onetime critic Adam Duffin.[89] Not long afterwards, Londonderry made his first appearance at two Orange 'Twelfth of July' demonstrations in County Antrim, at Finaghy and Lambeg. Colonel Wallace, Grand Master and fellow Convention delegate, introduced Londonderry to the Orangemen as the man who had initiated the debate that led Lloyd George to delay home rule (below).[90] With this specious re-branding, Londonderry went on to use his platform speech to attack the government's military recruitment policy. On 13 July he accompanied Carson to a meeting at Belfast of the newly formed Ulster Unionist Labour Association. The appearance of a marquess before this organization might seem a little out of place, but the UULA was deferential, socially conservative, strongly loyalist, and ultimately a failure.[91] Again, Londonderry summarized his views on the Convention in way that completely failed to acknowledge how close he had been to promoting a deal with Redmond and Midleton:

> ...as a member of the Convention he was convinced that there was nothing between the maintenance of the union and separation. There was no separate nationality in Ireland any more than in Scotland or Wales, and for military and commercial reasons as well as for social progress it was absolutely necessary to maintain the essential unity of the United Kingdom.[92]

If Ulster Unionists were recasting their wayward peer as a staunch Unionist then others hoped he might emerge as a leading advocate for federalism. The issue had become increasingly popular among the political elite towards the end of the First World War, especially after the failure of the Lloyd George settlement of 1916 and the growing feeling that the Irish question had to be settled for the good of the war. Londonderry had been a proponent of Oliver and Selborne's most recent pamphlet on federalism, *Suggestions for the Better Government of the United Kingdom*, a tract that had also influenced leading members of the cabinet committee charged with looking at home rule.[93] However, the announcement by Lloyd George on 25 June that home rule would, like Irish conscription, be delayed, effectively killed-off the need for the government to consider a federal solution. A delegation of federalists that included Selborne met with Lloyd George the following day, and although the Prime Minister was sympathetic he made it clear that there would be no radical reform to the United Kingdom while the war carried on. Not included in the delegation was the MP Moreton Frewen, a member of the Irish gentry with business interests in the USA, and a keen champion of landlord rights.[94] Responding to Londonderry's disappointment that the delay of home rule meant that federalism was off the agenda, Frewen suggested that the Marquess might head a campaign to bring it back:

we "have been had" ... I should value a quiet talk with you ... a talk on the wider subject of Federal Govt [sic] than merely ones hopes as to Ireland. Whether there is more of folly or danger in the sort of "deputation" Selborne has arranged for today, I know not. It will result in chaotic discussion of the issue by men utterly in the dark as to what it means & a strong set back for the principle of Federalism. If I am right, then is not this the right moment for you & Carson to take hold? I think it is. We others who have been working it will drop out & help as best we can, with our knowledge, in the background. If I might advise, you yourself might come out and advocate a "League of Federals" & be the first President. I could not only steer a lot of good fellows in, but I think send over a lot of funds from the US.

It wants a young man & a brand new man, all of us who have hunted in that line were too "previous" & previosity [sic] in a matter of this kind is never forgiven ... There is really no one of much importance in public life except AJB[alfour] who would not accept the Federal solution if it comes from the right quarter. You will have to advocate two States for Ireland & if you do this, bear in mind *en revanche* every Irishman will do his utmost to break up England ... But if you advocate Two Statehood [sic] for Ireland & make all sorts of good tempered alluring speeches "that when the right time comes Ulster will join at Dublin" – play that sort of hose on them & you will create a good federal atmosphere.[95]

By the end of June Frewen's enthusiasm had been diminished by the meeting between Selborne and Lloyd George, 'a deplorable mess'; but he did suggest that Londonderry could still 'do something', as long as it was 'along safe lines'.[96] With even such a long time enthusiast for federalism having given up hope, it is not surprising that Londonderry did not jeopardize his increasing prominence by heading a futile 'League of Federals'.

It is clear that Londonderry's political capital was significantly higher in 1918 than it had been ever before. And although an enquiring journalist may have been overly flattering when he wrote in July 1918 that Londonderry's 'views on the Irish situation ... carry great weight', Londonderry was no longer just a wealthy magnate, but like his father, a potentially useful and pragmatic voice in Ulster.[97] On 13 August he wrote to the Prime Minister to complain about the home rule sympathies of the Irish Chief Secretary, the Liberal MP Edward Shortt, and used the opportunity to again press for a federal scheme:

I have no desire to criticize Mr Shortt in any way but I am bound
to say that his handling of the Irish Question shows a profound
ignorance and will increase the difficulties which confront us in
plenty as it is…

Mr Short is pushing the course which many English politicians have done before and that is to raise hopes which cannot
be fulfilled. Home Rule on the lines of what is known as
Federalism can be given to Ireland as a portion of a much larger
system with which I will not weary you now when you are
engaged in matters of pressing importance. Dominion Home
Rule cannot be granted to Ireland for obvious reasons, and the
sooner a British Government definitely and deliberately takes up
this attitude the sooner will Ireland become peaceful and con-
tented.

The conflict in the Convention raged round Dominion
Home Rule and the middle parties, about which I am inclined to
think you received more information than about any other party,
had no following anywhere. The strength of the advocates of
Dominion Home Rule lay in the fact that utterances like Mr
Shortt's were taken to mean that some time or other Dominion
Home Rule will be granted.

I am not aware now what position Mr Shortt occupies in the
Ministry. I did understand that Lord French was the actual
Governor of Ireland and I welcomed the change from the usual
practice. By this change I understood that Mr Shortt was practi-
cally an Under Secretary and no more, otherwise I could not
understand how he came to be chosen to fill a post which
requires infinitely more than an English Constituency education
in Irish affairs … I have willingly done what I could to strength-
en the administration which you have set up in Ireland, but by
remaining silent now I run the risk of appearing to endorse Mr
Shortt's views and this is a situation I am not prepared to
accept.[98]

Irish conscription had been delayed until September 1918 to give
French some time to raise 50,000 recruits. On 18 August, with the dead-
line in sight, and only around 8,000 recruits, Londonderry took the
extraordinary step of informing the Viceroy that he was prepared to raise
his own Irish brigade to go to the front.[99] French refused the offer on the
basis that the War Office would reject it, but the letter may have brought
the Ulster noble to the general's attention just as he was looking for candidates for his new Advisory Council, or perhaps even confirmed

Londonderry's suitability.[100] Either way, the government chose to drop their plans for conscription.

On 23 August Londonderry was one of seven men formally invited to join the Viceroy's Advisory Council.[101] It was one of a series of military and civil committees that were created under French to assist this quasi-military governor in the administration of Ireland, but it would prove to be the most significant, even despite its untimely demise in December 1918. The Council was intended to represent 'men of position and standing in different parts of the country' but, as Eunan O'Halpin has noted: 'a less representative collection of Irishmen it would have been hard to find: they were simply rich men who were afraid of Sinn Féin. Apart from Londonderry'.[102] The members of this thoroughly patrician gathering included the fourth Earl of Dunraven and the eighth Earl of Granard, both southern Unionists; the nationalist Walter MacMorrough Kavanagh; Frank Brooke, of Ulster gentry stock; Sir Stanley Harrington, a bank director and railway chairman; and Sir Thomas Stafford. Those, like Londonderry, who were not already Irish privy councillors were elevated and thereby given access to Irish government files. And although the Council did not meet until October, Londonderry was quickly drawn into a heated row between the Ulster Unionists and Dublin Castle.

French's administration had originally hoped to reintroduce a policy of constructive unionism to Ireland, but while the imprisonment of many leading republicans in May 1918 and other draconian measures did create a more peaceful climate, increasing support for Sinn Féin was seemingly unstoppable. In line with the Castle's crackdown on violent groups, Shortt issued orders in August that the weapons of the Ulster Volunteer Force (UVF)—like those of the national volunteers—be seized and placed in military custody. Carson and Bates agreed that Londonderry, given his new association with the Viceroy, should be engaged to press their case.[103] Their position vis-à-vis the Castle was aided by the Viceroy's private secretary, Edward Saunderson, second son and namesake of the onetime leader of the Ulster Unionists. Initially, Ulster Unionist protests to Shortt were met with a stony resolution. Bates argued that the seizure of UVF arms would drive young Belfast men to the ranks of the 'Bolsheviks' and other left-wing groups, a deliberate play, perhaps, on French's strong dislike of the Irish trade union movement.[104] When French intervened to allow UVF weapons to be gathered at UVF armouries, and to be placed thereafter under military control, with permits granted to those who handed in weapons, Shortt halted the planned movement. However, following a request from Londonderry, the orders of Shortt were in turn rescinded by a furious Viceroy.[105] French and Saunderson now personally arranged for the storage of UVF weapons, thus ensuring that Unionist concerns were assuaged.[106] In subsequent correspondence with Carson, Londonderry referred to the question of UVF arms as a 'nuisance', but one he felt that needed to be addressed.[107]

French viewed the deteriorating political situation in the country as proof that, for the present, Ireland was incapable of governing itself. He confidently declared the problem to be one of insufficient infrastructure and wanted his new Advisory Council to focus on development.[108] The Council met for the first time on 10 October. Contrary to the wishes of French, Shortt arrived at the first meeting and suggested that the Council was a 'body in the nature of a Cabinet.'[109] Walter Long, who acted as a conduit between the coalition cabinet and Dublin Castle, also argued that he wanted to see the Council turn into 'a sort of Irish Cabinet.'[110] Londonderry took a more cautious approach, stating that while he hoped the Council would 'develop into something more substantial and responsible', he disagreed with the term 'cabinet', for it implied 'one conviction, one idea, one thought'.[111] He was similarly cautious about how the Council's activities would be made known to the public, and was successful in having publicity about it delayed for a few weeks after the first meeting.[112]

Collective responsibility was therefore not imposed upon the Council, and in the few months it sat, all were unaware as to the exact nature of their posts: were they advisors or governors? Its main and stated purpose was to look at economic matters, but the agenda for the second meeting included an examination of the general condition of the country, election precautions, and a scheme for granting land to soldiers.[113] There is little evidence that individual members were given portfolios, but Londonderry did become involved with agriculture, an issue he had only the slightest association with since his election to the House of Commons in 1906.[114] For his part, Frank Brooke appears to have been dealing with the Council's fears about the possibility of Sinn Féin county councils mistreating returning soldiers.[115] It is perhaps for this reason that the Irish Republican Army murdered Brooke on 30 July 1920.

It was this question of what the Council constituted, or more properly, what it might become, that framed its very public collapse in the second week of December 1918. Long and French had been discussing the possibility of turning the Council into something more like a government, one that might replace a scheme for home rule. But when the cabinet began to consider giving the Council new legal powers to aid its reconstruction work Shortt protested, rightly fearing it as a substitute for home rule. The increased confusion that surrounded the role of the Council led *The Times* on the 13 December to declare that it was in a 'muddle'. With that, no extra powers were granted to the Council and French quickly lost interest in it. No more meetings were convened.

Despite the failure of the Irish Convention and the Advisory Council, Londonderry had emerged from both with his authority enhanced. He had developed a reputation for being pragmatic, for putting the war above the concerns of Ulster Unionists, and yet of remaining loyal to that grouping even after a tense period in their ranks. For his role in these events, he was rewarded with a place in the post-war coalition government, and soon after, with the Order of the Garter. His outwardly steadfast association with the Ulster Unionists also gave him the opportunity to join the first government of Northern Ireland in 1921, and thus have a political career in both Britain and Ireland.

It is ironic that Londonderry's career started to progress at a time when the various species of unionism with which he was associated, directly or by temperament, began to unravel and part company. A period when Ulster unionism, in particular, had simplified, retreated and retrenched.[116] But this is at the heart of why his authority was enhanced in Ulster and at Westminster. The latter viewed him as conduit between Belfast and London, a reliable and safe pair of hands among an increasingly unreliable Belfast leadership; for the Ulster Unionists he provided a highly-placed political and social link with the front bench at Westminster. At a time when the landed elite of Britain and Ireland were feeling the effects of almost forty years of decline, Londonderry had survived marginality, earned positive prominence through his work in Ireland, and begun a government career that would last, intermittently, into the mid-1930s.

3

The Air Ministry, 1919–1921

If the scope of Lord Londonderry's political career had once seemed constrained by his aristocratic background, then, somewhat paradoxically, his inheritance of the Londonderry title and vast fortune in February 1915 helped to loosen those constraints. Political ability, or the perceived lack of it, still counted, but so did opportunity. As an immensely wealthy grandee peer, Londonderry may not have been able to imagine himself as Prime Minister, but his upbringing had inculcated him with a belief in his right to rule, and the socio-economic structures to realize this ambition. This background also afforded him the opportunity to have a political career on both sides of the Irish Sea, for aristocracy was still able to transcend localism and provincialism: a supra-national elite, at least in areas that shared the same nation-building aspirations.[1] Of course, individual agency was still important for political success, had Londonderry sided with the southern Unionists in the summer of 1916, or at the Irish Convention of 1917 to 1918, the Ulster Unionists would not have had him in their post-1921 government. And it hardly needs to be stated that he would not have been found a comparable place in the emergent Irish Free State, where a different nation-building project was stepping up a gear. Agency would also play a role in his ability to gain, remain and return to British politics, for no matter how wealthy he was or how grand his title, his political outlook had to acknowledge and espouse the credo of the post-war era: consensus and appeasement.

Londonderry's period in the post-war coalition government of Unionists and Lloyd George-Liberals is significant for three reasons. First, as has been mentioned, it reveals how his role in Irish affairs had made him a more viable candidate for government office at Westminster, and that the political spheres of Ireland and Britain were not wholly separate, especially for aristocrats. Second, for what he did in office.

Londonderry had learned to trim his sails and accept political realities, especially the consensus agenda espoused by the Prime Minister, David Lloyd George, and the cabinet Unionists who supported him. In particular, this meant overseeing the decimation of the nascent Royal Air Force, and raising no public protest at the increasing role of the state. Lastly, this brief period of office provided Londonderry with valuable ministerial experience that was not only useful for the offices he would later occupy, in Northern Ireland and at Westminster, but also for providing him with a more sustainable claim on those offices.

Even before the Armistice on 11 November 1918—an event that necessitated the first general election since December 1910— Londonderry had enjoyed some government patronage with his appointment to the Viceroy's Advisory Council earlier that year. Although this in no way bound him to the coalition, or the survival of it after the war, it no doubt impressed upon him the potential rewards awaiting those who swam with the tide of Unionist opinion, specifically, the acceptance of Lloyd George as the premier of a Unionist dominated government. Most Unionist leaders had realized that the post-war years would demand a consensus approach to domestic and foreign affairs, and were therefore prepared to continue to place their trust in the man who had led the country to victory in the First World War, at least for the time being.[2] Londonderry too would come to realize this. Having expressed concerns in May 1918 about the coalition, he was by the end of August that year, days after his appointment to the Viceroy's Council, a reluctant convert.[3]

This is not to say that Londonderry's attitude to Lloyd George and the coalition had remained static until he was offered a place on the Council, or that consensus politics were new to him. It has already been shown how Ireland gave Londonderry an arena in which to demonstrate pragmatism. But signs of this approach to politics were evident during his time in the House of Commons, albeit obscured by his unimportance and relative anonymity. Even if he was biased against reforms to taxation and parliament, and biased in favour of the coal owners, he was not immune to articulating the rhetoric of cooperation and moderation. In part, this may have represented a belief that such reforms were inevitable, and that they had to be made as palatable as possible; but as has been demonstrated, it also reflected his own estrangement from the bulk of his party. As he wrote to the government's Chief Whip, Lord Edmund Talbot, on 28 August 1918: 'Speaking for myself, I shall never forget their attitude to Home Rule, and when I look up Bonar Law's speeches in

Belfast before the war I see that his convictions are somewhat easily adjusted.'[4] He concluded the letter by hoping that Lloyd George would get on with winning the war instead of passing more controversial legislation.

Londonderry's support for the coalition could not be confined to rhetoric. Like his ancestors he was the head of the Unionist party in County Durham, and thus an influential voice in the selection of Unionist candidates for the county's parliamentary constituencies. The Great Reform Act of 1884 had done much to erode such influence, but as Cannadine observes: 'Provided they were still prepared to exert themselves as local political leaders, resident landowners remained potentially the most influential and significant element in the rural power structure.'[5] One prospective candidate for the Tory constituency of Stockton-on-Tees, Captain O. L. Martin, had assumed that the dowager Marchioness of Londonderry continued to perform this function in the county, even after her husband's death, for it was she and not her son who occupied Wynyard during the First World War. Lady Londonderry informed Martin that her son now took care of these affairs, and soon after the captain's case was impressed upon Lord Londonderry.[6] By the end of August 1918, a local Unionist organizer in County Durham, Major Stanley Appleby, wrote to Lord Londonderry to persuade him of the suitability of a Mr Watson as the Unionist candidate for Stockton. But Londonderry had already decided in favour of Captain Martin, and in response to some of the die-hard rhetoric of Appleby, added that it was 'the duty' of Unionists to support Lloyd George at the next general election.[7] In reply Appleby once again promoted Watson as the Unionist candidate, and added:

> If only we can clear out of this country all the alien blood and
> let the national characteristics of Englishmen carry their full
> weight in the government of the country, I think we shall find
> the greater portion of Labour coming out on the right side in
> favour of order and common sense.[8]

Appleby's statement was typical of contemporary die-hard opinion, set as it was against the backdrop of Unionist hostility towards the perceived leniency of the government's Aliens Restriction bill. Londonderry attempted to assuage Appleby's frustration:

> I fully agree with what you say about English Bolshevists, but I
> will ask you to remember that party politics and party organisa-

tions have been in existence for too long to establish anything in a moment in direct opposition to them. It is far better to capture the old organisations then to infuse those same organisations with the principles in which we believe.[9]

The conflation of race and political ideology was common in 1918, but it grew more so in the subsequent decades, and Londonderry would return to this question in the late 1930s in correspondence with Joachim von Ribbentrop.

A total of 533 seats were won by the coalition-Liberals and -Unionists at the December 1918 general election, the latter taking 339 seats. Lloyd George continued as Prime Minister, and Andrew Bonar Law acted as his deputy and the guardian of the Unionist interest. Winston Churchill, a coalition Liberal, was also returned to the cabinet. Having been refused a return to the Admiralty, Churchill was given charge over the ministries of War and Air, and was similarly successful in having his cousin, Londonderry, appointed to the Air Council.[10] Churchill's second cousin noted that 'friend Winston has come to the rescue just when I was going to turn into a 'Local Magnate'.'[11] However, not only did Churchill's patronage prove a mixed blessing, it is likely that even without it Londonderry would have received some minor office, especially given that he had a few other notable supporters, including Walter Long and Arthur Balfour.[12] Nevertheless, in the longer term Londonderry's relationship with Churchill continued to be of importance, helping him back into office in the late 1920s, and ensuring the polar opposite in the 1940s.

I

Although the Ministry of Air was under the control of the Secretary of State for War, it maintained its own structures and bureaucracy, in particular, the ruling Air Council, one of the few emergency bodies established during the First World War to outlive that conflict.[13] Churchill was president of the Air Council, and the Under Secretary of State for Air, John Seely, his deputy. It also contained other members with responsibilities for military and civil aviation. As Finance Member of the Air Council, Londonderry had responsibility for decreasing military funding and for encouraging private enterprise in civil aviation. Ironically, his membership of the House of Lords enhanced his limited authority within the Ministry, for it designated him spokesman for Air matters in the upper house.[14] But the Finance Member received no remuneration for his very junior post, something that upset his mother for reasons of status rather than income.[15] It led her to conclude that her son had 'never had the luck of the race.'[16] The dowager Marchioness never lived to see 'Charley' promoted to Under Secretary of State for Air in April 1920, for she died the year before on 16 March 1919.

It was inevitable that the end of the war would necessitate demobilization and drastic cuts to military expenditure. Londonderry's two years at the Air Ministry as Finance Member, then as Under Secretary of State, were therefore dominated with managing this task. The 'Ten Year Rule', agreed by the cabinet in August 1919, underscored this resolve, with its optimistic declaration that Britain would not be engaged in another great war for ten years.[17] Londonderry spent much of his time terminating government contracts for aircraft and selling off equipment and land. A fellow member of the Air Council, Sir James Stevenson, warned the Finance Member that the task might arouse public concern about the state subsidising this process: 'I should get down to these contracts as soon as possible. There are innumerable difficulties ahead and the sooner most of them are cleared away the less likelihood there is of anything bordering on public scandal. You won't sleep comfortably in your bed until these difficulties have been settled.'[18]

The Air Ministry was not entirely happy about giving away aircraft for what amounted to nothing—for example, Londonderry signed over 50 aeroplanes to Canada in February 1919—but it needed a buyer to cover the immense of costs of disposal.[19] This function was performed by a consortium fronted by Frederick Handley Page and Godfrey Isaacs, the younger brother of the first Earl of Reading, a favourite of Lloyd George. They agreed to purchase most of the former air force stock for one million pounds, paid in yearly instalments with the Ministry receiving half the profits from further sales. As the whole value had been estimated at roughly one hundred million pounds, the sale led to some public concern and accusations of creating a monopoly.[20] However, H. Montgomery Hyde in his history of air policy has noted how 'in the end … the taxpayers got back several millions of pounds from what, but for the skilful handling of sales, would have been scrap metal and timber.'[21] By the time Londonderry left the Air Ministry in the spring of 1921, he had completed this 'grim' task without arousing any scandal, no small achievement given the Anti-Waste movement then gaining ground within the Unionist party.[22]

Having been Secretary of State for War from June 1912 to March 1914, John Seely grew increasingly unhappy about his subordinate position at the Air Ministry, and finally left his post in December 1919. Prior to his resignation, Seely had urged Lloyd George to create a separate Air Ministry, no doubt in the expectation that it might return him to cabinet, but the Prime Minister demurred, citing the need for government to avoid increasing expenditure. Having attempted to assuage the frustrations of Seely, Londonderry emerged from this crisis with some credit, but when Churchill recommended that his cousin replace the outgoing minister, Lloyd George chose instead the Unionist MP George Tyron.[23] In his memoirs, Londonderry claimed that Lord Curzon had blocked his first attempt at promotion, and recorded Churchill's response: 'What can I do? ... your own people are against you.'[24] As for why Curzon should be so hostile to his ambitions, Londonderry attributed this to poor relations between them, in particular his recent refusal to grant early demobilization to Curzon's footman.[25] However, despite the anecdotal value of this explanation, it is more likely that Londonderry's association with Churchill caused Curzon to reject his promotion, for the latter had recently been appointed Foreign Secretary, and quickly grew to resent the War Secretary's role in external affairs.

Not even Londonderry's investiture as a knight of the Garter on 18 December 1919 could lift him out of his despair at having been passed over.[26] Churchill wrote to his cousin the following week, on Christmas Day, reminding him that he had been bestowed a great honour, and advising him to 'be entirely good tempered and apparently indifferent', to be 'guided' by him. '[T]hen I am sure that your public career will open out satisfactorily; whereas quarrelling with the present regime will only strand you on the mud flats.'[27] The Garter was indeed a prestigious honour for any aristocrat, and its award to Londonderry led Curzon to oppose the move in a letter to Law. But to Londonderry it may have appeared more as a sinecure than a reward for services rendered in Ireland. After all, his father had to serve as Viceroy of Ireland before he was given the Garter in 1888, and the third, fourth and fifth marquesses had received similar honours as an alternative to giving them political office.

Londonderry's failure to receive a promotion, coupled with his aristocratic aggrandizement as a knight of the Garter, caused him to lobby Law hard for a promotion, with help also from his wife and Churchill. This paid off on 2 April 1920 following Tyron's move to the Ministry of Pensions, when Londonderry was promoted to Under Secretary of State for Air, Curzon's opposition now having evaporated.[28] In reporting the appointment *The Times* commented:

> With the Irish question raised to the highest pitch of interest by the [fourth] Home Rule Bill, comment will no doubt be caused by the promotion of two of the leaders of Ulster Unionism, Sir James Craig and Lord Londonderry … The appointment of Lord Londonderry to succeed [Tyron] will not be questioned on personal grounds. He has given good service as Finance Member … But the House of Commons will assuredly object to an arrangement by which, with the Under-Secretary in the House of Lords, it can only secure information on air policy from Mr Churchill, whose predominant interest is in the Army.[29]

If Londonderry had to struggle to gain even this modest promotion, it did not stop him from having far greater ambitions. With a declining number of government posts for peers to occupy at home, many looked to the empire for satisfaction. As Cannadine has noted, 'the British Empire provided secure, comfortable, well-paid, and essentially ornamental employment opportunities in quite unprecedented numbers. And as a result was a system of outdoor relief for the upper classes'.[30] Londonderry felt that he too deserved a place in the sun, not a mere ornamental office, but one of the few that carried political weight: India. On 3 May 1920, only a month after his appointment as an under secretary of state, Londonderry wrote to Viscount Milner, Secretary of State for the Colonies and grand old man of Britain's imperial service. Londonderry intended his letter to end speculation that he might accept the post of Governor-General of Canada, claiming that he would not give up his place in the government and his commitments to Ireland for a purely ornamental role.[31] The implication of the letter was, however, that he would give up his political commitments for India. Milner was clearly unimpressed by Londonderry's claim on the viceroyalty and appalled by his dismissal of the Canadian post, the training ground of many Indian viceroys. So in his reply, he avoided mentioning the subcontinent and accepted Londonderry's refusal of Canada, adding that he for one thought more of Rideau Hall than the Under Secretary of State for Air.[32] In the end, Lord Reading was appointed to New Delhi, and Londonderry continued to delude himself about the possibility that he too might one day assume the post.

In contrast to his uneasy relationships with some senior ministers, Londonderry got along considerably well with Marshal of the Royal Air Force Sir Hugh Trenchard. Although the government had appointed Trenchard head of the air force to implement its policy of cut backs, in particular to prevent the development of an imperial air force, Trenchard and Londonderry shared a passion for promoting the use of military aeroplanes.[33] Londonderry fondly recalled their first meeting in his memoirs, noting how he ignored protocol by visiting the Marshal at his office, and not insisting that Trenchard come to see him:

> … after a formal greeting, [Trenchard] began to tell me what he intended to do with this and that. He delved among piles of papers and found the one he wanted immediately. Then he went on with his short, decisive phrases with so much energy that I was a little taken aback. After listening for a while I ventured to remark, 'But what if I don't agree with you?' He looked up in doubt: there was a moment of silence: then he laughed as energetically as he had been talking. From that moment there was a complete understanding between us.[34]

Trenchard recognized in Londonderry an agreeable and pliable ally in the Ministry, one who would aid him in his ongoing defence of the fledgling air force. The two men agreed on air policy instinctively—Trenchard assigning his proxy at meetings to Londonderry—and sought to protect the independence of the RAF from those within the military and government who, for differing motives, felt it could be absorbed by one of the older services.[35] Nor was the relationship all one-way. When the First Sea Lord, Admiral of the Fleet Lord Beatty, demanded that a Royal Naval Air Service be established, Trenchard was angered by the very public request, with its implication that the RAF was somehow inadequate. Londonderry assuaged Trenchard by claiming that the Royal Navy feared loosing major responsibilities to the RAF, and of being in 'dread that an air officer might one day be Commander-in-Chief.'[36] The two men became close friends, they shared confidences, and in the summer of 1920, Londonderry became godfather to Trenchard's newly born son.[37]

It may be that a degree of aristocratic embrace was at work between the two men. It is not inconceivable that Trenchard, the son of a bankrupt provincial lawyer, might have been delighted by the prospect of a marquess being the godfather of his son, and not just a mere under secretary of state. Indeed, Londonderry also brought a degree of aristocratic patronage to the belittled RAF. Londonderry House was a venue for formal and informal Air Ministry functions, helping Lady Londonderry to inherit her late mother-in-law's status as a leading political hostess. And with Churchill still overseeing War and Air, Lord Londonderry was looking more like the head of his own department, albeit not a particularly important ministry.

At one of the many public events he attended as Under Secretary, the sixth Aeronautical Exhibition at Olympia, in July 1920, Londonderry took the opportunity to criticize what he regarded as alarmist reports in the press about Germany rearming itself. In phraseology he would resurrect in the late 1930s as Secretary of State for Air, Londonderry informed the military and civil dignitaries who constituted his audience that a commission of control would ensure that any new German machines would be of no military use.[38]

Like his sympathy for Germany, Londonderry's admiration for military aeroplanes began during his time at the Western Front. And like many other contemporary aristocrats, he was keen to associate himself with and promote 'air-mindedness', thereby associating the apparently anachronistic landed elite with an innovative new technology. But it was his close relationship with Trenchard that transformed this from a mere appreciation into his becoming a staunch defender of the RAF. The importance of this would only really emerge when Londonderry returned to the Air Ministry in 1931 as Secretary of State. For his determination to safeguard the future of the RAF in the 1930s, especially at the Geneva Disarmament Conference, placed the government in some considerable difficulty. As he later noted:

> Through every phase [the Ministry] could always rely on Trenchard's good sense and clear thinking. He was never failing in sound advice, and it was my association with him which gave me such firm convictions of the ultimate importance of aviation in the future of international life. He gave me that sense of the air and the Air Force so that when the Service was threatened with extinction, about a decade later, I was already aware of the air possibilities whereas many of my colleagues were not.[39]

Cutbacks to spending and imperial commitments had an undoubted impact on the future viability of the RAF, especially when the economy began to falter in the winter of 1920 to 1921. It is ironic therefore that these same demands gave the air force a role that would safeguard its existence. Britain had emerged from the Paris peace conferences of 1919 with a larger empire, one that now included League of Nations mandates in the Middle East. With the army already stretched, the Air Ministry was able to take charge in Mesopotamia, for the RAF offered a faster and cheaper form of imperial policing.[40] This form of military intimidation had demonstrated its utility in 1920 when an uprising by 130,000 Arabs against British rule in Mesopotamia was 'broken primarily by RAF bombing and machine-gunning'.[41] Although the Under Secretary did not have to personally sanction such manoeuvres, the RAF's role in imperial security would become one of the main planks of his defence of aerial bombing in the early 1930s.[42]

The link between the Air Ministry and the Middle East became so strong that Londonderry acted as government spokesman in the House of Lords on the mandate of Palestine. On 20 April 1921 he dealt with questions from members of the Lords who were hostile to continued Jewish immigration to the mandate, and who pressed for the details of a recent US report on the subject to be released. Londonderry did not have any strong views on the Palestinian question and therefore unhesitatingly adopted the government line on the importance of the 1917 Balfour Declaration—that it was a precondition of the mandate—and denied that he could reveal the results of a foreign report.[43]

II

Civil aviation was in still in its very early stages during Londonderry's time as Under Secretary. One of his notable achievements was therefore the introduction and passage of the Air Navigation bill in May 1920, for this became the basis for the international law of the air. Londonderry was also involved in the provision of grants and subsidies to private aircraft companies in an attempt to boost private enterprise in air transport.[44] This role was enhanced in March 1921 when Churchill appointed Londonderry the chairman of the Cross-Channel Subsidies Committee. This development came in the wake of press criticism about the poor performance of British air transport companies in comparison to the their generously subsidized French rivals.[45] Nevertheless, Londonderry was all too aware that this did not mean that the increasingly stringent Treasury was willing to part with more money for the sake of national pride, especially with the Anti-Waste League fermenting discontent among Unionist backbenchers.

When he held the first conference between his committee and representatives of the aircraft industry on 10 March, Londonderry warned the
delegates that although the Ministry wanted to increase investment, they
would have the considerable task of constructing a good case for the
government to agree to this.[46] A week later he announced to the press
that the conference had agreed on two broad schemes: that the Ministry
should purchase British aircraft and then rent these to private companies,
or give them guarantees against losses.[47] However, Londonderry ruled
out any underwriting of private companies, but promised instead that
subsidies would be provided at least until the end of the summer season
so as to prevent the French from eclipsing British companies. It was a
patchy solution to a long-term problem, but it did signal Londonderry's
capitulation to government intervention in private enterprise. It was not
however a wholesale conversion, for Londonderry remained hostile to
the nationalization of industry, and still retained some ambivalence to
intervention inspired by social policy. But given that the government's initially enthusiastic attempts at social reform were by 1921 falling under the
Geddes axe, Londonderry's stance appeared more in harmony with the
coalition government than at any time before.

The recent criticism of Britain's civil aviation led the Prime Minister
to at last separate the ministries of War and Air; marked on 1 April 1921
with the appointment of the Liberal MP Freddie Guest as Secretary of
State for Air. Churchill had recommended Londonderry for the post, but
the appointment of a peer would have risked further hostility from the
press at a time when the government was coming under increasing criticism. After a few years of modest success, Londonderry's background,
specifically his membership of an unelected chamber, had put a brake on
his career at Westminster. For Londonderry, the blame also lay with Law
and other leading Unionists for failing to support his promotion.[48] If this
was a little sweeping, then it is likely that Curzon would have objected to
Londonderry's appointment, for the Foreign Secretary might have
viewed it as a further increase in the already considerable influence in
external affairs of the new Colonial Secretary, Winston Churchill.[49]

There is, however, another reason that would have made Londonderry
a controversial choice for promotion, one that he never acknowledged.
Enormous wealth certainly supported his political ambitions, but post-
war unrest in the British coal industry was placing its owners under more
public scrutiny than ever before. When Londonderry was cross-examined by the Sankey Coal Industry Commission on 8 May 1919, he admit-

ted that he would use his position as a member of the House of Lords to block reforms to the mining industry if he felt it was in his interests. His membership of the government was not raised during the hearing, perhaps because as Finance Member he had almost no say in policy, but it was clear from what Londonderry said that he was not prepared to submerge his private responsibilities beneath a lofty idea of public duty.[50] There is no record suggesting that this checked Londonderry's political ambitions, but the coalition government's poor relationship with the miners was a constant irritant to its ambition to represent the national interest. Moreover, Londonderry's failure to receive promotion occurred on 1 April 1921, the same day as the first post-war national miners' strike.

If Londonderry's background had finally caught up with him and halted his steady progress in the government, it still afforded him the option of returning to Irish politics. He had retained close links with the Ulster Unionists throughout his time in the government. Like the coal situation, this too might have played a part in checking his hopes for promotion, for Edward Carson and Ronald McNeill were prominent die-hard critics of the government. And yet the Ulster Unionists were not at variance with the government over their chief concern: supporting the 1920 Better Government of Ireland Act that gave parliaments to Northern Ireland and Southern Ireland.[51] On 31 May 1921, Law came across news that Londonderry was shortly to take up the combined post of Minister of Education and Leader of the Senate in the newly devolved parliament at Belfast. It prompted him to write to Londonderry, assuring him that he could find him another post at Westminster.[52] But the Irish peer had made up his mind, and probably felt that there was little Law could do, especially since he too had resigned from the government.

Londonderry left the Air Ministry on relatively good terms with its civilian and military personnel.[53] He had successfully steered through the Ministry's more controversial measures at a time when the government was coming under greater pressure to cut back on 'waste' and lessen its military commitments. He had also managed to avoid the bitter controversies that were to test the coalition government, particularly the debate about fusing the two coalition parties into one, and the even more divisive issue of social policy. Nor had he dabbled in foreign affairs, except to dampen down some of the wilder rumours about German rearmament.[54] But his close associations with Churchill, the Ulster Unionists, and the coal industry, and his membership of an unelected chamber all served to undermine his hopes of steady promotion. Moreover, he had shown himself to be rather too keen on advancement, particularly in his dealings with the respected Lord Milner. These were hardly matters that could decide the mortality of a political career, but they were relevant when the government had a considerable pool of experience from which to chose ministers.

In time Londonderry too would have more experience, and be offered the post of Secretary of State for Air in 1922 and in 1931. More immediately, his experience of running a government department made him an invaluable asset in the creation of a new devolved parliament at Belfast. Londonderry had resigned from the government because of his failure to be promoted, not because of any difference in ideology. This is notable in itself, for it demonstrated how far he had come from his many years of sniping at the sidelines of British politics. It was a lesson he had learnt remarkably quickly while at the Air Ministry and under the tutelage of Churchill, one that helped him regain office at Westminster in 1928, and enter the cabinet in 1931.

4

Northern Ireland, 1921–1926

In contrast to a peripheral and ornamental involvement with Ulster unionism before the First World War, Lord Londonderry thereafter achieved a prominent position in the provincial hierarchy that culminated in his appointment to the government of Northern Ireland in 1921. Like the five other ministers of this new administration, Londonderry was faced with the task of state building at a time when the very existence and legitimacy of the state was being challenged by politicians, British and Irish, and ongoing violence between Unionists and nationalists. However, Londonderry's reaction to these difficulties distinguished him from his colleagues. As Minister of Education, he was the only member of the cabinet who had to implement controversial social reform that required support from both protestants and Roman Catholics. As Leader of the Senate, he was the only minister appointed to the new parliament and not elected by the people. Londonderry was the wealthiest minister of a cabinet almost entirely made up of wealthy men, and although not the only landowner, he was the only titled nobleman. With the exception of Sir James Craig, the first Prime Minister of Northern Ireland, Londonderry was the only other minister with experience of office at Westminster. Unlike Craig, however, his career and political outlook had not been grounded in Edwardian Ulster unionism. Initially, Londonderry's distinctiveness made him an asset to the first government of Northern Ireland. But when he became a liability, it made him all the more vulnerable.

For these reasons it has been suggested that Londonderry's appointment was 'an anomaly', that his lack of conventionality guaranteed the emasculation of his education reforms in 1925.[1] This is perhaps overly deterministic, for there was in the very first years of the new state, as Patrick Buckland has argued, a fragile willingness to govern for everyone.[2] The aristocratic paternalism of Londonderry, and his successor at the Ministry of Education, the eighth Viscount Charlemont, did not make them anomalies. Rather, they were manifestations of a strain of constructive or anti-populist Ulster unionism that was often, but not exclusively, associated with Ulster politicians from the landed elite.[3] With his strong connections to England, his sense of Irish patriotism, and his belief that Ireland could only prosper under the union, Londonderry was the epitome of anti-populist and constructive unionism.[4] It has been argued that constructive unionism was ultimately destructive, raising nationalist expectations without being able to carry the support of die-hard Ulster Unionists.[5] However, this too, if not qualified, can be overly deterministic, for it was only at times of crisis that constructive Unionists found themselves sidelined by other wings of the movement. As Jennifer Todd explains:

> Tensions and contradictions existed in the body of [Unionist] thought. They were continually brought into view as the Union itself was consistently challenged in the Irish context. That these tensions fractured into competing theories, however, has more to do with the crisis of political unionism than with any logical incompatibility.[6]

In his memoirs, Londonderry outlined why he moved from the Air Ministry to Northern Ireland in June 1921:

> There was a real call of the blood in this invitation, for my family had been so long associated with Ulster. My father always sought to persuade me to make the Irish Question the main theme of my political activities, and when he died in 1915 I was expected to take his place, and if I had turned my back on the offer which James Craig had made to me, I should never have forgiven myself, or been forgiven by those with whom I had been associated for so many years. I also felt, notwithstanding my happy associations with the Air Ministry, that in view of the apparent opposition to myself amongst those whom I counted as my friends, I could do more useful work in Ulster.[7]

His decision to depart the Air Ministry was therefore not entirely one of chagrin, for Londonderry had a viable alternative by virtue of his family background. Even after his tense period representing Ulster Unionists at the Irish Convention of 1917 to 1918, he continued to represent their

interests, on the Viceroy's Advisory Council, at the Air Ministry, and in a
private capacity. For example, days after the Armistice of 11 November
1918, he wrote to David Lloyd George to protest about the King not visiting Belfast as part of the victory celebrations.[8] And exactly a year later,
he lobbied for Ministry of Munitions contracts to be given to Ulster.[9] His
ongoing association with the province was recognized on 8 April 1920
when he was awarded the freedom of Belfast, along with Field Marshal
Sir Henry Wilson and the Marchioness of Dufferin and Ava.[10]

Londonderry had therefore been accepted as a leading Ulster
Unionist, but it did not mean that he had conformed to popular expectations. Unlike Craig's indifference to the fate of south and west Ireland,
Londonderry, who as a member of the British government rarely spoke
publicly on Irish affairs, used those occasions when he did to address the
increasingly dire situation that faced the entire island.[11] Nor was his concern for all of Ireland restricted to ministerial rhetoric. Only days before
he was given the freedom of Belfast, Londonderry had offered to save
George Russell's journal *The Irish Statesman*. Few Ulster Unionists would
have understood why he wanted to help a Dublin journal edited by an
advanced nationalist, despite the constructive and establishment tone of
its contents.[12] For this reason it was perhaps fortunate for Londonderry
that his offer was declined and not made public. Nevertheless, his brand
of unionism was far from being a secret, as the readers of the staunchly
Unionist *Belfast News-Letter* discovered on Christmas Eve 1920 when they
read his comments on the Better Government of Ireland Act 1920:

> The setting up of two Parliaments … gives the best chance of
> ultimate unity. Those acute points of difference may disappear in
> the discharge of duties common to the whole of Ireland … I do
> venture to hope that every Irishman, whether he be of the North
> or of the South, will … give his wholehearted co-operation
> towards achieving success.

It was probably for this reason that he was appointed to the only Ministry
that was to engage meaningfully with the minority Catholic community.
Far from being an anomaly therefore, Londonderry was the most appropriate of Craig's ministers to take charge of Education. An additional factor might have been that Londonderry's father had sat in the British cabinet from 1902 to 1905 as President of the Board of Education.[13] This
would not have determined Craig's decision, but he might have felt it fit-
ting that the seventh Marquess oversee the reform of education in
Northern Ireland just as his father had in England.

I

On 29 April 1921, four weeks after Londonderry had been passed over for promotion at the Air Ministry, Craig formally asked him to accept nomination to the Senate of Northern Ireland.[14] Winston Churchill reacted badly to Londonderry's decision to leave the Westminster government, but given his own difficulties with colleagues in the coalition, he acknowledged his cousin's sense of duty to Ulster. He did however have reservations about the problems Londonderry would face.[15] During his time at the Air Ministry, Ireland had slipped into a routine of bloody tit-for-tat violence between the Irish Republican Army and Crown forces. In the meantime, the coalition government had passed the Better Government of Ireland Act 1920, creating parliaments in Northern Ireland and Southern Ireland. Only the Ulster Unionists were prepared to work the Act and sit in the Northern parliament; Sinn Féin preferring instead to constitute the Dáil Éireann.

By the time of the state opening of the Northern Ireland parliament at Belfast City Hall on 22 June 1921, Lloyd George had decided to seek an agreement with Sinn Féin on the future government of Ireland. The first public indications of this were, somewhat ironically, delivered in George V's speech to his new parliament at Belfast. Within weeks hostilities between the IRA and Crown forces had ceased, followed by months of protracted discussions, before formal negotiations between Sinn Féin and the British government finally began on 10 October. It had been agreed that the British would negotiate only with Sinn Féin, with the government of Northern Ireland attending as consultants. This arrangement suited all sides including the Ulster Unionists. It allowed them to avoid responsibility for the outcome of the negotiations, and their status as consultants went some way to meeting criticism from their own supporters that they should not negotiate with Sinn Féin. Addressing these critics from the Senate on 20 September, Londonderry defended his government's decision to attend the negotiations as consultants, arguing that to have refused would have placed them in the wrong before the British people and risked a settlement being made behind their backs.[16]

Whatever the intentions of the Ulster Unionists, it quickly became apparent that the continued existence of Northern Ireland was a bargaining device in negotiations about the proposed sovereignty of an independent Ireland. Like other Ulster Unionists, Londonderry was anxious about relying on coalition Unionists, his former colleagues, to safeguard the existence of Northern Ireland. In particular, he feared that the delay in transferring powers to the Belfast government had a deeper consequence. On 1 September, while the parties were still discussing formal negotiations, he outlined his thoughts to one of the leading Tory diehards, the fourth Marquess of Salisbury:

> ... our position as a Government is being hopelessly prejudiced. I don't know if you are aware that, although we are called the Cabinet of Northern Ireland, we have no power whatsoever. The offices are not yet transferred, but the police and the military are under the control of the British Government. Consequently, you will see that whereas everybody here looks upon us as the Government, we have no power to do anything on our initiative. If it were the Machiavellian plan to make the Northern Parliament a failure, this is by far the best way to do it.[17]

Londonderry was one of the Ulster Unionist consultants to the negotiations.[18] With Craig firmly in control of the delegation, it seemed as though there was little for Londonderry to do other than play host at Londonderry House, although even this could serve a political purpose. From 1915 Edith had made herself and Londonderry House the centre of a group of politicians and artists known as the Ark (see chapter 5). It was through this group, specifically the artist Sir John Lavery and his wife Hazel, that the Londonderrys were able to have some indirect communication with the Sinn Féin negotiators.[19]

The nationalist Lady Lavery felt that progress might be made if the leading Sinn Féin delegate Michael Collins met with Lord Londonderry.[20] She was not the only one who thought such an encounter might be productive, for Churchill, representing the British government at the negotiations, also considered a meeting between the two. On this occasion Londonderry declined to meet with Collins, claming that the IRA leader had been party to the murder of his fellow officers and friends.[21] But he must have also realized that such a meeting would produce very little, for even Craig had almost no room for manoeuvre had he wished to be more flexible.[22]

It was during these negotiations that the changing and problematic relationship between Ulster unionism and British unionism—more usually known from this time as the Conservative party—came sharply into focus. Austen Chamberlain had led the latter from March 1921, and as a

member of the cabinet negotiating with Sinn Féin, was willing to press
the Ulster Unionists to submit the Northern Ireland parliament to the
authority of a Dublin parliament in return for Ireland retaining links with
the empire. Whereas 'empire in danger' had necessitated Conservative
support for Ulster before the First World War, it now meant giving
Ireland a unitary state with dominion powers.[23] Had Londonderry
remained in the coalition government and outside the Ulster Unionist
party, he might have shared Chamberlain's view that Northern Ireland
was an obstacle to removing the sore of the Irish question from domestic and imperial politics. In reality, Londonderry felt that his former colleagues were reacting only to IRA violence. And like many Ulster
Unionists, he lashed out at the way leading Conservative newspapers took
the view of Chamberlain.[24] However, not all Conservatives agreed with
Chamberlain; a die-hard element threatened to wreck the party's
November conference at Liverpool if the government acted to undermine the Ulster Unionists. Andrew Bonar Law intervened decisively at
this point to ensure that the coalition government did not act against the
Ulster Unionists, therefore safeguarding the leadership of Chamberlain
for the time being. On 28 November Craig confidently informed his cabinet that they no longer needed to quarrel with London as 'the
Government was changing its attitude towards Ulster.'[25]

The 'Anglo-Irish Treaty' was signed on 6 December. Although committed to safeguarding the six counties, Lloyd George also conceded to
Sinn Féin the essential unity of Ireland. He reconciled these contradictory stances by allowing Northern Ireland to opt out of the dominion
scheme agreed with Sinn Féin: the Irish Free State. This, in turn, would
trigger the establishment of a Boundary Commission to readjust the border in accordance with local considerations. Despite this caveat, the
Ulster Unionists emerged from the negotiations with the most favourable
result. The Sinn Féin delegates had failed to achieve either recognition of
their republic or Irish unity; Ulster Unionists on the other hand had managed to keep their parliament within the United Kingdom and receive a
breathing space to prepare for the Boundary Commission.

This did not stop them from complaining. And for Londonderry, this
not only provided him with a chance to attack the government's conciliatory attitude to Sinn Féin, but also the leadership of Chamberlain.[26] As
the leading Ulster Unionist member of the House of Lords,
Londonderry led the opposition debate on the Treaty in the upper house
on 15 December. By doing do he associated himself and the Ulster

Unionists with the die-hard element of the Conservative party. However, rather than adopt a narrow Ulster Unionist perspective, Londonderry dismissed the ability of the Treaty to deliver lasting peace. With allusions to Viscount Castlereagh, he condemned the misuse of the Act of Union since it came into effect in 1801, arguing that the present situation arose because Ireland had not been governed properly or allowed to enjoy a long period of prosperity. He went even further by stating that the parliament to be established at Dublin only needed to prove itself worthy for Unionists to consider participating in it, as they had 'never expressed a determination to remain outside for all time.'[27]

The speech was in marked contrast to the 'brilliantly vulgar' tirade that poured from the mouth of Edward Carson, now Lord Carson, when he got up to speak.[28] It was probably for this reason that the Lord Chancellor and Treaty signatory, Viscount Birkenhead, formerly F. E. Smith, remarked that Londonderry had shown 'statesmanship' in his remarks.[29] Unlike Carson, Londonderry emerged from the Treaty debate with some credit, and this would serve him well in the coming years when he sought a return to the British government. However, in the short term, his opposition to the Treaty probably led to the decision being taken that he would not carry the Cap of Maintenance at the next state opening of the Westminster parliament, although court officials claimed this decision had been taken in the light of new constitutional arrangements. Londonderry, they claimed, was now associated with the Senate and government of Northern Ireland, and had acted as Minister in Attendance when George V opened the Belfast parliament earlier in the year. It is uncertain if the King had any part in this decision, but in any case, he made up for it when he and the Queen dined at Londonderry House a few months later, on the 10 March 1922.[30]

To many Ulster Unionists, however, such displays of 'statesmanship' portended Londonderry's suspect loyalty to their cause. For although he had expressed similar platitudes at the Irish Convention, he was now the supposed guardian of a parliament many Unionists felt to be their best line of defence against Dublin and London. Writing in September 1922, Londonderry outlined the pressure he felt himself to be under:

> I have always been criticised in Ulster and I always will be, because I am sometimes half a length in front of local ideas and this makes me suspect ... Somebody has got to tell the truth instead of agreeing with everybody, and I fancy it is a duty of mine ... I confess Belfast has always disappointed me a little ...

> Craig is so splendid about raising the whole thing out of the
> slough of parochialism, and I see so many agents doing their best
> to drag it down again. [31]

In a state that had struggled to survive political intrigue and often
bloody violence, it is not surprising that Londonderry's constructive
approach to governing Northern Ireland should meet with disapproval in
certain quarters.[32] For constructive Unionists, heavy policing could only
be one part of a broader strategy to secure the future of the state, for
they also felt a pragmatic and understanding attitude towards nationalists
was also necessary. If this meant Londonderry was suspected of leniency in Ulster, then it made him a benign figure to those in Dublin and
London who resented the apparent truculence of Craig. It was to
Londonderry, in April 1923, that the then premier of the Irish Free State,
W. T. Cosgrave, wrote in order to successfully ask for the release of a
southern prisoner.[33] It was also to Londonderry that the British turned
when faced with a deadlock in inter-Irish and Anglo-Irish relations, as in
December 1921, outlined above, and later in August 1924.

The violence that engulfed Northern Ireland before, during and
immediately after its creation in June 1921 worsened Unionist-nationalist
relations in the six counties and across Ireland generally. Between June
1920 and June 1922, 1,766 people were wounded and 428 killed as a result
of the violence, the majority of whom were Catholics.[34] It was widely
believed that Michael Collins, the first leader of the Irish Free State, had
a hand in IRA attacks on Northern Ireland, and it was feared by London
that this situation might damage the effectiveness of the Treaty. Churchill
therefore hosted a conference between Craig and Collins at the Colonial
Office in the third week of January 1922. The two Irishmen agreed on a
series of measures to cool tensions, but although they also agreed to deal
with the boundary question themselves, there was no agreement on how
much land might be transferred from the north to the south.[35]

Continuing unrest in Northern Ireland necessitated another meeting
at the end of March 1922.[36] Once again talks faltered on the possible size
of transfers from the north to the south. There was, however, some
agreement on other matters, such as the boycott of northern goods and
police reforms. If a number of Ulster Unionists felt that Craig had conceded too much, they would have been furious had they known about
Londonderry's informal meeting with Collins during this second attempt
at a pact. Both men had emerged from their meeting with nothing but

praise for the other. For Londonderry, he had 'spent three of the most delightful hours that I have ever spent in my life.'

> His enthusiasm was delightful as he unfolded his plans for the future in stirring phraseology. Perhaps I knew history a little better than he did and perhaps also I knew the power which he had over his followers and also the power which I had over mine when he entreated me to join with him in a really big conception.[37]

Londonderry also claimed that Collins had told him how he wanted to turn Ireland into a loyal portion of the empire as an inducement to Unionists, but when he made the claim Collins had been dead for over a month.[38] Another claim that arose from this meeting was that Lady Londonderry and Collins were having an affair. The basis of this being a letter from Collins to a 'Lady L'.[39] However, it was not to Lady Londonderry that the letter was addressed, but to Lady Lavery, who was reputed to have had affairs with both Collins and Lord Londonderry.

Also in March 1922, Craig announced the appointment of Sir Henry Wilson—recently retired Chief of the Imperial General Staff—as security advisor to the Belfast government. Wilson was a staunch supporter of the Ulster Unionists, and with the help of the Londonderrys he had been elected MP for North Down at the start of the year. Like them, his interests included developments in British politics, and he was keen to talk with them about the possibility of pulling the Conservative party out of the coalition government.[40] On 16 April 1922 Wilson and Londonderry addressed a meeting of Unionists at Newtownards at which the latter urged his audience not to blame the British government for the failure of the Craig-Collins pacts to deliver peace. A few days later Wilson wrote to Craig requesting that Londonderry replace Richard Dawson Bates at Home Affairs, the department responsible for security.[41] Both Londonderry and Wilson were critical of Bates' lack of experience, in particular his handling of relations between the police and the army.[42] Wilson argued that Londonderry would make a more suitable replacement because of his experience as a soldier and minister, his relationship with Churchill, and his influence at Westminster.[43] Wilson's advice was not acted on and two months later he was killed by the IRA outside his home in London.

By the time Wilson had made his suggestion, Craig and Bates had become almost solely responsible for security matters. Employing a double standard that discriminated against nationalists and in favour of Unionists, they were able to make on the spot decisions without dissent from the other.[44] This would not have been possible had Londonderry replaced Bates at Home Affairs. On 14 March 1922, a month before Wilson's suggestion, Londonderry became the first Ulster Unionist minister to publicly criticize the security policy of his own government. It was a gentle rebuke befitting the atmosphere of the Senate, but it was a serious departure from government rhetoric: 'a section of those who see eye to eye with us on the present political situation are implicated in outrages that are as reprehensible as those committed by Sinn Féin'.[45]

Craig did act on at least part of Wilson's advice, that concerning Londonderry's relationship with Churchill. Up until this point Craig personally dealt with the Colonial Office, demanding and more often than not receiving continued financial assistance from London for a range of services, from unemployment insurance to the Special Constabulary. However, in May and June 1922, Londonderry was also involved, perhaps to soften what were sometimes tense meetings between the Ulster premier and the Colonial Secretary.[46] From the British perspective, Londonderry was the acceptable face of a regime that continued to give London cause for concern, not only as a drain on finances at a time when the economy was in trouble, but also for its controversial use of the Special Constabulary.[47] In the early summer of 1922 Stephen Tallents was dispatched by the Colonial Office to report on Belfast's controversial security policy. It is notable that in his report no mention was made of the Education Minister, unlike his colleagues, except to say that Tallents had enjoyed the hospitality of the Londonderrys at Mount Stewart.[48] The eruption of the Irish Civil War at the end of June 1922 served to ease Northern Ireland's security difficulties a little, although border attacks did not entirely cease due to Collins' concern for nationalists in the six counties. For their part, the Londonderrys had the advantage of an armoured car and a guard of Special Constabulary at Mount Stewart.[49]

II

Continued tensions between Conservatives and Lloyd George led to the collapse of the coalition government on 19 October 1922. Within days Andrew Bonar Law was the Prime Minister of a wholly Conservative government, the first since 1905, and Londonderry was offered the post

of Secretary of State for Air.[50] Having left the coalition government in
May 1921 for the Ulster Unionist government of Northern Ireland,
Londonderry had some credit with Law. He had managed to avoid any
association with the more unpopular policies of the coalition, and he was
intimately involved with an issue that helped to ferment die-hard disqui-
et and thus return Law to the leadership.[51] Moreover, Law had been
pressed into giving Londonderry an appointment by Lord Salisbury, and
somewhat less effectively by Londonderry's father-in-law, Viscount
Chaplin.[52]

But if Londonderry had been associated indirectly with the die-hards,
he was not one of their number. Indeed, his experience of politics on
either side of the Irish Sea tempered his attitude to each political arena.
This dual commitment was exposed in September 1922, a month before
the downfall of the coalition. Despite his commitments to Ulster,
Londonderry had retained his family's almost hereditary presidency of
conservatism in County Durham. On 2 September he delivered a speech
to Conservatives at Wynyard Park in which he called for cooperation
between divided Conservatives and coalition Liberals so as to defeat the
challenge of Labour.[53] As a result Unionist newspapers in Belfast
attacked him as a supporter of Lloyd George. It did little to help his
standing in Northern Ireland, and betrayed Ulster's ignorance of affairs
in the north of England, for Londonderry was only adhering to his
party's strategy in that region.[54]

The episode greatly angered him. Writing to his Parliamentary
Secretary on 9 September, Londonderry complained about the 'narrow
and selfish Belfast spirit which ... is in my judgement fundamentally
destructive, and I find myself always up against it.' He felt that there
existed 'an element of jealousy and a desire to decry and destroy me,
which exists in fairly influential circles.' Nevertheless, he believed he had
a 'mission, and the moment that mission is in my judgement fulfilled, I
shall return to where I came from and leave Belfast to run the Six
Counties.'

> This brings me to the dual position which I occupy. First and
> foremost an Ulster Minister, as such negotiating with the British
> Government, it is not likely that I am going deliberately to
> wound the hand that feeds us, for the reason that if the British
> Government withdrew supplies, I do not see Belfast repairing
> the deficiency by voluntary subscription, or submitting to extra
> taxation. It is very easy to criticise the British Government, and

as I said in my speech no one can do it better than I can, but if I do that I include Winston Churchill who I know has fought our battle courageously from beginning to end, and he is a real personal friend to me too.

Secondly, I am President of the Unionist organisation controlling 19 seats in Durham, and my speech was expressly directed to this point. I know well what the menace is there and elsewhere. The menace is that if the Conservatives and Coalitionists fight each other on the old Conservative and Liberal prejudices, Labour slips in and wins all the seats.[55]

Londonderry was clearly troubled by his dual position, but not enough to make him accept Law's invitation to rejoin the government at Westminster. With his Education bill yet to be introduced, Londonderry felt he was 'pledged' to help Craig.[56] He wrote to his confidant Lady Desborough:

> I have made a sacrifice this time ... This may destroy my prospects, and although if I am really good enough it cannot do that, and if I am not good enough it doesn't matter. But judging dispassionately at this moment, as I have done, I have followed the right course. I came here to help deal with a crisis; that crisis is not over and it amounts to running away if I follow the path of my personal ambition ... I knew I was of a certain value here, that I filled a place which no one at the moment could fill, but I did not realise that my suggested departure would really create consternation.[57]

He made it clear to Law how tempting his offer had been:

> ...I am driven by the feeling that my duty is to give up what makes so strong an appeal to my personal feelings, and play my part here for a while longer. I believe you will understand the struggle in my heart far better even than I can explain it.[58]

What ultimately emboldened Londonderry to remain in Ulster, for the time being, was his sense of a historical mission, as he informed St Loe Strachey, editor of the *Spectator*:

> It is very difficult to know at this stage of Irish history, how far magnanimous concessions and the broad minded view are really operative. Some will say that anything in the nature of a concili-

ation is merely taken as a sign of cowardice and ineptitude. However, that may be, I have always got my eye on doing anything I can to remove the bitterness of feeling which exists at the present moment although I am restrained by the determination which [I] have fixed in my mind to do nothing, if I can help it to change our attitude of straight and fair dealing with everyone in the Six Counties.[59]

Another factor that might have contributed to his decision was a possible plan by Law to scrap the Royal Air Force and wind-up the Air Ministry. There is no evidence to suggest that Londonderry knew about this, but if he did know, his loyalty to Sir Hugh Trenchard and the RAF would have made the position very unappealing.[60] Whatever the cause of Londonderry's decision to stay in Ulster, he was still active in Conservative politics, both in County Durham and as a political host in London. Indeed, when Lady Londonderry wrote to Law to explain her husband's decision, she added that Londonderry House was Law's to 'command'.[61] The Prime Minister was sympathetic to Londonderry's position, and although he would not remain leader long enough to take up Lady Londonderry's offer, other Tory leaders would.[62]

It is also apparent that had Londonderry been offered a more distinguished office, he might have felt his duty to Northern Ireland was not so important after all. For example, at the start of November 1922, he responded favourably to a rumour that he might be offered the post of ambassador to Paris. It therefore must have pained him to learn that his very public commitment to remaining in Ulster had ruled him out of the running.[63] To add insult to injury, Londonderry was at the same time being discussed as a candidate for the ornamental post of Governor of Northern Ireland; needless to say, he did not accept it.[64] But it did lead him to complain that his October sacrifice had not been acknowledged properly in the pages of the *Spectator*. It was well and good remarking privately on his 'self-sacrifice' Londonderry wrote to Strachey, but why did this not appear in print?[65]

Had Londonderry accepted office at Westminster he would not have remained at the Air Ministry for very long. Baldwin, who had replaced Law in May 1923, called a general election for 6 December in the hope that his definite pledge to implement tariff reform might unite his party and win them victory at the polls. Instead, the number of Conservatives fell from the 483 returned the previous year—Law had called an election after the collapse of the coalition—to 258. With the support of 159

Liberals, and his own 191 Labour MPs, J. Ramsay MacDonald was able to form the first Labour government on 22 January 1924. At a dinner hosted by the King for his new Prime Minister at Buckingham Palace, Lady Londonderry quickly developed a friendship with MacDonald, in part based on their shared Scottish background. It was, of course, a triumphant example of aristocratic embrace. MacDonald invited the Londonderrys to Chequers the following month, and corresponded with them on the boundary crisis that dominated British-Irish relations in 1924. In the longer term, this relationship was to reap rewards that not even Edith could have foreseen.

III

The boundary crisis was slow to emerge and took even longer to resolve. The 1921 Treaty allowed Northern Ireland to vote itself out of the Irish Free State but only on condition that a Boundary Commission be established to adjust the border, although the exact meaning of what this meant was a source of controversy. The establishment of a commission was delayed by the Irish Civil War and Baldwin's decision to call an election at the end of 1923. But when the mechanisms for its establishment were being put in place by London and Dublin in May 1924, Belfast refused to nominate its appointee to the Boundary Commission.[66]

The boundary question gave Londonderry the opportunity to present himself as a steadfast Unionist to an increasingly restless public in Northern Ireland. But as it became clear that it would have a profound impact on the fate of the Conservative party, Londonderry became more hesitant. This added to his problems with fellow Ulster Unionists, for he was also receiving increasing criticism about his Education Act. To begin with, however, Londonderry toed the Ulster Unionist line, defending his government's refusal to appoint a commissioner in the Senate, the House of Lords, and on political platforms in England and Ulster.[67] And when he deputized for Craig at cabinet meetings in March 1924—the Ulster premier had one of his recurring bouts of ill health that year— Londonderry emulated his leader by refusing to allow for a planed reduction to the funding of the Special Constabulary. It has been noted that Londonderry had expressed some unease about Ulster's security policy, but he was also concerned with developments in southern Ireland. It was on this basis that he justified his stance to the British Home Secretary,

Herbert Morrison, who ultimately had to approve the funding, for he feared that the Irish army mutiny of 6 March might destabilize the Free State.[68] And when Unionist fears increased in May 1924 about the possibility that their leaders might back down and appoint a commissioner, Londonderry felt compelled to deny this outcome in the Senate.[69]

As Leader of the Senate, Londonderry also deputized for Craig at the intergovernmental conference held at London at the start of August. It was hoped that this meeting of ministers from London, Dublin and Belfast might finally resolve the boundary crisis.[70] However, Londonderry could do little other than to echo the view that Craig had expressed at similar conferences and discussions held throughout that year: that Belfast would not nominate a boundary commissioner. Thomas Jones, who as Deputy Cabinet Secretary was heavily involved in the crisis, noted in his diary for 2 August that Londonderry was 'the only reasonable negotiator', but 'too weak to bring along the rest of his party.'[71]

On 4 August Londonderry received a delegation of Ulster Unionist MPs at Londonderry House. Their spokesman, the die-hard Ronald McNeill, made it clear that the acting premier of Ulster was to stick to the 'not an inch' position that Craig had promised the Unionists of Northern Ireland. Afterwards, a 'largely attended' meeting of Ulster Unionist MPs and their supporters was held at Westminster to press home their resolution.[72] This public embarrassment was followed by further assurances from Londonderry that he had not made any agreement behind the back of Craig.[73]

This, of course, did not reveal his private thoughts. As Jones also noted in his diary, Londonderry felt that having made a display of defiance, the Ulster Unionists should make a concession, but that such a move would depend on Craig's heath. He also reassured Jones that there would be no violent resistance to the bill.[74] He went even further in a private letter to MacDonald. After complaining that the Prime Minister forgot about Ulster Unionists when he spoke of owing a debt of honour to the Irish, he went on to lament that the best way to govern Ireland was through 'ordinary local administration under the British Parliament.'[75]

Londonderry's frustration with the boundary crisis was not just a product of his precarious position in the Ulster Unionist party; it also reflected his fear about the future of the Conservative party. At the end of July 1924 the Judicial Committee of the Privy Council ruled that new legislation would be required if the British government wanted to appoint Northern Ireland's boundary commissioner. When the government decided to press ahead with this legislation in August, Baldwin feared that Conservative die-hards might risk the future of the party by throwing in their lot with the Ulster Unionists. This would risk not only splitting the party, and undermining its progress from territorial-unionism to One Nation conservatism, but also, if the House of Lords blocked the bill, an election in which the rallying call would be, like 1910, peers versus the people.[76] In public Baldwin gave the Ulster Unionists unenthusiastic support, in private he tried to persuade Craig to tell the die-hards to allow the bill to pass.

Towards the end of August it seemed as if Craig might be prepared to call off opposition to the bill. On 27 August Londonderry wrote to the Tory leader:

> I have had the opportunity of discussing the whole situation with [Sir Robert] Horne and Salisbury [leading die-hards] and while they seemed to have made up their minds that an election was inevitable by reason of the probable rejection of the Bill by the House of Lords, they have now somewhat changed their views after I had an opportunity of putting the whole situation, as we discussed it at Stormont [Castle], before them.
>
> They are fully alive to the many objections to the election being fought upon this particular issue but they hold the opinion that the Bill can only be allowed to pass through the House of Lords on a direct intimation being received from Northern Ireland that there will be no misunderstanding between the Conservative Party and Ulster on this particular point.
>
> I feel sure you will see the force of this argument and it appears to me that this had better be done in the form of a public letter from James Craig to yourself ... It was indeed good of you coming over to Belfast and I can assure you we are all most deeply grateful.[77]

When Londonderry wrote this letter, Craig was on a three-week sea cruise to help mend his ill health. By the time of his return in mid-September, Craig and his cabinet agreed that they would not encourage the upper house to oppose the bill, but that they would urge Baldwin to ensure that the Conservatives would pass amendments in favour of the Ulster Unionist position.[78] Londonderry was clearly unnerved by what was, in effect, Craig's continued determination to oppose the bill. On 18 September he wrote to Salisbury: 'Our people are very headstrong ... and they can only think for themselves. They cannot take the long view of

British politics which might be that an election on this point would not serve the interests of the Conservative Party.'[79]

At the end of September a rumour surfaced that Carson might be willing to represent Belfast on the Boundary Commission. Londonderry reported to his wife that when this was discussed at a cabinet meeting on 30 September, Craig had initially 'jumped' at the idea, but that other ministers rejected it on the basis that once the Commission was recognized by Belfast, they would be bound by its decisions.[80] Craig and Londonderry had been opposed by their colleagues on the boundary question before, back in February, when they favoured a solution involving a Council of Ireland.[81] But now Londonderry wondered if he might be called upon to replace Craig should his leader be removed by discontented elements in the party. Fortunately for his ambitions, Londonderry dismissed the idea, preferring instead to consider a return to Westminster politics.[82] For as Stephen Tallents noted in his 1922 report, should Craig ever be forced to resign, he would be replaced by a hard liner.

If Londonderry did not have much influence in the Ulster Unionist party, he played an imperceptible part in the Conservative victory at the general election of 19 October 1924. Earlier that month, Conservatives in the House of Commons gave up in their attempt to amend the Boundary Commission bill. But it was feared that the House of Lords would not be so passive, especially as Craig had failed to give a clear indication to them of what he wanted them to do. The situation was saved by Londonderry's close ally in the upper house and erstwhile die-hard, Lord Salisbury, who on 8 October reluctantly warned his colleagues of the electoral consequences that would face the Conservative party should they block the bill. The victory for common sense was not fully achieved, however, until Carson and Londonderry added their voices to Salisbury's, albeit in the same reluctant tones.[83] The bill was therefore passed, leaving the Labour government's Russian policy the only major issue on which the October election was fought. Just when it seemed as if the Conservatives might disappear as an electoral force, they were returned with a massive majority, 419 MPs in total. Indeed, it was the Liberals who suffered most at this election, for although Labour lost 40 MPs and government office, the Liberal party suffered its worst defeat to date with only 40 MPs returned.

Londonderry's role in this episode, and his campaigning in County Durham, only heightened his desire to return to British politics, especially as Churchill had returned to the Tory front bench as Chancellor of the

Exchequer.[84] It may be that Craig too wanted his Education Minister to consider this option, for it was the Ulster premier who recommended that Londonderry be made a British Privy Councillor in January 1925. This prompted one reader of *The Times* to point out that Londonderry was the only person to hold three such offices, in Ireland, Northern Ireland and Great Britain.[85] Craig had become increasingly estranged from Londonderry, especially as protestant opposition mounted to the 1923 Education Act, so much so that it threatened Unionist unity at the snap election called by Craig for 3 April 1925 as a challenge to the Boundary Commission. Having witnessed serious reverses to education policy before and after that election, Londonderry himself made efforts to secure another post at Westminster with help of Churchill, but nothing was available.[86] It was again suggested that he might be appointed Governor-General of Canada, but Londonderry was determined not be nudged into an ornamental office.[87]

It was clear therefore that by the end of 1925 the Education Minister had determined to leave office at some point in the near future, even if it meant being out of government altogether. Having decided to remain in post until the Boundary Commission delivered its report, Londonderry was astounded at the treatment he received from Craig once its findings were leaked to the *Morning Post* and published on 7 November. To the anger of Dublin and the relief of Belfast only minor alterations to the border were recommended. In the subsequent flurry of meetings between the three premiers at London, Cosgrave, Craig and Baldwin agreed to suppress the report and the leave the border unchanged.[88] Instead of bringing his unofficial deputy to this conference, Craig chose instead to have a senior civil servant, Charles Blackmore. Londonderry felt slighted, but took care not to resign until the following January, not least to demonstrate that he was not the sort of person to resign in a fit of pique, an important consideration for one who wanted a place in government at Westminster. In any case, it was not the main reason for his departure. For that, we must turn to his performance as Minister of Education.

IV

The Education Act 1923, also known as the Londonderry Act, was one of the most significant pieces of social legislation in the embryonic years of Northern Ireland. Not because of what it achieved, for it was ultimately reversed, but for its original intention: the attempt to end clerical control of schools and dismantle denominational segregation in what was a very divided society. Much ink has been spilled in examining education policy in the early years of Northern Ireland, although almost nothing of any substance is said about the role of Londonderry.[89]

The government of Northern Ireland set out to reform education in Northern Ireland following the lead but not the example of England.[90] The central plank of its proposals involved the transfer of clerical controlled elementary schools to the state sector. Ulster Unionists had supported previous attempts at similar reforms, however, opposition from the Catholic hierarchy and the Irish Parliamentary Party ensured that these measures were not passed. Two important factors determined that the Ulster Unionist government of Northern Ireland would pursue the course outlined above: a constitutional prohibition against funding religious bodies, and the willingness of key personnel in the government to pursue this object.

Section five of the Better Government of Ireland Act 1920 prohibited the Northern Ireland parliament from passing any law that directly or indirectly endowed, preferred or prejudiced any denomination or religious group. This was interpreted to include denominational schools. When the government came under increasing criticism for the 1923 Education Act, ministers often defended the legislation on the basis that anything else would be unconstitutional. However, Londonderry later undermined this defence when he admitted that he favoured non-denominational schools regardless of section five. Like constructive Unionists before and after, the Minister of Education believed that nationalists had to have an investment in the state. He believed this could be achieved by removing clerical influence in education and schooling children together regardless of their denominational background. He was not alone in this view. Craig also believed that clerical control had to be ended.[91] Moreover, Londonderry was assisted at the Ministry of Education by a group of talented and like-minded civil servants.[92]

On 23 June 1921, at the first meeting of the Senate, Londonderry signalled his desire for reform, admitting that there would be many difficulties ahead.[93] At this stage he was not so much thinking of possible organized opposition to his plans, but the structural and political difficulties of governing Northern Ireland at a time of violence and political instability. Like other ministries, Education was seriously hampered by delays in the transfer of powers and personnel from London and Dublin.[94] It had to build itself up from very little, and was therefore reliant on the previous experience and confidence of its minister.

In September 1921 Londonderry established a committee to examine education reform under the chairmanship of Robert Lynn.[95] Those involved in education, including clerics, were all invited to make submissions. Londonderry had hoped for Catholic representatives to sit on the committee or at least make submissions, and personally wrote to Cardinal Michael Logue, the Catholic Archbishop of Armagh.[96] Logue was in favour of a general boycott of the new state and was not prepared to allow any of his priests or teachers to engage with the Ministry. With all the deference one might expect from a cardinal to a marquess, Logue informed Londonderry that he viewed the Lynn Committee as the 'pretext' for an attack on Catholic schools, although he was careful to state that he knew that this was not the intention of the minister.[97] Before replying to Logue, Londonderry wrote to the Viceroy, a Catholic, in the hope that he might intervene positively, stressing that if Catholics sat on the committee, they would be allowed to frame a minority report if they so wished.[98] Nothing happened and Londonderry called a cabinet meeting to discuss the situation. At this meeting he took a bullish attitude, claiming that Logue was making a 'direct challenge' to the government; but his colleagues felt that the matter should simply be dropped.[99] Nevertheless, Londonderry wrote to Logue regretting his decision, and although he avoided directly asking him to reconsider his position, he made it clear that an opportunity was being missed.[100]

The Lynn Committee issued an interim report in June 1922; most of its structural recommendations found their way into the 1923 Education Act. These included the means by which elementary schools would be transferred to state control, the matter of control resting in the appointment of school managers. In those schools fully transferred to the state, the local education authority would appoint all school managers and the school would receive full funding. Schools that wished to remain independent were to receive minimal funding and retain their power to appoint managers. A third class of school would act as a bridge for those hesitant about full transfer. Known as four-and-two schools, the authorities were to appoint two managers, with the remaining four appointed by the existing school managers. It was hoped that under this system denominational schools would be persuaded to transfer totally, or at least partially, to the control of the state.

The Lynn Committee also recommended a programme of simple Bible instruction as part of the curriculum—a reflection of its exclusively protestant makeup and protestant clerical involvement. This was the one significant part of the report that Londonderry omitted from the 1923 bill. He also forbade managers at transferred schools from requiring teachers to come from a particular denomination. It was on these two issues—Bible instruction and appointments—that protestant opposition would focus, especially when it became clear that only protestant schools would be transferred to the state. For their part, the Catholic hierarchy had its own battle with the Ministry of Education on the question of teacher training.

Even before the bill became law, Londonderry had to persuade the cabinet that it was the right course to pursue. On the 15 December 1922, having satisfied his colleagues that there would be a right of entry for clergy and that funding would be drastically reduced for schools unwilling to transfer, the Education Minister was allowed to proceed with the bill.[101] Within a month however, the cabinet rejected Londonderry's proposal to establish small local education authorities that bore no relation to political boundaries, probably on the basis that it would further diminish local political influence.[102]

The first potentially serious attack came from the Lynn Committee's chairman, Robert Lynn. After reading the draft bill and Londonderry's cover note in February 1923, Lynn wrote a furiously critical reply attacking the bill and Londonderry's management of it.[103] He also threatened to mount an opposition campaign, something he had carried out the previous year, for it was Lynn, as editor of the *Northern Whig*, who had attacked Londonderry's speech to Conservatives in County Durham. It is not clear how, but within a month Lynn had been talked out of his opposition to the bill, moreover, he now became one of its leading advocates.[104] What is certain is that in 1924 Londonderry reluctantly contributed to Lynn's election expenses.[105]

Having seen off the threat of an opposition campaign, Londonderry faced another rumbling of dissent in the cabinet. On 16 April 1923 Craig suggested that the bill be amended to allow for religious education, but

that the burden for it be placed on local authorities and not the government. Londonderry admitted that at this stage he was coming under pressure from clergy to adopt this course, but that his own opinion was
'unchanged', adding that the bill allowed for 'moral instruction' of a non-
denominational character within school hours. The Minister for Labour,
John Andrews, and the Parliamentary Secretary to the Ministry of
Education, Robert McKeown added their voices in support of
Londonderry. He therefore won this round, but at a price. The cabinet
determined that the bill would not be altered unless 'the course of debate
made it clear that further concession was demanded' in which case 'the
scheme advocated by the Prime Minister would be adopted.'[106] With that
the Education bill was passed into law on 2 June 1923.

The 1923 Education Act repealed 17 earlier pieces of legislation and
introduced structural changes affecting the ownership, management and
financing of elementary schools. Londonderry emphasized its provisions
for local accountability, the democratic 'keystone of the arch of our new
system of education'.[107] At this stage the level of protestant hostility to
the Act was minimal, indeed Londonderry even received the support of
Orangemen from the staunchly loyalist Sandy Row district of Belfast.[108]
If protestant anxiety had not reached the heights it would in 1925, then
it certainly found an early advocate in the person of Craig. On 27
September 1923, he again called for an amendment that would satisfy
protestant critics, on this occasion, the lifting of the prohibition on transferred schools from employing a denominational test in teacher appointments.[109] Londonderry had been absent at this meeting and it was decided to await his return. At the next meeting of the cabinet, on 2 October,
Londonderry dismissed the proposal as unconstitutional, and for being
'against the general principle of a Secular Education Bill'. As for the risk
that opposition might be widespread, Londonderry claimed it was not 'of
a serious character', that 'it was largely manufactured by certain interested ecclesiastics.'[110]

It was only protestant opposition that bothered Craig, for this threatened to damage the image of unity he was so carefully cultivating in order
to see off threats to Northern Ireland from within and without. As he
had warned Londonderry in January 1923, while being 'satisfied that
sticking to the strict letter of the law always pays in the end; in any event
it is better to have trouble with enemies rather than with friends'.[111] The
following month he asked Londonderry in cabinet 'whether any particular denomination could, in his opinion, with justice assert that it had

been penalised.' Charles Hendriks, Londonderry's Private Secretary, stepped into rescue his Minister, arguing that it would be the Catholic sector that would feel penalized due to reduced funding. On the basis of this the cabinet somewhat incredulously concluded that 'the proposals of the Bill are impartial in their dealings with the denominations.'[112]

If Londonderry felt he had seen off the opposition, he had seriously underestimated the ability of protestant clerics to ferment mass opposition to the Education Act through the populist Orange Order. The failure of Catholic schools to transfer to the state allowed protestant critics to argue that it was only their denominations that were obliged to end religious instruction. It therefore became increasingly clear that the benefits of the Act depended on co-operation from all quarters, for without this each denomination could claim a separate grievance. Nowhere was this clearer than in the area of teacher appointments. Protestant opposition focussed on the ability of Catholic teachers to be allowed to teach at protestant schools, but not vice versa. Given that the Ministry's teacher training college at Stranmillis had managed to enrol almost two hundred Catholic applicants in 1923, it was not an altogether paranoid claim, especially as the Catholic hierarchy warned the students that they would not be employed in Catholic schools.[113]

Protestant opposition grew throughout 1924, with the Ministry of Education having to deal with frequent letters of complaint and deputations seeking to persuade the Minister to change his mind. Having always displayed an aloof attitude towards the protesters, he appealed over their heads to the people, and on 1 April 1924 announced that the government had not endangered the moral upbringing of children by entrusting it to their parents and teachers.[114] It was clear that Londonderry was not prepared to budge. Opposition therefore moved up a gear with the formation of the United Education Committee of the Protestant Churches (UEC) in December 1924.

The early months of 1925 witnessed further clashes between Londonderry and his opponents. Moderate members of the higher clergy and the very senior ranks of the Orange Order began to call on the Education Minister to make at least some gesture to temper the opposition, not least because populist agitation threatened their own authority.[115] This was particularly notable in the case of the Orange Order. On 4 February 1925 the Grand Orange Lodge of Belfast informed Londonderry that while they appreciated the many 'popular benefits' contained in the 1923 Act, they opposed the absence of religious instruction and the prohibition of a denominational test for teachers.[116] Hendriks subsequently informed Londonderry that Sir Edward Archdale—Minister for Agriculture and Commerce, and Grand Master of the Grand Orange Lodge of Ireland—had responded to this by dismissing the Belfast Orangemen as 'riff-raff'.[117] Hendriks then met with the Grand Secretary of Belfast and was informed that both he and Sir Joseph Davidson, Grand Master of Belfast, 'had the greatest difficulty in restraining the hot-heads amongst the Orangemen, who are being persuaded by the clergy that the Bible is in danger.'[118] With this knowledge Londonderry felt he could deal personally with the 'malcontents'. At his meeting with them on 23 February, the Grand Master of Belfast asked if any amendment might be possible, Londonderry replied that the Orange Order's objections were simply too late.[119]

On 5 March the UEC held a demonstration at the Presbyterian Assembly Hall in Belfast. Londonderry's contention that their cause was unrepresentative began to look deeply flawed. Worse still, the meeting coincided with Craig's decision to call a snap general election on the boundary question for 3 April. Having called the poll in order to demonstrate the determination of Northern Ireland to remain separate from the Irish Free State, Craig was not about to allow the education row to overshadow his campaign. With Londonderry absent due to ill health, Craig met with a deputation from the UEC on 6 March. The next day, with Londonderry still absent, the cabinet agreed that the Education Act would be amended to remove the prohibitions on Bible instruction and teacher selection on the basis of denomination.[120]

When Londonderry moved the second reading of the amendment bill on 13 March, he emphasized that the measure only sought to clarify existing law. He claimed that although the bill had lifted the prohibition on religious instruction in schools, it remained voluntary for both teachers and pupils. Furthermore, school management committees would only have an advisory role in teacher appointments, not the determining one that the UEC had demanded.[121]

It became apparent to the UEC that Craig had misled them about the effect of the Amendment Act.[122] On 2 April, the day before the general election, a deputation visited Londonderry to demand a further amendment. He refused and threatened to resign if they persisted. According to the minutes Londonderry 'pointed out that circumstances had radically changed with self-government in Ulster, that the decentralization in education under the Education Act was a necessary corollary to the new position, and that the Churches must be prepared to surrender their privileged position in education.' In reply the clerics said they would surrender the teaching of religious instruction if teachers were compelled to take it. Londonderry declined their demand.[123] There is nothing to suggest that this very late development had any effect on the results of the general election, but the number of Ulster Unionist MPs returned did fall from 40 to 32. If anything it was proportional representation that hammered the Unionist vote the hardest, for it also returned three Labour MPs, ten nationalists, four independent Unionists, two Sinn Féin, and one farmers' representative.

With the election out of the way the UEC had lost a major opportunity to reverse the 1923 Education Act. But this did not end their agitation. On 17 April Londonderry gave a provocative address to the annual Congress of the Irish National Teachers' Organization on their freedom *of* employment and their freedom *in* employment.[124] This provoked the UEC on 24 April to again demand that the Ministry of Education allow transferred schools to compel their teachers to give religious instruction. Londonderry refused, and also denied their call for a denominational test for teachers. The agitation continued throughout May and June.

At the start of June lawyers for the UEC challenged the government's interpretation of section five of the Government of Ireland Act 1920. Despite the advice of the Attorney General that the UEC were incorrect in their assessment of the constitution, Craig suggested on 4 June that the cabinet seek a ruling on the matter from the Judicial Committee of the Privy Council. Londonderry successfully countered this by arguing that it would create 'an awkward situation' for the government if the court agreed with the UEC.[125]

On 12 June the Presbyterian General Assembly upped the stakes by calling on local councillors to withdraw levies to the Education Ministry if further amendments were not made. The situation was getting worse, and Londonderry seemed incapable of dealing with it effectively. He again protested that voluntary religious instruction was permitted under current legislation, but on this occasion added fuel to the fire by admitting that even if it could be proved legally that there was no constitutional bar, he for one would not change his position.[126]

Somewhat surprisingly, Craig supported Londonderry after this admission, agreeing in cabinet that nothing further should be conceded.[127] However, his colleagues were not so sure. John Andrews, hitherto a supporter of Londonderry, complained of being subjected to pulpit harangues at his church about the loss of protestant rights.[128] Other ministers feared that they too would be verbally attacked at the upcoming 'Twelfth' of July Orange Order demonstrations, and that this would undermine the authority of the government in advance of the Boundary Commission's report. Stephen Tallents had forecast such an outcome in his 1922 report: 'Ministers are too close to their community and cannot treat their supporters as from a distance.'[129] After 'exhaustive conversations' between Craig and Londonderry in the third week of June, the latter was persuaded to meet with the UEC and reach an agreement.[130] At this ill tempered meeting, the Education Minister refused to give in to demands concerning the appointment of teachers, but did offer to allow local authorities to permit non-denominational Bible instruction. He also agreed to compulsory religious instruction for teachers if it met with the approval of their union.[131] On 23 June he informed Craig that if the teachers refused he would resign. He went on, claiming that he had 'handled all this controversy very badly … I never have understood Orangemen and Presbyterians and it is always difficult to know under the shouting and the threats what the people really want and what is best for them to have.'[132] In what was a sympathetic response, Craig urged his Education Minister not to resign.[133]

On 24 June Londonderry met with the teachers' representatives and secured their consent to compulsion. The following day he met again with the UEC and the row was fully resolved. He consoled himself in the knowledge that he had stood firm in the face of growing opposition, although it did not occur to him that this defiance might have exacerbated the situation. On 25 June his erstwhile critic turned supporter Robert Lynn reported that Craig had not spoken to him since he attacked the policy reversal.[134] On the same day however, in a letter to the Ulster Unionist Chief Whip, Herbert Dixon, Craig remarked that Londonderry had 'very cleverly handled the Education question'.[135] As a gesture of goodwill, and in keeping with landlord tradition, Londonderry held a garden party at Mount Stewart on 10 July. Press reports claimed that five thousand people attended, mostly from the Ulster Unionist Council and the Orange Order. Craig was the only notable absence.[136]

V

If Londonderry's difficulties with protestant opponents to his reforms ultimately ended in 'surrender', then his relations with the Catholic hierarchy followed a different course.[137] At the end of 1922 all Catholic teachers came under the authority of the Northern Ireland Ministry of Education, Dublin having stopped payments to the minority of teachers who had held out in the hope that Northern Ireland would wither away. Although Londonderry took a tough line with this minority, refusing to backdate the pay they had lost until their transfer to Belfast, he had a benign attitude to Catholic educational concerns generally.[138] On 1 December 1922, in a letter to his British counterpart, Edward Wood, he noted that many Catholics regarded 'the present system of government in Northern Ireland as an attempt at Protestant domination and, consequently, as part of the long-standing feud between the Protestants and themselves.'[139] At a cabinet meeting on 29 October 1923, he unsuccessfully opposed Craig's decision to include all teachers paid by the state in a scheme to compel civil servants to make an oath of allegiance. Londonderry informed his colleagues that the Christian Brothers teaching order had asked him not to impose it for religious and political reasons and that he 'had a certain amount of sympathy with the representations made by those who were merely influenced by their desire to advocate a union with the South on constitutional lines'.[140] Perhaps Londonderry heard such views articulated most effectively by the leader of constitutional nationalism in Ulster, Joseph Devlin, an occasional guest at receptions organized by Lady Londonderry.[141]

Londonderry's sympathies, however, should not be overstated. He did not, for example, permit the use of the Irish language in examinations other than those specifically designed to test that subject.[142] In part this reflected an assumption that Irish should be treated like any other European language, except of course English. But Londonderry was also of the belief that the promotion of the language by education authorities in the Irish Free State was ultimately harmful to the place of Ireland in the world, for he felt it would make the country a 'little Irish speaking island'.[143] Nevertheless, the main source of controversy between the hierarchy and Londonderry was in the end handled successfully.

In January 1922 the cabinet agreed to implement new teacher training arrangements in place of the existing system of sending students to southern Ireland.[144] They established Stranmillis College for this purpose but Catholic bishops refused to allow their male student teachers to attend, insisting instead that they continued to attend colleges in the Irish Free State. As the southern colleges refused to teach the Northern Ireland curriculum, the Ministry felt it had to find some compromise. St Mary's College in Belfast already trained Catholic women but refused to admit men. In June 1924 Londonderry dispatched the very able Catholic civil servant Andrew Bonaparte Wyse to negotiate with representatives of the Catholic hierarchy. Some progress was made with proposals for separate lectures, grounds and residences at Stranmillis. However, the government was concerned about the extra costs this would impose, and further progress appeared to be blocked by Cardinal Logue. Londonderry then attempted to move things along by writing to his old adversary at the Irish Convention, Bishop Patrick O'Donnell; but he too refused to join a government committee.[145] Despite this initial setback, O'Donnell replaced Logue as Archbishop of Armagh in January 1925 and thereafter initiated a more cooperative attitude to the Ministry of Education.[146] By the end of the month an agreement was reached to send male Catholic students to the Catholic teacher training college at Strawberry Hill near London. Not only did this outcome allow Londonderry to quell Unionist discontent about building another college, it also meant that Catholic students would be trained outside Ireland.[147]

VI

Londonderry's attitude to Northern Ireland politics was fundamentally paternalistic, a reflection of his landlord background and unelected seat in the parliament. Lacking a popular mandate for his reforms, he made no attempt to assuage protestant critics. For them it appeared as if Londonderry was trying to undermine the *raison d'etre* of Ulster unionism. With the creation of Northern Ireland, Ulster Unionists had developed from an 'ethnic association'—in which the members develop common interests and political organizations—into an 'ethnic community', possessing a permanent, physically bounded territory over and above its political organizations.[148] Having played only a tenuous part in Ulster Unionist mobilization before the First World War, Londonderry had only a tenuous link with it as an ethnic association, so it is unsurprising that he should have found it difficult to be part of it as an ethnic community. As

Jennifer Todd explains: 'Northern Ireland ... was founded on an exclusivist legitimating principle, which was impervious to more generalized and universalistic pleas for justice and democracy if these were to conflict with unionists' basic interest in the survival of the state and the union.'[149]

This is not to suggest however that the outcome was certain. Constructive or anti-populist unionism had achieved some moderate success in the past, and in the person of Londonderry it had helped to defrost relations with the Catholic hierarchy. But their boycott of the state, its violent birth, and the ongoing fear of the Boundary Commission all served to undermine Londonderry's position. He had failed as a politician in Northern Ireland. But far from harming his chances of returning to government at Westminster, the fact that he had attempted to resist the worst excesses of the new state only provided him with credit.

5

Catering his way to the Cabinet?
1926–1931

General assessments of Lord Londonderry's political career typically neglect the years between his departure from the government of Northern Ireland in January 1926 and his appointment to British cabinet in October 1928, and again in November 1931. Without any analysis of this period, writers have attributed Londonderry's 1928 appointment to the role of Londonderry House as one of the leading political salons of its time, quoting Lord Birkenhead's comment that Londonderry was engaged in 'catering his way to the Cabinet'.[1] Not dissimilarly, many regard the close friendship between Lady Londonderry and Ramsay MacDonald as being the main reason for her husband's two appointments to the National Government in 1931. It is true that these factors played a part in Londonderry's return to government, but they are not the only explanations.

It has already been argued that plutocratic aristocrats could still utilize wealth, status, confidence and opportunity in their pursuit of government office. The frequent but ultimately limited satisfaction of Londonderry's political aspirations therefore serves to demonstrate that the political culture of the nineteenth century had not been entirely extinguished by the onward march of democracy. But this is not to say that he just slipped into high office by virtue of his noble birth and enormous wealth. He was, to some extent, the master of his own destiny. Irish politics, both during the war and after, had cast Londonderry as a champion of conciliatory government. His association with Belfast also meant that he was on the winning side when the coalition fell in October 1922. The chief beneficiary of this development, Andrew Bonar Law, offered Londonderry the non-cabinet post of Secretary of State for Air, and although he chose to remain in Northern Ireland, Londonderry actively ensured that the Conservative party would not be sacrificed on the altar of old fidelities.

All this risked being undermined by events in 1926. Londonderry's ownership of relatively successful collieries was, after all, a double-edged sword. It gave him industrial wealth at a time when many in the landed elite had been struggling for decades to overcome a declining agricultural economy.[2] But it also made him a hate figure for Labour, and therefore a liability for Baldwin's voter conscious Conservative party. The General Strike and miners' strike of 1926 should therefore have ended his ambitions to re-enter the British government. But Londonderry had learnt a lesson in Northern Ireland: efforts at conciliation and active appeasement not only helped to solve difficult disputes, they also enhanced the reputation of those who espoused this form of politics.

If Londonderry's reputation survived '1926 and all that', then acting as host for the Conservative party at Londonderry House certainly served to remind his leaders that he was available for work. He was not disappointed. In 1927 he was given the chairmanship of a royal commission, and then asked to quell die-hard unrest at the annual party conference later that year. A cabinet reshuffle in 1928 had him appointed First Commissioner of Works, and re-appointed to the post in the emergency National Government of August to October 1931, this time outside the cabinet. The importance of Lady Londonderry's friendship with MacDonald has therefore been overplayed, for it was only one of several factors that allowed her husband to enter the cabinet for the second time in November 1931. Moreover, as Secretary of State for Air he had not been given a prestigious office. It would take the threat of another world war for that to change.

I

Londonderry's resignation letter to Craig was published in the press on 9 January 1926, and made it clear that the former Education Minister wished to devote more time to his mining interests in County Durham. His real concern was, of course, a return to government, but without any sign of that in the immediate future he wondered if his political career had just ended.

I am rather liking the free lance complex and expect to continue
in that state altogether … I have time now to do all sorts of
things I have always wanted to do without trammels and collective responsibility which is in one scale, whilst the honour and
prestige and importance of being a member of the Government
are in the other.

I don't care about the Government either and I am sure I
should not agree. They have all served together for years and are
a sort of executive of a Trade Union speaking a language which
I don't understand and should never learn. No, I regret India
very much. It would have been just the climax and after it I could
have come home and adopted the sort of life I am leading now.
I apologise for the egotism.[3]

It seemed as though his life might now be confined to country pursuits
and London society. With the exception of the press baron Lord
Beaverbrook, no leading politicians seemed to take an interest in his decision to concentrate on mining.[4]

Londonderry could never accept as consolation the numerous ceremonial offices he had been given by virtue of his aristocratic background,
such as his role as Chancellor of the Queen's University of Belfast, for
although Londonderry enjoyed ceremony, he resented it as an alternative
to power.[5] Some aristocratic appointments still retained a degree of political power; he was after all a member of the House of Lords, and
remained a Northern Ireland Senator until 1929. He had also retained his
presidency of the Conservative party in County Durham, although this
too was becoming politically irrelevant. Nor could the Londonderrys'
patronage of local organizations in County Durham stem the rising tide
of support for Labour in the area, although local patronage did keep
many of the county's remaining Tory voters happy, and it has been
argued elsewhere that it may even have helped to marshal the female vote
against the Labour party.[6]

The erosion of the Londonderrys' political authority in County
Durham was not just observable in the popular vote for Labour, but also
in the attitude and expectations of the county's leading Conservatives. If
some in the middle class enjoyed garden parties at Wynyard Park, then
others resented the continued political pretensions of a class they viewed
as anachronistic. Constituency chairmen and MPs were no longer prepared to cow-tow to the hereditary area-president, especially when the
rising Labour vote was feeding off discontent among Londonderry's

employees.[7] Landlord decline in provincial politics was underscored by its declining contribution to party funds. This added to the tension already existing between the landed elite and their political inheritors. It led the Tory MP for Barnard Castle, Cuthbert Headlam, to complain in October 1926 that the local party's finances were in a dire state because of Lord Durham and Lord Londonderry.[8] Despite his desire that they contribute to party funds, and because he felt that what they did give was inadequate, Headlam was deeply critical of their continued involvement in the management of the local party, going so far as to blame them personally for its defeat, including his own, at the general election of 1929.[9] Lady Londonderry, however, took the opposite view, attributing the local party's poor showing on that occasion to the decision by London to subsume County Durham into the Central Office Northern Area.[10]

II

Whatever his standing in the Conservative party, the main challenge to Londonderry's authority in County Durham came from local branches of the Miners' Federation of Great Britain (MFGB) and the Labour party. Throughout Londonderry's lifetime, trade unions had successfully unbound the bonds of paternalism in pit-village life, stripping the employer-employee relationship to its economic core. As Huw Benyon and Terry Austrin have noted: 'In villages where once there were only Chapels and where they were dependent upon the patronage of the employer, there were now cooperative stores, reading rooms and all manner of clubs.'[11]

After the First World War British collieries employed around 1,250,000 men. In February 1919 the MFGB threatened a strike unless miners' wages were increased to take account of the post-war boom. They also called for wartime nationalization to be made permanent. To avoid an economically disastrous confrontation the government asked Sir John Sankey to chair a commission on the future of the industry. The results of the Sankey Coal Industry Commission shook the public, government and miners alike, for the owners had been obliged to divulge details hitherto kept from the public gaze.

Londonderry gave his evidence on 8 May 1919, while he was serving, unpaid, as Finance Member of the Air Council. He informed the Commission that he was the sole shareholder of the Londonderry

Collieries Limited. That it owned 5,808 acres of mineral rich land in County Durham, which included three collieries near Seaham Harbour: Dawdon Colliery, sunk by the sixth Marquess between 1900 and 1906; Seaham Colliery, purchased by Frances Anne, Marchioness of Londonderry in 1849; and Silksworth Colliery, sunk by the fifth Marquess in 1872 and now held under a lease. At these pits a total of seven thousand men and boys were employed. Londonderry was then obliged to reveal that the average annual output of his collieries was 546,720 tons, around half of which was worked by lessee companies. Royalties paid to him were fixed to tonnage, the average being 4½ d. per ton, totalling £9,608 annually. A further £5,726 was paid each year to Londonderry for way-leaves. He was also cross-examined by the secretary of the MFGB, Frank Hodges, and briefly at the end by Arthur Balfour. They focussed on Londonderry's opposition to nationalization, the former ensuring that the witness delivered a defensive performance, forcing him to concede that nationalization during the war had benefited 'the community at large'.[12]

The Sankey Commission decided by a majority of one that it was in favour of nationalization, but the coalition government were not prepared to go that far, especially as the industry had begun operating at a loss. The mines were therefore handed back to the owners on 1 April 1921. But the owners' insistence that wages be reduced led the MFGB to call a national strike for the same day. They would remain on strike for three months, despite loosing the support of other major unions on 15 April. Prior to his departure from the coalition government, Londonderry attempted to offer a solution via the press baron Lord Northcliffe, whose newspapers were taking a moderate line on the strike. Londonderry felt that the demands of the MFGB were 'mere palliatives', that they did nothing to make the industry more competitive or efficient. Instead he suggested to Northcliffe that this could be achieved through an 'amalgamation' or 'trustification' of the industry. After making his own investigations in mid-May Northcliffe agreed with Londonderry's proposal, especially having learnt that many small US mines had amalgamated in the mid-nineteenth century.[13] However, nothing came of the proposal, for on 1 July 1921 the miners returned to work on lower wages and district settlements, and economic decline ensured a fall in the number of strikes, at least until 1925.

The British coal industry achieved a brief period of success in 1924 and was therefore able to raise wages, but by the following year it was again running at a loss. This led the owners' Mining Association of Great Britain (MAGB) to insist on wage cuts and longer hours.[14] With the support of the Trade Union Congress the MFGB rejected the owners' demands and again called for nationalization. Fears grew of another strike until Baldwin intervened at the end of July 1925, giving the industry a nine-month subsidy and establishing a royal commission on the matter under Sir Herbert Samuel. Having just left the government of Northern Ireland at the beginning of January 1926, Londonderry delivered his first public reaction to these developments at Seaham on the 8th, blaming the difficulties of the industry on state interference rather than international competition.[15] It appeared as though he had reverted to the opinions he had once expressed as a backbench MP.

Very soon after, however, Londonderry was presenting himself as a moderate owner, more publicly than he had in 1921, and now with a reputation for having done something similar in Northern Ireland. On 10 January 1926 he informed a meeting of the Dawdon Colliery Officials' Association that those in authority had to treat their employees as individuals and not machines.[16] But he remained hostile to the MFGB, assuring an audience of Conservatives at New Seaham the following night of his great dislike for the MFGB leader A. J. Cook.[17] Londonderry's hostility about the MFGB reflected his belief that it was somehow misleading the miners. Therefore, on 22 January, he spoke at the Dawdon Working Men's Club, advocating cooperation to safeguard the industry, adding that he and many others did not want to reduce wages, but that the industry needed to change to replicate the success of mining in the USA.[18] His other important speech that month was delivered on the 27th to an audience of 10,000 people gathered at Sunderland Stadium to hear the Prime Minister. Londonderry used the opportunity to advertise his 'One Nation' credentials, and to refer to his recent efforts to promote peace in the industry:

> I have taken this decided step in the past few days because I feel that we are bound to follow the example which the Prime Minister gives us, and to do every single thing we can to stimulate the spirit and feeling of sympathy, fellowship, and cooperation … They had seen the same phenomenon in Ireland…[19]

The miners' leader, A. J. Cook, initially welcomed Londonderry's intervention, regarding it as a weakening of the owners' position. But he soon became hostile upon the realization that Londonderry's position was not that different from the owners, that like them he wanted disputes to be settled on district lines and not nationally. Cook was therefore concerned that Londonderry might attract support, and warned him publicly to give his views only through the MAGB.[20] For its part the MAGB also felt that Londonderry was saying nothing new. But in his recent statement to the Dawdon miners, Londonderry had gone beyond Association policy by envisaging district settlements subject to national agreements. This is not to say that Londonderry had a clearly worked out strategy for rescuing the industry. But he had at least returned to public prominence in a favourable light, and for him that was just as important. As his son Lord Castlereagh noted: 'My father has now come out as the coal King and at the moment is the central figure in the picture'.[21]

Londonderry had been given an advanced copy of the Samuel Report before its publication on the 10 March 1926.[22] The report did not shy away from criticising the owners, and although it did not recommend nationalization, it proposed instead that royalties be nationalized, and that the industry be streamlined through amalgamation. It also called for wage cuts as an immediate solution to the industry's difficulties, but refused the MAGB demand for longer working hours. With the nine month subsidy due to run out at the end of April time was short, but the MAGB and MFGB were unable to reach an agreement, the former taking little heed of the more moderate owners in its ranks. Indeed, with the notable exception of Sir Alfred Mond, moderates were pressed into public silence. Nor was Baldwin prepared to coerce the owners; he wanted to see an end to the state's role in the industry, an unwelcome legacy of the coalition government he had helped to topple. Londonderry was not involved in negotiations between the Association and the Federation, but he did feel that their deadlock obliged the Prime Minister to intervene:

> I put this to you with all respect and humility because we collec-
> tively, owners and men, have failed to do what I earnestly hoped
> and prayed we could do, which was to join together and work out
> a solution to the problem. If our failure is due to deeper reasons
> than those which appear on the surface, it is for those outside the
> industry to diagnose the causes which are nullifying the best ele-
> ments in the representatives of each side.[23]

Without any real movement from the MAGB, the MFGB, or the government, the owners forced the miners to accept lower wages and longer
hours. The Federation refused and its members were locked out on 30
April 1926.

This prompted last minute negotiations between the cabinet and leaders from the MFGB and Trades Union Congress (TUC). The TUC were keen to avoid a national strike but they felt morally obliged to help the miners. One of their leaders, the Labour MP J. H. Thomas, had even been in correspondence with Londonderry in the hope that a settlement might be reached between moderates.[24] Negotiations on 3 May went on late into the early hours of the morning. Margaret Morris has suggested that despite the urgency, Baldwin did not inform his colleagues that Londonderry and one of Mond's managers had contacted him to express their unhappiness about the hardline position of the MAGB.[25] Then came the news in the early hours of the morning that unauthorized industrial action had been called by printers at the *Daily Mail*. Negotiations were broken off and so began the General Strike. In solidarity, two and a half million workers from the engineering and transport unions joined the one million striking miners.

The MFGB handed control of the General Strike over to the TUC. Unlike the government, however, the TUC was badly prepared for the strike, and divisions soon became apparent between moderates like Thomas and the more leftwing miners' leaders. On 7 May a deputation of ten major colliery owners, including Mond and Londonderry, met in secret with Baldwin to promote a compromise based on the Samuel Report. Baldwin, however, did not want to press a particular settlement and continued instead to appeal to the public for trust.

The government was also instrumental in quashing another attempt involving Londonderry to broker a settlement. On 5 May Londonderry was one of several prominent politicians and churchmen to visit the Archbishop of Canterbury, Randall Davidson, who was known to sympathize with the plight of the strikers. Both Baldwin and MacDonald discouraged Davidson from making an immediate overture to end the strike, but he was persuaded to do otherwise by Londonderry: 'the one mine owner whom I have found to possess suggestiveness or resource is Londonderry, of whom I myself should hardly have expected it.'[26] However, the Archbishop's appeal for a negotiated settlement was not as effective as it might have been, for the British Broadcasting Company refused to air it after coming under pressure from the government. Nevertheless, the appeal did make it into the provincial and national press, receiving a mixed reaction from politicians and churchmen alike.[27]

The TUC called off the General Strike on 12 May under the impression that Baldwin would act on the their recent talks with Sir Herbert

Samuel.[28] Baldwin had no such intention and the MFGB remained locked out. However, the Prime Minister did make efforts to suggest a compromise, including a temporary resumption of the subsidy and the creation of a national wages board. Londonderry wrote to him on 15 May to offer his help, repeating his view that all sides needed to give something if a solution was to be reached.[29] But the collapse of the TUC's support for the strike also made Londonderry even more venomous about the MFGB, allowing him to claim retrospectively that the owners had done all they reasonably could to avoid the strike.[30]

Toward the end of June, and after a consultation with Baldwin, Londonderry published his latest proposals for a settlement in the pro-miner *Colliery Guardian*.[31] As well as a national wages board and better conditions for miners, Londonderry argued that the industry could only be returned to profitability if local pits were organized so that 'co-partnership and cooperation' existed between miners and owners.[32] The effect of this article is uncertain, but it coincided with some movement towards a compromise on the part of the increasingly desperate MFGB.

Londonderry soon returned to a more defensive position, however, upon learning towards the end of August that MacDonald had been seeking US aid for distressed mining families. He attacked this as black propaganda and invited the Labour leader to inspect conditions at the Londonderry collieries. Moreover, he published a long letter in *The Times* defending conditions at his collieries, listing what the miners' children ate in their two meals a day, advertising his company's welfare schemes, and reminding readers that miners' lived rent free in colliery houses and received a coal allowance.[33] However accurate or otherwise his statements might have been, the letter displayed a lack of judgement and poor timing, for its publication coincided with the MFGB's decision to enter negotiations unconditionally, a development that was in many ways a reaction to the worsening conditions of many miners and their families. They were subsequently informed that the owners would not accept anything other than a complete surrender.

Even Churchill was now coming round to the view that it was the MAGB that was the real obstacle to a settlement.[34] The Chancellor had been dismayed by the inability of even the moderate owners to formulate acceptable terms, and therefore arranged to meet with them again at his house, Chartwell, in early September.[35] According to Thomas Jones' account of this meeting, Churchill was 'discussing it from every conceivable angle ... walking the grounds with "Charley" Londonderry and owing to the echo his voice can be heard a quarter of a mile away'.[36] Churchill hoped that his cousin might persuade the owners to compromise, or at least offer information on their thinking. After this meeting Londonderry wrote to the Chancellor about his dealings with the MAGB:

> I attended our meeting today and with difficulty I was able to carry the meeting with me on these lines. I accepted the Federation as a body which in some form was bound to be in existence, and we agreed that our district arrangement should be subject to the acceptance or rejection of the Federation, but not if we could help it to variation by the Federation. That means that wages, loans and conditions of working should be district arrangements and that other matters should be for the Federation to discuss and arrange with the Association ... Cook and [Herbert] Smith want Nationalisation and to save their faces, the owners want to get back to work and make money but are obsessed with the idea that they cannot make money on National lines. They trace all the troubles to the growth of the National idea and the case is a very strong one indeed ... when I pressed my friends as to how far they would go in National lines, the answer was, they could accept a national agreement which allowed for the working at a profit of the poorest district ... The great point for the district settlements which is being lost sight of is that a trivial local dispute would not have the effect of holding the country up to ransom which is what Cook and Smith want ... My idea is that if the Federation (Cook and Smith) are judiciously handled Cook and Smith will be only too glad to climb out on the bare recognition of the Miners Federation, but if you give them the smallest inkling that your mind is moving from the equilibrium away from the owners side of the table even by a hairs breath then they will fight like tigers for the National agreement and nothing but the National agreement.[37]

The partisan tone of this letter worsened relations between Churchill and his cousin. Londonderry feared that the Chancellor was going to move against the owners and even complained about Churchill's handling of the issue to the Prime Minister.[38] Baldwin was not impressed and sent only the briefest of acknowledgements.[39] Tensions between the two cousins worsened in October after Churchill had publicly criticized both the miners and the owners. Londonderry again defended the owners, arguing that they were 'fighting socialism ... one of the most powerful army corps in the field against us'.[40] Churchill replied angrily:

> It is not the business of Coal Owners as Coal Owners to fight
> Socialism. If they declare it their duty, how can they blame the
> Miners' Federation for pursuing political ends? The business of
> the Coal Owners is to manage their industry successfully, to insist
> upon sound economic conditions as regards hours and wages,
> and to fight Socialism as citizens and not as owners of a partic-
> ular class of property.[41]

Londonderry had tarnished his image as a moderate, he might still argue for a settlement, but it was accompanied increasingly by partisan attacks on the Labour party and the MFGB.[42] Even after the miners' were forced to return to work at the end of November, Londonderry blamed the strike for the industry's difficulties and for preventing him from sinking new mines.[43] It was hardly what the dejected and utterly defeated miners wanted to hear, but Londonderry could barely stop himself from attacking the strike. He had, in effect, backtracked on the position he had adopted before the General Strike. The apparent contrariness of his position was exemplified by two speeches he delivered within days of each other in January 1927. On the 8th he addressed his colliery officials at Dawdon on Cook's revolutionary leanings, his 'wicked and insane ideals', and his allies in Moscow.[44] On the 13th, however, while still taking time to criticize Cook and the MFGB, he addressed a branch of the Industrial Peace Union at Sunderland that his son, Castlereagh, had established, informing his audience of how he still insisted on the need for industrial peace.[45]

It is clear that Londonderry viewed the MFGB with contempt, as an obstacle to industrial peace. Like other Tories, he may also have felt that attacking the unionized working class might entrench existing working class support for the Conservatives, especially in areas like Stockton.[46] He therefore backed the Trade Disputes Act 1927, a measure forced on Baldwin by die-hards in the cabinet to declare strikes illegal if they inflicted hardship on the community or the government. Explaining his support for the Act to a meeting of Conservative 'working men', Londonderry declared that it would prevent unpatriotic union leaders from manipulating their members to oppose the country.[47] He was able therefore to inform the House of Lords on 30 June 1927 that he 'dreaded the introduction of politics into the industry,' that he regarded 'the trade union movement as one of the greatest forces in modern social evolution, a movement which had remedied abuses which all were now agreed should be remedied', but that they could be subject to malign influences such as communism.[48] In the end, the owners' attitude to the General Strike, the miners' strike, and their support of the 1927 Act only heightened the bitterness felt by miners. The Act became a rallying point for the Labour movement and hardened their resolve to one day nationalize the industry.

As the owner of a relatively large and successful mining company Londonderry was able to take a moderate stance at the start of the miners' strike and a more partisan position towards the end. But his wealth, and no doubt his realization that Labour would never forgive the owners, also compelled him to take a more benign attitude towards his employees in the years that followed their defeat.[49] He publicly supported the industrial peace talks between Mond and the leading trade unionist Ernest Bevin during the winter of 1927 to 1928.[50] In 1928 he reversed a decision to terminate the employment of almost three thousand miners at his failing New Seaham colliery.[51] On 9 January 1932, in what he called 'a red letter day', he opened new pit baths at Dawdon, and received praise from an official of the 133,000 strong Durham Miners' Association who claimed that ninety percent of his employees would ballot to maintain the mine under Londonderry's ownership. On this occasion he addressed his family's history in the area:

> …some persons seemed to think from what they read from time to time in the newspapers that there was a quarrel existing between Dawdon people and his family. 'So far as I am concerned,' he declared, 'that quarrel never existed and never will exist. (Cheers.) Some of you—and I believe you do it more good-naturedly than otherwise—are inclined to express your criticism not only of me but of my forebears in very forcible language. (Laughter.) Whatever condemnation you pass on my forebears, it is not correct. They have always tried to inculcate in those of us who came after them a sense of our responsibilities, and I sincerely hope that I have been able to carry out with some success those duties … My sympathies and my hopes are with the people in this neighbourhood to which I am proud to belong.[52]

In September 1933 he declined to donate money to a new non-political miners' union for fear of antagonising the Durham Miners' Association, a decision that angered some local Conservatives including Headlam.[53] This public reticence did contrast, however, with his willingness in private to support the owners.[54] He also remained sensitive to public accusations about his role as a coal owner, although by 1931 it was his wife who submitted long letters to *The Times* on behalf of her husband the government minister.[55] But by and large, as one of Londonderry's Conservative critics remarked: 'as a mine-owner in Durham he had quite a good reputation, but the people who were his agents were regarded as a pretty hard lot.'[56]

III

In July 1927 Londonderry was appointed chairman of the Royal Commission on London Squares.[57] It is hard to judge whether this marginal appointment was intended by the government to test him, or if it was to merely to buy off his claims to a higher office. After all, it could hardly be described as a step up from under secretary of state, and yet it preceded his appointment the following year to the not unrelated Office of Works. Indeed, as First Commissioner of Works he would implement the report he had prepared in 1927.[58] It was, however, the sort of appointment that was given out typically to aristocrats. As David Cannadine has noted, aristocrats were well suited to chairing royal commissions, they possessed 'those attributes of leisure, dignity, a broad view, and a disinterested tone' necessary for the task, and were 'less inclined to be controversial or acrimonious'.[59] The two other royal commissions appointed in 1927 were also chaired by aristocrats, one of whom was a very junior minister in the government, and the other a leading diplomatist. It is therefore difficult to determine if the government had any long-term plans for Londonderry when they gave him the royal commission; but if they did, they soon found a sharper test for their would-be minister.

    If Londonderry's reputation for moderation in the mining industry had been somewhat tarnished towards the end of 1926, then the annual Conservative party conference in October 1927 gave him the opportunity to fully extricate himself from any association with the die-hards.[60] Several motions at the Cardiff conference called for the powers of the House of Lords to be strengthened as a bulwark against a future Labour government, but Baldwin was determined to see off this threat to his One Nation agenda.[61] On the recommendation of Harold Macmillan he asked Londonderry to move the leadership's amendment to the die-hards' motion.[62] It is also possible that Baldwin remembered the small role Londonderry had played in opposing die-hard designs on the House of Lords in the past.

In his speech to conference, Londonderry claimed that there was no need to alter the constitution, especially as it had been vindicated during the General Strike. Altering the powers of the House of Lords, he argued, would create suspicion among the electorate that they were moderating the free exercise of the vote.[63] Although he did not succeed in placating the die-hard faction, the speech did earn him the praise of moderates. The most notable praise came from Churchill who assured Londonderry on 22 October that his contribution would serve him well.[64]

IV

The prominence of the Londonderrys as political hosts has been interpreted by some as their sole claim on office, when in fact it should be viewed as one manifestation of their claim. It has already been noted several times that wealthy territorial magnates could still claim an office in the gift of the state, and although the incidences of this had been diminishing from the 1880s, it remained a feature of British public life for much of the twentieth century. There was, of course, a serious qualitative decline in what they could receive. While many aristocrats could easily claim a deputy lieutenancy in their county, far fewer could ever hope to enter the government, let alone the cabinet. But even here their decline was far from sudden. When Londonderry's father entered Salisbury's second government in 1886, he was one of ten aristocrats in a cabinet of 15 men. In Balfour's cabinet he was one of 9 in a cabinet of 19 men. When Law asked the seventh Marquess to join his government in 1922, half of his 16-man cabinet came from the aristocracy. And when Baldwin formed a cabinet of 21 in 1924, it included nine aristocrats.

It was therefore not so much the existence of Londonderry's claim on office in the 1920s that aroused criticism, but the way it manifested itself. When many aristocrat-politicians had abandoned the more overt and extravagant methods of gaining political patronage, the Londonderrys continued as if nothing had changed.[65] In 1935 the MP and socialite Henry Channon noted in his diary that Lady Londonderry was 'the only political hostess left'.[66] And writing in the 1950s, Robert Vansittart recalled that Londonderry House was 'the last great house in London.'[67]

When Lord Londonderry inherited his father's title and property in 1915, Edith also inherited the role of leading political hostess that her mother-in-law had cultivated from the 1880s. This meant carrying on the tradition of holding grand receptions at Londonderry House. But Edith distinguished herself from previous form in two notable ways. First, Londonderry House hosted evening parties of the type that character-ized 1920s London, with live music and a guest list that included politi-cians, writers and ambassadors. Second, Edith formed a dining club in 1915 called the Ark, with an exclusive but varied membership of leading figures from politics, society and the arts. This divergence from previous socialising was an adaptation to changing times to ensure continuity, but, as Ross McKibbin has highlighted, it also hastened the 'Americanization' of London society, a process that Edith lamented but by her own actions encouraged.[68]

The Ark was outwardly superficial, its members having pet names, and its activities normally involving frivolity and general entertainment. But it also allowed the Londonderrys to have a more intimate relationship with leading political figures. Throughout its two decades or so of existence Ark members included Churchill, Edward Wood, Samuel Hoare, Lady Astor, Edward Carson, Arthur Balfour, Harold Macmillan, Stanley Baldwin and Neville Chamberlain. The more artistic of its members included Sir William Orpen, Sean O'Casey, Sir John Lavery, St John Gogarty, George Bernard Shaw, Rutland Boughton and John Buchan.[69] This intimacy extended even to the royal family, and the Londonderrys did not shy away from using it to attempt a royal match. After the First World War, George V's second son, Prince Albert, became a member of the Ark, known as the Unicorn. Try as they might, the Londonderrys could not get their eldest daughter, the eighteen-year-old Maureen, to take an interest in Albert, for she preferred and eventually married Lord Derby's son Oliver Stanley. The full ramifications of this failed match became apparent in 1936 when Albert unexpectedly became King George VI.

If they were never to be part of the royal family, the Londonderrys' Ark did include Ramsay MacDonald, who became a member in 1929 after being appointed Prime Minister for the second time. Although cor-respondence between Edith and MacDonald had lapsed by the time the latter left office at the end of 1924, it was rejuvenated again in 1926 just after the return of the Londonderrys to County Durham.[70] The friend-ship became even more intense and controversial when MacDonald replaced Sidney Webb as the MP for Seaham in 1929, followed soon after by his assumption of the premiership. The spotlight therefore intensified on the Londonderrys' social activities. Gossip columnists made frequent reference to Edith and MacDonald, and Labour MPs expressed unease about the high society company their leader was keeping.[71] The relationship was even fictionalized by Howard Spring in his 1940 political novel *Fame is the Spur*, the satirical account of a MacDonald-like Labour politician who befriends a 'Lady Lostwithiel'. When MacDonald appointed Londonderry to his emergency National Government in August 1931, and to the cabinet three months later, it was attributed by almost everyone to Lady Londonderry's friendship with the Prime Minister. Receptions at Londonderry House thereafter cemented the link in people's imagination, particularly the image of MacDonald in full evening dress standing atop the staircase of Londonderry House with a diamond bedecked Edith beside him greeting guests as they arrived.[72] But few considered Londonderry's previous experience, or the appointment of five other aristocrats to the cabinet, or that he had been appointed to Baldwin's government in 1928. The 1931 appointment just seemed less justifiable than previous appointments, even though criticism was nothing new.

Throughout the 1920s popular daily newspapers were keen to give their readers news of the social activities of London's Bright Young Things. The decadence and frivolity of the post First World War period captured the public imagination, but not always in a flattering light.[73] The upper classes were often portrayed as grotesquely extravagant at a time when the country struggled economically, especially after the 1929 Wall Street Crash. On 30 December 1930 Headlam referred to Edith as 'that wretched woman ... a perfectly valueless person politically ... is only too willing to entertain the Party in London.'[74] He was somewhat less hostile, however, three years later when found himself invited to Londonderry House by Lord Castlereagh, and introduced to the Prime Minister and other leading figures of the day.[75]

The presence of senior politicians on this occasion is a useful reminder that Londonderry House remained popular among its exclusive set well into the 1930s. But this did not mean that Lord Londonderry was ignorant of criticism. On 11 October 1930 he responded to the latest request for him to host a reception by writing to Baldwin:

> I am always glad to give the party, as you know, if it is necessary ... My difficulty is ... when the newspapers write us up as the perpetrators of Bacchanalian orgies. I hope Neville [Chamberlain] is

right when he thinks these parties do a great deal of good. We get the smug-faced citizens of London with their wives and daughters who vote Conservative anyway. I always wish that we could touch the other strata where the bulk of the votes lie: but please rest assured that we are always delighted to do anything that gives you the smallest assistance ... [76]

Baldwin later criticized Londonderry's use of grand entertainments as a political expediency to help his career with MacDonald. But in doing so he seemed to have forgotten his own frequent attendance, and worse still, his view that they were useful.[77] The truth may be that the Tory hierarchy simply enjoyed the functions, and that these occasions helped them replenish party coffers through the aristocratic embrace of wealthy businessmen and other potential donors.[78]

Nevertheless, reports in the press about parties at Londonderry House continued to concern Londonderry. They made him appear extravagant and associated him with the vacuous social world captured by Evelyn Waugh in his 1930 novel *Vile Bodies*.[79] His unease intensified after his appointment to the National Government in August 1931. By January 1932 he had enough and wrote to the proprietor of the *Daily Express*, Lord Beaverbrook, to explain how reports of lavish functions at Londonderry House showed little consideration for his employees and friends in County Durham and Northern Ireland. He informed Beaverbrook that he had been obliged to cut back on socialising at his provincial bases, but that he could not avoid the duties expected of him at London. Beaverbrook was unimpressed and replied by suggesting that Londonderry's lavish spending was an ideal cure for the ailing economy. Londonderry then accused the press baron of espionage.[80] Before denying this charge, Beaverbrook contributed a leader to the *Sunday Express* on 10 January 1932 in which he defended lavish spending on entertainments.[81] With this Londonderry ended their correspondence.[82] But it would not be the last time they would clash over reports in the *Daily Express*.

V

Lord Birkenhead's resignation in October 1928 left a vacancy in the cabinet, one Baldwin decided that Londonderry would fill as First Commissioner of Works. According to Headlam the Prime Minister had no choice: 'One can't use a man's hospitality and not give him a job if he wants it.'[83] Indeed, Baldwin went so far so to visit Londonderry House to make the offer, rather than summon Londonderry to Downing Street.[84] However, it has been demonstrated that this was not the only factor in Baldwin's decision; had it been, Londonderry's appointment as Lord Lieutenant of County Durham earlier in the year would have been seen as an adequate payment for the services rendered at Londonderry House.[85]

In fact, Londonderry's appointment owed much to Churchill, who had assured him in 1927 that his conference speech would serve him well. The new First Commissioner, however, was under the impression that he owed his gratitude to Sir James Craig, now Viscount Craigavon.[86] This mistake probably arose from the fact that Churchill and Londonderry had just emerged from a tense period in their relationship. In March 1926, when Londonderry conferred an honorary degree on Churchill at Queen's University, all had seemed well between the two.[87] By the end of the year, however, the ongoing miners' dispute created tensions between them that lasted well into the following year. In August 1927 Londonderry complained to the Chancellor of the Exchequer about increases in company tax. Churchill denied he had done this and asked bluntly that his friends do not write to him on public issues unless they had suggestions of their own.[88] When Londonderry replied that his cousin was being 'unfriendly', Churchill accused him of giving him 'a lecture on my public misdeeds and short comings':

> Then you say in effect 'aren't we friends after all'? Of course we are; but it is not part of friendship to neglect to reply to criticism. I take criticism in good heart, but not if I am to be gagged. Even in the House of Commons I am allowed to reply and if any member had used your tone of arguments to me there I should have tried to answer them suitably. But that would have had nothing to do with personal relations.[89]

Nevertheless, within a few months relations had improved, and the following year Londonderry joined his cousin around the cabinet table.

Londonderry's re-entry to the government was marked in ceremonial style when the new First Commissioner was allowed to carry the Cap of Maintenance at the opening of parliament in November 1928.[90] Otherwise, it was difficult for Londonderry do anything remarkable during his first period at the Ministry of Works. Not only because it lasted less than nine months, but also because the department mainly dealt with the mundane task of maintaining government buildings at home and abroad.[91] It is not surprising therefore that unlike his previous appointments, Londonderry enjoyed his time at the Ministry of Works, for it aroused almost no controversy and yet still provided him with a seat in the cabinet. For all these reasons Londonderry did little of note, but several decisions he took in office are worthy of record. In February 1929 he refused to support a proposal to create 'National Parks' through the transfer of Forestry Commission land to the Ministry of Works, arguing that the costs involved did not justify it.[92] Somewhat more controversially, he approved the statue in Whitehall of Field Marshal the Earl Haig. It had been criticized on ascetic grounds by Lady Haig, and on moral grounds by the King, who desired that its site be moved further away from the Cenotaph.[93] If Londonderry's portfolio was not of itself demanding, then as one of six peers in the cabinet he did sometimes find himself representing the government on a wide range of matters in the House of Lords. These could vary from unemployment to electricity supply, to his small part in curtailing Viscount Cecil of Chelwood's attempt to introduce a bill that would have created driving tests for both drivers and their vehicles.[94]

Londonderry's portfolio might have kept him out of trouble with the electorate, but he still managed to have a major disagreement with Baldwin over the Prime Minister's decision in January 1929 to allow the Prince of Wales to visit pit villages in Northumberland and County Durham. Londonderry was furious with the negative publicity generated by the visit and condemned the Prince's reference to 'appalling conditions', claiming that this failed to take into consideration the special rent arrangements he had reached with his employees.[95]

It was an apathetic Conservative party that fought the 30 May 1929 general election; Baldwin's policy of moderation had caused unease in the party and fears that he was pushing through semi-socialist measures.[96] It was apathy that Londonderry addressed during his own attempt to drum up support for the Conservatives in County Durham.[97] He also had to deal with an ongoing strike by his miners at Dawdon, something he used in an attempt to marshal the Tory vote, but even the presence of Communists at Dawdon failed to excite the electorate.[98] The results of the general election reflected this nationally, for the Conservatives polled around the same number of votes as they had in 1924, but the Labour party went from around five and half million to almost eight and a half, giving it 288 seats to the Conservatives' 260. But the second Labour government was a minority government like the first, and no one expected it to last long, especially after the Wall Street Crash in the last week of October 1929.[99]

During the Tories' interregnum Londonderry's loyalty to the leadership of Baldwin was twice tested, over Labour's Coal Mines bill, and once again over tariff reform. Despite the somewhat retaliatory intentions of the Coal Mines bill, Londonderry adhered to Salisbury's view that the House of Lords would only try to amend the bill but not reject it.[100] Having done so much in the past to avoid a clash between the Lords and Commons, both men agreed that it would be futile to create too many obstacles.[101] Londonderry therefore restricted himself to voicing concerns about the impact the bill would have on the market, although he did suggest on 29 April 1930 that the measure was stepping stone towards nationalization.[102]

The deteriorating international economic situation obliged the Conservative party to once again consider their position on tariff reform. Baldwin did not want to repeat his defeat at the 1924 election and so opposed those in the party who called on him to advocate imperial preference. Above all, he was concerned that Labour would use the scare of food taxes to take more seats from the Tories in the industrial north. However, with most countries opting to raise tariffs in the wake of the Wall Street Crash, even Londonderry drastically revised his earlier opposition to tariff reform. As he later noted in his memoirs: 'I have always looked on Protection as an evil in itself but rendered absolutely necessary by events.'[103]

After almost half a year out of office Londonderry gave cautious support to Beaverbrook's increasingly popular campaign for imperial preference. On 16 December 1929 he offered his car for the press baron's tour of County Durham, but subsequently declined Beaverbrook's invitation to join him on the campaign trail.[104] In February 1930 Beaverbrook moved his campaign up a gear by forming the Empire Crusade party. On the 14th of that month Londonderry chaired a meeting of the Ulster Unionist Council at Belfast at which Baldwin was the guest speaker. As presiding officer, he used his opening remarks to welcome the leader's statement on the need for the liberal use of safeguarding—the targeted protection of struggling industries as opposed to general tariffs—delivered to a meeting of Unionists the previous night. Londonderry then proceeded to outline the problems faced by the Irish linen industry in dealing with international competition. Baldwin avoided the implicit invitation to recommend that Irish linen be safeguarded and instead focussed on the loyalty of Ulster to the empire.[105]

Like many Conservatives, Londonderry's attitude to Baldwin and Beaverbrook remained equivocal throughout 1930. On 16 July he informed an audience at Rothbury, Northumberland, that:

> The country owed a debt of gratitude to Lord Beaverbrook for bringing forward his great policy of Empire free trade, which must form the main plank in the Conservative platform. Some people said that there were two camps in the Conservative Party, but there was nothing of the sort. There was only one ... he was not prepared to go as far as Lord Beaverbrook and go to the country on the question of food taxes until he knew what business-like arrangement could be made for the mutual benefit of the country and the Dominions.[106]

He repeated these statements to Beaverbrook three days later, adding that he could not agree with the press baron using his newspapers and campaign to harm the Tory leadership.[107] By August Londonderry was trimming his sails even further, informing an audience at the Ulster Reform Club, Belfast, that:

> Empire Free Trade was an inspiring ideal which they hoped one day to attain, the sooner the better. Safeguarding was a practical policy, gaining fresh supporters from all parties every day. He had no patience with any one, whoever he might be, who sought to create dissensions [sic] in their ranks on matters of pure detail. On great principles they were clearly and obviously united...[108]

On 8 October, at the Imperial Conference at London, Baldwin took the wind out of Beaverbrook's sails by welcoming the Canadian Prime Minister's offer of a reciprocity agreement with the United Kingdom. Londonderry, who hosted a reception for the Imperial Conference at Londonderry House, was privately apprehensive about the success or otherwise of Baldwin's position, informing his leader that safeguarding would be a mere palliative until a international trade agreement could be reached.[109] In public, however, he displayed no such doubts:

> The great policy upon which the Conservative Party was desirous of educating the country was an extension of safeguarding

which would enable them to place in healthy and remunerative
work a great many of the unemployed. On the other side of their
policy was Imperial preference, a policy with which he had always
been associated.[110]

The last claim was of course a gross distortion, for he had always been a
free trader, and had addressed an audience at Birmingham, of all places,
on the perils of protection as recently as 28 February 1929.[111] He made
a similar claim exactly two years later, when moving a bill on import
duties, informing the House of Lords that he always had 'little sympathy'
with free trade; an untruth, but one that earned him the praise of John
Buchan.[112]

At a crucial meeting on 30 October 1930 Baldwin received the support of his party for a free hand in trade negotiations with the dominions. Londonderry wrote afterwards to congratulate his leader on his 'victory'.[113] Like many others in the party Londonderry now felt he could
back Baldwin without equivocation. On 22 November 1930 he informed
an audience at Gateshead that Baldwin commanded a strong party, but
contradicted this unintentionally by 'making an appeal for a free hand to
be given to Mr Baldwin in negotiations with the Dominions'.[114] The final
crisis on this issue for Baldwin occurred on 1 March 1931 when his shadow cabinet came close to asking him to resign. Within a fortnight however Baldwin had recaptured his party's support. In the intervening period, Londonderry wrote to Beaverbrook on 5 March to declare that the
Tories were now united, and that their previous divisions had only helped
Labour remain in power. On 8 March Beaverbrook disbanded his Empire
Crusade party in the belief that Baldwin had given in to his demands. He
wrote to Londonderry the following day saying he had decided to back
down as his campaign was destroying the only party that could deliver
what he wanted.[115] After that there was only a transient reactivation of
Empire Crusade in the spring of 1931—attracting the covert support of
many Tories including Londonderry—but for Baldwin the crisis had
effectively ended.[116]

VI

Londonderry's engagement with and attitude to the whole episode
demonstrated his desire to re-enter a Conservative government. Out of
office he had only part time and ornamental roles to fulfil, as a lord lieu-

tenant twice over, as a coal owner, a director on the boards of several companies, and now chancellor of two universities, Belfast and Durham.[117] In January 1931 George V offered Londonderry the post of Governor-General of Canada. The idea had originated with the Prime Minister of Canada, Richard Bennett, who had enjoyed a reception at Londonderry House during the Imperial Conference in October 1930.[118] For the third and final time, Londonderry declined the purely ornamental office, visiting Buckingham Palace personally to deliver his refusal.[119]

It proved to be a wise decision. The increasingly dire state of the British and international economy had been fuelling divisions in the Labour party and its collapse seemed inevitable; yet unpopular economic decisions would have to be taken by whatever government replaced it. On 24 August 1931, with the blessing of the King, the three party leaders formed an emergency National Government to take these decisions and thus avoid a divisive general election. Like most other Tories, Londonderry supported Baldwin's decision to enter an alliance with the Liberals and those Labour MPs who remained with MacDonald—it was also agreed that the Labour leader would continue as Prime Minister. He was rewarded with a reappointment to the Ministry of Works, although on this unique occasion it did not carry with it a seat in the cabinet.[120]

Having taken some preliminary measures to avert further economic disaster, the National Government sought a doctor's mandate to continue in office and called a general election for 27 October. In his campaigning, Londonderry called for tariff reform and asked the people to do their duty to the country by supporting the 'National' parties.[121] At the very least his performance pleased Churchill.[122]

But Londonderry was also an election issue, at least for MacDonald. When the Prime Minister stood for re-election at Seaham he faced criticism for appointing a local colliery owner to his most recent cabinet. MacDonald denied the charge, claiming that it was the Conservatives who nominated Londonderry to the Ministry of Works and not him.[123] But deny it as he might, the belief was widespread, even Headlam noted in his diary that Lady Londonderry had been playing her cards well. Beatrice Webb was even more blunt: 'Evil communications corrupt good manners'.[124] Whoever chose Londonderry, it is undeniable that MacDonald's troubled leadership of the second Labour government had made him more reliant on Edith.[125] Indeed, it has been suggested that Lady Londonderry had been in favour of a coalition government since 1930.[126] However, it is likely that this reflected her very personal empathy with MacDonald and not the view of her husband, for he used almost every speech he made between 1928 and 1931 to criticize the Labour party and its leader.

The general election returned 554 MPs supporting the National Government, a staggering majority that completely eclipsed those who refused to join it. Within a week it was announced that Londonderry had been appointed to the cabinet as Secretary of State for Air.[127] What role MacDonald had in Londonderry's second appointment to the National Government is not certain, but as the new Secretary of State for Air later noted, he was from this time marked out as 'Ramsay's man'.[128] Subsequent events may have played a part in fostering the belief that it was MacDonald and not Baldwin who appointed Londonderry to the cabinet. For the latter two had an increasingly poor relationship that led Baldwin to remove Londonderry from the Air Ministry in June 1935. MacDonald intervened at that point to ensure that Londonderry was given another post, but by the end of the year he was out of the government altogether. In this light a retrospective judgement is understandable, but it has ignored Londonderry's other claims to office and overshadowed his personal involvement in issues that were crucial to the future success of Stanley Baldwin and the Conservative party.

6

Secretary of State for Air, 1931–1935

As Secretary of State for Air with a seat in the cabinet, Londonderry had reached the highpoint of his political career. His period in office coincided with a crucial stage in international relations, a time when, according to Piers Brendon, the world 'traversed a dark valley inhabited by the giants of unemployment, hardship, strife and fear.'[1] In this sense the period inflated Londonderry's importance; had he served as Secretary of State for Air during the 1920s his term of office would have aroused little notice and barely any controversy. No one expected that the Air Ministry would, in the words of Winston Churchill, 'become one of the most important offices in the State', but, as it became just that, especially following Adolf Hitler's assumption of power in 1933, Londonderry's position was increasingly precarious.[2] He was particularly vulnerable because his appointment to the National Government had been the subject of controversy. But it would be his deteriorating relationship with Baldwin that ultimately sealed his fate. Ideologically they had contradictory views on aerial bombing, and, on a more practical level, overlapping parliamentary responsibilities. The latter was a result of the peculiar position of both men in the government: Londonderry an increasingly prominent cabinet minister in the House of Lords, and Baldwin a prime minister in all but name in the House of Commons with a premier's interest in foreign affairs. It was Londonderry's difference of opinion with Baldwin, and the majority of the cabinet, and his unwillingness to forsake Air Ministry dogma for popular politics that determined his fate in 1935; in this respect it was a repeat of his experience in Northern Ireland. In both instances Londonderry believed himself to be in the right as the defender of ministry wisdom, and in both he disregarded the need to appease public concerns, no matter how much they conflicted with his own potential for remaining in office.

I

The continuing international economic crisis ensured that the temporary National Government of August 1931 evolved into a permanent one. The 'National' parties went to the polls as a unified body in October 1931 and won an overwhelming mandate to continue in power. Conservatives now dominated the House of Commons, with Ramsay MacDonald's Labour supporters winning a dozen seats and the official Labour party only retaining fifty-two. The new National cabinet reflected the parliamentary arithmetic, and although MacDonald remained Prime Minister, Baldwin acted as his deputy and guardian of the Conservative interest through the office of Lord President of the Council. Aside from the two Liberals occupying the Foreign and Home Offices respectively, the Tories and the four MacDonald-Labour members received between them the remaining 16 posts; six of which went to aristocrats.

Londonderry made his first formal policy announcement in the House of Lords on 17 November 1931.[3] It dealt with the question of air routes, a policy that gave preference in some instances to foreign states over British possessions. It was one example of how the Air portfolio and collective cabinet responsibility would demand a large measure of flexibility on the part of Londonderry.[4] As a government minister and one of its spokesmen in the upper house, he was, like other Tory ministers, compelled to advocate policies he had once attacked. Therefore, when Londonderry moved the second reading of the Finance bill in 1932, he referred to it as a necessary sacrifice despite the damaging cutbacks it inflicted on the Air Ministry.[5] On another occasion, Londonderry defended trade with the Soviet Union, a country whose Communist system he both feared and despised. He informed the House of Lords that although he sympathized with critics of the policy—notably on this occasion they included lords Mount Temple and Lothian—trade relations would prevent further hostilities, promote domestic employment and positively effect Russian development.[6] On yet another occasion, he responded to accusations of Soviet activity in India by reminding the Lords that the market afforded by 180,000,000 people was not one that could be lightly ignored.[7] As one of four peers in the cabinet Londonderry took his responsibilities in the House of Lords very seriously. It was, of course, the basis of his right to sit in parliament, and it was perhaps for that reason that he could chide peers for low attendance, and yet defend the chamber's existence against those who sought to introduce life peerages. If reform had to occur he argued, then it had to be substantial and not a further dilution of the institution he cherished.[8]

Among his range of responsibilities in the upper house Londonderry dealt with maters concerning the Transport Ministry, in particular the London Passenger Transport bill 1933.[9] Aware of some Conservative unrest with the direction of policy he reassured the Lords that the bill had been 'purged of any Socialist character'.[10] When he introduced the Petroleum (Production) bill 1934, Londonderry anticipated a much later defence of globalization by advancing the argument that increasingly larger business corporations were part of the 'development of modern civilisation', that they 'imposed upon us all a certain measure of surrender of individual and private rights.'[11] Similarly, addressing the Lords in 1935, he defended the 'national' aspect of the government by arguing that people recognized the increasing need to control certain activities by the state: 'they had been willing to surrender part of their personal sovereignty in the belief that this control … was beneficial to the community.'[12] When visiting Jarrow in October 1934, two years before the famous hunger march, he remarked that he would support 'any measures' to restore prosperity to the area.[13] He again demonstrated how much he had changed when he moved the Lotteries bill on 30 May 1934. In contrast to his backbench campaign against government restrictions on the lifestyle of 'working men', he now agreed with the finding of a royal commission that deplored 'the general detriment to the character of young persons in poor neighbourhoods due to the excitement of day-to-day betting on greyhound tracks.[14] His advocacy of the Lotteries bill prompted Headlam to note in his diary that Londonderry had promoted 'a very socialistic measure'.[15] He countered such accusations by claiming that he had his own concerns, but that such measures were in the best interests of the Conservative party and national unity.[16]

Londonderry's advocacy of limited interventionism and concomitant defensiveness against accusations of socialism should not exaggerate the political distance he travelled. Like other Conservatives, he sought to preserve the National Government by appealing to national unity through measures that sometimes owed more to socialist interventionism than Tory ideals, a calculated precaution against the growth of an increasingly doctrinaire Labour opposition and the populist ideals of fascism and communism.[17] The Conservative ideals of pre-war Britain could therefore no longer be sustained, and the growing international trend towards protectionism helped to heal internal party wounds by compelling the adoption of the Import Duties Act 1932. Londonderry therefore had little choice other than to welcome this measure of protectionism, especially as it was he who moved the bill in the House of Lords, leading the first Viscount Snowden to note that he did so by 'praising it with faint damns.'[18] He still took some care, however, to defend certain libertarian doctrines, in particular press freedom and the commercial freedom of the City of London.[19]

Although Air policy in the early 1930s was dominated by military concerns, Londonderry's Ministry also occupied itself with the expanding civil aviation industry. With cut-backs to the budget of the RAF there was little of significance the Ministry could do to support civil aviation other than through influence and encouragement. For example, in performing the latter Londonderry used newspaper coverage of the many conferences and functions he attended as Air Minister to champion civil aviation.[20] This aspect of the Ministry's work took on more importance towards the end of 1933 as the Geneva Disarmament Conference teetered on the brink of collapse. The conference had attempted to internationalize civil aviation as a means of preventing aerial bombing, indeed, the failure to do so made Londonderry a sceptic of any possible agreement. But it also prompted him to champion the peaceful and unifying benefits of civil aviation:

> discovery of the means of flight had too often lately been represented as a misfortune rather than as a blessing to mankind ... The aeroplane ... was destined to be a more potent instrument for peace in the world and for union among the nations than any other which at present they possessed.[21]

Limited in what he could spend, and with his attention concentrated on the RAF, Londonderry did what he could to advocate and celebrate developments in civil aviation such as the internationalization of aerial law and the construction of airports by local authorities.[22] And although Imperial Airways was the Ministry's preferred instrument for international air routes, Londonderry also encouraged private companies to put forward viable proposals and thus open the market.[23] He soon took up this cause personally with the construction of an aerodrome at his Newtownards estate.[24] Within a year the first civil airport in Northern Ireland was opened with a circus-like demonstration of wireless technology, Londonderry giving a speech from an aeroplane three thousand feet from the ground. After some difficulties it was reported that he could be heard 'fairly distinctly over quite a large area.'[25] Having learnt to fly in 1932, and having opened his own airport in 1934, Londonderry was thus devoted not only to his Ministry, but also to the very concept of aviation.[26]

Unintentionally, Londonderry's emphasis on the importance of civil aviation undermined his control of it, despite the report of the Gorell Committee in July 1934. This had favoured the Air Ministry retaining control of civil aviation on financial and structural grounds, but it failed to stem growing criticisms that the Ministry was too occupied with military matters. On 27 September 1934 Londonderry urged the Chief Whip to ensure that no debate took place on the Gorell Report, but he still could not escape the mounting criticisms of Britain's relatively poor record in civil aviation.[27] By the second week of December 1934 a serious disagreement on the issue led to a row between the Permanent Secretary of the Air Ministry, Sir Christopher Bullock, and the Air Minister. The result of this was the appointment of a Director General of Civil Aviation to reassure critics of a new dispensation for civil aviation.[28] It would be the first of several events that undermined incrementally Londonderry's position at the Air Ministry. The episode also heightened tensions between the Air Minister and his Under Secretary of State, Philip Sassoon, who along with Baldwin was appropriating more Air Ministry business for the House of Commons.[29]

II

As Secretary of State for Air Londonderry found himself embroiled in one of the most controversial issues of the early 1930s, disarmament and the abolition of aerial bombing. Within days of his appointment he accompanied the Prime Minister to the Lord Mayor of London's banquet at the Guildhall. The new Air Minister made it clear to his audience that, while he thought that all methods towards peace should be pursued, the drive for disarmament, which was necessitated by economic stringency, should go no further due to continued threats of aggression.[30] This earned him a parliamentary rebuke from the Labour MP Sir Stafford Cripps, who criticized the timing of Londonderry's 'unfortunate' statement, coming as it did before the Disarmament Conference had even met.[31] Cripps demanded to know if the government had approved Londonderry's speech. It was not an easy question for this government of individuals to answer, and it was one that would continue to trouble Londonderry's relationship with his colleagues. The Air Minister's opening shot in the debate highlighted publicly his underlying fear that the decline of the British economy was dictating external policy. Like Bernard Porter, Paul Kennedy has argued that this was 'the most critical conditioning element in the formulation of the country's external policy'.[32] Although Londonderry preferred to believe political choices could still be made regardless of financial considerations, pre-empting the thesis of David Reynolds, he would later lament that the choices he believed to be correct were never effectively made because of Neville Chamberlain's economic policy.[33]

As with his previous tenure at the Air Ministry Londonderry sided with and promoted the interests of the commanding officers of the RAF, sharing their belief in the maintenance of an independent air force and their faith in armed deterrent. Within weeks of taking office he warned his cabinet colleagues of Britain's weakness in the air, informing them that it had fallen to fifth among the world powers for aviation spending.[34] Like other proponents of the RAF he highlighted their role in the Middle East, where the threat and occasional use of aerial bombing had been more financially prudent than using the army.[35] Like the Air Staff, he felt that if aerial bombing was banned it would not only be unenforceable, but that it would also spell the end of the RAF and Britain's influence in the Middle East. Londonderry's relationship with his military chiefs was not unusual for a service minister; as A. J. P. Taylor has noted, such politicians 'became little more than agents for those who were in theory their subordinates.'[36] And although service chiefs and ministers scored a victory with the abandonment of the Ten Year Rule in March 1932, they still had to contend with more senior cabinet ministers who continued to respond to the public mood by pressing for an agreement on disarmament.[37]

On 2 February 1932 the League of Nations Disarmament Conference held its first session at Geneva. Londonderry was uneasy about the idealistic aims of the conference from the outset. He disliked the venue and later argued that it was too removed from the real world, that Geneva was 'full of old women and sentimental cranks.'[38] Despite the stated aim of disarmament the conference fell victim to several factors: the competing interests of its 61 delegations, ongoing hostile relations between France and Germany, and a moralistic crusade to formulate a ban on aerial bombing, an effort given extra impetus by the recent Japanese invasion of Manchuria.[39]

British delegates to the Disarmament Conference, like the government, were divided on the prohibition of aerial bombing. Some agreed with the view of the Air Ministry and RAF, while others felt under pressure to abandon it. The main difficulty lay in the fact that while the Foreign Secretary, Sir John Simon, and most other cabinet ministers disagreed with Londonderry, he was nevertheless Secretary of State for Air and therefore responsible for aerial bombing. Moreover, he often received the cautious support of the Prime Minister, who was also, at least officially, the chief British delegate to the Disarmament Conference. But MacDonald's ill health meant he rarely attended, leaving representation to Simon, Londonderry and the other two service ministers.[40] Back in London the Committee of Imperial Defence (CID) struggled through its subcommittees to mediate between the three services, the Foreign Office, and public opinion.[41]

After only two weeks Londonderry assumed that the conference would never succeed in its aims.[42] However, unlike any government position he had held before, Londonderry was aware that the expectations of the country demanded that he ignore his own doubts and pursue a policy with which he disagreed, although this did not stop him from fighting his case in private.[43] He had little choice; with the exception of Simon, he was more involved with the conference than any other minister. And as the sole British member of the conference's General Committee, he also reported personally to MacDonald, Baldwin, and even the King.[44] On 22 February he sent his early impressions of the conference to Baldwin:

> This is the most terrible place. It is bitterly cold outside, and the hotels inside are like furnaces … I find the complete League of Nations atmosphere very interesting, but I am fully conscious that it is quite a different atmosphere to any other … I am sure, however, that it is of the highest importance that we should maintain the League of Nations, and it depends on Great Britain whether the League will develop or whether it will languish … If it receives no more than favourable acquiescence from us it may not be worth while to go on spending money that we do in this connection, but on the other hand if we are determined to maintain the position which we now hold, then I am inclined to think we shall have to take a more active participation in its activities. We have some excellent Foreign Office officials here in the shape of [Alexander] Cadogan and [Walford] Selby, and I know this is their view [45]

Londonderry also pressed Baldwin to make Simon a permanent delegate to the conference, an indication, given Simon's reluctance to protect the RAF, that Londonderry knew that the real power lay not with the delegates, but with the CID's disarmament subcommittee at London, an echo of his experience at the Irish Convention. His request also represented his frustration at being, very often, the sole British representative at Geneva, giving an opinion with which he did not concur.[46]

The ongoing Sino-Japanese crisis dominated the first meetings of the conference. Londonderry argued—in reasoning identical to the attitude he adopted with Nazi Germany in the late 1930s—that once the damaged prestige of the Japanese was alleviated a settlement would be easier to reach. Referring to the League of Nations' decision to reprimand Japan, Londonderry, temporarily taking the place of Simon, informed Baldwin of his attempt to accommodate them both:

> [Dr Koto] Matsudaira [the Japanese ambassador] came to see me, and said that he thought that public opinion in Japan would take grave exception to the [reprimand], but I did my best to point out to him that there was no indictment and no criticism but an appeal to Japan as a strong power. I especially made this point in the few remarks I had to make at the public meeting of the Council, that we had made an appeal to the strength of the honour of Japan, but I see there was no mention of that in *The Times*.[47]

The press reports of Londonderry's efforts were mixed. On 17 February 1932 the *Daily Express* reported that he had 'objected strongly to the dispatch of a drastic warning to Tokyo' but was 'outnumbered and overruled' by smaller powers without Far Eastern interests, who 'clamoured for a sharply worded Note to placate China'.[48] While the *Guardian* and *Daily Telegraph* correspondents contradicted one another by reporting respectively that he had been 'particularly firm' and conciliatory.[49]

By 10 March Londonderry was worried about the prevalence of anti-Japanese sentiment at Geneva and warned Baldwin that 'the smaller States are hoping to establish some League of Nations doctrine which will safeguard their own boundaries no matter what crime they may have committed.'[50] MacDonald agreed with a line of appeasement and informed Londonderry that he should privately let the Japanese know the British position, that the affair must be straightened out without conflict and that British prestige in the Far East should be maintained.[51] As a

result Londonderry encouraged Japan and China to avoid further inci-
dents without condemning the former, a position that greatly irritated the
USA.[52] The episode demonstrates that Londonderry's rationale for
appeasement was not restricted to Germany. He had accepted in 1932 the
principle that Britain was incapable of a war in the Far East due to the
neglect of its armed forces. And although he attempted in private to
blame the crisis on British and US arms suppliers, he never condemned
the real source of the problem: Japanese aggrandizement.[53]

Despite its private disagreements, the British delegation gave the
impression of unity at the start of the Disarmament Conference, pressing for air force limitation and taking the lead by ending its post-war programme for 52 squadrons, a measure Londonderry announced on 3
March 1932.[54] Their call for disarmament was not entirely selfless, the
RAF being only fourth in the world in first-line strength, but this also
meant their strategy was a gamble, one that Londonderry openly admitted was a 'direct and inevitable result of the current financial crisis'.[55] But
this apparent unity was only on the surface. The Foreign Office sought
more than mere limitation and had begun to consider the curtailment of
aerial bombing. On 19 March 1932 Simon proposed this in a memo circulated to the cabinet. For his part, Londonderry had been aware of
Simon's views from late January and had acted at the end of that month
to try and delay conference procedure by using his position on the
General Council.[56]

Following Simon's memo Londonderry registered his opposition to
Baldwin's Cabinet Disarmament Committee—the CID subcommittee
that oversaw the British position at Geneva—of which the Air Minister
was a member.[57] The Air Ministry took exception to Simon's deviation
from the original policy and argued that while the Foreign Office proposal allowed Britain to continue police bombing its own subjects in the
Middle East mandates, it prevented its use against enemy warships outside territorial waters on course to attack British possessions. They also
felt strongly that such an agreement would be ignored in a war scenario.
Despite Simon gaining the support of the Admiralty and the Chief of
the Imperial General Staff, the cabinet and its Disarmament Committee
agreed with the Air Ministry that a counter-offensive was necessary.[58]
However, Baldwin and the Disarmament Committee did differ with the
Air Ministry on what the desired end should be, for the Lord President
believed that the best solution would not be a mere prohibition of aerial
bombing but its outright abolition.[59] He raised it at cabinet on 4 May

1932 while Londonderry was making his way back from Geneva to address Conservatives in Cumbria on the need for 'realism' at Geneva.[60] With the support of the Admiralty, War Office and cabinet, Simon and Sir Maurice Hankey, the Cabinet Secretary, devised a draft proposal to ban military and naval air forces and to internationalize civil aviation so as to prevent states from using civil aircraft for military purposes.[61]

The Air Staff, and consequently the Air Ministry, was up in arms about the proposal despite friendly overtures from Simon.[62] Sir John Salmond, Chief of the Air Staff, warned Londonderry on 8 June that the proposal would mean the end of the RAF and suggested that the Air Minister press both MacDonald and the King to intervene.[63] Londonderry then informed MacDonald on 9 June that his Ministry was furious and that he needed to be persuaded that their fears were unnecessary.[64] Following an audience with George V on the 10 June, Londonderry informed the Prime Minister that the sovereign was 'very indignant with any attempt to do away with the Air Force'.[65] His confidence led him to declare his dissatisfaction with MacDonald's handling of the situation, and repeat his view that air power could only be abolished if all weapons were abolished.[66]

Londonderry's opposition was sufficient, according to Sir Maurice Hankey, to make MacDonald and Simon unenthusiastic in their attempts to woo the disinterested French and German governments. However, it was not Londonderry who was the decisive factor, but those who supported his position, as he admitted the following month, the King's 'views were very valuable at that particular moment.'[67] The Simon proposal was therefore scrapped and British officials began anew to examine ways of dealing with aerial bombing. Londonderry's own solution to international tensions, as delivered to his Cumbrian audience on 4 May 1932, was that success could only come through security, and that could only be achieved by removing the fear and mistrust that bedevilled Franco-German relations. He went further, and warned that unless this was addressed, German support for Hitler would increase. He concluded his address by calling for immediate disarmament, although he also argued that Britain could not take the lead in case it jeopardized imperial security.[68] It was one of the many contradictions that hindered the Disarmament Conference.

Two months later a compromise between the positions of Foreign Office and Air Ministry was embodied in a government white paper dated 7 July 1932. This prohibited aerial bombing on civilians with further limits to be laid down by an international convention. It went further than Londonderry and the Air Staff felt necessary and was published while the Air Minister was at Geneva supporting the admission of Turkey to the League; nonetheless, Salmond reassured him that the Ministry would fight this latest attack.[69] The British delegation at Geneva, however, went even further than the new proposal by agreeing to the Beneš resolution that called for the abolition of aerial bombing subject to an agreement on how it could be made effective. Londonderry was angered by the departure and wrote to MacDonald blaming the Foreign Office for surrendering 'all along the line' at Geneva, adding that he would be more anxious about Beneš had he thought such a solution could be found. Londonderry felt that they should have 'brushed aside' the 'unreal' suggestion of a ban but not restrictions, and that Britain could find support for such a position from France, Japan and Argentina.[70]

The Air Minister was convinced of the impracticability of this solution because he did not trust the intentions of foreign states and feared the loss of British possessions. MacDonald shared his view that the sentimentality of the smaller countries was harming hopes of a more effective agreement between the great powers, one that could repeat the success of the Washington Naval Treaty.[71] Encouraged by this, and MacDonald's antipathy to the French, Londonderry wrote optimistically to Hankey requesting that the Prime Minister direct foreign policy and not the Foreign Office.[72] However, any influence Londonderry might have had on MacDonald was waning. Days after his suggestion, MacDonald met Hankey and discussed what was perceived to be the main weakness of the Air Minister's position: that the maintenance of aerial bombing would allow other countries to attack Britain.[73]

By this stage Londonderry felt increasingly isolated from the majority of his cabinet colleagues, although he maintained a good relationship with the Foreign Office officials he worked with at Geneva.[74] He found it hard to deal with Baldwin and attempted get around this difficulty by writing to MacDonald and the King. In one such letter to the sovereign he expressed his unease about representing a government policy with which he did not agree. Adding that, despite what was being attempted at Geneva, air power 'will play the leading part in any future war should we be faced with such a dreadful calamity'.[75]

In response to Londonderry's continuing opposition the Cabinet Disarmament Committee asked him to submit a draft proposal. In his September proposal, the Air Minister advocated limitation on both the use and size of air forces and on the weight of individual aeroplanes. He

also recommended that the French air force be cut by a third and that all
other forces be fixed in relation to it, and that aerial bombing be confined
to military purposes and not against civilians. But events conspired to
make these proposals inoperable. Throughout the summer the German
government of Franz von Papen had been repeating its calls for equal
treatment with the other powers, but it could not break the continued
opposition of France. Although the British did not want to upset the
French, Londonderry was sympathetic to Germany, fearing the growth
of 'Hitlerism' if its concerns were not appeased.[76] As the German
demand for rearmament was not addressed by the other powers Berlin
announced its departure from the conference in September.
Londonderry's prediction of failure appeared fulfilled. The following
month, as president of the County Durham Scout Association, he
explained his lack of faith in the conference to an audience that included
Lord Baden-Powell:

> The world is sighing for security. But, however far the nations
> may disarm materially, they cannot make war impossible without
> a disarmament of the spirit and the mind to war. Weapons once
> cast away can be reforged. It is the will to make use of weapons
> that makes weapons dangerous, and the spirit of aggression that
> makes wars possible.[77]

In the wake of Germany's withdrawal the British attempted a new policy, but a final decision was delayed by continued disagreements between
the Air Ministry and Foreign Office over the abolition of military and
naval aircraft.[78] With only days to go before Baldwin's 10 November
announcement on a new proposal, Salmond and Bullock pressed
Londonderry to present their view to the cabinet at this 'critical juncture';
as a result the cabinet agreed on 8 November to propose only an inquiry
into abolition.[79] Nevertheless, MacDonald warned Londonderry after-
ward that 'some gesture has got to be made if our influence in the world
is not to be completely lost.'[80] Baldwin outlined the new policy to the
House of Commons on 10 November. He expressed his preference for
abolition as 'the bomber will always get through', but that an offensive
capability was needed, especially as peacetime rules could be abandoned
under wartime conditions.[81] Salmond wrote to Londonderry: 'You must
have had a great battle yesterday to induce the cabinet to shift the ground
as far as they have done.'[82]

The following week Simon submitted the new draft proposals to the Disarmament Conference, stating that Britain wanted to abolish aerial bombing and air forces except for police purposes in outlying places, and calling for an international civil aviation scheme. He also proposed weight limitations for aircraft and the reduction of all air forces to a level equal to the RAF, which would be followed by a further reduction of one third. The proposals helped to restore confidence to the conference. Further progress was made in December when, in an effort to reengage Germany, a formula of words was agreed upon by the USA, Britain, Germany, France and Italy that acknowledged the right of Germany to 'equality of rights in a system which would provide security for all nations.'[83]

Londonderry followed this promising renewal in January 1933 with a tour of RAF bases in the Middle East, declaring that they 'played the part which the British Navy had for so many years played on the sea.'[84] On his return journey Londonderry had his first brush with the theatrics of fascism when he met General Italo Balbo, the Italian Air Minister, at Rome on 30 January 1933. By coincidence it was the same day that Hitler assumed power in Germany. Along with the diplomatic meetings Londonderry was taken to see an exhibition on the 'Fascist revolution', and when leaving Rome his train was accompanied by formations of aeroplanes.[85]

Despite the progress of November 1932 and the new Nazi regime, the British remained divided in their attitude to aerial bombing when the conference reconvened in February 1933. Anthony Eden, deputising for Simon, used the opportunity to omit the reservation of police bombing much to the anger of both Simon and Londonderry, although Eden not surprisingly found Simon the more unreasonable of the two.[86] Londonderry was able to correct the omission when he presented the compromise British position to the Air Committee of the conference on 20 February.[87] However, the following week the Air Committee agreed to the abolition of military and naval aircraft provided that their subcommittees discussed schemes for the internationalization of civil aircraft. Fortunately for the Air Minister nothing was done and the subcommittees disappeared. Londonderry returned to London to brief the King and his government.[88]

Motivated by both financial constraints and gesture politics, the cabinet decided upon a slight reduction to the 1933 air estimates, thereby maintaining the RAF at 75 formations. On 8 March the Air Minister announced this reluctantly to the House of Lords.[89] On the same day he addressed his objections privately to the Secretary of State for War, Viscount Hailsham—who was also hostile to the Disarmament Conference—referring to the air estimates as an attempt to 'destroy the independent Air Force' that was becoming their first line of defence.[90] It was certainly in sharp contrast to substantial increases among the other leading air powers, but it was hoped that this would make an impact at Geneva. Indications that it would in the long run damage the government came when Churchill attacked the move. Although Churchill would continually criticize air policy up to and after his cousin's downfall in 1935, Londonderry privately welcomed Churchill's initial intervention.[91]

On 16 March 1933, following Japan's withdrawal from the Disarmament Conference, the chief British delegate made a rare appearance to address the conference on the importance of reaching an agreement. He brought with him the British draft convention, or 'MacDonald Plan', which embodied the proposals that Eden and MacDonald felt would be most acceptable to the conference. These included the limitation of armaments and the abolition of aerial bombing except for policing purposes. The plan, which did not specifically mention Germany, envisaged that an international commission would oversee disarmament and that the air forces of major countries would be reduced to 500 aircraft, with a decreasing scale for lesser powers. Londonderry felt that this definite agenda had 'set Geneva by the ears'.[92]

When the conference met again in May it used the MacDonald Plan as the basis for discussion, but it was by no means universally accepted. At home Churchill raised new fears by claiming that Hitler was rearming, while at Geneva the majority of delegates still hoped for the abolition of aerial bombing and air forces; the USA and France in particular criticized MacDonald's reservation of police bombing.[93] This led Londonderry to fear that the British would bend under pressure and concede police bombing; he therefore reminded Baldwin that both he and MacDonald had promised this would not happen. Fearing a decision in his absence, especially as he was to replace Simon as head of the British delegation, Londonderry wrote to Baldwin on 29 May to ask the Lord President not to dispatch him to Geneva.[94] Despite this he was compelled to go, not to avoid a decision on the retention of police bombing but rather, as was well publicized, to explain it.[95] Basil Liddell Hart, a contemporary observer at Geneva, recorded Londonderry's replacement of Simon in a very positive light, that he:

> contrary to expectation … succeeded wonderfully well in restor-
> ing Britain's shaken prestige. He achieved this by combining a
> maximum of 'presence' with a minimum of words, playing his
> role with such gracious dignity and apparent sincerity as to evoke
> from many foreign observers admiring comments about '*le grand
> seigneur*' and references to the guidance of his great ancestor,
> Castlereagh …

Liddell Hart was so impressed that he confessed in his memoirs that although he felt that the defects of the hereditary system outweigh its advantages, he was 'glad to record a case where its value was manifest.'[96]

As a result of further deliberations at Geneva an agreement was reached on 7 June that the MacDonald plan would be the basis of a future international convention to be drawn up following the summer adjournment.[97] This was immediately followed with further talks between the British, represented by Eden and Londonderry, and the French and Americans, but little progress was made and they soon broke up.[98] The cabinet then agreed that the MacDonald plan would be the furthest Britain would go. Londonderry had succeeded in retaining police bomb-ing, although he was unhappy with Eden's lack of enthusiasm for the compromise.[99]

If the Air Minister had won a temporary victory, it did nothing to increase his standing in the cabinet or in parliament; indeed, it only served to exacerbate existing tensions. In contrast to previously cordial relations, Londonderry was disappointed with Sir Austen Chamberlain's call for the police bombing reservation to be given up if it blocked agree-ment.[100] Londonderry subsequently complained to Chamberlain that the former party leader had not consulted him before making his statement. The Air Minister went on to claim that a British withdrawal of the reser-vation would have little effect until Germany and France sorted out their differences. Chamberlain disagreed with Londonderry's preference for limitation, arguing that if the reservation was kept other countries would use it to flout the agreement.[101]

By July the cabinet had backed down from their earlier position and authorized Eden to drop the police bombing reservation if it blocked a settlement.[102] Londonderry resigned himself to sniping from the side-lines. On 24 July he addressed a well attended meeting of the parliamen-tary Air Committee on Disarmament, using the occasion to question the likelihood of any agreement being reached to internationalize civil avia-tion. He also 'reminded the committee that only about 12 of the nations represented at the Disarmament Conference had air forces of their own, and it was therefore easy for them to support proposals for complete abolition.'[103] Kurdish disturbances in Iraq during the summer of 1933 prompted him to remind MacDonald that British control over the newly independent client state depended on the RAF: 'we make a great mistake apologizing for the manner in which we police the world.'[104]

In the meantime Londonderry spent most of June and July at Mount Stewart from where he engaged in various social events connected with the Ministry. Although Londonderry's connection with the Ministry was not merely social, as some critics were apt to remark, he did bring it social prestige.[105] Aside from overseas tours of RAF stations, Londonderry made ceremonial and Ministry visits to various units throughout the United Kingdom and gave addresses regularly on air matters. His appearances at such events were given an added flair when he was made an Honorary Air Commodore in 1934, a position that entitled him to wear a RAF uniform.[106]

On 22 June 1933 Londonderry House entertained King Feisal of Iraq—someone Londonderry felt to be of 'no use at all'—along with the British cabinet and royal family.[107] He hosted anther function the following month for the Air Council and dominion and imperial representatives with air interests.[108] On 2 July he opened Liverpool Municipal Airport alongside MacDonald and used the occasion to declare that it would 'be idle to pretend that armaments could in fact be abolished at the end of the existing Conference.'[109] The following day he flew to the city of Londonderry where he met General Balbo.[110] The Italian Air Minister was en route to the USA to demonstrate the skills and abilities of the Italian air force.[111] Londonderry felt privately that the stunt reflected the Italian's 'inferiority complex', but he used the opportunity of a meeting to smooth relations between the two countries.[112] When asked afterwards in the House of Lords why the RAF did not engage in such feats, or attempt to break speed records, the Air Minister admitted that it would be too expensive.[113]

III

The failure of Paris and London to reach an agreement with Berlin led to Germany's withdrawal from the conference and the League of Nations on 14 October 1933. By this action the Disarmament

Conference had effectively been terminated. Hitler's withdrawal led to mounting fears of another war, one that would involve aerial bombing, and this in turn led to a shift of opinion in Britain. Despite the mixed benefits it would bring to the Air Ministry, Londonderry not only failed to capitalize on this change of opinion, but was perceived to be actively against it. He had become fixed on the need for peace through limitation and felt that German grievances had been exacerbated by France and ignored by Britain.[114] Therefore, when many in the country were calling for increased armaments, Londonderry was calling for the peaceful resolution of differences through the League of Nations.[115]

Londonderry undertook a well-publicized tour of RAF units throughout the empire between December 1933 and February 1934.[116] After Christmas in Cairo with his wife and daughters, he flew to Sudan, Iraq and India.[117] Spending a fortnight in the subcontinent he had once hoped to rule as viceroy, Londonderry promoted the growth of internal air services and toured the Northwest Frontier in his own aeroplane, posing in his jumpsuit for press photographers.[118] The visit also served to underscore the RAF's role in policing India, one that the Viceroy, Viscount Willingdon, was keen to safeguard. On his return from Karachi, Londonderry met with the Italian dictator, Benito Mussolini, at Rome, securing a deal to allow British aviation companies to use Italy as an air route to the mandates and India.[119]

As a figure associated with the failed Disarmament Conference, Londonderry soon encountered criticisms from various quarters. He was blamed, along with Simon, for the government's unpopularity, and some Tories made 'subterranean' calls for their removal.[120] The Labour party attacked him personally for wrecking the possibility of ever reaching an agreement at Geneva. This criticism grew in potency following the Labour by-election victory at East Fulham on 23 October, viewed by many at the time as an expression of pacifism and one that threatened moves toward rearmament.[121] Focussing on his Labour critics, Londonderry made it known on 4 November that the government 'would exert every effort to secure the continuance of international cooperation towards securing that atmosphere of appeasement, mutual trust, and security without which a general measure of disarmament was impossible'. He also warned his audience at Newtownards that 'nothing was more dangerous ... than to talk of war for the mere purpose of securing party advantage.'[122] To reassure Conservatives he was careful to make it clear that although he viewed disarmament as solution to international tensions, no further steps would be taken in this direction.[123] But this view was out of step with a growing body of opinion in his party that felt the country needed to rearm immediately, and Londonderry soon found himself denying press speculation that the government was about to announce a new policy of rapid expansion.[124] Nonetheless, this was exactly what the government did announce months later, in March 1934, compelled by the failure of the Disarmament Conference, the report of the Defence Requirements Committee, and growing evidence that Germany was rearming illegally.

On 2 March 1934 Londonderry announced a modest expansion to the RAF, justifying it on the basis that other powers had failed to reduce their air forces in line with the MacDonald plan.[125] Although he had welcomed Baldwin's 'definite statement' on RAF expansion, Londonderry failed to appreciate fully that the public demand that had initiated the policy u-turn would also dictate its pace.[126] Nevertheless, for a while it seemed as if Londonderry and his colleagues were in harmony. Therefore, when further schemes for an international disarmament agreement circulated the cabinet in April 1934, both Londonderry and Baldwin were pessimistic of such a move, especially with increasing rumours of significant German rearmament.[127] On 17 May 1934 the Cabinet Disarmament Committee, which had hitherto been reluctant to approve Air Ministry views, now ratified its plans for expansion. On 24 May, Empire Day, Londonderry justified the government's policy in a radio broadcast by saying that they had failed to persuade others of the need for limitation and now needed to protect the country.[128] He was once again responding to Labour critics, while at the same time failing to harness a populist cause. However, he was also conscious that some in the government and the Foreign Office still hankered for an international disarmament agreement. To them he addressed some remarks on 16 June: 'The last thing we desired was to enter upon a race in armaments, but we could not remain impassive while all other nations were increasing the strength of their forces.'[129]

Not surprisingly, this did little to allay criticisms from either the right or the left. Churchill criticized the government for not arming fast enough, while Labour attacked it for risking the destruction of another war through their failure at Geneva. Restricted to the upper house, Londonderry could not spar directly with Clement Attlee, the rising star of Labour and by now one of his most vociferous critics. Instead, he used a graduation ceremony on 10 July at Queen's University to warn

against the spread of rumours of another war, attributing it to the growing number of people who lacked experience of the First World War.[130]
In advance of a question from Attlee scheduled for 19 July, Londonderry
wrote to Baldwin arguing that although there was no total protection for
the country against aerial bombing, this should be a reason for rearmament and not another fruitless quest for the abolition of aerial bombing.
In the House of Commons Baldwin took a more moderate approach,
announcing that RAF expansion did not diminish the National
Government's goal of international disarmament.[131]

Just as Baldwin's statement reflected his own mixed feelings,
Londonderry confidently asserted in the House of Lords that the proposed expansion would be a deterrent, not merely to war, but also to an
armaments race. He was careful to couch this in terms similar to Baldwin:

> although we still ought not to abandon all hope of something
> materialising at Geneva, the idea of parity in the air with any
> Power within striking distance must be a cardinal principal of
> policy. If this new policy was effectively carried it would
> strengthen our influence for peace, and, far from inaugurating a
> new race in armaments, might effectively stop one.[132]

In his memoirs Londonderry attributed the government's change of
heart on rearmament to his own efforts; it was also the view of at least
one member of the Air Staff, Sir Edward Ellington.[133] However,
Baldwin's change of attitude had not been sudden and was certainly not
a response to the views of the Air Minister; it owed more to an intuitive
awareness public opinion, the collapse of the disarmament conference,
and the hectoring of Churchill.

Fear of German rearmament during the latter half of 1934 transformed the debate about RAF expansion from whether it should happen
to the rate and size of the increase. Air Ministry sources recorded that
Germany was steadily expanding its air strength throughout the year, but
Churchill attacked the Ministry's estimates for failing to take account of
the potential for enlarged production. Londonderry, however, was determined to avoid the implications of Churchill's scare mongering. Speaking
at Darlington on 22 October, he declared that the new policy 'had no element of panic'. He went on, somewhat belatedly, to address Conservative
critics, in particular Churchill and Viscount Rothermere:

From those who were crying out for a vast armament of aeroplanes immediately, he would ask first to what purpose they were
to be put and for what immediate crisis they were intended.
Then he would inquire where they were to be housed, and how
they were to be manned. Demands of this kind might be
inspired by patriotism, but they were certainly not inspired by
statesmanship. We obviously had no need of an enormous fleet
of aeroplanes of this kind now.[134]

On 9 November Londonderry gave an address to the Lord Mayor of
London's banquet at the Guildhall, three years after his first controversial
address to a similar gathering. In many ways the two speeches were the
same, but the first was made at a time of expectation, prior to the
Disarmament Conference, while the latter was made in its ruins.
Addressing Labour critics, Londonderry defended expansion on the basis
that Britain needed protection as others had failed to limit their air forces.
He went on to argue that 'No armaments which we might provide for our
defences would ever be regarded by the rest of the world as containing a
menace to the world's peace'. Instead, 'they would minister to the cause
of peace, for they would aid the establishment of a general sense of security and greatly diminish that fatal fever of suspicion and the international tension to which it gave rise'.[135]

Londonderry's underlying rationale was his belief that a militarily
strong Britain could pressure Germany into a limitation agreement; but
he was not on the subcommittee now considering German rearmament.
Nonetheless, he had encouraged his daughter Maureen and her husband
Oliver Stanley, the Minister for Labour, to use their trip to Berlin in
October 1934 to meet the German Air Minister Hermann Göring. At the
meeting Göring expressed his desire for an air force that would present
no threat to Britain.[136] This prompted Londonderry to write to his friend
Hailsham, who sat on the subcommittee considering German rearmament. In his letter the Air Minister advocated the readmission of
Germany into the League; this, he argued, could have three alternative
outcomes:

The first is that we should be successful in converting them into
helpful partners in the scheme of the world; the second is that if
the first fails we should be in a position, by knowing what the
Germans are doing, to immobilize their hostile activities; and the
third is that if the Germans are determined, as some think they

are, to be wholly aggressive and unwilling to join in a peaceful comity of nations, then they will stand arraigned in their true colours before the world. [137]

Londonderry's experience at Geneva had reinforced his sympathies for Germany and filled him with contempt for the French, whose leaders he blamed for ruining any possible agreement.[138] Readmitting Germany, he pointed out to Hailsham, would not be surrendering to them, it would, rather, re-establish their lost prestige and help bring about a limitation agreement that would enable the world to be certain of what the Germans possessed:

> If I am entirely wrong, I do not see that the situation is rendered more difficult than it is at the present moment. The practical view which appeals to me at this moment is that whereas we may move some distance along the road of idealism by reason of the Germans not being in a position to challenge the world, this situation will be entirely altered in a comparatively short space of time, and we shall then find ourselves up against ultimatums from Germany and a power behind those ultimatums which will plunge the world once more into the catastrophe of war.[139]

Hailsham later noted that Baldwin adjourned the subcommittee after Londonderry's letter was read, deciding to wait for the Saar plebiscite on rejoining Germany before making a decision.[140]

Baldwin and Simon subsequently decided that something had to be done and so began months of diplomatic efforts to secure Italian and French backing for an arrangement with Germany, culminating in the defence white paper of 1935 and the visit of Eden and Simon to Hitler.[141] Although Londonderry encouraged this process he would later attach a different importance to his letters to Hailsham.[142] Privately and in print he argued that the letters justified his later stance on appeasement, that had his advice been adopted in 1934, Germany would not have become as powerful or uncontrollable as it would be in the late 1930s.

In anticipation of Churchill questioning the figures for German air strength the cabinet met on 28 November 1934 to agree on Baldwin's statement. Londonderry, like the Air Staff, was wary of the consequences of making definite statements. He advised that specific figures should be avoided and assured his colleagues that his Ministry, contrary to the claims of Churchill, was monitoring German expansion accurately. Still hoping for a limitation agreement, Londonderry warned MacDonald prior to the cabinet meeting that any announcement would reveal that the government had known all along about German rearmament and that they had only the policy of an arms race to counter it.[143] But it soon became apparent at the cabinet meeting that there was a serious difference of opinion as to what the figures for German rearmament actually were. The Foreign Office regarded the French claim of over one thousand first line aircraft to be excessive, preferring instead the figure of 600. For his part, Londonderry argued that the figure stood at one thousand military aircraft, including first line and training aeroplanes, with an estimated production rate of between 160 to 180 aircraft per month. These contradictory statements not only revealed inter-departmental fractures, but also the Air Ministry's internal problems, for the Foreign Office received their figures directly from the British Air Attaché at Berlin.[144]

Despite Londonderry's concerns about stating figures, Baldwin wanted his Commons statement to be a warning that Britain was aware of German rearmament. During the course of the debate Churchill asserted that by 1936 the Luftwaffe would overtake the RAF, and double its size the following year. Baldwin accused him of exaggerating; arguing that it was impossible to predict beyond two years. He then countered Churchill's claims by citing the figures given in cabinet—that Germany possessed between 600 and 1,000 aircraft in total, that this was not its first line strength, and that, however rapidly they might try to rearm, Germany lacked the infrastructure possessed by Britain. His statement, based largely on Air Ministry advice, was correct inasmuch as it referred to first line aircraft, with Britain at over 500, not including its strength overseas, and Germany 300. Accepting Londonderry's figures, the Lord President assured the country that British production would keep a position 'not inferior' to the Germans.[145]

It appeared that Londonderry's views were once again in line with those of his colleagues; his figures were used to challenge a volatile and potentially destabilising attack from Churchill, and his hopes of a rapprochement with Germany were shared by Baldwin and the Foreign Office. However, he remained outside the formal diplomatic efforts to pursue this policy and could only exercise influence from the sidelines.[146] He wrote to Simon in December, blaming the French for the breakdown of the Disarmament Conference, and promoting the recognition of equal treatment for Germany within a limitation agreement.[147] It is notable that by this stage even Simon had moved to a more pro-German attitude, one that compelled Baldwin to exercise restraint over him during discussions with the French.[148] Londonderry's attention was also drawn to the unofficial meeting between Hitler and the eleventh Marquess of Lothian in January 1935; the two peers subsequently exchanged positive views on the German Chancellor.[149]

IV

The 'fateful year' of 1935 witnessed Londonderry's decline and fall from government.[150] Superficially his position appeared secure. He had spent the Christmas break relaxing at Mount Stewart from where he reminisced with Lord Craigavon, and then at County Durham where echoed the views of others in the National Government by giving a cautious welcome to David Lloyd George's plans for national recovery.[151] More importantly, Londonderry spoke in favour of the government's plans to reform Indian government, siding with Baldwin in an issue that was the cause of bitter tensions within the Tory party. Londonderry's support for Indian reform was not, however, like his statements on Russia, a mere pragmatic affirmation of government policy, for he had been in favour of reform since 1905. Speaking to a large meeting of Conservatives at Torquay on 16 March 1933, Londonderry defended the government's India white paper against accusations that it was socialist in origin and inspiration.[152] Again in October 1934, when the bill began its year long journey through parliament, he argued that the reforms were progressive and in tune with developments throughout the empire: 'Why should we make so great an exception in the case of India, by seeking to maintain an old-fashioned method of Government'.[153] A month later he claimed that he could understand the objections made by some conscientious Conservatives, but that he supported reform as one 'who wished to preserve the unity' of the party and discharge British obligations of justice to their 'fellow subjects' in India.[154] His response to the party crisis over India in the early months of 1935 was therefore to increase his calls for party unity, and to host a talk at Londonderry House by the former Viceroy and architect of Indian devolution, Viscount Halifax.[155] Baldwin could not fault Londonderry for his position on India, but not even this would be enough to save his position at the Air Ministry in the months that followed.

On 4 March 1935 the government published its defence white paper on conditions for German rearmament and Britain's increased investment. RAF expansion was outlined the following day when Londonderry released the Air Ministry estimates for 1935.[156] However, on the 8 March, the day before the House of Commons was due to discuss the white paper, Göring publicly admitted that his country possessed an air force. Londonderry attempted to ease fears by assuring the parliamentary Air Committee on 13 March that: 'nearly twice as many machines would be ordered' for the RAF in the coming year.[157] Growing public unease prompted Baldwin to seek further assurances from Londonderry that measures were being developed to counter an air attack; he was assured that progress was being made.[158] Then, on 16 March, Hitler announced the introduction of conscription to raise his army to 500,000 men.

The cabinet met two days later to agree that Simon and Eden would visit Hitler and other major leaders as previously arranged, but that they would convey their government's protest about Germany's breach of Versailles. When they met Hitler on 25 and 26 March Simon and Eden failed to persuade the Chancellor of the need for limitation, but they did come away with something fatal to diplomatic efforts up to that point. When asked Hitler declared that the Luftwaffe had already reached parity with the RAF and would soon reach it with the French air force. Although Londonderry maintained at the time, and subsequently, that Hitler's statement was wrong, and was, after the fact, judged correct, the panic created by the statement and his own distance from Baldwin ensured that his view was ignored.

The claim to parity with the RAF created a furore in the cabinet and country at large; Londonderry was even summoned to Buckingham Palace to explain himself.[159] Hitler's claim received widespread press attention and the Air Minister in particular was singled out for blame by the newspapers of Lord Rothermere.[160] The government was thus faced with two contradictory views, and as J. C. C. Davidson noted, this meant they were compelled to prepare for the worst-case scenario.[161] The chief mandarin at the Foreign Office, Robert Vansittart, then entered 'a vigorous battle of half truths' with Londonderry on German figures.[162] Simon panicked and like Vansittart believed Hitler rather than the Air Ministry.[163] The Foreign Secretary then circulated a letter to his cabinet colleagues declaring that the Germans had no motive to exaggerate Luftwaffe figures and that they had indeed reached parity. Convinced that Hitler had deceived Simon, Londonderry denied the claim and on that basis the Air Ministry made preparations for a comparatively modest expansion of the RAF.[164] It appears, with hindsight, that the Air Ministry had relatively accurate figures for the composition of the Luftwaffe in 1935. But it was their assumption that German expansion would be as efficiently executed as RAF expansion that undermined their position, for not only was it not, but they also underestimated Hitler's determination to rearm.

After years of dealing with a critical public sphere that demanded reductions in defence spending, Londonderry found the country and his fellow ministers clamouring for rapid expansion. In an attempt to remain aloof from such calls the Air Ministry conceded that German aircraft output was necessarily greater than that in Britain, but that RAF expansion must proceed carefully as the Ministry and Air Staff regarded efficiency, resources and industrial organization as more important to an air force than numbers. Moreover, the RAF, they argued, could not simply expand rapidly after years of neglect.[165] By taking this line Londonderry may have felt he was doing the best thing for the air force, but as Churchill later noted, it was at the expense of vital political considerations.[166]

With pressure for rapid expansion from all quarters Londonderry's scheme was sidelined. Instead, a new subcommittee of the Cabinet Disarmament Committee was established on 30 April 1935 under Philip Cunliffe-Lister. This new subcommittee, in consultation with the Air Ministry, discussed schemes for a more accelerated expansion of the RAF. The subcommittee undermined Londonderry not only by its very existence, but also through its deliberations. After a series of interviews with Londonderry, Ellington and various intelligence officers, Cunliffe-Lister reported to Baldwin on 10 May that Hitler's assertion was correct.[167] Despite this, J. C. C. Davidson's conclusion was closer to the truth: 'Although it was clear that the Air Ministry was absolutely right ... there seemed to be a certain lack of drive in their programme. I know that SB [Baldwin] attributed the responsibility to Londonderry personally'. Davidson had a poor opinion of the Air Minister's political abilities:

> Londonderry had the reputation of being a rather soft, Regency-beau type of man. Although he had a certain amount of cunning and capacity, he was not really equipped for thinking ... He was never really fit for Cabinet rank, and his association with the Air Force was, although keen, rather on the social than the technical side. Amongst the politicians of the Party – people like

> [Viscount] Bridgeman and [Edward] Wood and Sam Hoare, he
> was regarded as a lightweight and only fit for an under-secretary-
> ship ... He hadn't got the capacity to deal with his Air Council
> or to give them a positive lead, and their intelligence department
> was always regarded by the two other fighting departments and
> by the Foreign Office as extremely weak. But Londonderry took
> himself very seriously...[168]

The establishment of the parity subcommittee was not the fist time
that Londonderry had been undermined. Countering charges that Britain
had no air defences, thereby leaving it with only bombers as deterrent,
Londonderry had in January 1935 established a committee of scientists
under Henry Tizard that eventually pioneered radar detection. It attract-
ed the critical attention of Professor F. A. Lindemann who, supported by
Austen Chamberlain and Churchill, pressed MacDonald for a new committee to be formed, this time independent of the Air Ministry.
Londonderry mounted a successful defence of Tizard's committee by
claiming it was making progress and that the Air Ministry was able to
supply it promptly with funds whenever it was necessary.[169] Nevertheless,
while the Air Ministry's committee continued its vital work, another committee was established in March 1935 to examine air defences under the
chairmanship of Baldwin's preferred candidate, Philip Cunliffe-Lister.

Not for the first time Churchill warned Londonderry at a royal banquet on 9 May about 'intrigues' to remove him from the Air Ministry, that
'there was very strong opposition' to his remaining in office. When
Londonderry replied that he was aware of it but that he had 'succeeded'
in establishing expansion, his cousin warned him: 'Look out, they are
going to kick you out. I should resign if I were you'.[170] Londonderry later
claimed that Churchill then tried to persuade him to tour the country on
a campaign for rearmament, but that his loyalty to the government prevented it. At the time however, the Air Minister knew that an alliance with
Churchill—who had resigned from Baldwin's front bench in 1931 over
Indian reform—would end his government career and consign him to
the political wilderness along with his cousin. Moreover, he did not agree
with Churchill's calls for rapid rearmament.

Far more serious for Londonderry's future prospects was the attitude
of MacDonald. Baldwin had been taking over many of the ailing Prime
Minister's duties, and without his political patron Londonderry despaired
that his career was at an end. He wrote to his wife on 27 April:

> I have several enemies and now the election approaches there
> are one or two who would like to have my place. If I survive I
> think it will be on your merits. I am sure the P.M. would never
> sponsor me again and SB has always resented (I think) our sup-
> port of the P.M. … I see myself being squeezed out. I do not
> know that I mind very much as I am sure my present post is
> already allotted, but I should be sorry to leave the Air. Anyway in
> the 4 years we have sown a good crop at the Air Ministry and my
> would be successors want to reap the harvest.[171]

If Londonderry did not join Churchill in a campaign for rapid rearmament, then he did use his remaining time in office to disagree with the
government's new air policy. He also criticized cabinet colleagues for failing to defend him against press attacks and for their failure to invest in
the RAF at an earlier date.[172] Because of this, even relations between
MacDonald and Londonderry worsened. In response to warnings from
the Prime Minister that the Conservatives were against him remaining in
office, Londonderry attributed the inability of the Air Ministry to defend
itself to the Prime Minister's lack of a 'dictator spirit', that while he himself had it, he lacked the power to enforce it.[173]

Cunliffe-Lister produced his report at a full meeting of the Cabinet
Disarmament Committee on 12 May. Londonderry was present and
claimed that there were 4,000 trained pilots in Germany, despite knowing
beforehand that Cunliffe-Lister estimated it at double that figure. The
committee, somewhat inevitably, preferred the figure given by Cunliffe-
Lister.[174] Londonderry's nerve began to crack. On 20 May he protested
at cabinet that he had been criticized at Geneva for maintaining the RAF
and that he was now criticized for not rearming at a speed satisfactory to
his critics, when 'all he had done was to warn his colleagues of the consequence of an attempt to expand very rapidly.'[175] The cabinet ignored
the Air Minister and formally approved a scheme for the rapid expansion.

On 22 May Churchill informed in the House of Commons that the
Luftwaffe was superior to the RAF and that by the end of 1935 it would
be three to four times as great. In reply Baldwin admitted that although
he was sure that his previous figures for current strength were accurate,
he had been misled about future estimates and that the only facts came
from Hitler himself. He added that no one minister was responsible and
that the government as a whole was at fault.[176] As J. C. C. Davidson
noted, Baldwin 'knew it was no longer practicable politics to try to argue
in defence of the [Air Ministry] figures. The only practicable and right
course was to assume the worst and prepare for it'.[177]

The speech earned Baldwin cheers from his backbenches; in contrast, Londonderry's contribution in the House of Lords was far from apologetic. He used his speech to justify his position at the Disarmament Conference and his role in the subsequent rearmament crisis. He was, after all, aware of Conservative pressure to have him removed from office. But the defiant statement he made regarding his role in safeguarding the use of 'the bombing aeroplane' meant that he also handed the Labour party a weapon to attack the National Government.[178] Caught up in his ministerial statement, knowing it might be his last, the Air Minister was too proud of what he regarded as a success to care or understand how politically damaging his words might be. A normally unapologetic Londonderry later realized how misjudged, even vindictive, his speech had been:

> My name became forthwith associated with air bombing and all its attendant horrors ... It was soon made clear to me that my statement of fact had been unfortunate, however much it was justified. It was not calculated to catch votes, and after all a General Election was in the offing. From a purely political point of view my statement of fact had made me an embarrassment. My personal position was not made easier by certain intrigues against me in the Government, intrigues which became so apparent that they were the subject of comment in the public Press.[179]

A fortnight after the speech Londonderry was out of the Air Ministry.[180]

A combination of factors compelled Londonderry's removal in the first week of June 1935. His uneasy relationship with cabinet colleagues, his aloofness from the need to court public opinion, and the controversial House of Lords speech that was symptomatic of both. This led some to think that he would be removed from government altogether. A month prior to the speech on 30 April, Baldwin had indicated to an ailing MacDonald that Londonderry, Simon, and Oliver Stanley had to go.[181] That Londonderry remained in the cabinet, as Lord Privy Seal and Leader of the House of Lords, was therefore remarkable in view of opposition to him. However, as with previous appointments, it was facilitated through highly placed connections. Hailsham had contacted Baldwin to remind him that Londonderry 'had worked very hard and loyally for four years' and that he should therefore be retained.[182] Others, like the MP Henry Channon, ascribed Londonderry's 'surprise' retention to Lady Londonderry's hold over MacDonald. It may have played a part, but the Prime Minister's relationship with the Londonderrys had been deteriorating in the run-up to the reshuffle.[183] The then Transport Minister, Leslie Hore-Belisha, later attributed Londonderry's retention to Britain's political culture:

> The trouble ... in all this Cabinet making was that 'claims' counted for so much. Meat was all right for the Bar and journalism; if a man did badly at the Bar he failed, while if he did badly at journalism he lost his job, but in politics 'claims' counted enormously. Lord Londonderry was an instance. He was a second-rate man, not capable at all and really ignorant, yet when they got him out of the Air Ministry he was made Lord Privy Seal.[184]

After swapping offices with MacDonald to become Prime Minister, Baldwin informed Londonderry that Cunliffe-Lister would replace him as Secretary of State for Air, explaining that representation for such an important office needed to be in the House of Commons. It was obvious to Londonderry's wife, among others, that his sinecure as Lord Privy Seal was merely a staggered dismissal, but Londonderry was too keen on political office to relinquish this temporary reprieve. Accepting Baldwin's offer, he admitted his disappointment in giving up 'at this point the work of development which after a long struggle is now decided upon, to say nothing of leaving those in the Ministry who have never spared themselves all the years to help me.' He also took exception to the suggestion that Cunliffe-Lister would succeed better at 'hustling' in the House of Commons: 'I think I can claim to be as capable of that as any one ... and the record of my work here, especially when as recently the occasion demanded it, will prove what I say.'[185] In his friendly reply Baldwin was 'relieved' with Londonderry's response and reassured him that his cabinet colleagues wanted him to remain.[186] Despite this, Londonderry knew he had 'been got rid off'.[187] The reshuffle was announced on the 8 June 1935 and on the 17th Londonderry gave his farewell message to the RAF.[188]

V

As Leader of the House of Lords and Lord Privy Seal, Londonderry acted as the Conservative and government leader in the upper chamber. Maurice Cowling has claimed that in this role Londonderry was a 'makeweight to Salisbury among peers.'[189] However, such a judgement can easily overlook the difficult position in which Londonderry now found himself. He had lost his own department, and encountered opposition from Baldwin when he attempted to be nominated to both the Committee of Imperial Defence and the Defence Requirements Committee.[190] Baldwin, of course, had no intention of returning the controversial former Air Minister to any post involving defence. Londonderry appears to have then contemplated resigning, that is until Hailsham reminded him how important it was for the government to stay united at this delicate moment in international affairs.[191]

Londonderry's hope that he be consulted in matters of defence was made even more unlikely following his determined stance on the planned transatlantic air route from Canada to the Irish Free State.[192] Despite assurances that it had already been settled at the 1932 Commonwealth Conference, Londonderry—who wanted the route to utilize Northern Ireland and not the Free State—sought to raise it in cabinet, but was informed in late September by his private secretary that it was being kept off the agenda.[193] He also wrote to Lord Craigavon, who had agreed to the proposal, accusing him of ignoring the political aspect of the issue.[194] On 17 October he voiced his concern to Baldwin: 'I ought to be fully aware of the question of the Atlantic Flight from which I have been definitely and deliberately excluded.' Still refusing to fade gracefully Londonderry complained that his position as Leader of the Lords was impossible unless he had close contact with Baldwin and 'those who control policy.' Referring to the decision made the day before to call an election:

> You asked me if I should be happy in a different kind of life. Happy is a relative term. I am happy in all work, the more strenuous the better: but I am uneasy in the position in which I stand now because I bear full responsibility and have neither power or knowledge.[195]

Londonderry's third office of state in the National Government was dogged by his feelings of exclusion and continued personal attacks from Labour. The latter was given added impact by Italy's use of aerial bombing in their recent invasion of Abyssinia. However, even before this Londonderry seemed to be spoiling for a fight with his Labour critics. On 27 July he addressed a Conservative fête at Southampton on how he drew a distinction between Conservative and socialist views of the League of

Nations. The former, he argued, did not view the League as a super-state controlling its members, but as the embodiment of collective responsibility for the maintenance of peace. The socialist view, he felt, 'was nothing more or less than the employment in the last resort of compulsion by force of arms.'[196] A few days later, Attlee, Labour's chief spokesman on defence, used the speech to embarrass Baldwin in the House of Commons.[197] Attlee consistently pressed the government to clarify their position on the League by asking if Londonderry had challenged the power of its council to recommend what forces each state should contribute to protect League covenants. Baldwin countered this by attempting to focus on the Lord Privy Seal's reference to collective security. Attlee, however, continued to press him on why Londonderry made a distinction between Conservative and socialist views, leaving the Prime Minister little option but to duck the question by remarking that press coverage of the speech was 'considerably truncated'. When Baldwin suggested that Attlee look at the speech again with this in mind and forgetting that the Lord Privy Seal is 'a colleague', the floor erupted in laughter. Sir Austen Chamberlain then stepped in to successfully end the discussion.[198]

In what would be his last statement as a member of the cabinet, on 22 October, Londonderry defended the government's position on the Abyssinian crisis: that it could only support collective sanctions and not unilateral action by the League.[199] Baldwin then had parliament dissolved—taking advantage of the economic upturn and internal Labour divisions—for a general election on 14 November. One of the major issues that divided the two parties in an otherwise confusing election was the question of disarmament, and any suspicion that Londonderry might damage Conservative success at the polls was confirmed when Labour published its manifesto:

> The Government has a terrible responsibility for the present international situation … It has wrecked the Disarmament Conference by resisting all the constructive proposals made by other States. As regards air armaments, in particular, Lord Londonderry has boasted that he succeeded, though with great difficulty, in preventing an agreement for the abolition of all national air forces.[200]

Not for the first time Londonderry had become an election issue. But on the few occasions that he was invited to address Conservative meetings, at Barnstable, Southampton and Wallasey, he compounded the situation by directly repudiating the accusations made by Labour. In long speeches he accused them of taking his infamous Lords speech out of context and defended his role at Geneva.[201] Londonderry's last election speech, on the day before polling, was at his former Maidstone constituency. In exasperation and desperation he lashed out at Labour, accusing them of using deliberately organized 'rowdyism' to prevent free speech at the election.[202] He had in mind MacDonald's heckled and ultimately unsuccessful campaign at Seaham and regretted that his lord lieutenancy had forbidden him from helping his ailing colleague.[203]

Baldwin remained in power with a decreased majority; the voters, preferring social issues, had little interest in foreign policy. Free of MacDonald's influence and with his own mandate for government, Baldwin wrote to Londonderry on 21 November:

> I am profoundly distressed that I find myself unable to offer you a place in the new Government ... I have more men than places.
>
> You remember our talk in the House: you know what I feel. You have ever been a loyal and trusted friend; I think I know what you will feel. Yet I have faith to believe that our friendship is too firmly based to be broken by a cruel political necessity which obliges a PM—and none have escaped it—to inflict pain on those they hold not only in regard but in affection.[204]

Castlereagh found his father in Londonderry House after the sacking:

> He was a tragic sight ... I never really knew before the meaning of the phrase 'A broken man'. He was sitting sideways in his chair with his legs dangling over the arm. Holding a letter in his hand and with the tears running down his cheeks, he kept muttering: 'I've been sacked—kicked out.'[205]

Londonderry responded to Baldwin with a correspondence of bitter complaint that lasted for many years, much of which the Prime Minister simply ignored. Although his dislike for Baldwin was based on his personal experience, it is notable that it occurred at a time when Baldwin's popularity began to plummet from its earlier peaks. Indeed, Austen Chamberlain recorded at the time that Londonderry's resentment would only add to the Prime Minister's problems.[206] This deep sense of grievance led Londonderry in 1938 to publish a defence of his pro-German and pro-RAF views at Geneva in *Ourselves and Germany*, an article defending aerial bombing the following year, and ultimately his memoirs in 1943.[207] It was the only way he felt he could defend himself without directly and openly attacking his former colleagues. Much of his grievance centred on a belief that he had been betrayed by Baldwin: 'I recollect that you very expressly said that if I joined your Government in June I might retain the leadership of the House of Lords as long as I wished to do so. This hardly corresponds with your present decisions'.[208] His bitterness only deepened when in May 1936 his successor at Air, Cunliffe-Lister, was created Viscount Swinton, with a seat in the House of Lords.[209]

In the short term, however, Londonderry's dismissal led him to search for issues through which he could again make his voice heard. Throughout December 1935 he attempted to cast himself once again in the role of a moderate mine owner. But his attempt to recapture the role he had occupied a decade earlier quickly failed.[210] With that he concentrated instead on eradicating Labour criticisms that he had been a warmonger, and within less than a month he found himself at the door of Adolf Hitler.

VI

The limited analysis of Londonderry's period in the National Government that does exist tends to be sympathetic to his difficult role at Geneva, although there is a general tendency to dismiss him as ineffective. To J. C. C. Davidson he was a regency beau, to Vansittart he lacked the strength to impress parliament.[211] Londonderry himself would later lament that he lacked 'the force of personality or, perhaps, the presence' needed for the job.[212] However, not all his contemporaries were so dismissive. Hailsham, Londonderry's knight errant, declared that his friend's final dismissal made him 'very miserable'.[213] Lord Templemore informed Londonderry that he was not surprised in the light of his earlier removal.[214] Cunliffe-Lister recorded that: 'Londonderry had a thankless and impossible task' and 'had no opportunity to give the [aircraft] industry either orders or encouragement. He and his colleagues deserve credit for having maintained the spirit, the tradition and the training of our small Air Force in those disappointing days.'[215] His close friends Lord Salisbury and Lady Desborough made contradictory comments, the for-

mer attempting to congratulate him on regaining a private life of privilege, and the latter assuring him that 'this is not the political end. You are
too much needed in the future.'[216] Following the obligatory meeting with
the King to hand back his seals of office, Londonderry received a letter
from Baldwin's cousin, Rudyard Kipling, two months before the writer's
death:

> I am writing to you to say how sorry I am that after your coura-
> geous stand and speech on Re-Armament you are not to lead the
> debates in the Upper House on this vital matter. I had thought
> that, even now, the sincerity of fear should have driven the
> administration along this road. Once again, with very many oth-
> ers, I am disappointed and disheartened: but at any rate, you have
> put yourself on record, and we shall not forget it.[217]

Churchill took the view that Londonderry had only misled Baldwin
about German air estimates because the Air Ministry had misinformed
him. Indeed, despite their almost non-existent relationship from the mid-
1930s, Churchill's treatment of Londonderry in *The Gathering Storm* is
sympathetic, possibly a reaction to the not entirely genuine praise of
Churchill in *Wings of Destiny*. Although he noted that Londonderry lacked
the political potency of his successor at Air, Churchill argued that his
cousin's great achievement 'was the designing and promotion of the ever-
famous Hurricane and Spitfire fighters', something he rightly claimed
that Londonderry never mentioned in his own defence, at least in
print.[218] Similarly, Vansittart later claimed that he was 'sorry' to have
embarrassed Londonderry in the wake of Hitler's statement, regarding
him as having all the good intentions and vagueness of MacDonald.[219]

Opposition Labour opinion was divided on Londonderry. Attlee
attached great blame to him for wrecking the Disarmament Conference,
an accusation Londonderry took the trouble to deny in a letter to *The
Times* following the general election.[220] On the other hand, Michael Foot
et al omit him from their 'cast' in *Guilty Men*; Londonderry had, after all,
challenged Baldwin on the need for investment in the RAF from 1931.[221]
The journalist Malcolm Muggeridge took a more benign view than
Attlee:

> Even if this meant that, but for Lord Londonderry's reservation,
> an agreement abolishing air-bombardment would have been
> concluded, it is highly improbable that, in view of subsequent

developments, such an agreement would ever have become oper-
ative. At most, Lord Londonderry's guilt may be compared to
that of a small boy who, seeing a gang of men bent on setting
fire to a house, allowed them to strike a match on the sole of his
shoe.[222]

In his contemporary analysis of the period, John F. Kennedy, then a student at the University of London, argued that while British leaders were
responsible for underestimating German rearmament capabilities, the
public were equally to blame for their hostility to rearmament.[223]

Those historians who have dealt with Londonderry's period at Air,
usually with a brief one-line synopsis, have been equally varied in their
views. In his *English History*, A. J. P. Taylor argued that the failure of the
Disarmament Conference 'had little to do' with Londonderry's defence
of police bombing, the 'real deadlock' was between France and
Germany.[224] The military historian Basil Liddell Hart noted that:
'Londonderry's influence with the Prime Minister enabled him to be
more helpful to the RAF than expected, and he served it well in many
ways, but it was not in him to take a strong lead in urging radical
changes'.[225] In his biography of Eden, David Carlton suggests that
Londonderry's stance on the policing reservation for the RAF made
Baldwin and Eden appear more 'progressive' than they 'wholly deserved';
it could be similarly argued that their priorities made Londonderry appear
more intransigent than he actually was.[226] Robert Shay, in his study of the
economics of rearmament, highlights the overriding restraint placed on
Londonderry by the Treasury.[227] Conversely, Martin Gilbert and Richard
Gott view Londonderry's period at the Air Ministry as typical of an
appeasement tendency that sought to avoid war.[228] For Robert Rhodes
James, Londonderry's eventual downfall was attributable to many factors,
his role as a society host, his pro-German views, his ownership of mines,
and his role as a 'bomber' in the disarmament debate.[229]

The argument that Londonderry was out of his depth at the Air
Ministry, and his own belief that he had always acted dutifully, both
reflect the fact that he was not a typical politician. Although he was usually willing to make an effort to fit in with the consensus generated by the
leadership, he never easily took to the increasing demands of a unified,
voter-conscious and increasingly middle-class party. Londonderry echoed
the views of the Air Staff to a government preoccupied with handling
the economic crisis that followed 1929. His increasing personal interest

in air matters was only symptomatic of his self imposed duty to represent a particular view in government against the opposition of competing ministries, namely Admiralty, War, the Foreign Office, and Neville Chamberlain's Treasury. This he might have managed better had he not performed in parliament with little regard to the political sensitivities of Baldwin and the general public. Londonderry felt that the meeting of Simon and Eden with Hitler was connected with his sacking, but he seemed to forget that he had encouraged such a meeting and would carry on encouraging such meetings in the belief that Hitler could be trusted.[230] When the public mood in Britain changed to allow for a more open rearmament programme, far from associating himself with it, Londonderry once again retreated to Air Staff dogma and criticized its hurried implementation. His unwillingness and inability to shelter under Baldwin's popular views made him appear both a warmonger and a military appeaser, earning him the hatred of Labour and the mistrust of Tories. His sinecure in the House of Lords, if he had remained quiet, might have allowed him a prolonged role in the government, but he failed to keep a low profile and fulfilled Labour's hopes by continuing his defence of aerial bombing at a time when the newspapers were filled with horrific images of the Abyssinian invasion. Just as when he was Education Minister in Northern Ireland, Londonderry had become a liability to the leadership. His unquestionable failure was therefore not the Disarmament Conference or rearmament, but his continued mishandling of political expectations.

Ourselves and Germany, 1936–1949

L ondonderry's political life from 1936 until the outbreak of the Second World War in September 1939 is the most infamous portion of his career. Just as he had during the 1926 general strike, Londonderry attempted once again to play a role outside government in the hope of decelerating his declining power and influence. However, in choosing the avoidance of war through the improvement of Anglo-German relations, he discredited himself at the time and ever since as a 'pure pro-Nazi apologist'.[1] Historical memory has been dismissive at best and scathing at worst about this period of his life. Those who have dealt with it, albeit briefly, neglect to examine properly the motives and context of Londonderry's actions; some taking his utterances too literally while others dismiss him as a misguided and foolish aristocrat.[2] His contradictory public and private statements, underlying motives, and role in events completely out of his control, complicate an analysis of Londonderry's relationship to Adolf Hitler's regime. It is therefore necessary to examine the various political and social contexts before Londonderry's interaction with the British and German governments can be fully understood.

I

It is a popular perception that the British aristocracy were leading proponents of appeasement, 'the search for peace by the redress of German grievances.'[3] There is also the belief that many were inclined to fascism, and even that they harboured a desire to establish a fascist government in the United Kingdom. The fictional character of Lord Darlington in Kazuo Ishiguro's 1989 novel *The Remains of the Day* embodies these perceptions and in some respects resembles the eponymous subject of this study.

Many aristocrats were indeed favourable towards appeasement and some even played a prominent role in promoting better Anglo-German relations. However, although aristocrats were in a much better position to engage in high profile politics outside of government, appeasement was by no means exclusive to the wealthy. The bulk of the British people backed the government's policy of appeasement, at least until after the Munich agreement in 1938. No one wanted another war, especially one that would involve aerial bombing. In this respect the aristocracy reflected British society. But their prominence, wealth, political contacts and sense of leadership meant that some, if they chose, could act upon this.

Given the general support among all sections of British society for diplomatic initiatives that kept Britain out of potential European wars, it does not necessarily follow that all agreed on what this meant in practice, or that they shared a view of international relations. Indeed, in a society noted for its class divisions, the rationale of the British aristocracy differed to some extent from their now dominant political rivals in the middle- and working-classes.

By the 1930s, the aristocracy had suffered half a century of political and economic decline. Most prominent aristocratic appeasers—for example, Edward VIII, the dukes of Westminster and Buccleuch, Sir Oswald Mosley, and the marquesses of Lothian and Londonderry—were all outside the government, at least from 1936. What they did possess in abundance was status and wealth, two attributes that Nazis such as Joachim von Ribbentrop confused with direct political power. In reality, aristocratic interference in foreign policy had to compete with that of other politicians, and even they had to contend with the power of the press, military and civil service.[4] However, it was the very phenomenon of declining influence that led many aristocrats to strongly advocate appeasement. Lost in an inter-war world of mass democracy, declining power and wealth, the aristocracy like other traditionalists looked upon Hitler's regime as a bulwark against communism. Fascist governments also had a deep resonance for aristocrats, as David Cannadine has argued, for they could see in those regimes, on a national scale, the benevolent paternalism of a landed estate.[5]

Undoubtedly there were cultural influences that could distinguish aristocratic forms of appeasement from the concerns of the average reader of Lord Rothermere's *Daily Mail*. Their actions, however, were largely determined by structural factors both domestically and internationally. Sympathy for Hitler's Germany did not necessarily translate into a belief that Britain required a similar government. Indeed, the rationale of many British traditionalists for appeasement, even those critical of mass democracy, was to preserve Britain and its way of life against external and internal threats, especially from the left.[6] Fascism was still perceived as a threat, hence appeasement, but communism, as Eric Hobsbawm has highlighted, was viewed as a greater threat, challenging as it did the social order on which everything rested.[7] And if most European traditionalists placed the fear of communism above that of fascism, then the way this affected relations with the fascist governments and domestic fascism depended on the individual state.

Unlike old ruling elites elsewhere in Europe, the British aristocracy had not been swept from power after the First World War; they still enjoyed a significant, if diminishing, political influence in the United Kingdom and its overseas empire. They therefore did not seek German support to give them political power. Rather, a number of aristocrats hoped to use their remaining influence to foster an informal alliance between British traditionalism and German fascism, institutionalized by the Anglo-German Fellowship, and to use this to promote better diplomatic relations between London and Berlin. Consequently, there was no need to support a British fascist party. Like his mainly working-class followers, Mosley was an exception.[8]

II

Londonderry's amateur diplomacy was, on the surface, unnecessary for a retired politician with enormous wealth and leisure at his disposal, but he was animated by several factors originating from his time in government. Indeed, far from being what his silent collaborator in *Wings of Destiny* called an 'incidental' part of his life, Londonderry's interaction with the Nazi leadership was the very summation of his political career, one that he thought might place him in the pantheon of outstanding diplomatists alongside his famous ancestor Viscount Castlereagh.[9]

The ultimate motive for Londonderry was the same as that which had stirred him since his involvement in Irish politics during the First World War: the need to play a significant role in society and thereby continue the family tradition at a time when aristocratic participation and power was irrevocably under siege. This lifelong desire was thrown into crisis when he was removed from the cabinet by Stanley Baldwin in November 1935.

Without office it appeared as though there was nothing the 57 year old Londonderry could do to continue his prominent role in European affairs. One solution was to imitate many others and engage in amateur diplomacy in the hope of promoting better Anglo-German relations. Characteristically, he would treat his crusade for 'Anglo-German under-standing' as if it was a ministerial portfolio; his subsequent complaints of non-recognition by senior government figures certainly echoed many of his earlier grievances when serving under MacDonald and Baldwin. And like his profound support for both the Royal Air Force and Ulster union-ism, Londonderry, a fellow traveller of the right, was sympathetic and receptive to German grievances long before his first meeting with the Nazis in January 1936.

The underlying rationale for appeasement for many people was the fear of another war with Germany. As Londonderry wrote in 1937: 'We beat the Germans and I am very glad we did, and it is just because I don't want to have to do it again that I have gone all out to capture the Germans another way.'[10] However, on its own this fails to explain fully why Londonderry, among others, acted upon this, why he took steps to meet the Nazi leadership, and why he defended its policies in Britain and pleaded for moderation in Berlin.

Londonderry's bitter reaction to his removal from the National Government has been considered already. Nevertheless, it is essential to note here that his grievance towards Baldwin continued for many years, fuelled by a belief that he had not been treated fairly and that his reputa-tion as Air Minister had been badly tarnished. He resented Baldwin's claim about being misled over the strength of the Luftwaffe, and informed him of this in a voluminous correspondence that carried on even after Baldwin had retired from the premiership.[11] This angry preoc-cupation was exacerbated by a belief that his appeasement activities were not being given the attention they deserved because Baldwin had discred-ited him.[12]

Londonderry's experience in the National Government also haunted him in another way. Labour's attacks on him as a warmonger cut deep, and had led him in 1935 to make rash statements in parliament and on the hustings that increased Conservative concerns about him being an electoral liability. In this respect his decision to engage in amateur diplo-macy the following year was a continuation of his defence against Labour's critique, for he believed that by engaging in appeasement he might demonstrate his credentials as a peacemaker.

Contrary to suggestions in previous scholarship, Londonderry's belief in a better understanding between Germany and Britain was not novel in

1936.[13] Rather, the evidence is clear that he was, for strategic and ideo-logical reasons, a pro-German advocate from the early 1920s. Reflecting on Castlereagh's non-punitive treatment of the French following the Napoleonic Wars, Londonderry felt that Germany had not been treated in a similar spirit by the allies after the First World War. In August 1923 he publicly called into question the French government's determined pur-suance of reparations from Germany.[14] A month later he gave another speech on the 'destruction of Germany', arguing that although Germany needed some punishment 'it was necessary to consider the future of the world and the best basis on which peace could be established.'[15] The fol-lowing year in an Armistice Day radio broadcast for the British Broadcasting Company, Londonderry called on the country not to har-bour animosities when remembering the war.[16] In 1929, as a cabinet min-ister, he praised the Locarno Treaty for bringing Germany into the League of Nations and hoped it would establish 'for all time and under-standing throughout the world that there was a desire for peace'.[17] And just prior to his appointment to the emergency National Government in 1931, he praised the decision of the US President, Herbert Hoover, to postpone Germany's payments of international debts as a 'brave deci-sion.'[18]

Ideologically, Londonderry viewed Germany as a physical barrier against the expansion of Soviet Russia. He outlined his view at St Helens in 1931:

> the worlds danger was a German collapse … The Communists would welcome it. They were out to destroy everything in which this country believed. If there were not a satisfactory end to the deliberations of the nations Germany would be driven into the hands of the Communists, with consequent rebellion and the country torn from top to bottom by dissensions. That would have a grave repercussion on the whole civilized world, and it was our duty to give all the assistance we could to prevent it.[19]

His sympathy for Germany while serving in the National Government was constrained by the difficulties and deliberations of the League of Nations, although he did little to hide his dislike for French foreign poli-cy. His plea to Baldwin and others in November 1934 that Germany should be readmitted to the League of Nations in order to reach a new settlement was another manifestation of his pro-German leanings, more notable than on previous occasions because the Nazis were now in

power. This call for the acceptance of Germany also influenced his jus-
tification of later appeasement activities by allowing him to argue that
when he had pressed for an Anglo-German agreement in 1934, it was
because Britain was in a position of strength and could therefore direct
the settlement.[20] Such a diagnosis was not without merit, but it also
became a useful moral prop for Londonderry to air when accused of
wanting to make peace at all costs.

From his first entry into politics in 1905 Londonderry was expected
to uphold the family tradition and take a leading role in the affairs of
Britain and Ireland. Although his father had pressed him into politics and
initially guided him, it was the reputation of the second Marquess, Lord
Castlereagh, who activated him to a greater extent. From his childhood
he was tutored to admire Britain's famous Foreign Secretary, and it is not
surprising that he should look back to this most influential member of
the family when judging his own successes and failures. Indeed, the comparison, despite very different social and political contexts, was an easy
one to make given their involvement with Irish, British and European
affairs. But it also had obvious problems. The seventh Marquess operat-
ed in a timeframe when, in stark contrast to Castlereagh, the hold of the
aristocracy over government and politics was declining significantly. Even
if he had the intellectual ability, which he often regretted lacking, aristocrats would have to be especially favoured and talented to repeat the successes of Castlereagh.[21]

Londonderry not only looked back and admired the work of his
ancestor in Europe, he sought to apply it to the 1930s. In the conclusion
of *Ourselves and Germany*, which opens with a quotation of Castlereagh,
Londonderry argued that the great powers of western Europe had to col-
laborate to find a solution to the political crisis.[22] The method by which
this agreement would be reached—as he wrote to Viscount Halifax in
December 1936—was one that 'resembled' the Congress of Vienna.[23]
Londonderry could not avoid seeing direct parallels between 1815 and
1914. Writing in January 1938 he admitted:

> I have always been guided by the doctrines of Castlereagh and
> the Duke of Wellington who recognised that as soon as the
> indemnity ... was paid by France after the Napoleonic Wars,
> occupation should come to an end and France should have the
> full opportunity of regaining her equilibrium and playing her part
> in international affairs.[24]

Although he never stated it explicitly, it is evident from Londonderry's words and deeds that he believed he might replicate Castlereagh's success by advocating a similar policy in the language of détente. His repeated invocation of Castlereagh was therefore not only a personal preoccupation but also an attempt to associate with and inherit his success at a time of political isolation. This is certainly the impression he sought to give the German Chancellor in 1938 when he sent a copy of a book about the Congress of Vienna to Hitler's translator; Londonderry had already encouraged the author to publish it in German.[25] As such, the eventual failure of his appeasement mission weighed heavily on his sense of family duty:

> I sometimes feel rather sham faced vis-à-vis my ancestors. I feel that they are murmuring: 'Well, he might have done better than that,' and with the motto I have always had graven on my heart: 'Luck is the superstition of the incompetent', I find I have no answer to make.[26]

Another important factor when considering the interaction between Londonderry and the Nazi leadership was that it served the purposes of both parties, that is until Hitler changed his foreign policy in 1937. Outside government, Londonderry had searched for a new role and found one in the active cultivation of Anglo-German friendship. The Nazis, under the mistaken belief that the aristocracy still exercised some control over British politics, relied on those like Londonderry to influence the British government, to spread propaganda, and provide them with general information on British opinion. Hitler was anxious to avoid a war with Britain, so amateur diplomats like Londonderry were welcomed and encouraged by Berlin. The key to this policy was Joachim von Ribbentrop, Hitler's party advisor on foreign affairs and the Nazi with whom, to his later embarrassment, Londonderry would develop the closest association.[27]

Hitler had little regard for normal diplomacy and sought relations with foreign interests outside the orthodox channels of the Wilhelmstrasse.[28] Reporting directly to Hitler, Ribbentrop was given his own foreign affairs bureau in 1934, the Dienststelle Ribbentrop, which engaged in a policy of influencing prominent people in Britain and exploiting the sympathies of those who were already pro-German and anticommunist. It arranged visits with various peers in order to prepare the ground for direct meetings between Hitler and the British government, in the hope that such meetings would repeat the success of the Anglo-German Naval Agreement of 1935. The work of the bureau had begun prior to Londonderry's visits, and many of the rhetorical devices Londonderry would later utter had been well practised on the Marquess of Lothian. They included Hitler's desire for Anglo-German friendship and the need for direct contacts between British and German statesmen to quickly seize vital issues. These two points framed Londonderry's advocacy for dealing with Hitler directly, a very personal mission underscored by a mistaken belief that the Chancellor did not want to go to war.[29]

Through the work of the Dienststelle Ribbentrop the former Air Minister was injected with a new sense of purpose, encouraged to believe that he had a vital role to play. The refusal of the Foreign Office to act on his advice frustrated Londonderry and led him to conclude—as he had done throughout the early thirties—that they were ignorant of European affairs. It was, after all, preferable to believe foreign diplomats when they assured him of an innate influence than it was to support a government department with which he had a history of bad blood.

With hindsight, however, we know it was Londonderry, like so many others, who was blind to Hitler's intentions. Under the robust management of Robert Vansittart—with whom Londonderry had clashed during his time at the Air Ministry—the Foreign Office believed that the Germans were duplicitous in their dealings with Lothian, and that Hitler only wished to drive a wedge between Britain and France. But far from stopping diplomatic tourists like Londonderry, the Foreign Office was without authority to prevent their contacts and the subsequent promotion of Anglo-German relations in the press. We know now, after the fact, that far from promoting Anglo-German understanding, such contacts damaged relations by allowing Hitler to believe that an exclusive deal could be reached with Britain, rather than force him to accept the French and British preference for a general settlement. However, until Hitler's change of policy at the end of 1937, both the Dienststelle Ribbentrop and Londonderry benefited and fed off each another's existence, caring little for the delusions of either party to the arrangement.

III

Londonderry initiated his new political role with a private visit to Germany at the end of January 1936. His stated purpose was to visit the German Air Minister, Hermann Göring, and to ascertain German opinion. Londonderry noted the 'lavish' treatment and hospitality he received during a seven week tour that concluded with the Winter Olympics.[30] In keeping with the policy of Ribbentrop's bureau, Londonderry enjoyed entrée to leading politicians including Hitler, the Foreign Minister, Baron von Neurath, and the Deputy Führer, Rudolf Hess. He was also given access to aircraft factories and Luftwaffe training facilities.

At his meeting with Hess and Ribbentrop on 1 February, Londonderry was repeatedly informed of the 'danger of Bolshevism' and the need for the British empire and Germany to forge an anticommunist alliance. Their discussion also dealt with the return of former German colonies, something that Londonderry felt reflected an 'inferiority complex'. Ribbentrop continued conversing with Londonderry in this vein for the remainder of the day, drumming into him the need for a French-backed 'Anglo-German arrangement of all the complex problems surrounding present-day international affairs'.[31]

Several days later, on 4 February, Londonderry had a two-hour audience with Hitler, accompanied by Hess and Ribbentrop. In response to Londonderry's appreciation that he was treated like an official representative, Hitler replied that he welcomed 'unofficial' visits. Like his lieutenants, the Führer was keen to press for an anticommunist alliance and gave a long 'tirade' on the threat of Russia. For the remainder of the meeting questions from Londonderry on rearmament, German aims, and the League of Nations were ignored or deflected with veiled threats about the failure of Anglo-German understanding, especially in relation to Hitler's desire to recover the former German colonies. Despite Londonderry's inability to receive clear answers, he would use much of what his hosts told him to justify the German position in *Ourselves and Germany*. Before returning to Britain he, his wife and their youngest daughter, Mairi, also enjoyed the hospitality of prominent pro-Nazi German aristocrats, including the Prince of Hesse, the Duke and Duchess of Brunswick, and the Duke of Saxe-Coburg.[32] Like their British counterparts, Hitler also used the German aristocracy for tactical purposes, for he wanted to create a new racial and meritocratic élite and held the existing aristocratic order in contempt, remarking in 1938 that the upper class were 'in reality no more than the scum produced by societal mutation gone haywire from having had its blood and thinking infected by cosmopolitanism.'[33]

Contrary to his expectation, only one of Londonderry's former cabinet colleagues, Oliver Stanley, expressed interest in his visit, and Stanley was his son-in-law.[34] Neither Baldwin or Vansittart were initially concerned with Londonderry's self-declared mission, except insofar as encouragement might do harm. Nevertheless there was some interest. The *Times* had followed his tour, the Cabinet Secretary, Sir Maurice Hankey, also took note of his findings, and in June the backbench 1922 Committee included him in their programme of speakers.[35]

In contrast, hostility to the visit was more noticeable, arousing concern among the society and political salons in which the Londonderrys had played a leading part, Harold Nicolson noted:

> My new pal Maureen Stanley asked me to come round and meet her father who is just back from hob-nobbing with Hitler. Now I admire Londonderry in a way, since it is fine to remain 1760 in 1936; besides he is a real gent. But I do deeply disapprove of ex-Cabinet ministers trotting across to Germany at this moment. It gives the impression of secret negotiations ...[36]

Londonderry was aware of such hostility and warned his wife: 'we shall be left out of everything and it will be a trifle galling, but if you understand it, and are ready for it, and I have got you, I feel I don't mind.'[37]

More controversially, Londonderry returned the hospitality of his German hosts with invitations to visit his estates in Northern Ireland and County Durham. And in 1937 he even invited Göring to attend the coronation of George VI, although the Air Minister had to turn him down owing to organized opposition to the visit.[38] Only Ribbentrop was able to avail himself of the Londonderry hospitality, especially after he became German ambassador to London in October 1936.[39] Ribbentrop would become so associated with Londonderry through these visits and other social engagements that he earned the sobriquet 'the Londonderry Herr'.[40] Londonderry later claimed that he did not like Ribbentrop, but at the time he was a perfect host to the ambassador, and he in turn repaid him with further visits to Germany and a sense of playing an important part in a great endeavour. Nevertheless, Ribbentrop did not entirely deceive Londonderry, for both men shared a nineteenth century view of European power politics. It was Hitler who did not hold this view, preferring instead to see the world in ideological and racial terms.[41]

On 6 March, two months after Londonderry's visit to Germany, the Wehrmacht occupied the demilitarized Rhineland. In what would prove a recurring strategy, Hitler accompanied this with calls for a new peace settlement. In contrast to the majority of British Conservatives who outwardly showed restraint, Londonderry defended the occupation in a letter to *The Times*. Repeating German arguments against Versailles and the French, he advocated the right of Germans to run their country as they pleased.[42] The letter created a poor reaction and firmly placed him among the most notable of active appeasers. This made him question whether he should continue in his new role, but his sense of mission was emboldened by his wife's enthusiasm. For her part, she continued to enjoy her own, more informal, correspondence with Hitler and Göring.[43] Londonderry also received encouragement from Lord Beaverbrook who praised his *Times* letter as 'brilliantly done'.[44] In reply Londonderry admitted:

> I am megalomaniac enough to think that we can dominate the whole situation but Baldwin can't do it. Neville is too parochial, in fact I see no one who can fill my bill. I should like to do it myself but my record is not good enough. I could not carry the people. Whilst I know what ought to be done I have too many gaps in my intelligence to do it. Whether a democracy could do what I want I am not quite sure. So I am looking on ...[45]

Beaverbrook replied: 'It is your duty to go back into public life. And, if you will allow me to say so, you should go without the slightest feeling against Baldwin.'[46]

Many in the Conservative party felt that the Rhineland occupation would be Hitler's furthest expansion west, and the government was reluctant to use sanctions in case it drove Germany into an alliance with Italy. A Conservative split was avoided by changes in foreign policy including recognition of Italian rule in Abyssinia, further diplomatic efforts with Germany, and increased rearmament. Although Londonderry had always been in favour of rearmament, he grew concerned that it was not being balanced with diplomacy.[47] In April he repeated his earlier call for a settlement with Hitler.[48]

Many Conservatives were concerned that any deal with Hitler would involve the return of the colonies. Having advocated a deal, Londonderry silently sat out the subsequent party crisis knowing that he could not win by adopting any position. If he spoke against the return he would damage his relationship with the Nazis, if in favour he would entirely alienate himself from the party. Caught in the middle he privately encouraged Churchill to 'go easy with Baldwin' and urged Göring to avoid policies that created anxiety in Britain.[49]

By July the government had begun to take some interest in Londonderry's visit; a sea-change facilitated by improved relations with

Baldwin and the abandonment of the colonial solution.[50] On 21 May
Londonderry wrote yet another letter to the Prime Minister complaining
about his removal from the cabinet, but of more interest to Baldwin he
added: 'I have had a most interesting letter from Göring to-day. It is
meant for propaganda but it has a value'.[51] Londonderry followed the letter with a press statement denying that he had misled Baldwin about air
parity with Germany in 1935. Baldwin had no political reason to assuage
his former Air Minister, so it may have been curiosity that led the Prime
Minister days later to declare to the House of Commons that he had not
meant anyone to think that Londonderry had misled him.[52]

The way was thus paved for Halifax to meet with Londonderry and
discuss his findings, followed by correspondence on the latter's proposals for better Anglo-German relations.[53] The rapprochement was short
lived. Londonderry—echoing Hitler's suggestion at their first meeting—
pressed Halifax to adopt an anticommunist policy that would be the basis
of further understandings between the two states.[54] Halifax stressed the
need for a general settlement and cautioned against the alienation of
Russia.[55] In turn Londonderry criticized foreign policy 'drift', accused the
government of 'misunderstanding' him, and warned that war loomed if
they merely re-armed and avoided talking to Hitler.[56]

In reacting badly to Halifax, Londonderry had not only misjudged
British foreign policy and his own role, but recklessly harmed his already
low standing among former colleagues. The government was not so
much interested in Londonderry's personal opinion, but rather what
Hitler and other senior Nazis were communicating through him.
Therefore, the Lord Privy Seal, renowned for his good nature, easily
ignored his predecessor's outburst and assured him that he had no intention of alienating Germany.[57]

Londonderry's very public advocacy of a deal with Germany made
him increasingly defensive about accusations that he was pro-Nazi.[58] In
September he wrote to Halifax condemning recent speeches at the
Nuremberg Rally.[59] He also dropped his rejected proposals for direct
agreements between London and Berlin in favour of a conference of
great powers, these included Britain, France, Germany and Italy, but not
Russia.[60]

> My desire is to pin Hitler down to peace under all circumstances
> for a period of time if necessary ... if the four great powers of
> Europe with no reservations took this line, there can be no war

> … it is no use crediting the smaller nations with any actual power
> in this issue … In default of a definite reply from Hitler in a con-
> ference of actual plenipotentiaries, which on the lines I suggest
> has a resemblance to Vienna … we should announce at once that
> we were proposing to take the definite line of power politics and
> give up for the time being the doctrines which we have sought to
> develop.[61]

At the end of October, on his return from a tour of eastern Europe—
during which he had met with King Carol and the rightwing Prince
Bibesco of Romania— Londonderry had a second meeting with Hitler.[62]
He did not record what was said at the meeting, or if Hitler approved, or
indeed acknowledged his four power proposal, but it is likely from
Londonderry's subsequent correspondence with Halifax that the meeting
dealt with the former German colonies, eastward expansion, and Hitler's
dislike of Anthony Eden. It is also certain, from what Londonderry told
Halifax, that Hitler informed his guest of Germany's next move a year in
advance of the Czech crisis: 'it appears to me that German policy is moving in the direction of Danzig and Polish interests, and also
Czechoslovakia, and it would not surprise me if the next sudden
demarche were not some movement in that direction.'[63]

The years of foreign policy drift under Baldwin ended in May 1937
with the appointment of Neville Chamberlain as Prime Minister. Now the
government pursued officially a policy of appeasement and rearmament.
Londonderry had always held a grudge against Chamberlain, but he welcomed the end of drift. Moreover, he agreed with the new leader's belief
in the sincerity of Hitler's requests for a peaceful settlement, and both
men believed this could be brought about by an agreement between the
great powers. Londonderry did not, however, share Chamberlain's
emphasis on economic appeasement, preferring instead to focus on the
balance of power and anticommunism. Nevertheless, despite many other
ideas in common, most notably the four-power pact, and Londonderry's
public support for Chamberlain, the two men rarely corresponded or met.

Following a promising start to 1937 Anglo-German relations thereafter suffered a series of setbacks, culminating in the September 1937
Nuremberg Rally at which Hitler demanded the return of former
colonies. This brazen confrontation with Britain was more than a rhetorical outburst. Prior to the rally, Ribbentrop had belatedly come to the bitter realization—influenced at least in part by Londonderry—that British
power did not lie with the aristocracy. Hitler was now determined to seek

other allies and the usefulness of Londonderry and others to the Nazis was severely diminished. However, Ribbentrop continued to use sympathizers, especially through the 900 strong Anglo-German Fellowship—of which Londonderry had been a member since February 1936—to disseminate words of reassurance and goodwill in Britain. The pro-German lobby thus continued its quest for Anglo-German understanding unaware that the cause they served was a sham.

Londonderry returned to Germany in September 1937, the same month that Hitler hosted Mussolini for a state visit. Accepting Göring's invitation to join him for a hunt, the Marquess found his host 'less conciliatory', defensive about Germany's newly acquired Italian and Japanese allies, and condemnatory of Britain's refusal to engage in friendly relations with Germany.[64] Londonderry informed Ribbentrop that the meeting was unsatisfactory and put the blame for this on the arrival of Mussolini.[65] Unwittingly, in his subsequent correspondence with Göring, Londonderry reaffirmed the new direction in Nazi foreign policy by protesting that he had barely any influence over his former government colleagues. He recommended instead that they deal with the new British ambassador in Berlin, Nevile Henderson, a keen advocate of appeasement.[66]

Indeed, it may be that it was Londonderry's insistence that he had no power that finally persuaded Ribbentrop to change his mind on Anglo-German rapprochement, that and the former ambassador's own inability to find acceptance in London society. As the Labour MP Hugh Dalton commented in his diary on 5 September 1938: 'All really depends on Hitler, whom it is very difficult to reach. In so far as he is reached by Ribbentrop he is misled, for Ribbentrop saw too much of Londonderry and Mayfair and too little of England.'[67] When the ambassador made his final report to Berlin in January 1938, before becoming Hitler's Foreign Minister, he cited a letter from Londonderry to illustrate his realization that the aristocracy lacked any authority over the government. His mission had been a failure. Without the possibility of an agreement on the lines that he and his British allies had been advocating, Britain, he concluded, was the Reich's main enemy.[68]

IV

Just as the Nazis were downgrading Londonderry's value as a man of influence, the British, contrary to his later complaints, renewed their interest in his recent findings. Ironically, worsened relations between London and Berlin made informal contacts more valuable. Following his visit to Göring, Londonderry met with Chamberlain, and even Baldwin asked for a meeting.[69] A poker-faced Prime Minister left Londonderry unhappy, but Halifax compensated through his increased interest.[70] By coincidence, Londonderry was at the same time appointed President of the National Union of Conservatives and Unionists. The 'loud cheers' from the conference floor that greeted his appointment must have warmed Londonderry, for he had always lacked a following within the party and recent events appeared to have ostracized him completely.[71] However, this ornamental appointment had little to do with the government and a lot to do with his prominence in northern English conservatism. But that did not stop Londonderry from reasserting himself, not only in the area of Anglo-German relations, but also in the affairs of the Air Ministry and Northern Ireland.

It is highly probable that the reason for Londonderry's new found favour can be traced to Chamberlain's desire to arrange a meeting between Halifax and Hitler in the aftermath of Germany's pact with Italy and Japan. Londonderry was secretly given prior knowledge of the proposed visit and discussed the idea at length with Halifax.[72] Although it is not certain how much influence Londonderry exerted, Eden noted at the time that Halifax's ideas for the visit included a 'Four-Power Pact.'[73] Officially, the visit was in response to a hunting invitation, but its main purpose was for a meeting between the Führer and Halifax on 19 November 1937. Prior to the visit, Londonderry went to Germany himself and briefed Halifax on his own discussions.[74]

The Halifax-Hitler meeting inevitably heightened tensions within the government. Against the wishes of Vansittart and Eden, Chamberlain and his emissary were keen to inform Hitler that any revision to eastern European borders should come through the course of peaceful evolution. More controversially, it was Halifax and not Hitler who first named the areas where Versailles might be revised. Halifax has often been criticized for allowing Hitler to know, without prompting, that Britain would consent to German expansion in eastern Europe. However, it was Halifax who had been prompted, albeit indirectly, as Hitler must have known that his conversations with Londonderry were being passed on to the British government. Although this is not certain, it is likely that Londonderry would have informed Hitler, not least to highlight his own importance as an unofficial link between the two governments.

Londonderry was disappointed that Halifax and Hitler did not reach a settlement.[75] And although he recognized that the Nazis no longer seemed responsive to British concerns, he failed to realise why. Consequently, his letters to Ribbentrop continued to hope for a four-power conference, but he now more readily added his concern for the damage being done to British opinion by Nazi policies.[76]

To his lasting misfortune, the cooling of Anglo-German relations also led Londonderry to conclude that more efforts at promoting them were necessary. At a time when more pamphlets and books on foreign affairs were published than ever before, his contribution was *Ourselves and Germany*, a short book, serialized in the *Evening Standard*, that sought to explain the German position to a British audience. It also included a defence of his role at Geneva and subsequent amateur diplomacy.[77] With this small book, which sold enough to warrant several reprints as a 'Penguin Special' throughout 1938, Londonderry cemented his reputation as an arch-appeaser and apologist for the Nazi regime.

Londonderry was selectively clandestine about his visits. Much of what was said between the author and the Nazi leaders during his first visit was included in the book; what was not we know through his correspondence with Halifax. But even partial openness would backfire. The book contained correspondence with Ribbentrop in which Londonderry addressed the Jewish question. Intended as a warning, it was also unthinkingly offensive:

> I should be wrong if I minimized in any way the anxiety which is felt here in relation to your policy towards the Jews, for there is the feeling that we do not like persecution, but in addition to this there is the material feeling that you are taking on a tremendous force which is capable of having repercussions all over the world.

Then the reassuring admission:

> I have no great affection for the Jews. It is possible to trace their participation in most of those international disturbances … on the other hand, one can find many Jews strongly ranged on the other side who have done their best … to counteract those malevolent and mischievous activities of fellow Jews.[78]

Londonderry earned a severe rebuke for this from a family friend, Anthony de Rothschild, who accused him of promoting myths about the international influence of the Jews and for giving respectability to Nazi prejudices.[79]

Like many others with similar views, Londonderry did not regard himself as actively anti-Semitic. Indeed, he had learned to tame an initial dislike for his Jewish son-in-law, Lord Jessel, and Nazi brutality towards the Jews only reinforced the perceived harmlessness of his own prejudices. Nevertheless, his statements reveal not only poor judgement, but also the pervasiveness and casualness of his own anti-Semitism and that existing in the country at large.[80] But the Jewish question only mattered to appeasers inasmuch as it harmed hopes for Anglo-German understanding. There was a general tendency among them to treat German Jews, like the new states of eastern Europe, as expendable for the sake of domestic security.[81] Nevertheless, the bad reaction to the letter and personal lobbying from British religious groups encouraged Londonderry to complain about the issue more frequently to his Nazi contacts. And in April 1938 he wrote to Hitler about the harm being done to Anglo-German relations by 'reports of the plight of the Jews and those who differed from or opposed the Nazi policy'.[82] He was still convinced Hitler cared.

Hitler's unpredictable actions troubled the appeasers, but for many including Londonderry it made their resolve even stronger. So when Halifax replaced Eden as Foreign Secretary in February 1938, appeasers were dismayed by the Führer's announcement of a more militant foreign policy. Fearing that a solution was slipping away, Londonderry wrote a conciliatory letter to Ribbentrop, and in parliament called on Chamberlain not to allow differences to prevent an agreement with Germany.[83] By way of contrast, he privately informed a colleague in the Anglo-German Fellowship that he 'condemned the methods employed' by Hitler and predicted a bleak future.[84] And yet the forbidden *Anschluss* with Austria on 13 March 1938 only encouraged appeasers that a solution had to be reached. It demonstrated, after all, Hitler's ability to seize control of events and the inability of others to control him. Londonderry openly criticized the suddenness of the *Anschluss*, but also warned of war unless there was a better understanding of German aspirations.[85] But again, in private, he admitted to a German correspondent that he neither knew of nor understood Hitler's recent actions, including his continued persecution of the Jews.[86] For her part, Lady Londonderry complained about mass arrests in Vienna and ended her flattering correspondence with Göring and Ribbentrop.[87]

Like other appeasers Londonderry's sense of mission blinded him from the reality of Nazism. He attributed worsening relations between himself and the regime to commentary on their policies in the very book he had written to promote understanding, *Ourselves and Germany*. On 5 April 1938 he wrote to Hitler defending his published views on the basis that he needed to address issues that aroused concern in Britain. And he again emphasized the damage being done to Anglo-German relations by the persecution of Jews and the *Anschluss*. Appealing to sentiments expressed by the dictator at their first meeting in 1936, Londonderry claimed that if an agreement could be reached between them, Britain and Germany could rule the world.[88] There was no mention of whether this should be reached bilaterally or through a four-power pact, but it is the only correspondence in which such a stark outcome is touted by Londonderry. Given his obvious inability to deliver such a development, it was more a desperate attempt to replenish the almost non-existent understanding between the two men than a serious proposition. Hitler sent a curt acknowledgement thanking Londonderry for a copy of *Ourselves and Germany*. The book was subsequently refused publication in Germany until its author leant on Göring.[89]

At the same time Londonderry grew increasingly sensitive about suggestions in the *Daily Express* that he was 'pro-Nazi'. He wrote to its proprietor Beaverbrook, who had originally encouraged his activities. Far from being apologetic, the press baron retorted that the *Express* reflected public opinion.[90] Londonderry replied:

> I have had a pretty difficult time since I left the Government. I have a friendship and an understanding with Neville, because he knows I don't want anything; but he and his colleagues are just a little frightened of me and just a little jealous. I am beginning to think of throwing my hand in altogether. Why should I bother about public life? I find the Socialists proclaiming me a Nazi and Fascist in my judgement two insulting terms and contrary to the whole of my point of view. Now the *Daily Express* joins in and I feel that if after all these years I can't get it across, then I am disposed to leave it all alone and fly aeroplanes, travel, play Bridge ... I can't go on saying I am not a Nazi, but have pleaded for justice for Germany.[91]

Following another report on the 'pro-Nazi' Londonderrys, Beaverbrook responded to further complaints by assuring Londonderry that he had instructed his editors to 'give special consideration to everything that comes into the office concerning you.'[92] Londonderry paid a short visit to Germany at the end of June 1938. Contrary to his claim in the second postscript of *Ourselves and Germany*, the visit was not of an entirely private character. Although attending a conference of the Fédération Aéronautique Internationale as its Vice-President, he had also arranged a meeting with Göring.[93] The British Air Ministry was kept in the dark about the meeting, although Halifax had briefed Londonderry before his departure.[94] Halifax's private secretary, Oliver Harvey, noted on 14 June:

> I learn also that Londonderry is off shortly to Berlin to see Hitler and Goering and it is strongly rumoured that he will bear some sort of 'appeal' from the P.M. to Hitler. H[alfiax] has asked him to come and see him before he goes, as I hope, to stiffen him up a bit.[95]

In his report to the Foreign Secretary, Londonderry noted a change in the German leadership's attitude to Britain, especially Göring who he felt was less truculent, a Nazi with whom business could be done. Göring informed his guest that Germany's final demands would be satisfied by the settlement of the Sudeten question. Conversely, Ribbentrop and Himmler spoke as though they had 'rehearsed parts'.[96] Once again Londonderry was left with the impression that a solution was within reach. Little wonder, for Göring's suggestion had been deliberately designed to encourage British appeasers and to counter French opposition to any alteration to Czechoslovakia. And although Chamberlain was prepared to reach an accommodation with Hitler on the issue, Halifax did not appreciate Londonderry's truculent conclusion that Prague was to blame for the crisis and that Czechoslovakia was 'one of the unfortunate post-war developments'.[97]

As the crisis intensified Chamberlain flew to Germany for a meeting with Hitler at Berchtesgaden on 15 September. Londonderry's informal contacts were no longer useful now that the Prime Minister was meeting Hitler face to face. However, Londonderry was pleased that his hoped-for summit between the two leaders was finally happening.[98] After some initial difficulties, the Munich Conference between the four powers convened on 29 September. The resulting agreement gave Hitler the Sudeten territories and guaranteed, through an agreement with France and Italy, the remainder of Czechoslovakia. The following day Chamberlain had Hitler sign the infamous letter declaring their intention never to go to war. As Churchill admitted, the conference and subsequent agreement was almost exactly what Londonderry had advocated: 'Your policy is certainly being tried'.[99]

If not part of the deliberations, then Londonderry sought to associate himself with what appeared to be a victory for peace.[100] He was in Munich at the time, talking with journalists, local people, and his contacts in the Nazi leadership.[101] But far from enjoying a hero's welcome like Chamberlain, the only attention Londonderry received was from leftwing critics, and rather than ignoring the taunts he characteristically rushed to his own defence in the press.[102] He further alienated himself from mainstream opinion when he added his name to a letter in *The Times* from the pro-Nazi 'Link' group of politicians, praising the Munich agreement.[103] He was not the only non-member to add his name, but his status as an ex-cabinet minister and the group's reputed connections to Berlin made it scandalous. He paid for it with what he called a 'conspiracy of silence'.[104]

The murderous outrage of *Kristallnacht* in November 1938 decapitated the campaign for Anglo-German friendship and left most appeasers with little choice but to outwardly abandon their support for Germany. Londonderry wrote angrily to Göring, complaining that on each occasion he had acted for Germany, Hitler embarked on a sudden action or policy that he could not explain.[105] It ended his direct contacts with the Nazi leadership but not, in contrast to most appeasers, his public calls for an agreement between the two countries.[106]

International tension increased in the early months of 1939, signalled by Franco's victory in Spain.[107] The Londonderrys stayed in Stockholm during March as guests of the Swedish royal family. It was reported in the press that Londonderry held a meeting with the German Legation, although nothing was recorded of their exchanges.[108] While in Sweden, events took a turn for the worse with the collapse of an increasingly fractured Czechoslovakia on 15 March and its subsequent division between Germany, Poland and Hungary.

To British public opinion this was a breach of the understanding reached at Munich; Hitler could no longer be believed and it was felt that Germany should be stopped. Londonderry similarly argued that Hitler had 'overstepped all limits' and that he no longer had any confidence in him.[109] At last he realized what had been happening, though pride prevented him from admitting that he had been manipulated. Like other pro-Germans he feared for his reputation, if he had been deceived then surely he had deceived the British public? Like many others in a similar position, he dropped the cause of peace for that of the patriot.[110] In private, however, like Chamberlain and some others, Londonderry did not abandon his hopes that war could still be averted through renewed dialogue.[111]

In response to Chamberlain's tougher stance announced on 17 March 1939, which included the protection of Poland, Londonderry informed Göring—with whom he had reopened communication after a break of five months—that he had little choice but to support the Prime Minister. He argued that nobody in Britain would listen to his calls for better understanding as Hitler had 'destroyed' all his efforts.[112] In early June 1939 he indicated to the former German Chancellor, Franz von Papen, now ambassador to Turkey, that he regretted it had taken the invasion of Prague for him to change his mind about Hitler.[113]

Despite an assurance to Halifax that he had left politics, Londonderry could not quell the need to play a role that might cast him as a peace-broker.[114] On 17 June he unsuccessfully demanded that the German ambassador to London save Anglo-German relations by challenging press reports about Nazi brutality.[115] And in a letter to *The Times* on the 22nd he called for yet another peace settlement between the 'Great Powers'.[116]

Although Londonderry threw his weight behind a new agreement, he had abandoned his sympathy for the Nazi leadership. In early July, Philip Conwell-Evans—an ex-appeaser who had forged links with German opposition groups—arranged for Londonderry to meet the 'moderate' Lieutenant Colonel Schwerin of the German General Staff.[117] Schwerin was one of a number of aristocratic senior officers who regarded Hitler's military plans as disastrous. Following the meeting Londonderry dutifully renewed contact with Halifax and relayed Schwerin's desire for British militarily force:

> He ... conveyed that Hitler, being a soldier, would only be impressed by arguments given to him by soldiers, and that the political points made very little impression upon him. I, of course, retorted that if he wanted a soldier's answer the only way that that could be given was in war, which I was quite certain all peoples ... were longing to avoid.[118]

Halifax appreciated the information, despite the addition of his infor-
mant's unsought-after scepticism.[119] But this gratitude only led
Londonderry to believe that he could perform a useful role again. It was
this, and not as he later claimed a request from Lord Winterton, that led
Londonderry to plan another visit to Hitler.[120]

As soon as Halifax was informed of Londonderry's proposed mission,
at the start of August, he made moves to stop it. Londonderry had over-
inflated his own usefulness, and in any event the government had its own
special intermediary. Initially, Londonderry was defensive, arguing that he
had unique contacts with the German leadership that would allow him to
declare that he had been betrayed by Nazi assurances and that he 'represented the spirit of the British Government and people in being determined to resist any further aggression.'[121] It was Hitler's style to leave his
guests with the impression that they mattered. Halifax, himself a victim
of this, retorted that the visit would betray British anxiety and look too
much like a negotiation.[122] With that Londonderry's attempt at amateur
diplomacy was at an end. He responded with chagrin, bitterly attacking
the Prime Minister for the failures of the National Government.[123] His
anger was also a response to the Nazi-Soviet Pact of 23 August, for the
agreement demonstrated how badly the appeasers had misjudged Hitler.
Politically ostracized, Londonderry abandoned Londonderry House and
moved to his Ulster estate a few weeks prior to the outbreak of war on
3 September 1939.[124]

V

Even the outbreak of war did not halt Londonderry's energies for long.
Not only did he still desire a role in the affairs of state, but the war also
provided its own necessities and opportunities. Chief among his priorities throughout the Second World War was his need to vindicate his
actions as Secretary of State for Air and his prominent role in promoting
Anglo-German friendship. Not unrelated to this were his other concerns,
the removal of Neville Chamberlain from the premiership, the political
and military defence of Northern Ireland, and the performance of the
Air Ministry.

Londonderry disliked Chamberlain for a host of reasons, ranging
from the clash between their fathers over tariff reform, through to the
Prime Minister's reluctance to take a personal interest in Londonderry's

amateur diplomacy. His main grievance however seems to have focussed on Chamberlain's stringent control of defence spending in the early 1930s, a policy Londonderry adhered to reluctantly at the time, but subsequently used in an attempt to absolve himself from any responsibility for Britain's relatively weak military capability. Indeed, it was Londonderry's overweening need to explain and excuse his role in recent events that prompted his most bitter falling out with Chamberlain.

Even before war was declared at the start of September, Londonderry was keen to publish his two 1934 letters to Lord Hailsham in which he called for Britain to deal with Germany from a position of strength. As outlined in the previous chapter, the former Air Minister believed that these letters vindicated his role at the Air Ministry and his later promotion of Anglo-German friendship.[125] On 27 September, Chamberlain contacted Londonderry to deny him permission to publish the letters, adding that he too had suffered from bad press.[126] It is unlikely that publication of the letters would have changed popular perceptions of Londonderry, after all, his actions subsequent to 1934 demonstrated that he had wanted to negotiate with Germany regardless of Britain's strength. Nevertheless, he took it as a personal blow and an obstacle to the vindication of his name. On 1 October he replied to the Prime Minister, lamenting that 'I personally should have been destroyed and that my reputation for all time must suffer is only a matter of importance to myself and my family.'[127]

If Londonderry was bitter towards his government, did he go as far as some have suggested and seek to make peace with Nazi Germany even after the start of the Second World War?[128] That Londonderry should be considered a traitor is not that surprising given his prominent campaign for Anglo-German understanding. Such ideas were very quick to emerge, with the press reporting on 20 September 1939 that Londonderry had been interned at Mount Stewart because of his German sympathies.[129] While this was not true, he had not abandoned his rationale for appeasement. In one of many unrequited letters to Halifax on how the war should be conducted, Londonderry made it clear that he still harboured fears of Soviet expansion following a conflict between Britain and Germany.[130] If this view was somewhat understandable, then there was something stubborn about Londonderry's decision not to stand down as president of the Anglo-Hungarian Society until August 1940, after Budapest congratulated Mussolini on his conquest of British Somalia.[131] Another piece of potentially damning evidence came on board an aeroplane with Rudolf Hess when he made his mysterious flight to Scotland in May 1941. Hess carried with him a list of British peers whom he believed had constituted a peace party. Although it was true that some peers favoured a truce, in particular the Duke of Westminster and the Duke of Buccleuch, the letter only revealed how deluded some Nazis continued to be about the influence of the aristocracy.[132]

If anything Londonderry had aligned himself since 1940 with the 'war party', albeit with a deep regret that could make him appear equivocal. This view is not based on the occasional anti-German speech he made, or his family's patronage of war measures in counties Down and Durham, but his actions beyond the public gaze.[133] For example, on 21 October 1939 he wrote to the then Secretary of State for Air, Sir Kingsley Wood, asking if he might be able to join the RAF. Needless to say, the 60 year old former-cabinet minister's offer was politely turned down.[134] Far more relevant, however, was his association with the Marquess of Salisbury's self-styled 'Watching Committee'. Even before the formation of this group in April 1940, Londonderry had been a keen behind-the-scenes critic of the government's handling of the war. In part this reflected his anger toward Chamberlain, and his hope that by sending supportive letters to Churchill—brought back into the cabinet by popular demand—he might ingratiate himself with a leading voice in the war cabinet.[135] The First Lord of the Admiralty did not reciprocate his cousin's efforts, but Londonderry continued to back Churchill in the knowledge that it was the best means of attacking Chamberlain. In one of his many letters to the Foreign Secretary, Londonderry informed him that that Churchill was the only member of the war cabinet qualified to 'carry us through these difficulties', and that he was by far the most inspiring minister, especially in his radio broadcasts.[136]

With his credentials as an anti-Chamberlainite well established, it is still remarkable that committed anti-appeasers like Salisbury and Leo Amery should chose to welcome Londonderry into their Watching Committee, despite his ongoing friendships with the two men.[137] But foremost in the mind of the Watching Committee was Londonderry's experience at the Air Ministry, although how the committee came to reach this decision owed much to the contrivance of the former Air Minister.[138] In the same month that Salisbury formed his Watching Committee, Londonderry wrote to his immediate successor at the Air Ministry, Viscount Swinton, now out of office, advocating the reformation of the 'Independent Peers': a Tory ginger group that had pressed for the unrelenting prosecution of the First World War. For good measure he also suggested that it should scrutinize the government through a private committee.[139] Having described Salisbury's Watching Committee, it is not surprising that on 1 April Salisbury asked him to join.[140] Mere membership of the committee boosted Londonderry's self esteem, and he was not the only one:

> The formation of the Watching Committee unleashed a thrust of constructive assessment and encouraged the dissidents to believe that they had a vehicle with which to influence government reform, shape policy, and make a positive contribution to the administration of the war.[141]

Londonderry did not have a good record of attendance at meetings of the Watching Committee, mainly because he had thrown himself into the role of wartime landlord in counties Down and Durham.[142] However, along with fellow committee member Lord Trenchard, Londonderry was active in the committee's deliberations about how the RAF might be better used.[143] He also added his concern about the need to improve the role of women in the services, a reflection of his wife's lifelong campaign for women's participation in the armed forces.[144] With his poor attendance and the inability of peers on the committee to intervene directly during the Norway debate of 7–8 May 1940, Londonderry was only associated by implication with the subsequent replacement of Chamberlain with Churchill. If he took some satisfaction at this turn of events then he was soon disappointed by the new Prime Minister's refusal to communicate with him. This only encouraged Londonderry to carry on 'watching' the government's management of the war, to write his memoirs, and to assume once again a role in the affairs of Northern Ireland.

VI

Londonderry had never abandoned his interest in Northern Ireland after resigning from its government in January 1926. Indeed, he took advantage of his place in the British cabinet to promote and defend the Ulster Unionist government. As Secretary of State for Air, for example, he discussed with MacDonald possible British reactions to the formation of Eamon de Valera's first government of the Irish Free State, including military intervention.[145] His later attempt, as Lord Privy Seal, to address the transatlantic air route, was less welcome.

Out of office there was little to restrain Londonderry in his defence of Ulster unionism. Despite sharing much of Chamberlain's rationale for appeasing Germany, he took exception to the Prime Minister's overtures to de Valera.[146] During discussions between the two premiers he leant on Samuel Hoare to ensure that further concessions were granted to Northern Ireland in what became the 1938 Anglo-Irish Treaty.[147] When the IRA launched a campaign in 1939 he successfully pressed Chamberlain to give guarantees that the British government would not cave in to terrorist demands.[148]

The outbreak of war saw Londonderry spend most of his time at Mount Stewart. Here, and in County Durham, the Londonderrys busied themselves with local organizations associated with the war effort. This involvement in local affairs was not new, for Londonderry had continued to play a part in the life of Northern Ireland after 1926, as Lord Lieutenant of County Down, Chancellor of Queen's University, and at various political events. On one such occasion, in July 1933, he spoke at the unveiling of Lord Carson's statue outside the new Parliament Buildings at Stormont, waxing lyrical about the Ulster Crisis of 1912 to 1914 even though he had found it a bore at the time.[149]

Therefore, when he offered his services to the government of Northern Ireland on 8 September 1939, it was hard for them to turn him down despite some concern about his German sympathies. Sir Basil Brooke—a fellow Ulster landowner and Belfast's Minister for Agriculture—was keen to use the former Education Minister in his recruitment campaign.[150] It was, by coincidence, an issue that Londonderry had raised earlier in the year with Kingsley Wood. On 12 July he warned the Air Minister that in the eventuality of another war with Germany it would be difficult to recruit in Northern Ireland. This he felt was attributable to the confidence of Unionists having been shaken by Chamberlain's dealings with de Valera, and a by now embedded desire that 'they must get whatever they can out of the British Government.'[151]

Londonderry's need to involve himself in Ulster affairs had by 1940 soured relations between him and his former colleagues. As part of his general critique of the government's handling of the war, Londonderry wrote to Churchill's new war cabinet to warn of the threat of German fifth columnists in the Irish Free State. These warnings were accompanied by his protest about the possibility of Northern Ireland being the price for de Valera ending his neutrality. The Secretary of State for War, Anthony Eden, responded politely by saying that he had the situation under control.[152] This was followed by further complaints in June, this time about the inadequate protection of Belfast's dockyards against an aerial attack. In particular, Londonderry criticized Eden's decision to accept Lord Craigavon's use of the Ulster Special Constabulary for anti-parachute defence duties.[153] Actions like this made him despair about his former colleague's ability to govern Northern Ireland during the wartime emergency, and suggest to Eden that he appoint a military governor to take charge of Ulster's defence.[154]

When he finally went over Eden's head and wrote to Churchill on the matter on 21 June 1940, the Prime Minister responded with a terse and angry rebuke.[155] Londonderry then unsuccessfully attempted to press Salisbury to take up his concerns.[156] When his ally of so many previous occasions replied by politely rebuffing his efforts, Londonderry responded by blaming Eden and others for a disastrous foreign policy that he felt had led the country to its present difficulties.[157] This was followed in August with accusations that his correspondence to and from England was being opened. In his reply Eden justified this on the basis that Northern Ireland did not censor its mail with the Irish Free State.[158]

VII

Northern Ireland was not the only area of interest Londonderry had maintained since leaving office. He had continued to corresponded with key personnel at the Air Ministry long after his departure, exchanging opinions, and sometimes receiving briefings for debates in the House of Lords. In 1938 he was rewarded for his services to the Ministry when it appointed him chairman of the Air Guard Commissioners.[159] But this did not mean that Londonderry possessed much influence over his former colleagues. His failure to change the transatlantic air route has already been noted. He was also unable to make them address in April 1939 what he and his wife regarded as the Ministry's need to promote the women's section of the RAF.[160] A more personal blow to his prestige came a few months later when the Ministry decided to locate an Auxiliary RAF base at a site near Belfast instead of Londonderry's existing airfield outside Newtownards.[161] He had been similarly unable to stop the

Ministry from moving civil aviation from Newtownards to Belfast the previous year.[162]

Having upset Churchill and Salisbury in June 1940 there were few in the wartime government who would now listen to Londonderry. With no one else to turn to in the government Londonderry began to correspond with Lord Beaverbrook, from May 1940 to June 1945, successively, Minister of Aircraft Production, Minister of State, Minister of Supply, Minister of War Production, and Lord Privy Seal. Londonderry—who believed that it was his criticisms of government policy that had prompted Beaverbrook's appointment—informed the press baron-come-minister that he was the only independent voice in the cabinet who could counter Churchill's dominating style of leadership.[163] It is unlikely that Beaverbrook took Londonderry's claims too seriously, but he did utilize the former Air Minister's help in the early part of 1944, passing on confidential government documents in the hope that it might help him defend legislation intended to reform civil aviation.[164] Londonderry was certainly under the impression that he was playing a valuable role, although it is clear from a later claim—that he would not serve in a government under Churchill—that he still overvalued his importance.[165] In the end, Beaverbrook's polite solicitations to a former Air Minister could not hide the fact that, for all purposes, Londonderry was a finished politician with a bitter sense of grievance towards those in office. Outside of his communications with Beaverbrook, his political role had become wholly negative. Even his other political concern of the mid-forties— reform of the Foreign Office—was motivated almost entirely by his experience in the 1930s.[166]

VIII

Out of office, out of favour, and unwilling to remain silent, Londonderry began to consider his vindication. Assurances from friends like Sir Robert Lynn that he was not viewed as pro-German meant little; for in the midst of a war against foes he had once courted, Londonderry was compelled to place his version of history on record.[167] According to Montgomery Hyde, Londonderry decided to start writing *Wings of Destiny* in 1942 as a means of distracting his mind from the death of his daughter Maureen Stanley.[168] However, this is inaccurate on two points, authorship and date.

An undated memorandum among the Londonderry papers indicates that Londonderry was assisted in writing *Wings of Destiny*, and that his assistant was keen to concentrate the work on his career at the Air Ministry, describing the appeasement period as 'incidental'.[169] The memorandum gives advice on presentation and layout that closely resemble the final product. Hyde, a barrister and historian, had collaborated with Londonderry in the writing of *Ourselves and Germany*, and it is possible that he did so again for *Wings of Destiny*.[170] Hyde's assertion that Maureen's death was the catalyst for the book is also misleading. In June 1941, a year prior to the tragedy, Londonderry boasted to Beaverbrook that his November 1934 letters to Hailsham would soon 'see the light of day', and the following month he received permission from the war cabinet to consult cabinet papers for his research.[171]

In fact, the proofs of *Wings of Destiny* were ready by the end of 1941. Instead of writing the book, the following year was taken up in negotiations with the war cabinet for permission to publish particular documents, and in undertaking several re-workings of the manuscript following government objections to certain passages.[172] Churchill was dismissive of Londonderry's 'twaddle' and 'tale-telling', but he still took the precaution of ordering a cabinet committee to examine the potentially embarrassing manuscript.[173] Unknown to a frustrated Londonderry, the Lord Privy Seal, Sir Stafford Cripps, was assigned the task and by November permission was granted with the proviso that certain passages be removed.[174] Londonderry subsequently complained that the deletions had spoilt his book and that delays had cost him a place on the Christmas list. He did not seem to acknowledge the cabinet's more pressing duties; even the normally considerate Halifax was moved to complain that Londonderry had reacted unfairly.[175]

But Londonderry no longer cared about his standing with the government. Through correspondence and in parliament, Londonderry continued his 'watching', openly questioning the management of the war from issues as varied as mining to the surrender of Singapore.[176] Speaking in the House of Lords in 1942 he proclaimed: 'The whole conduct of the war up to now had shown a lack of appreciation of the magnitude of the issues involved, and there had been a lack of planning and foresight.'[177] Chips Channon noted Londonderry's acrimonious attitude to Churchill when he had lunch with him in December 1943: 'Charlie held forth about his cousin Winston, who, he maintains, has few Churchillian qualities'.[178] As Channon was aware, Londonderry attributed his fall out with

Churchill to a disagreement they had at a dinner party given by Lady Cunard before the war. It was a simplistic and often repeated view that grossly underestimated the breadth and depth of the political gulf between the two men. It may have been a catalyst for the breakdown of their relationship, but the divisions could be traced as far back as 1926.

If Londonderry was presumptive and occasionally arrogant in the way he expected his former colleagues to treat him, then he was not entirely ignorant of his failings. In 1943 he wrote to his lifetime confidant Lady Desborough:

> When Baldwin removed me I instinctively knew that I was finished, that my active life was over and that I had to fall back on resources which it is difficult to cultivate when you have been in the middle of politics as I had been since the end of the war. In your last letter you say so kindly, 'The swing of the pendulum will come.' But of course I know it won't be for me and I confess that knowing this, as I have known it, I have touched almost the lowest depths of despair ... So the war, the crisis of our lives, finds me completely isolated and under a sort of shadow which I cannot get away from. Politicians burn their boats ... I want you to know that I have no illusions about it and that I am bitterly disappointed. I had great chances and I missed them by not being good enough and that really sums up the whole thing ... It all has worked out badly and I know it is some inherent fault in myself. However I know I have got to carry on and I am doing my best.[179]

In November 1945 a gliding accident put Londonderry out of action in the short term and contributed to a series of strokes in the last three years of his life.[180] It was also in November 1945, in what must have been a painful reminder, that Ribbentrop's defence lawyers successfully requested that Londonderry deliver an interrogatory to the Nuremberg war trial, although interrogatories were also requested from Halifax, Derby, Beaverbrook and Vansittart.[181]

IX

Londonderry's support for appeasement was not unusual, indeed, it was typical of many British observers of foreign affairs. More interestingly, he closely resembled Chamberlain in his application of appeasement, and there is evidence to suggest that he may have had some indirect influence on the otherwise solitary premier, especially on the occasion of Halifax's meeting with Hitler. And like Chamberlain, Londonderry's continued appeasement after 1938, largely hidden from the electorate, barely wavered even after the invasion of Prague. Both men were compelled to avoid war, holding that it was not only futile, but that it would leave western Europe vulnerable to Soviet expansion. They hoped a benign, almost gentlemanly, approach to diplomacy would tame Hitler, who encouraged such notions, and in doing so spectacularly underestimated the dictator's ambitions. The main distinction between Londonderry and Chamberlain was that it was the latter's job to engage in diplomacy. Londonderry took it upon himself to play a part, encouraged by the Nazis, and in doing so overestimated his usefulness to both London and Berlin. He did nevertheless have limited if unintended uses for both governments, as evidenced by Ribbentrop's memorandum and Halifax's consultations, but Londonderry mistook this for high-level influence. By making himself an arch proponent of appeasement through his speeches, books and visits to Germany, he suffered the fate of those other 'guilty men' whose reputations have suffered enormously ever since. In the end Hitler destroyed the nineteenth-century world that Londonderry and others had hoped to save. The appeasers had grossly misjudged the Nazi leader, but in their prediction that war would end European hegemony and lead to Soviet expansion, they were proven correct.

For many aristocrats the promotion of Anglo-German relations provided a renewed sense of political input after decades of being steadily marginalized. Their participation was intensified by the lack of a clear British foreign policy, Nazi encouragement, and the universal fear in Britain of another European war, with its concomitant danger of Soviet expansion and further imperial decline. Having played such a prominent role, Hitler's breach of Munich and the consequent descent into war ensured that the aristocracy would, as a class, bear much of the guilt for appeasement. It was easier to recall the deeds of those whose prominence appeared to have led Britain into a Faustian pact than it was to acknowledge a general reluctance to fight Germany, especially when the depths of Nazi evil were fully realized towards the end of the Second World War. In remembering the aristocracy as being somehow responsible for appeasement, the general public, then and now, have not only made a similar mistake to the Nazis in overestimating aristocratic influence, but also, more disturbingly, abdicated responsibility for shaping the actions of those who led them.

Conclusion

On 8 May 1945, 'VE Day', Harold Nicolson recorded a memorable meeting with Londonderry:

> I left early and in haste leaving my coat behind me. A voice hailed me in Belgrave Square. It was Charles, seventh Marquess of Londonderry, Hitler's friend. As we walked towards his mansion in Park Lane, he explained to me how he had warned the Government about Hitler; how they would not listen to him; how, but for him, we should not have had Spitfires and 'all this', waving a thin arm at the glow above a floodlit Buckingham Palace, at the sound of cheering in the park, and at the cone of searchlights which joined each other like a Maypole above our heads.
>
> Enraged by this, I left him in Park Lane and walked back through the happy but quite sober crowds to Trafalgar Square...[1]

It was unfortunate for Londonderry that he was so obsessed with his reputation that he failed to show obvious humility to anyone outside his family circle and closest friends. To one such friend, Lady Desborough, he wrote a long letter in 1943 in which he admitted many of the flaws that others attributed to him.

Londonderry's downfall from the National Government and subsequent condemnation for appeasement had been so markedly detrimental that he had come to have the impression that his career before that lacked the struggles of his later years:

> Whatever I touched seemed to turn to gold. I seemed to succeed in everything, not brilliantly or exceptionally, but still everything went well, everyone helped me, and I seemed to have so many friends and well wishers, and then suddenly it all came to an end. I tried loyally to carry on outside, then I dabbled in diplomacy with an idea which I know was correct but I could not somehow

work it with anyone who counted. Then I did a lot of flying. I
made speeches which people seemed to want to hear; we went
on entertaining and everyone seemed to want to come.

In his letter Londonderry admitted that he had failed, attributing this to
his poor relationship with various party leaders rather than his failure to
grasp or share their concern for public opinion.[2] However, he remained
unapologetic for his beliefs and actions:

> Then I had some bitter exchanges with Baldwin and
> Chamberlain whom I knew were wrong although I commended
> Chamberlain for Munich but regretted everything he subse-
> quently did. Then I fell out with Winston because I wanted to
> achieve by what I thought was statesmanship what he wanted to
> achieve by war. That quarrel I think originated sometime before
> because I was never really fond of F. E. [Smith] who complete-
> ly absorbed Winston to the exclusion of W's allies like myself,
> and I disagreed with both and rightly disagreed over their Irish
> policy which has had such fatal results. So I really planned a bad
> crash and was not strong enough or clever enough to strike out
> on my own...

Londonderry not only had cause to look back to his career with frustration, but also to a future that he knew would condemn him as a Nazi
sympathizer:

> I get so impatient about the attitude towards me in books and
> articles with reference to my German activities and I hate special
> pleading, and if I do write retorts ... no one seems to read them
> or notice them. Winston has been distinctly unfriendly and I
> often wonder why he never would take the trouble to find out
> what I was at. W. did suggest to me to resign when Chamberlain
> at last consented to re-arm and I wish I had done so because my
> loyalty to my old colleagues afterwards precluded me from join-
> ing Winston which I would like to have done.

He also expressed a fear that his lack of any political role might somehow weaken him:

> I am intensely lucky. But for this cussed war I am quite happy at
> home and I pray that will go on. A politician who has missed is
> really terribly out of a job. You are not wanted for the big things

and there is really no place in the smaller things. All the many figure head duties were very good accompaniments to the central
and dominating duty, but they are uninteresting by themselves
and it is so difficult to keep oneself up to the mark … I was
always so sorry for Hailsham, because the moment he took off
his harness he became an old man.[3]

Londonderry's gliding accident in November 1945 put an end to his last
involvement in politics, a campaign with the former Foreign Office mandarin Sir Walford Selby for Foreign Office reform.[4] It did not, however,
tame his desire to rescue his reputation. When news reached him that
Samuel Hoare, now Viscount Templewood, would be allowed to publish
government letters in his memoirs, Londonderry protested to Sir Edward
Bridges of the Cabinet Secretariat that he had not been given the same
right.[5] But this only prompted Bridges to make enquiries about the need
for definite mechanisms to avoid future disputes.[6] Having initially dismissed the idea of writing yet another vindication of his career, Bridges'
legalistic and unconvincing explanation for why Londonderry could not
now publish his 1934 letters angered him to the point that he accused
Churchill of selling stories to the American press.[7] It also led him to consider writing a comparative history of the RAF and Luftwaffe in the
1930s, with the intention, of course, of vindicating his reputation.
Following internal enquiries about granting Londonderry access to government documents, Bridges—who was clearly ruffled by Londonderry's
attempt to compare the British and German air forces in the light of subsequent knowledge—prevented access and asserted that the former Air
Minister 'is more a controversialist than an historian.'[8] While the accusation was partly accurate, if a little unfair, Bridges' response suggests that
the Churchillian view of the war and its causes was already censoring
those who sought to challenge it. With Churchill out of office after 1945,
a solution appeared to be on offer from the Air Minister, Philip Noel-
Baker, when he suggested that Londonderry use parliamentary privilege
to ask questions in the House of Lords on matters contained in the
closed papers.[9] Knowing how impractical this situation would be—consistent questions in the public arena on pre-war policies that implied criticisms of Churchill—Londonderry dismissed the suggestion and regretted what he viewed as the inevitable development of a pro-Churchill historiography.[10] He received some comfort however when the editor of the
Belfast Telegraph, Jack Sayers, agreed to publish correspondence between
Londonderry and Franz von Papen.[11]

Londonderry's final years coincided with the post-war electoral triumph of the Labour party under the helm of Clement Attlee, the man who had so effectively attacked his handling of the Disarmament Conference. Londonderry met their reforms with some success and magnanimity. In particular, he died a millionaire, leaving the bulk of his fortune to his grandson, the ninth Marquess of Londonderry.[12] And rather than fight Labour's plans to the nationalize the collieries, the seventh Marquess sounded a note of regret when he addressed his employees in January 1946:

> I wish I had been forceful enough to get my plan across [in 1926]. Instead of that the colliery owners as a whole have taken for granted that the coal industry will be nationalised and have taken steps accordingly. The Mining Association have spoken for the coal trade, but I have not found myself in agreement with the attitude they took up, beyond full agreement with the undertaking to do everything in their power to increase production.[13]

By the end of 1947 successive strokes curtailed Londonderry's power of speech, and soon after his ability to write. Before that, on 21 September 1947, he wrote his last letter to Lady Desborough:

> I really am not bothering about politics. I think all the politicians are quite useless. I have been reading the histories of the last century and all the politicians were actually the most terrible liars, foreign affairs was a game, and no one ever wrote a letter or a dispatch without his tongue in his cheek. I now see why I failed to understand the very second-class people I had to deal with and how glad they must have been to get me out of the way. I am sorry I failed to handle Winston because he really could have saved the war instead of gaining the credit which he fully deserves for winning it, and we are now paying the price ... If only someone had been powerful enough to combine Chamberlain with his passion for peace with Winston ... we need never have had the war with its ghastly results as the price for Winston gaining an everlasting historical name ... I am getting much interest from letters I am getting from a few people, who think I was right and everyone else wrong, who come across my books at libraries, but that the historian will deal with in years to come I think.[14]

Londonderry died at the age of 70 on the night of the 10–11 February 1949 at Mount Stewart.[15] Unlike his parents he was buried in the grounds of the County Down estate, on St Valentine's Day, surrounded by statues of four Irish saints in a graveyard named in Irish, '*Tir-Na-nOge*', land of the forever young. On the 16 February a memorial service was held at St Anne's Cathedral, Belfast, and on the following day at Westminster Abbey.[16]

Londonderry's last years were spent in relative obscurity. His pre-war pre-occupations were of little concern to a nation that had endured the Second World War and its immediate aftermath. More than ever before he seemed to belong to a bygone age. His obituary in *The Times* gave a comprehensive overview of his political life and concluded that his promotion of Anglo-German friendship had lost him a lot in public esteem.[17] Viscount Trenchard felt the need to add his own obituary notice the following week, emphasising Londonderry's role alongside him in preserving the RAF. Similarly, an anonymous 'old friend' compared him to Castlereagh: 'In spite of his obvious advantages he was curiously diffident about himself … he possessed the moral courage which enabled him to take the course which he believed to be right and to hold his road, deeply distressed, but outwardly indifferent to misrepresentation and abuse.'[18]

Ever since his death memories of Londonderry, both historical and popular, have been mixed and disjointed, failing to link the contrasting aspects of his life in order to explain his actions. In part this is due to the perceived failure of Londonderry in each phase of his political life, as a backbencher, an Ulster Unionist, a coal owner, and as Secretary of State for Air. In each of these positions he left no obvious or lasting mark and therefore failed to enter the pantheon of Great Men. However, this ignores the real significance of his political life, its overtly aristocratic character at a time when traditional authority was irrevocably in decline. Lord and Lady Londonderry are an example of how the aristocratic political culture of the nineteenth century had survived the growth of democracy. It of course had limitations that increased over time, but by his actions and their results we can see that traditional authority had survived the onslaught of legal-rational and bureaucratic authority. This is not to say that all aristocrat-politicians were like Londonderry. Rather, that he was a relic of an era when they were born to rule, someone who used the methods of nineteenth-century politics with mixed success. Knowing that everyone loves a lord, and playing up to it, won him election to the House of Commons in 1906. It also, through his continued role alongside his wife as prominent political hosts, made him useful to Baldwin and the Conservatives in the late 1920s, and it charmed the Labour leader Ramsay MacDonald into a close friendship that aided Londonderry's entry and survival in the National Government. His patrician distance from the electorate also allowed him to play a more paternalistic and moderate part at the Irish Convention, in the Northern Ireland government, and during the miners' strike of 1926.

However, it was Londonderry's senatorial outlook that helped to guarantee his failure as a politician. As an aristocrat brought up to fulfil family duties, including participation in government, it is unsurprising that he found it hard to shake off the class assumptions with which he was imbued. He never questioned his right to govern and often resented his reliance on elected politicians. Although he admired those who had 'started from nowhere' in contrast to his 'pampered life', Londonderry believed they had few scruples.[19] When surveying the political landscape, he looked to the top but not, like most politicians, also to the electorate. This prevented him from carrying Ulster Unionists with him at the Irish Convention and in the Northern Ireland government. It also made him indifferent to Baldwin's attitude to rearmament policy in the 1930s. Instead, Londonderry allied himself with the Air Ministry and RAF when, as a politician, he was expected to appease the concerns of a mercurial public.

This should not imply that Londonderry was totally inflexible. He demonstrated pragmatism from his time in the House of Commons when, in contrast to the die-hard Tory peers, he called for a more considered attitude from the Liberal government in both House of Lords reform and Irish home rule. He supported the six-county exclusion agreement in 1916 and continued to do so when hard-liners in Ulster and Britain, seeking his aid, conspired to topple their party leaders. When he was censored at the Irish Convention he did not abandon the Ulster Unionists; instead he expressed his frustrations privately.

His pragmatism in Irish affairs earned him the admiration of some Tory grandees. Coupled with his active support for the Lloyd George coalition, after years of hostility, Londonderry received a junior ministerial post in 1919. In office he supported government interference in civil aviation after years of vocal opposition to such measures as an MP. In the Northern Ireland government his diplomacy towards the Catholic hierarchy facilitated their cooperation in educational affairs. Londonderry's moderation is also evident from his role in the 1926 miners' strike, in his challenge to the die-hards at the Conservative party conference in 1927, and his conversion to tariff reform in the wake of the Wall Street Crash. It is also possible to discern Londonderry's pragmatism at the Disarmament Conference, when he loyally represented a policy at Geneva that he challenged in private. During his years of amateur diplomacy, he attempted to persuade both the British and German governments to moderate their attitude to one another, but he was out of his depth and like many others he greatly underestimated the motives and ambitions of Hitler.

Despite this flexibility, Londonderry's equally characteristic stubbornness and single-mindedness damaged his relations with political colleagues. His open support for free trade hindered his early career in the House of Commons, and his attitude to protestant critics in Northern Ireland made it almost impossible for him to remain in the Belfast government. His conflicts with fellow cabinet ministers in the National Government were exacerbated by his passionate support of the RAF and its chiefs, his dislike of the Foreign Office, and his refusal to agree with policies that sought to assuage the electorate. His continued public spats with Labour in the run up to the 1935 election—when the Tories hoped to minimize critical attention about rearmament—left Baldwin with little choice but to remove him. Most fatally of all, Londonderry's continued and enthusiastic advocacy of Anglo-German relations, even after almost all others had abandoned the cause, ensured not only his own alienation from contemporaries, but also that his reputation would be tarnished long after his death.

What made Londonderry pragmatic in some instances and immovable in others was his fundamental motivation for continuing in politics against the odds and in the face of more legitimate competition and opposition. He believed that he had a right to be in government, one that on the one hand called for paternalist moderation and on the other for a more definite stance born of a sense of duty. He was fundamentally an aristocrat in practice, temperament and outlook. But unlike others of his social rank who made it into and upward in government, he did not adjust to the priorities of a mass democracy. It is little wonder therefore that Londonderry has been described as a political failure. However, this ignores the less tangible qualities and legacies of his political career. He was a highly placed internal critic of Unionist policy in the first government of Northern Ireland, one who partly reconciled an ambivalent

Catholic hierarchy to a largely disinterested Belfast government. He brought social prestige to an otherwise ridiculed air force after the First World War and in the 1930s. His defence of the RAF also ensured that no premature disarmament took place in the early 1930s, and that Britain maintained the core of an air force that would eventually repel the Luftwaffe in what was later called 'Britain's finest hour'. He also oversaw investment that led to the development of radar, and the Spitfire and Hurricane fighters, at a time when others had demanded disinvestment. He challenged the lack of defence spending upon taking office in 1931, precipitating Churchill's campaign by two years, and his caution in building up the RAF, even in 1935, ensured that priority was not given to the building of bombers.

Londonderry's approach to his own career also revealed a degree of sagacity. His move to Northern Ireland in 1921 did not, as Churchill suggested at the time, end his hopes of office at Westminster. His decision to avoid the fate of other aristocrats by refusing, on three separate occasions, the governor generalship of Canada allowed him to take a seat in the cabinet until 1935. His amateur appeasement led to some rapprochement with Chamberlain and Halifax who, like Hitler and von Ribbentrop, initially welcomed and used Londonderry's self-proclaimed role as a go-between. His determination to fight for the future of the RAF ensured he was not subjected to the same post-Second World War condemnation as that suffered by Baldwin and Chamberlain; indeed, Londonderry pre-empted such attacks.

None of this means that Londonderry was necessarily always correct, or even a good politician. When it mattered his view was often sidelined and undermined by his own failure to communicate effectively in a highly critical public sphere. His delivery was old fashioned and his message often unpopular. He impressed people by his presence but not his presentation; some finding it scattered, rambling, and diffuse.[20] His calm demeanour led some to accuse him of being 'slow on the uptake'; even Londonderry occasionally lamented his lack of academic ability.[21] Assessments of Londonderry's intelligence are subjective, but two points are worth noting. In not communicating with or fully comprehending modern, media driven and voter conscious politics, Londonderry's utterances would naturally appear outdated; a major critic of his style, A. L. Kennedy, was after all a *Times* journalist. This touches on the other factor, highlighted elsewhere by David Cannadine. Aristocrats were easily labelled 'stupid' by the younger men who rejected ideas about being born to rule, who resented aristocrats clinging to senior positions, and who had striven to enter parliament and the government despite lacking all the privileges of the landed elite.[22]

On the day of Londonderry's death one of his critics, Cuthbert Headlam, noted in his diary: 'He was extraordinarily conscientious—modest and unassuming—and is a real loss to the community—he was often misunderstood and never rightly appreciated.'[23] On the same day Chips Channon recorded a similar view:

> In the long run [Londonderry] will be proven right politically; he always maintained that there were only two possible courses for us: either to make friends with Germany, or, if this was impossible, to re-arm. We did neither, and war was the result. But he was unpopular and much criticised at the time for his views.[24]

The maverick Tory MP Robert Boothby later referred to this as Londonderry's 'simple but irrefutable logic'.[25] Following the memorial service at Westminster Abbey, Arthur Henderson, former Labour Foreign Secretary and chairman of the Disarmament Conference, turned to Channon and remarked 'possibly Londonderry was right all the time.' Channon replied: 'of course he was.'[26] A recent assessment of Londonderry by the poet Tom Paulin also raises this question, fusing Londonderry's reputation with that of his famous ancestor, Viscount Castlereagh, and concluding that both 'were sheer bad luck'.[27] Londonderry certainly believed he had bad luck. Had he not been ambitious politically then he might have thought otherwise.

Notes

Introduction

1 *The Sunday Chronicle*, 13 December 1908.

2 Margot Oxford, *More Memories* (London, 1933), p. 78.

3 H. C. Plunkett, *The Irish Convention: Confidential Report to His Majesty the King by the Chairman* (Dublin, 1918), pp. 11–12.

4 James Lees-Milne, *Harold Nicolson: A Biography, 1886–1929* (London, 1980), p. 366.

5 Channon, diary, 11 February 1949 (Robert Rhodes James, *'Chips': The Diaries of Sir Henry Channon* (rep. edn., London, 1999), p. 434).

6 Annabel Goldsmith, *Annabel, An Unconventional Life: The Memoirs of Lady Annabel Goldsmith* (London, 2004), pp. 15–17.

7 Ross McKibbin, *Class and Cultures: England 1918–1951* (Oxford, 1998), p. 20.

8 As this book was going to press Ian Kershaw published his *Making Friends with Hitler: Lord Londonderry and Britain's Road to War* (London, 2004). I reciprocate Professor Kershaw's kind acknowledgement of my own work, and hope, as does he, that our books are viewed as complementary.

9 Anne de Courcy, *Circe: The Life of Edith, Marchioness of Londonderry* (London, 1993); Diane Urquhart, 'Peeresses, patronage and power: the politics of ladies Frances Anne, Theresa and Edith Londonderry, 1800–1959', in Alan Hayes and Diane Urquhart (eds), *Irish Women's History* (Dublin, 2004), pp. 43–59; A. Susan Williams, *Ladies of Influence: Women of the Elite in Interwar Britain* (London, 2000), pp. 13–38. See also J. A. Pauley, 'The social and political roles of Edith, Marchioness of Londonderry, 1878–1959', Ph.D. thesis (University of Ulster, 1994).

10 Edith's other publications include *Henry Chaplin: A Memoir* (London, 1926); *Character and Tradition* (London, 1934); *Mount Stewart* (privately printed, 1956); *Frances Anne. The Life and Times of Frances Anne, Marchioness of Londonderry and her Husband Charles, Third Marquess of Londonderry* (London, 1958).

11 For scholarly approach to critical biography see Philip Williamson, *Stanley Baldwin: Conservative Leadership and National Values* (Cambridge, 1999), pp. 1–20.

12 See Patrick O'Brien, 'Is political biography a good thing', *Contemporary British History*, 10, no. 4 (winter, 1996), p. 60; Friedrich Nietzsche, 'On the uses and disadvantages of history for life', *Untimely Meditations* (Cambridge, 1983), pp. 57–123; N. C. Fleming, 'New Ireland, same old heroes', *Fortnight*, no. 405 (June 2002), p. 33.

13 Londonderry to Wickham Steed, 1 August 1940 (PRONI, Londonderry papers hereafter cited as D/3099, D/3099/2/21/A/246).

14 Jonathan Powis, *Aristocracy* (Oxford, 1984), p. 3

15 Aristotle, *The Politics* (trans. T. A. Sinclair) (rep. edn., London, 1992), pp. 256–60.

16 For importance of pedigree to aristocracy see J. V. Beckett, *The Aristocracy in England, 1660–1914* (Oxford, 1988), p. 3.

17 See A. P. W. Malcomson, *The Pursuit of the Heiress: Aristocratic Marriage in Ireland, 1750–1820* (Belfast, 1982), p. 13.

18 F. M. L. Thompson, *English Landed Society in the Nineteenth Century* (London, 1963), pp. 9–11.

19 Urquhart, 'Peeresses, Patronage and Power', pp. 44–50.

20 W. D. Rubinstein, *Men of Property: The Very Wealthy in Britain Since the Industrial Revolution* (London, 1981), pp. 194, 209.

21 Urquhart, 'Peeresses and Power', pp. 43–59.

22 David Gilmour, *Curzon* (London, 1994), p. 233.

23 The Londonderrys were depicted as the characters of Lord and Lady Roehampton.

24 Andrew Adonis, *Making Aristocracy Work: The Peerage and the Political System in Britain, 1884–1914* (Oxford, 1993), *passim.*

25 Marquess of Londonderry, 'In the days of my youth', *T.P.'s & Cassell's Weekly*, 21 March 1925, p. 806.

26 David Cannadine, *Aspects of Aristocracy: Grandeur and Decline in Modern Britain* (New Haven and London, 1994), pp. 22, 55; Castlereagh to Theresa, Lady Londonderry, n.d. (DCRO, D/Lo/C/682).

27 Londonderry, 'my youth', pp. 806–10.

28 Political notes by Theresa, Lady Londonderry, 29 November 1915 (PRONI, D/3084/C/C/B/1/7).

29 Marchioness of Londonderry, *Retrospect* (London, 1938), pp. 28–9.

30 They included Emperor Francis Joseph of Austria-Hungary, the Queen of Rumania, King Alexander of Serbia, and Sultan Abdul Hamid of Turkey (Londonderry, 'my youth', p. 806; Castlereagh to Theresa, Lady Londonderry, 9, 13 and 18 April 1901 (DCRO, D/Lo/C/682 (20–3)).

31 Londonderry, *Retrospect*, pp. 40, 43, 45.

32 Castlereagh to Theresa, Lady Londonderry, 12 August 1905 (DCRO, D/Lo/C/682 (47)).

33 Londonderry, 'my youth', p. 810.

34 Edith Londonderry, *Retrospect*, p. 73.

35 Viscount Chilston, *Chief Whip: The Political Life and Times of Aretas Akers-Douglas, 1st Viscount Chilston* (London, 1961), p. 4.

36 A. K. Russell, *Liberal Landslide: The General Election of 1906* (Newton Abbot, 1973), pp. 66, 83.

37 *The Kent Times*, 16 December 1905; Edward Carson to Theresa, Lady

Londonderry, 17 December 1905 (D/3099/12). For a more cynical report of the meeting see *The Northampton Mercury*, 13 June 1908.

38 See Austin Chamberlain to Balfour, 12 September 1904 (Charles Petrie (ed.), *The Life and Letters of the Right Hon. Sir Austin Chamberlain K.G., P.C., M.P.* (London, 1939), pp. 152–5).

39 Richard A. Rempel, *Unionists Divided: Arthur Balfour, Joseph Chamberlain and the Unionist Free Traders* (Newton Abbot, 1972), pp. 132–3; Alan Sykes, *Tariff Reform in British Politics 1903–1913* (Oxford, 1979), p. 95.

40 Blanche E. C. Dugdale, *Arthur James Balfour, First Earl of Balfour, K.G., O.M., F.R.S., etc.* (2 vols, London, 1936), vol. 1, p. 127.

41 Castlereagh to Theresa, Lady Londonderry, 24 December 1905 (DCRO, D/Lo/C/682 (51)).

42 Castlereagh to Theresa, Lady Londonderry, 24 December 1905 (DCRO, D/Lo/C 682 (50)); Castlereagh to Theresa, Lady Londonderry, 28 December 1905 (DCRO, D/Lo/C 682 (52)).

43 Castlereagh to Theresa, Lady Londonderry, 28 December 1905 (DCRO, D/Lo/C 682 (52)).

44 *The World*, 23 January 1906.

45 'Maidstone's reputation in regard to political morals is not a good one. The present petition is probably the ninth, or possibly the tenth, since 1800' (*The South Eastern Gazette*, 13 February 1906).

46 G. Gordon to Castlereagh, 13 February 1906 (D/3099/2/4/2).

47 Edith, Lady Londonderry, *Retrospect*, p. 77.

48 *The South Eastern Gazette*, 17 May 1906; *The Tribune*, 10 May 1906. Londonderry was involved in another court case concerning breach of contract with an election employee (*The Times*, 29 July 1932).

49 *The Newtownards Chronicle*, 29 July 1899.

1. Politics and War, 1905–1918

1 George Dangerfield, *The Strange Death of Liberal England* (rep. edn., London, 1966), pp. 90–1, 137, 291.

2 Philip Williamson and Edward Baldwin, *Baldwin Papers: A Conservative Statesman, 1908–1947* (Cambridge, 2005), forthcoming.

3 Marquess of Londonderry, 'In the days of my youth', *T.P.'s & Cassell's Weekly*, 21 March 1925, p. 810; *Hansard 4 (Commons)*, 152, 400 (21 February 1906); see also *The Morning Post*, 22 February 1906.

4 *The Standard*, 17 July 1908.

5 Castlereagh to Theresa, Lady Londonderry, 25 October 1906 (DCRO, D/Lo/C 682 (53)).

6 Londonderry, 'my youth', p. 810; E. H. H. Green, *The Crisis of Conservatism: The Politics, Economics and Ideology of the British Conservative Party, 1880–1914* (London, 1995), p. 6; Earl Winterton, *Orders of the Day* (London, 1953), p. 44.

7 During his first five year term Castlereagh's speeches covered the army, coal

mining, alcohol licensing, tenant law, Ireland, access to mountains, pensions, death duties, land taxation and horse breeding (*The Westminster Gazette*, 22 February 1906).

8 *The Sunday Chronicle*, 13 December 1908.

9 *Hansard 4 (Commons)*, 198, 1303 (14 December 1908).

10 See *Hansard 4 (Commons)*, 189, 386–8 (20 May 1908).

11 *Hansard 4 (Commons)*, 172, 147–52 (9 April 1907). See also ibid., 174, 1727, 1730–1 (29 May 1907); ibid., 176, 227–30, 240 (17 June 1907); ibid., 176, 391, 397, 417 (18 June 1907).

12 David Cannadine, *Decline and Fall of the British Aristocracy* (rep. edn., London, 1992), pp. 277–8.

13 See Arthur Marwick, *The Deluge: British Society and the First World War* (rep. edn., London, 1978), pp. 155–6.

14 Colin Nicholson, 'Edwardian England and the coming of the First World War', in Alan O'Day (ed.), *The Edwardian Age: Conflict and Stability, 1900–1914* (London, 1979), p. 153.

15 *Hansard 4 (Commons)*, 172, 528–31 (12 April 1907).

16 *Hansard 4 (Commons)*, 172, 528–31 (12 April 1907).

17 Quoted from *The Times*, 10 December 1908; *Hansard 4 (Commons)*, 198, 520 (9 December 1908); *The Sunday Chronicle*, 13 December 1908.

18 *Hansard 5 (Commons)*, ii, 2075 (26 March 1909).

19 Robert Pearce, *Britain: Industrial Relations and the Economy, 1900–39* (London, 1993), p. 19.

20 *Hansard 5 (Commons)*, xxxi, 1552 (24 November 1911); ibid., xxxii, 1290–3 (5 December 1911).

21 Ibid., xxxv, 2244–5 (22 March 1912).

22 Ibid., xxxvi, 245 (26 March 1912).

23 Ibid., 397–409 (26 March 1912).

24 *Hansard 4 (Commons)*, 195, 1322 (4 November 1908).

25 Stephen Koss, *Nonconformity in Modern British Politics* (London, 1975), pp. 16–17.

26 *Hansard 4 (Commons)*, 173, 403–6 (26 April 1907).

27 Gwylmor Prys Williams and George Thompson Brake, *Drink in Great Britain 1900–1979* (London, 1980), p. 42.

28 *Hansard 4 (Commons)*, 178, 1388, 1397, 1425, 1429 (23 July 1907); ibid., 179, 1385–92 (2 August 1907).

29 *Hansard 5 (Commons)*, i, 666 (23 February 1909).

30 Bruce K. Murray, *The People's Budget 1909/10: Lloyd George and Liberal Politics* (Oxford, 1980), *passim*, in particular pp. 178–9.

31 Cannadine, *Decline and Fall*, p. 48.

32 *The Times*, 14 March 1914.

33 Ibid., 20 July 1909.

34 David Dutton, *'His Majesty's Loyal Opposition': The Unionist Party in Opposition, 1905–1915* (Liverpool, 1992), pp. 69–77.

35 *The Times*, 8 January 1910.

36 Ibid., 16 April 1910.

37 During discussion of the Accession Declaration bill, Castlereagh gave a rare public airing of his religious outlook by asking the government to clarify the term 'Protestant' in the declaration. He felt this would ensure that only actual protestants could sit on the throne in case the 'meaning of the word "Protestant" might alter in years to come'. He did not elaborate on what he thought protestant meant, nor did he mention Catholics, but he did refer to atheists taking advantage of changing meanings (*Hansard 5* (*Commons*), xix, 2488 (28 July 1910)).

38 At this time Lord Castlereagh, through his wife's involvement with promoting women's healthcare, became president of the Chelsea Hospital for Sick Women, a position he held for much of his life (*The Times*, 19 April 1910).

39 J. A. Pauley, 'The Social and political Roles of Edith, Marchioness of Londonderry, 1878–1959', Ph.D. thesis (University of Ulster, 1994), chapters 2 and 3.

40 *The Times*, 19 April 1910. See also *Hansard 5* (*Commons*), xliii, 1083–4 (5 November 1912).

41 David R. Morgan, *Suffragists and Liberals: The Politics of Women's Suffrage in England* (Oxford, 1975), p. 71.

42 Brian Harrison, *Separate Spheres: The Opposition to Women's Suffrage in Britain* (London, 1978), p. 33.

43 Jose Harris, *Private Lives, Public Spirit: Britain 1870–1914* (London, 1994), pp. 29–32.

44 John D. Fair, *British Interparty Conferences: A study of the Procedure of Conciliation in British Politics, 1867–1921* (Oxford, 1980), pp. 77–102.

45 *Hansard 5* (*Commons*), xix, 1793–6 (25 July 1910).

46 Neal Blewett, *The Peers, the Parties and the People: The General Elections of 1910* (London, 1972), pp. 93–4.

47 *The Times*, 5 December 1910.

48 Ibid., 2 March 1911.

49 *Hansard 5* (*Commons*), xxiii, 2075 (4 April 1911).

50 Ibid., xxv, 238 (2 May 1911).

51 *The Times*, 28 July 1911.

52 Andrew Adonis, *Making Aristocracy Work: The Peerage and the Political System in Britain, 1884–1914* (rep. edn., Oxford, 2002), pp. 157–61.

53 Cannadine, *Decline and Fall*, p. 53.

54 Dutton, '*His Majesty's Loyal Opposition*', pp. 183–8; Anthony Howe, *Free Trade and Liberal England 1846–1946* (Oxford, 1997), pp. 237–9; David Dutton, *Austen Chamberlain: Gentleman in Politics* (Bolton, 1985), p. 42.

55 *The Times*, 8 January 1913; Castlereagh to Theresa, Lady Londonderry, 29 January 1912 (DCRO, D/Lo/C/682 (86)).

56 *Hansard 5* (*Commons*), xxxvi, 1459–66 (11 April 1912).

57 Alvin Jackson, *Home Rule: An Irish History, 1800–2000* (London, 2003), p. 187.

58 N. C. Fleming, 'The landed elite, power and northern unionism', in D. George Boyce and Alan O'Day (eds), *The Ulster Crisis* (London, 2005), forthcoming.

59 *Hansard 5 (Commons)*, xxxix, 1536–7 (18 June 1912).

60 Jennifer Todd, 'Unionist political thought, 1920–72', in D. George Boyce, Robert Eccleshall and Vincent Geoghegan (eds), *Political Thought in Ireland since the Seventeenth Century* (London, 1993), p. 192.

61 F. M. L. Thompson, 'Britain', in David Spring (ed.), *European Landed Elites in the Nineteenth Century* (London, 1977), pp. 22–3.

62 Edward Marjoribanks, *The Life of Lord Carson* (3 vols, 3rd edn., London, 1932), vol. 1, pp. 115, 163.

63 R. J. Q. Adams, *Bonar Law* (London, 1999), p. 65; Diane Urquhart, 'Peeresses, patronage and power: The politics of ladies Frances Anne, Theresa and Edith Londonderry, 1800–1959', in Alan Hayes and Diane Urquhart (eds), *Irish Women's History* (Dublin, 2004), p. 52.

64 A. T. Q. Stewart, *The Ulster Crisis: Resistance to Home Rule 1912–1914* (rep. edn., Belfast, 1999), pp. 50–2, 76–7; Paul Bew, *Ideology and the Irish question: Ulster Unionism and Irish Nationalism, 1912–1916* (Oxford, 1998), p. 92.

65 See for example *The Ulster Unionist Demonstration of 1912: In Royal Agricultural Show grounds, Balmoral, Belfast*, 9 April 1912 (PRONI, D/1507/A/3/14).

66 Castlereagh to Edith, Lady Castlereagh, 23 September 1912 (D/3099/13).

67 *The Times*, 26 September 1912.

68 Castlereagh to Theresa, Lady Londonderry, 24 September 1912 (DCRO, D/Lo/C 682 (93)); Castlereagh to Bonar Law, 7 December 1911 (HLRO, BL/24/5/114); Bonar Law to Castlereagh, 8 December 1911 (ibid., BL/33/3/30); Marquess of Londonderry, *Wings of Destiny* (London, 1943), p. 29.

69 Castlereagh to Edith, Lady Castlereagh, 25 September 1912 (D/3099/13).

70 Ronald McNeill, *Ulster's Stand for the Union* (London, 1922), p. 121; Andrew Gailey, 'King Carson: an essay on the invention of leadership', *Irish Historical Studies*, xxx, no. 117 (May 1996), pp. 66–87.

71 *Hansard 5 (Commons)*, xlii, 845–6 (14 October 1912).

72 Ibid., xxxix, 1760–63 (19 June 1912).

73 Ibid., xlii, 1347–51 (16 October 1912); *The Times*, 24 October 1912.

74 *Hansard 5 (Commons)*, xlii, 2483–6 (24 October 1912).

75 *The Times*, 29 October 1912; *Hansard 5 (Commons)*, xliii, 201–4 (28 October 1912).

76 Stewart, *Ulster Crisis*, pp. 67–8.

77 H. Montgomery Hyde, *Carson: The Life of Sir Edward Carson, Lord Carson of Duncairn* (London, 1953), pp. 340–1.

78 Stewart, *Ulster Crisis*, p. 77.

79 McNeill, *Ulster's Stand*, p. 230.

80 Copy notes detailing personnel and logistics of 'the North Belfast Regiment' (D/3099/8/1).

81 Stewart, *Ulster Crisis*, p. 122.

82 Records of the Ulster Volunteer Force (PRONI, Ulster Unionist Council papers, D/1327/4).

83 Trevor McCavery, *Newtown: A History of Newtownards* (Belfast, 1994), p. 181.

84 Ian Colvin, *The Life of Lord Carson*, vol. 2 (3 vols, London, 1934), p. 349.

85 Richardson to Londonderry, 29 April 1919 (D/3099/2/7/41).

86 Theresa, Lady Londonderry, 29 September 1915 (PRONI, D/3084/C/C/B/1/5).

87 Ill-health indisposed him during May 1913 (*The Times*, 1–3, 5, 10, 23 May 1913).

88 *Hansard* (*Commons*) (*General Index for 1913 session*), lvii, pp. 79–80; (*General index for 1914 session*), lxvii, pp. 110–11.

89 It is notable that Baldwin in 1913 spoke on eight different occasions but only five the following year. None of these speeches dealt with Ireland (*Hansard* (*Commons*) (*General index for 1913 session*), lvii, p 27; (*General Index for 1914 Session*), lxvii, pp. 44–5).

90 *The Times*, 19 April 1913. This followed an earlier denial that he was leaving Maidstone (ibid., 30 March 1913).

91 Paul Fussell, *The Great War and Modern Memory* (London, 1977), p. 21.

92 Cannadine, *Decline and Fall*, pp. 73–4.

93 Castlereagh to Lady Castlereagh, 26 September 1914 (D/3099/13)

94 Castlereagh to Lady Castlereagh, 2 September 1914 (ibid.).

95 Castlereagh to Lady Castlereagh, 24 September 1914 (D/3099/13)

96 Castlereagh to Lady Castlereagh, 7 December 1914 (ibid.). Castlereagh also expressed anger about Churchill's influence following the promotion of his political contemporary F. E. Smith to rank of major and general-staff officer, second grade (Castlereagh to Lady Castlereagh, 8 October 1914 (ibid.)).

97 Castlereagh to Lady Castlereagh, 5 September 1914 (ibid.)

98 Castlereagh to Lady Castlereagh, 8 November 1914 (ibid.).

99 Castlereagh to Lady Castlereagh, 24 September 1914 (ibid.)

100 Castlereagh to Lady Castlereagh, 22 December 1914 (D/3099/13).

101 H. Montgomery Hyde, *The Londonderrys: A Family Portrait* (London, 1979), p. 116.

102 *The Times*, 26 February 1915; Pulteney to Edith, Lady Londonderry, February 1915 (D/3099/3).

103 *The Times*, 17 February 1915.

104 Pulteney to Edith, Lady Londonderry, February 1915 (D/3099/13).

105 It is an irony, enjoyed by aristocrats, that Londonderry did achieve high rank in the army but in an honorary capacity. In April 1915 he was appointed Honorary Colonel of the fourth battalion, the Royal Irish Rifles and in August 1916 he held the same rank in the Durham Light Infantry (*The Times*, 14 April 1915, 13 August 1916).

106 Maureen Helen (1900–42); Edward Charles Stewart Robert (Robin) (1902–55); Margaret Frances Anne (1910–68); Helen Maglona (1911–86).

Mairi Elizabeth was born in 1921.

107 Theresa, Lady Londonderry, 15 September 1915 (PRONI, D/3084/C/C/B/1/4).

108 Londonderry to Blumenfeld, 22 June 1915 (HLRO, Blu/Lon/3).

109 E. A. Aston to Londonderry, 23 June 1915 (D/3099/8/1); 1 July 1916 (D/3099/2/7/1).

110 Londonderry to Lady Fingall, 26 November 1917 (D/3099/2/7/15).

111 *The Times*, 14 December 1917.

112 *The Times*, 11 August 1915.

113 Bates to Law, 12 February 1915 (HLRO, BL/36/3/33); Londonderry to Law, 18 February 1915 (ibid., BL/36/4/52).

114 Wimborne to Londonderry, 22 September 1915 (D/3099/8/2A).

115 Crawford to Londonderry, 8 October 1915 (D/3099/8/2).

116 Philip [L]ambury [?] to Londonderry, 12 October 1915 (D/3099/8/2E, F); [L]ambury to Londonderry, 13 October 1915 (D/3099/8/2G).

117 Londonderry to Lloyd George, 14 June 1916 (D/3099/2/7/6).

118 Lord Bangor to Londonderry, 9 October 1915 (D/3099/8/2C); Bates to Londonderry, 23 October 1915 (D/3099/8/2I). Bates even tried to persuade Londonderry to overturn the government's recommendation (Bates to Londonderry, 20 November 1915 (D/3099/8/2J); T. G. G. Mackintosh to D. W. Macklejohn (Wynyard estate office), 13 October 1915 (D/3099/8/2H). A Mr Daniel McCartan was appointed).

119 Theresa, Lady Londonderry, 20 October 1915 (PRONI, D/3084/C/C/B/1/6).

120 Londonderry to Lord French, 18 August 1918 (D/3099/8/3).

121 Theresa, Lady Londonderry, 13 December 1915 (PRONI, D/3084/C/C/B/1/9).

122 Theresa, Lady Londonderry, 29 November 1915 (ibid., D/3084/C/C/B/1/7).

123 Theresa, Lady Londonderry, 20 December 1915 (ibid., D/3084/C/C/B/1/10).

124 Londonderry to Hankey, 16 July 1916 (D/3099/2/4/7).

125 Hyde, *Londonderrys*, p. 128.

126 Theresa, Lady Londonderry, 3 September 1916 (PRONI, D/3084/C/C/B/1/13).

127 See Herbert Buckmaster, *Buck's Book: Ventures-Adventures and Misadventures* (London, 1933), pp. 134, 162.

128 Londonderry's military records were destroyed along with many others during a Luftwaffe raid on London (PRO, WO/374/70388).

129 C. A. Court Repington to Lloyd George, 17 July 1917 (HLRO, LG/F/43/4/2).

130 Capper to Londonderry, 25 July 1917 (D/3099/2/4/13).

131 Derby to Londonderry, 10 October 1917 (D/3099/2/8/4).

132 Derby to Londonderry, 7 December 1917 (D/3099/2/8/5).

133 Londonderry to Edith, Lady Londonderry, 6 December 1917 (D/3099/2/8/13).

134 Derby to Londonderry, 31 May 1918 (D/3099/2/8/10).

2. Ireland, 1916–1918

1 *The Times*, 16 May 1916 (dated the 14th).

2 A. R. Preston to Londonderry, 17 May 1916 (PRONI, Londonderry papers hereafter cited as D/3099, D/3099/2/7/3A); Rev. Dr Francis Knight to Londonderry, 19 May 1916 (D/3099/2/7/3B)); William Buchan to Londonderry, 24 May 1916 (D/3099/2/7/4). See also Col. Rowan Hamilton to Londonderry, 14 May 1916 (D/3099/2/7/2).

3 John D. Fair, *British Interparty Conferences: A Study of the Procedure of Conciliation in British Politics, 1867–1921* (Oxford, 1980), pp. 125–6.

4 Theresa, Lady Londonderry, 10 August 1916 (PRONI, D/3084/C/C/B/1/11).

5 Londonderry to Theresa, Lady Londonderry, 13 June 1916 (DCRO, D/Lo/C/682).

6 Patrick Buckland, *Irish Unionism: One: The Anglo-Irish and the New Ireland 1885–1922* (Dublin, 1972), p. 60.

7 Alvin Jackson, *Home Rule: An Irish History, 1800–2000* (London, 2003), pp. 155–74

8 Long to Eaith, Lady Londonderry, 1 June 1916 (D/3099/8/3).

9 Londonderry to Lloyd George, 14 June 1916 (D/3099/2/7/6).

10 Edith, Lady Londonderry to McNeill, 3 July 1916 (D/3099/8/3).

11 McNeill to Edith, Lady Londonderry, 1 July 1916 (ibid.).

12 Long to Londonderry, 2 July 1916 (ibid.).

13 Londonderry, notes for a letter to Edith, Lady Londonderry, n.d. (ibid.).

14 Kenneth O. Morgan, *Consensus and Disunity: The Lloyd George Coalition Government, 1918–1922* (Oxford, 1979), p. 14 and *passim*.

15 Nicholas Mansergh, *The Unresolved Question: The Anglo-Irish Settlement and its Undoing 1912–72* (London, 1991), p. 103. See also Alan O'Day, *Irish Home Rule 1867–1921* (Manchester, 1998), p. 278.

16 R. B. McDowell, *Irish Convention, 1917–18* (London, 1970), pp. 77–8; Carson to Dawson Bates, 23 May 1917 (D/3099/2/7/7).

17 H. C. Plunkett, *The Irish Convention: Confidential Report to His Majesty The King by the Chairman* (Dublin, 1918), p. 5.

18 Midleton to Londonderry, 15 June 1917 (D/3099/2/7/8).

19 Lloyd George to Londonderry, 22 June 1917 (D/3099/2/7/9); William Sutherland to Londonderry, 17 July 1917 (D/3099/2/7/10A).

20 *Hansard 5 (Lords)*, xxv, 224–5 (21 May 1917). Londonderry had an audience with George V the following day.

21 *The Times*, 22 May 1917.

22 'Minutes of the Ulster Unionist Delegation to the Irish Convention' (PRONI, D/1327/3/17).

23 Ulster delegation minutes, 21 July, 7 August 1917 (ibid.).
24 H. C. Plunkett, *Report of the Proceedings of the Irish Convention* (Dublin, 1918), pp. 9–10; Carla King, 'Defenders of the union: Sir Horace Plunkett', in D. George Boyce and Alan O'Day (eds), *Defenders of the Union: A Survey of British and Irish Unionism since 1801* (London, 2001), pp. 137–54.
25 *Confidential Report*, pp. 11–12.
26 Londonderry to Theresa, Lady Londonderry, 29 August 1917 (DCRO, D/Lo/C/682 (241)); Jackson, *Home Rule*, p. 185.
27 *Confidential Report*, p. 13.
28 Nicholas Allen, 'National Reconstruction: George Russell (Æ) and the Irish Convention', in D. George Boyce and Alan O'Day (eds), *Ireland in Transition, 1867–1921* (London, 2004), p. 132.
29 *Confidential Report*, p. 18.
30 McDowell, *Irish Convention*, p. 112.
31 Londonderry to Desborough, 1 September 1917 (PRONI, T/3201/29).
32 Derby to Londonderry, 8 September 1917 (D/3099/2/8/2).
33 Londonderry to Theresa, Lady Londonderry, 23 September 1917 (DCRO, D/Lo/C/682 (245)).
34 *Confidential Report*, pp. 7–8. Pollock had replaced Sir Alexander McDowell due to the latter's illness.
35 Four representatives of labour were also permitted seats (*Confidential Report*, p. 42).
36 Midleton to Londonderry, 25 October 1917 (D/3099/2/7/14).
37 McDowell, *Irish Convention*, pp. 121–2.
38 *Report of the Proceedings*, p. 16.
39 Barrie and Londonderry to Plunkett, 14 November 1917 (*Report of the Proceedings*, pp. 68–9).
40 *Confidential Report*, p. 51.
41 John Kendle, *Ireland and the Federal Solution: The Debate over the United Kingdom Constitution, 1870–1921* (Kingston and Montreal, 1989), p. 188; Grey to Dunraven, August, 1917 (D/3099/2/7/12).
42 John Turner, *Lloyd George's Secretariat* (Cambridge, 1980), p. 103; Jackson, *Home Rule*, p. 189.
43 *Confidential Report*, p. 51.
44 Duffin to Londonderry, 16 November 1917 (Patrick Buckland (ed.), *Irish Unionism 1885–1923: A Documentary History* (Belfast, 1973), pp. 422–3).
45 The Ulster delegation minutes jump from 12 November to the 17 December 1917 (PRONI, D/1327/3/17).
46 *Confidential Report*, p. 52.
47 Londonderry to Fingall, 26 November 1917 (D/3099/2/7/15).
48 Fingall to Londonderry, 28 November 1917 (D/3099/2/7/16).
49 Adams to Lloyd George, 10 December 1917 (Turner, *Lloyd George's Secretariat*, p. 104); Southborough to Adams, 17 December 1917 (McDowell, *Irish Convention*, p. 136); Plunkett to Londonderry, 21 December 1917 (ibid.).

50 *Report of the Proceedings*, p. 18; Ulster delegation minutes, 18 December 1917 (PRONI, D/1327/3/17).

51 Mahon to Londonderry, 3 December 1917 (D/3099/2/7/17).

52 See Ulster delegation minutes, 20, 22, 27 August 1917 (PRONI, D/1327/3/17)).

53 McDowell, *Irish Convention*, p. 143.

54 Ulster delegation minutes, 1 January 1918 (PRONI, D/1327/3/17).

55 Ulster delegation minutes, 3 January 1918 (PRONI, D/1327/3/17); *Confidential Report*, p. 62.

56 *Confidential Report*, p. 62.

57 McDowell, *Irish Convention*, p. 146.

58 Ibid.

59 Londonderry to Theresa, Lady Londonderry, 21 January 1918 (DCRO, D/Lo/C/682 (258)); Earl of Midleton, *Records and Reactions, 1856–1939* (New York, 1939), p. 242.

60 *The Times*, 12, 25 January 1918.

61 *Confidential Report*, p. 67.

62 Londonderry to Theresa, Lady Londonderry, 21 January 1918 (DCRO, D/Lo/C/682 (258)).

63 Londonderry to Edith, Lady Londonderry, 3 February 1918 (D/3099/13/1/886).

64 McDowell, *Irish Convention*, p. 156.

65 Jackson, *Home Rule*, p. 191.

66 McDowell, *Irish Convention*, p. 162.

67 Barrie to Londonderry, 16 February 1918 (D/3099/8/3).

68 Lloyd George to Barrie, 21 February 1918 (McDowell, *Irish Convention*, p. 163).

69 Londonderry to Carson, 21 February 1918 (D/3099/8/3).

70 Ulster delegation minutes, 25 February 1918 (PRONI, D/1327/3/17).

71 Montgomery to Londonderry, 26 February 1918 (Buckland, *Irish Unionism*, pp. 425–6).

72 Londonderry to Theresa, Lady Londonderry, 27 February 1918 (DCRO, D/Lo/C/682 (99)).

73 Theresa, Lady Londonderry to Law, 13 January 1918 (HLRO, BL/102/1/22); Balfour to Law, 28 February 1918 (HLRO, BL/82/9/20).

74 McDowell, *Irish Convention*, p. 168.

75 Londonderry to Lady Desborough, 16 March 1918 (PRONI, T/3201/31).

76 *Report of the Proceedings*, p. 116

77 Ibid., pp. 30–4; *Confidential Report*, pp. 134–7.

78 McDowell, *Irish Convention*, p. 188.

79 David Lloyd George, *War Memoirs of David Lloyd George*, vol. 2 (2 vols, London, 1938), p. 1600.

80 *The Times*, 18 April 1918.

81 Ibid., 21 June 1918.

82 Eunan O'Halpin, *The Decline of the Union: British Government in Ireland, 1892–1920* (Dublin, 1997), p. 159.

83 *Hansard 5 (Lords)*, 30, 289–99 (20 June 1918).

84 Theresa, Lady Londonderry to Law, 13 January 1918 (HLRO, BL/102/1/22).

85 Balfour to Law, 28 February 1918 (HLRO, BL/82/9/20).

86 Law to Balfour, 1 March 1918 (HLRO, BL/84/7/8).

87 *The Times*, 31 July 1918.

88 Derby to Londonderry, 14 June 1918 (D/3099/2/8/11); Andrew Adonis, *Making Aristocracy Work: The Peerage and the Political System in Britain, 1884–1914* (rep. edn., Oxford, 2002), pp. 35–40.

89 Duffin to Londonderry, 23 June 1918 (D/3099/2/7/26).

90 *The Belfast News-Letter*, 13 July 1918. The sixth Marquess had attended a 'Twelfth' at Finaghy in 1911, remarking that it was the first occasion a former Viceroy had done so (H. Montgomery Hyde, *Carson: The Life of Sir Edward Carson, Lord Carson of Duncairn* (London, 1953), p. 286); the seventh Marquess later spoke at a 'Twelfth' at Ballymanoch (*The Times*, 14 July 1919).

91 Austen Morgan, *Labour and Partition: The Belfast Working Class, 1905–23* (London, 1991), pp. 215–28.

92 *The Times*, 15 July 1918.

93 Barrie to Londonderry, 24 April 1918 (D/3099/8/3).

94 Kendle, *Federal Solution*, pp. 110, 187.

95 Frewen to Londonderry, 26 June 1918 (D/3099/8/3).

96 Frewen to Londonderry, 30 June 1918 (D/3099/8/3).

97 Literary Editor of the *National News* to A. D. Mayhew (Londonderry House), 30 July 1918 (D/3099/8/3).

98 Londonderry to Lloyd George, 13 August 1918 (D/3099/2/7/27).

99 Londonderry to French, 18 August 1918 (D/3099/8/3).

100 French to Londonderry, 19 August 1918 (D/3099/2/7/29).

101 Saunderson to Londonderry, 23 August 1918 (D/3099/2/7/30).

102 O'Halpin, *The Decline*, p. 171.

103 Londonderry to Carson, 4 September 1918 (PRONI, D/1507/A/19/1).

104 Bates, memorandum, 31 August 1918 (D/3099/8/3); O'Halpin, *The Decline*, p. 168.

105 Bates to Carson, 26 August 1918 (D/3099/8/3), Bates to Londonderry, 26 August 1918 (D/3099/8/3); Londonderry to Saunderson, 27 August 1918 (D/3099/8/3).

106 Bates to Londonderry, 3 September 1918 (ibid.).

107 Londonderry to Carson, 4 September 1918 (PRONI, D/1507/A/19/1).

108 O'Halpin, *The Decline*, p. 171.

109 Council minutes, 10 October 1918 (D/3099/8/3).

110 Long, memorandum, 9 October 1918 (ibid.).

111 Council minutes, 10 October 1918 (ibid.).

112 Council minutes, 10 October 1918 (ibid.); *The Times*, 24 October, 29 November 1918.

113 Viceroy's advisory council notice, October 1918 (D/3099/8/3).

114 *The Maidstone Journal*, 14 December 1905. See series of letters from T. P. Gill to Londonderry, 1918 (D/3099/8/3); P. J. McAndrew to Londonderry, 19 December 1918 (D/3099/2/7/36)). Londonderry exhibited an interest in Irish agriculture when he served in the Northern Ireland government (see Salisbury to Law, 22 February 1923 (HLRO, BL/111/29/145); *The Times*, 23 February 1923).

115 Saunderson to Londonderry, enclosing a series of letters on the issue from Frank Brooke and others, 2 November 1918 (D/3099/8/3).

116 Alvin Jackson, 'Irish unionism, 1870–1922', in D. George Boyce and Alan O'Day (eds), *Defenders of the Union: A Survey of British and Irish Unionism Since 1801* (London, 2001), p. 115.

3. The Air Ministry, 1919–1921

1 Jim Mac Loughlin, *Reimagining the Nation-State: The Contested Terrains of Nation-Building* (London, 2001), *passim*; David Cannadine, *Aspects of Aristocracy: Grandeur and Decline in Modern Britain* (London, 1994), pp. 9–36. See also Linda Colley, *Britons: Forging the Nation, 1707–1837* (London, 1992), pp. 155–9. For dissenting view see Ellis Wasson, *Born to Rule: British Political Elites* (London, 2000), p. 146.

2 A. J. P. Taylor, *English History, 1914–1945* (rep. edn., Oxford, 1990), pp. 126–8.

3 Londonderry to Lord Derby, 12 May 1918 (John Turner, *British politics and the Great War: Coalition and Conflict, 1915–1918* (New Haven, 1992), p. 300).

4 Londonderry to Lord Edmund Talbot, 28 August 1918 (PRONI, Londonderry papers hereafter cited as D/3099, D/3099/7/1).

5 David Cannadine, *Decline and Fall of the British Aristocracy* (rev. edn., London, 1996), p. 143.

6 Martin to Londonderry, 31 August 1918 (D/3099/7/1).

7 Londonderry to Appleby, 28 August 1918 (D/3099/7/1); Londonderry to Martin, 10 September 1918 (D/3099/7/1).

8 Appleby to Londonderry, 2 September 1918 (D/3099/7/1).

9 Londonderry to Appleby, 7 September 1918 (D/3099/7/1).

10 John Grigg, 'Churchill and Lloyd George', in Robert Blake and Wm. Roger Louis (eds), *Churchill* (Oxford, 1996), p. 104.

11 Londonderry to Theresa, Lady Londonderry, 13 January 1919 (DCRO, D/Lo/C 682 (256)).

12 Long to Lloyd George, n.d. [1918] (HLRO, LG/F/33/2/5).

13 Kathleen Burk, 'The Treasury: from impotence to power', in Kathleen Burk (ed.), *War and the State: The Transformation of Government, 1914–1919* (London, 1982), p. 97.

14 *The Times*, 16 January, 12 February 1919.

15 Theresa, Lady Londonderry, 23 December 1918 (PRONI, D/3084/C/C/B/1/15).

230   THE MARQUESS OF LONDONDERRY

16   Theresa, Lady Londonderry, 5 December 1918 (PRONI, D/3084/C/C/B/1/14).

17 H. Montgomery Hyde, *British Air Policy Between the Wars, 1918–1939* (London, 1976), p. 59.

18 Marquess of Londonderry, *Wings of Destiny* (London, 1943), p. 14.

19 *The Times*, 5 February 1919.

20 Londonderry, *Wings of Destiny*, p. 17.

21 Hyde, *Air Policy*, p. 74.

22 Londonderry, *Wings of Destiny*, p. 14.

23 Seely to Londonderry, 4 April 1920 (D/3099/2/9/7).

24 Londonderry, *Wings of Destiny*, p. 18.

25 Curzon to Law, 17 June 1918 (HLRO, BL/83/4/12). It was characteristic of Londonderry, e.g., during his second term at the Air Ministry, in 1934, he had his daughter Margaret officially reprimanded by the ministry for flying too low over Windsor Castle (Londonderry to Sir F. Humphrys, 13 March 1934 (D/3099/2/16/34)). The sixth Marquess of Londonderry had helped Curzon acquire his Irish peerage (David Gilmour, *Curzon* (London, 1994), p. 375).

26 *The Times*, 19 December 1919; he had the King and Queen to dinner in Londonderry House the following year (*The Times*, 24 June 1920); Curzon to Lloyd George, 27 November 1919 (HLRO, LG/F/12/2/6).

27 Churchill to Londonderry, 25 December 1919 (D/3099/2/5/5).

28 Londonderry to Law, 28 January 1920 (HLRO, BL/100/1/46); Edith, Lady Londonderry to Law, 29 January 1920 (HLRO, BL/100/1/47); Law to Tyron, 31 March 1920 (HLRO, BL/101/4/22); Londonderry, *Wings of Destiny*, p. 19; Churchill to Londonderry, 7 April 1920 (D/3099/2/5/6); Seely to Londonderry, 4 April 1920 (D/3099/2/9/7).

29 *The Times*, 3 April 1920.

30 Cannadine, *Decline and Fall*, p. 588.

31 Londonderry to Milner, 3 May 1920 (D/3099/2/7/52; D/3099/2/4/23). During his 1911 visit to Canada Londonderry recorded a mild dislike of Canadians (Castlereagh to Theresa, Lady Londonderry, 21 September 1911 (DCRO, D/Lo/C/682 (78))). See also *The Times*, 13 September 1911; Castlereagh to Lord Robin Vane-Tempest-Stewart, 21 September 1911 (DCRO, D/Lo/C/682 (77)).

32 Milner to Londonderry, 5 May 1920 (D/3099/2/4/24).

33 John Robert Ferris, *Men, Money, and Diplomacy: The Evolution of British Strategic Policy, 1919–26* (New York, 1989), p. 68.

34 Londonderry, *Wings of Destiny*, p. 9.

35 Trenchard to Londonderry, 26 September 1919 (D/3099/2/9/4).

36 Hyde, *Air Policy*, p. 99.

37 Trenchard to Londonderry, June 1920 (D/3099/2/9/11); Trenchard to Londonderry, 16 June 1920 (D/3099/2/9/6).

38 *The Times*, 10 July 1920. See also ibid., 22 April 1920.

39 Londonderry, *Wings of Destiny*, p. 14.

40 G. H. Bennett, *British Foreign Policy During the Curzon Period, 1919–24* (New York, 1995), p. 107.

41 Anthony Clayton, 'Imperial defence and security, 1900–1968', in Judith M. Brown and Wm. Roger Louis (eds), *The Oxford History of the British Empire, vol. iv: The Twentieth Century* (Oxford, 1999), p. 287.

42 Trenchard to Londonderry, 26 August 1920 (D/3099/2/9/8).

43 *Hansard 5 (Lords)*, 44, 1064–71 (20 April 1921); Glen Balfour-Paul, 'Britain's informal empire in the middle east', in Judith M. Brown and W. Roger Louis (eds), *The Oxford History of the British Empire, vol. iv: The Twentieth Century* (Oxford, 1999), p. 498.

44 *Hansard 5 (Lords)*, 40, 223–33 (11 May 1920). He later proposed that the City of London be allowed to have an aerodrome despite the obvious lack of space: 'developments might take place in aviation which would change the position in that respect' (*The Times*, 10 June 1920).

45 Ibid., 8 March 1921.

46 Ibid., 11 March 1921.

47 Ibid., 19 March 1921.

48 Londonderry, *Wings of Destiny*, p. 19.

49 Morgan, *Consensus and Disunity*, p. 115.

50 *Coal Industry Commission: Report and Minutes of Evidence*, vol. 2 (Cmd. 360), P.P. (1919), XII, 631–3.

51 Carson to Londonderry, 8 January 1921 (D/3099/2/7/56); Carson to Londonderry, 6 June 1921 (D/3099/2/7/59)). When the Better Government of Ireland bill was going through parliament Carson warned Londonderry that there was 'a good deal of comment' that they were not speaking up for unionism (Carson to Londonderry, 5 December 1920 (D/3099/2/7/54)). When Londonderry supported the bill he noted the paradox of an anti-home rule campaigner voting for a home rule parliament (*Hansard 5 (Lords)*, 42, 541–49 (24 November 1920)).

52 *The Times*, 31 May 1921; Law to Londonderry, 31 May 1921 (HLRO, BL/101/5/30).

53 Guest to Londonderry, 23 July 1921 (Londonderry, *Wings of Destiny*, p. 20).

54 He was given a permit to fly to the Paris peace conferences on 11 March 1919, but there is little otherwise to indicate that he had any involvement with the negotiations (Air Ministry permit, 10 March 1919 (D/3099/2/9/3)).

4. Northern Ireland, 1921–1926

1 Mary Harris, *The Catholic Church and the Foundation of the Northern Irish State* (Cork, 1993), p. 197.

2 Patrick Buckland, *Irish Unionism: Two: Ulster Unionism and the Origins of Northern Ireland, 1886–1922* (Dublin, 1973), pp. 127–46.

3 Paul Bew, Peter Gibbon and Henry Patterson, *Northern Ireland 1921/2001:*

Political Forces and Social Classes (London, 2002), p. 60; Duke of Abercorn to Home Secretary, 13 January 1926 (PRO, HO/276/195).

4 See for example his call for Northern Ireland to become an agent of rapprochement between England and Ireland (*The Times*, 18 October 1923).

5 Andrew Gailey, 'The destructiveness of constructive unionism: theories and practice, 1890s–1960s', in D. George Boyce and Alan O'Day (eds), *Defenders of the Union: A Survey of British and Irish Unionism since 1801* (London, 2001), pp. 227–46.

6 Jennifer Todd, 'Unionist political thought, 1920–72', in D. George Boyce, Robert Eccleshall and Vincent Geoghegan (eds), *Political thought in Ireland since the Seventeenth Century* (London, 1993), p. 191.

7 Marquess of Londonderry, *Wings of Destiny* (London, 1943), pp. 20–1.

8 Londonderry to Lloyd George, 17 November 1918 (HLRO, KG/F/29/2/65).

9 Londonderry to F. G. Kellaway (Ministry of Munitions), 21 November 1919 (PRO, MUN/4/5847); Kellaway to Londonderry, 22 November 1919 (PRO, MUN/4/5847).

10 *The Times*, 8 April 1920.

11 Ibid., 25 January, 17, 24 June 1921; D. George Boyce, 'Conservative opinion, the Ulster question, and the partition of Ireland, 1912–21', *Irish Historical Studies*, xvii, no. 65 (March 1970), p. 103.

12 George Russell to Londonderry, 2 April [1920] (PRONI, Londonderry papers hereafter cited as D/3099, D/3099/2/7/58); F. S. L. Lyons, *Culture and Anarchy in Ireland, 1890–1939* (Oxford, 1979), p. 111.

13 Blanche E. C. Dugdale, *Arthur James Balfour, First Earl of Balfour, K.G., O.M., F.R.S., etc.* (2 vols, London, 1936), vol. 1, pp. 324–5.

14 Craig to Londonderry, 29 April 1921 (D/3099/2/10/1); *The Times*, 31 May, 8 June 1921; Hugh O'Neill to Londonderry, 11 June 1921 (DCRO, D/Lo/F/593 (2)).

15 Churchill to Londonderry, 20 May 1921 (D/3099/2/5/14).

16 *Hansard N.I. (Senate)*, i, 30–8, 42–3 (20 September 1921). Londonderry had been hostile to direct talks between Sinn Féin and the government earlier in the year (Cabinet Conclusions, 16 July 1921 (PRONI, CAB/4/8/3)).

17 Londonderry to Salisbury, 1 September 1921 (D/3099/8/1); see also Londonderry to Salisbury, 2 September 1921 (D/3099/8/1).

18 *The Times*, 7 December 1921.

19 Sinead McCoole, *Hazel: A Life of Lady Lavery 1880–1935* (Dublin, 1996), pp. 77–82.

20 Lady Lavery to Michael Collins, undated but probably 14 December 1921 (Leon Ó Bróin (ed.), *In Great Haste: The Letters of Michael Collins and Kitty Kiernan* (Dublin, 1996), p. 90).

21 Hyde, *Londonderrys*, p. 150.

22 Londonderry later dismissed the idea of a Londonderry-Collins pact as a 'complete fallacy' (Londonderry to Churchill, 5 August 1922 (DCRO, D/Lo/C/242 (6))).

23 Boyce, 'Conservative opinion', p. 107.

24 *The Times*, 16 December 1921; Londonderry to R. D. Blumenfeld (editor of the *Daily Express*), 12 November 1921 (HLRO, Blu/Lon/6).

25 Cabinet Conclusions, 28 November 1921 (PRONI, CAB/4/27/4).

26 Maurice Cowling, *The Impact of Labour 1920–40: The Beginning of Modern British Politics* (Cambridge, 1971), p. 143.

27 *Hansard 5 (Lords)*, 48, 58–70 (15 December 1921).

28 Alvin Jackson, *Sir Edward Carson* (Dundalk, 1993), pp. 61–2.

29 J. Mulhall to Londonderry, 16 December 1921 (D/3099/2/7/65); John Ross to Londonderry, 19 December 1921 (D/3099/2/7/66).

30 *The Times*, 24 June 1921; Lord Fitz-Alan to Londonderry, 10 December 1921 (D/3099/2/4/28); Lord Stamfordham to Londonderry, 10 December 1921 (D/3099/2/4/29); *The Times*, 10 March 1922.

31 Londonderry to Robert McKeown, 11 September 1922 (D/3099/2/7/77).

32 This was not restricted to constitutional questions, e.g., Londonderry successfully opposed a bill that would have prevented women from being jurors (Cabinet Conclusions, 25 February 1925 (PRONI, CAB/4/135/18)).

33 Bates to Londonderry, 20 April 1923 (D/3099/2/7/82); Cosgrave to Londonderry, 1 May 1923 (D/3099/2/7/83).

34 Buckland, *Irish Unionism: Two*, p. 176. See also Brian Follis, *A State Under Siege: The Establishment of Northern Ireland, 1920–1925* (Oxford, 1995), *passim*.

35 Cabinet Conclusions, 26 January 1922 (PRONI, CAB/4/30/1).

36 Cabinet Conclusions, 13 March 1922 (PRONI, CAB/4/35/16).

37 Londonderry to Pakenham, 30 October 1935 (Hyde, *Londonderrys*, p. 152).

38 Londonderry to Lionel Curtis, 5 October 1922 (DCRO, D/Lo/C/242 (2)).

39 Anne de Courcy, *Circe: The Life of Edith, Marchioness of Londonderry* (London, 1993), pp. 166–7; McCoole, *Hazel*, pp. 86–8.

40 Wilson, diary, 14 January 1922 (C. E. Callwell (ed.), *Field Marshal Sir Henry Wilson: His Life and Diaries* (London, 1927), p. 320).

41 *The Times*, 17 April 1922; Londonderry to Strachey, 15 April 1922 (HLRO, STR/9/15/8).

42 Londonderry to Strachey, 31 December 1922 (HLRO, STR/9/15/9).

43 Wilson to Craig, 19 April 1922 (PRONI, T/3775/17/2); Londonderry to Churchill, 2 April 1922 (DCRO, D/Lo/C/242(16)).

44 Patrick Buckland, *The Factory of Grievances: Devolved Government in Northern Ireland, 1921–39* (Dublin, 1979), p. 206.

45 *Hansard N.I. (Senate)*, 2, 10 (14 March 1922); Michael Farrell, *Northern Ireland: The Orange State* (rep. edn., London, 1992), p. 51.

46 Cabinet Conclusions, 23 May 1922 (PRONI, CAB/4/44); *The Times*, 14 July 1922; Paul Canning, *British Policy Towards Ireland 1921–1941* (Oxford, 1985), p. 61.

47 See Strachey to Londonderry, 10 April 1922 (HLRO, STR/9/15/8).

48 Bew, Gibbon and Patterson, *Northern Ireland*, pp. 24–6; Tallents' report to the British Cabinet and diary, June 1922 (PRO, PRO/CO/906/24).

49 Marchioness of Londonderry, *Retrospect* (London, 1938), p. 212.

50 R. J. Q. Adams, *Bonar Law* (London, 1999), pp. 350–2; Londonderry, *Wings of Destiny*, pp. 28–9.

51 Londonderry to Law, 1 December 1921 (HLRO, BL/107/1/82); *The Times*, 28 July 1922.

52 Chaplin to Law, 20 October 1922 (ibid., BL/109/1/19); Salisbury to Law, 22 October 1922 (ibid., BL/109/2/32).

53 *The Times*, 4 September 1922.

54 Stuart Ball, *The Conservative Party and British Politics, 1902–1951* (London, 1995), p. 76.

55 Londonderry to Robert McKeown, 9 September 1922 (D/3099/2/7/76).

56 Londonderry to Law, 24 October 1922 (HLRO, BL/109/2/27a).

57 Londonderry to Desborough, 25 October 1922 (PRONI, T/3201/33).

58 Londonderry to Law, 25 October 1922 (HLRO, BL/109/2/27b).

59 Londonderry to Strachey, 31 December 1922 (ibid., STR/9/15/9).

60 For Law's intentions see Peter Townsend, *Duel of the Skies: The Struggle for the Skies from the First World War to the Battle of Britain* (rep. edn., London, 2000), p. 50.

61 Edith, Lady Londonderry to Law, 26 October 1922 (HLRO, BL/109/2/13a).

62 Law to Edith, Lady Londonderry, 2 November 1922 (ibid., BL/109/2/13b).

63 Ralph Lambton to Londonderry, 6 November 1922 (D/3099/2/7/79); *The Times*, 25 October 1922.

64 Archbishop D'Arcy of Armagh to Craig, 8 November 1922 (PRONI, CAB/9T/3/1); Londonderry to Churchill, n.d. [1940s] (D/3099/2/17/78).

65 Strachey to Londonderry, 2 January 1923 (HLRO, STR/9/15/9); Londonderry to Strachey, 3 January 1923 (ibid., STR/9/15/9). It was not the only occasion that Londonderry complained about reports of his work in *The Spectator* (Strachey to Londonderry, 21 May 1919 (ibid.); Strachey to Londonderry, 14 March 1923 (ibid.)).

66 Cabinet Conclusions, 7 May 1924 (PRONI, CAB/4/113/9).

67 *Hansard N.I. (Senate)*, 4, 17 (11 March 1924); *The Times*, 2, 12 May, 12 June, 25 August 1924.

68 Londonderry to Henderson, 26 March 1924 (PRO, PREM/1/43); Londonderry to Henderson, 11 March 1924 (ibid., PREM/1/43).

69 *Hansard N.I. (Senate)*, 4, 117 (13 May 1924).

70 *The Times*, 4 August 1924.

71 Thomas Jones, diary, 2 February, 1924 (Keith Middlemas (ed.), *Thomas Jones Whitehall Diary, vol. 3: Ireland, 1918–1925* (London, 1971), p. 226.

72 *The Times*, 5 August 1924.

73 Ibid., 8 August 1924.

74 Jones, 8 August 1924 (Middlemas, *Jones Whitehall Diary*, vol. 3, p. 235).

75 Londonderry to McDonald, 9 August 1924 (D/3099/2/7/93).

76 See Stephen Evans, 'The conservatives and the redefinition of unionism, 1912–21', *Twentieth Century British History*, 9, no. 1 (1998).

77 Londonderry to Baldwin, 27 August 1924 (CUL, Baldwin 99, ff. 128–9).

78 Cabinet Conclusions, 16 September 1924 (PRONI, CAB/4/121).

79 Londonderry to Salisbury, 18 September 1924 (Kevin Matthews, *Fatal Influence: The Impact of Ireland on British Politics, 1920–1925* (Dublin, 2004), p. 177).

80 Londonderry to Lady Londonderry, 2 October 1924 (Hyde, *Londonderrys*, p. 162).

81 Matthews, *Fatal Influence*, p. 140.

82 Despite his low standing in the party the nationalist *Irish News* speculated in 1926 that Londonderry had an agreement with Craig to succeed him as Prime Minister (*The Irish News*, 9 January 1926). Craig later sentimentally referred to Londonderry as his 'right hand man' in speech given to the Lord Mayor's luncheon at Belfast, of course at this stage Londonderry had resigned (*The Times*, 26 January 1926).

83 Matthews, *Fatal Influence*, pp. 189–90.

84 For personal views of campaign see Londonderry to Blumenfeld, 2 November 1924 (HLRO, Blu/Lon/7) and Londonderry to Baldwin, 7 November 1924 (CUL, Baldwin 42, f 263); Londonderry to Churchill, 7 October 1924 (PRONI, D/3084/C/C/3/1); Londonderry to Churchill, 2 December 1923 (PRONI, D/3084/C/C/3/5).

85 *The Times*, 3 January 1925.

86 Londonderry   to   Churchill,   26   October   1925   (PRONI, D/3084/C/C/3/6A–D); Churchill to Londonderry, 30 October 1925 (D/3099/2/5/16); Londonderry to Churchill, 2 November 1925 (PRONI, D/3084/C/C/3/7A–B); Londonderry to Desborough, 21 November 1926 (PRONI, T/3201/48).

87 Lynn to Londonderry, 3 October 1925 (D/3099/2/11/8).

88 It is also clear that Craig was kept informed of the Commission's delibera-tions and that he did so with the greatest discretion, even denying such knowledge when challenged by Londonderry (Alvin Jackson, *Home Rule: An Irish History, 1800–2000* (London, 2003), p. 211).

89 Buckland, *Factory of Grievances*, pp. 247–65; Harris, *The Catholic Church*; Sean Farren, *The Politics of Irish Education, 1920–65* (Belfast, 1995); Michael McGrath, *The Catholic Church and Catholic Schools in Northern Ireland: The Price of Faith* (Dublin, 2000). For exception see D. H. Akenson, *Education and Enmity: The Control of Schooling in Northern Ireland, 1920–50* (London, 1973).

90 See Sydney H. Zebel, *Balfour: A Political Biography* (Cambridge, 1973), p. 118; Tony Taylor, *The Politics of Reaction: The Ideology of the Cecils and the Challenge of Secular Education, 1889–1902* (Leeds, 1997), *passim*.

91 St John Ervine, *Craigavon: Ulsterman* (London, 1949), p. 119.

92 For fond recollection of Londonderry by his departmental staff see Akenson, *Education and Enmity*, p. 41.

93 *Hansard N.I. (Senate)*, 1, 24 (23 June 1921). See also *The Times*, 6 December 1922; *Teacher's World*, no. 1 (10 January 1923).

94 Delays in transfer stretched into 1922 (Lewis McQuibban's notes, 10 May 1922 (D/3099/5/1).

95 Londonderry to Lynn, 30 August 1921 (PRONI, D/3480/59/42).

96 Londonderry to Logue, 29 August 1921 (PRONI, CAB/4/18/1).

97 Logue to Londonderry, 2 September 1921 (D/3099/2/7/61).

98 Londonderry to Fitz-Alan, 4 September 1921 (PRONI, CAB/4/18/13).

99 Cabinet Conclusions, 9 September 1921 (ibid., CAB/4/18/21).

100 Londonderry to Logue, 10 September 1921 (ibid., CAB/4/18/19).

101 Cabinet Conclusions, 15 December 1922 (PRONI, CAB/4/61/12); Bates to Londonderry, 28 November 1922 (D/3099/5/5).

102 Cabinet Conclusions, 11 January 1923 (ibid., CAB/4/66/21).

103 Londonderry to Lynn, 8 February 1923 (ibid., D/3480/59/44); Lynn to Londonderry, 19 February 1923 (ibid.).

104 Lynn to Senator Sam Cunningham, 16 March 1923 (D/3099/2/4/19B); Londonderry to Lynn, 10 June 1923 (PRONI, D/3480/59/46); Londonderry to Lynn, 21 February 1923 (ibid., D/3480/59/44).

105 Lynn to Londonderry, 6 October 1924 (D/3099/2/11/3); Lynn to Londonderry, 9 October 1924 (D/3099/2/11/4).

106 Cabinet Conclusions, 16 April 1923 (PRONI, CAB/4/77/15).

107 Address by Londonderry to members of the Ulster Reform Club, Belfast, 9 November 1923 (ibid., CAB/9D/1/4).

108 *Belfast Evening Telegraph*, 24 November 1922.

109 Cabinet Conclusions, 27 September 1923 (PRONI, CAB/4/86).

110 Ibid., 2 October 1923 (ibid., CAB/4/88).

111 Craig to Londonderry, 2 January 1923 (D/3099/2/10/2).

112 Cabinet Conclusions, 28 February 1923 (PRONI, CAB/4/72/16).

113 *Hansard N.I. (Commons)*, 3, 356 (17 April 1923).

114 *The Times*, 2 April 1924.

115 Archbishop D'Arcy to Londonderry, 9 March 1925 (D/3099/5/14/2); D'Arcy to Londonderry, 10 March 1925 (ibid.).

116 Secretary of the Grand Orange Lodge to Londonderry, 4 February 1925 (D/3099/5/9).

117 Hendriks to Londonderry, 3 February 1925 (D/3099/5/9). Orange leaders had always struggled to maintain control over populist working-class members, see Dominic Bryan, *Orange Parades: The Politics of Ritual, Tradition and Control* (London, 2000), *passim.*

118 Hendriks to Londonderry, 4 February 1925 (D/3099/5/9).

119 Minutes of the meeting between the Education Minister and a delegation from the Grand Orange Lodge of Belfast, 23 February 1925 (D/3099/5/9).

120 Cabinet Conclusions, 7 March 1925 (PRONI, CAB/4/137/10).

121 *The Times*, 13 March 1925; *Hansard N.I. (Senate)*, 5, 29–31 (13 March 1925). See also D'Arcy to Londonderry, 10 March 1925 (D/3099/5/14/2); *The Times*, 14 March 1925.

122 Buckland, *Factory*, pp. 254–5; Craig to Londonderry, 25 June 1925 (PRONI, CAB/9D/1/5).

123 Minutes of meeting of protestant church leaders and the Minister of Education, 2 April 1925 (D/3099/5/9).

124 *The Times*, 18 April 1925.

125 Cabinet Conclusions, 4 June 1925 (PRONI, CAB/4/145/15).

126 *The Times*, 12 June 1915.

127 Craig to Londonderry, 13 June 1925 (PRONI, CAB/9D/1/5).

128 Andrews to Craig, 17 June 1925 (ibid., CAB/9D/1/5).

129 Tallents' report to British Cabinet and diary, June 1922 (PRO, PRO/CO/906/24).

130 Craig to Wilfred Spender, 19 June 1925 (PRONI, CAB/9D/1/5).

131 Londonderry to Craig, 23 June 1925 (ibid., CAB/9D/1/5).

132 Londonderry to Craig, 23 June 1925 (ibid.).

133 Craig to Londonderry, 25 June 1925 (ibid.).

134 Lynn to Londonderry, 25 June 1925 (D/3099/2/11/7).

135 Craig to Dixon, 26 June 1925 (PRONI, CAB/9D/1/5).

136 *The Times*, 10 July 1925; Craig to Londonderry, 2 July 1925 (PRONI, CAB/9D/1/5).

137 Londonderry to Lynn, 29 July 1925 (ibid., D/3480/59/57).

138 Londonderry to Lionel Curtis, 5 October 1922 (DCRO, D/Lo/C/242 (2)); Cabinet Conclusions, 6 October 1922 (PRONI, CAB/4/54/13).

139 Londonderry to Wood, 1 December 1922 (D/3099/5/4).

140 Cabinet Conclusions, 29 October 1923 (PRONI, CAB/4/91/21).

141 J. A. Pauley, 'The Social and political Roles of Edith, Marchioness of Londonderry, 1878–1959', Ph.D. thesis (University of Ulster, 1994), p. 255.

142 Farren, *Education*, p. 43.

143 Londonderry to Churchill, 5 August 1922 (DCRO, D/Lo/C/242).

144 Cabinet Conclusions, 10 January 1922 (PRONI, CAB/4/29/15).

145 O'Donnell to Londonderry, 27 December 1924 (ibid., ED/21/1/4).

146 Londonderry to O'Donnell, January 1925 (ibid., ED/32/B/6/1/62).

147 Cabinet Conclusions, 27 January 1925 (ibid., CAB/4/134/28).

148 Don Handelman, cited in John Hutchinson and Anthony D. Smith (eds), *Ethnicity* (Oxford, 1996), p. 6.

149 Todd, 'Unionist political thought, 1920–72', p. 197.

5. Catering his way to the Cabinet? 1926–1931

1 John Campbell, *F. E. Smith, First Earl of Birkenhead* (London, 1983), p. 805.

2 Londonderry to Stanley Baldwin, 13 April 1926 (Keith Middlemas (ed.), *Thomas Jones Whitehall Diary: vol. 2: 1926–1930* (2 vols, London, 1969), p. 10).

3 Londonderry to Lady Desborough, 1926 (H. Montgomery Hyde, *The Londonderrys: A Family Portrait* (London, 1979), pp. 168–9).

4 *The Times*, 11 January 1926; Beaverbrook to Londonderry, 23 January 1926 (HLRO, BBK/C/224).

5 T. W. Moody and J. C. Beckett, *Queen's, Belfast 1845–1949: The History of a*

University (2 vols, London, 1959), vol. 2, p. 485.

6 Pauline Lynn, 'The impact of women. The shaping of political allegiance in county Durham 1918–1945', *The Local Historian* (August, 1998), pp. 159–75.

7 Huw Benyon and Terry Austrin, *Masters and Servants, Class Patronage in the Making of a Labour Organisation: The Durham Miners and the English Political Tradition* (London, 1994) p. 323; Stuart Ball, 'The national and regional party structure', in Anthony Seldon and Stuart Ball (eds), *Conservative Century: The Conservative Party since 1900* (Oxford, 1994), p. 209); Stuart Ball, 'Introduction', in Stuart Ball (ed.), *Parliament and Politics in the Age of Baldwin and MacDonald: The Headlam Diaries, 1923–1935* (London, 1992), p. 9.

8 Headlam, 3, 22 October 1926 (Ball, *Headlam Diaries*, p. 100).

9 Headlam, 30 November 1926, 20 July 1929, 22 February 1930 (*Headlam Diaries*, pp. 105, 177–8, 185).

10 Lady Londonderry to J. C. C. Davidson, 11 December 1929 (Robert Rhodes James (ed.), *Memoirs of a Conservative: J. C. C. Davidson's Memoirs and Papers, 1910–37* (London, 1969), pp. 311–2).

11 Benyon and Austrin, *Masters and Servants*, pp. 204–5.

12 *Coal Industry Commission: Report and Minutes of Evidence*, vol. 2 (Cmd. 360), P.P. (1919), XII, pp. 631–3.

13 J. Lee Thompson, *Northcliffe: Press Baron in Politics, 1865–1922* (London, 2000), pp. 349–53.

14 M. W. Kirby, *The British Coalmining Industry, 1870–1946* (London, 1977), pp. 66–91.

15 *The Times*, 9 January 1926; Barry Supple, *The History of the British Coal Industry: vol. 4: 1913–1946: The Political Economy of Decline* (Oxford, 1987), pp. 6–16. See also Londonderry to Strachey, 17 May 1924 (HLRO, STR/9/15/9); Strachey to Londonderry, 20 May 1924 (ibid., STR/9/15/11); Londonderry to Baldwin, 18 December 1925 (CUL, Baldwin 13, ff. 105–7)).

16 *The Times*, 11 January 1926.

17 Ibid., 12 January 1926.

18 Ibid., 23 January 1926; Marquess of Londonderry, *Wings of Destiny* (London, 1943), p. 34.

19 *The Times*, 28 January 1926. See Chris Cook, *The Age of Alignment: Electoral Politics in Britain, 1922–1929* (London, 1975), *passim*.

20 *The Times*, 27 January 1926.

21 Castlereagh to Adrian Holman, 1926 (Hyde, *Londonderrys*, p. 169). Castlereagh was sent to the USA in January 1926 to study its successful coal industry (*The Sunderland Echo*, 23 January 1926).

22 Londonderry to Sir Ronald Waterhouse (Prime Minister's Office), 1 March 1926 (CUL, Baldwin 13, f. 144); Waterhouse to Londonderry, 2 March 1926 (ibid., f. 145).

23 Londonderry to Baldwin, 13 April 1926 (Middlemas, *Jones Whitehall Diary*, vol. 2, p. 10).

24 Thomas to Londonderry, 14 April 1926 (PRONI, Londonderry papers here-after cited as D/3099, D/3099/2/4/36). See also Thomas to Londonderry, 18 May 1926 (D/3099/2/4/7).

25 Margaret Morris, *The General Strike* (Harmondsworth, 1976), p. 224.

26 Stuart Mews, 'The Churches', in Morris, *General Strike*, p. 326.

27 Julian Symons, *The General Strike: A Historical Portrait* (London, 1957), pp. 182–6.

28 Joyce Howson, 'The General Strike: a bluff which was called?', *Modern History Review*, 8, part 1 (September 1996), p. 21.

29 Londonderry to Baldwin, 15 May 1926 (CUL, Baldwin 137, f. 87).

30 *The Times*, 1 June 1926; Londonderry to Beaverbrook, 25 May 1926 (HLRO, BBK/C/224); Beaverbrook to Londonderry, 31 May 1926 (ibid.). Beaverbrook's initial enthusiasm for Londonderry was lessened by an invita-tion from the Londonderrys to support and report on an 'Anti Socialist Propaganda Ball' organised by Lady Londonderry at the Kit Kat Club, London. Annoyed, Beaverbrook declined (Edith, Lady Londonderry to Beaverbrook, 4 February 1926 (ibid.); Beaverbrook to Edith, Lady Londonderry, 6 February 1926 (ibid.)).

31 Londonderry to Jones, n.d. [June 1926] (CUL, Baldwin 20, f. 235).

32 *The Times* quotes from the *Colliery Guardian* article (*The Times*, 18 June 1926).

33 *The Times*, 18, 20 August 1926.

34 Henry Pelling, 'Churchill and the labour movement', in Robert Blake and Wm. Roger Louis (eds), *Churchill* (Oxford, 1996), p. 121.

35 Jones, 26 August 1926 (Middlemas, *Thomas Jones Diary*, vol. 2, p. 68).

36 Jones, 5 September 1926 (ibid., pp. 76–7).

37 Londonderry to Churchill, 6 September 1926 (PRONI, D/3084/C/C/3/8). See also Londonderry and D. R. Llewellyn to Baldwin, 6 September 1926 (CUL, Baldwin 18, f. 64).

38 Londonderry to Baldwin, 12 September 1926 (CUL, Baldwin 18, ff. 149–54).

39 Baldwin's office to Londonderry, 20 September 1926 (ibid., f. 155).

40 Londonderry to Churchill, 1926 (Hyde, *Londonderrys*, p. 172).

41 Churchill to Londonderry, 3 November 1926 (D/3099/2/5).

42 Open letter from Londonderry to Sidney Webb, 26 October 1926 (*The Times*, 26 October 1926). See also ibid., 16 October, 7 November, 4 December 1926.

43 Ibid., 17 December 1926.

44 Ibid., 10 January 1926.

45 Ibid., 14 January 1926; W. R. Garside, *The Durham Miners, 1919–1960* (London, 1971), p. 234.

46 Ross McKibbin, *The Ideologies of Class: Social Relations in Britain, 1880–1950* (rep. edn., Oxford, 1991), pp. 289–90.

47 *The Times*, 12, 13 April 1927.

48 *Hansard 5 (Lords)*, 68, 28–9 (30 June 1927).

49 Benyon and Austrin, *Masters and Servants*, p. 348.

50 *The Times*, 23, 30 December 1927, 18 June 1928.

51 Ibid., 14, 15 September 1928.

52 Ibid., 11 January 1932.

53 Benyon and Austrin, *Masters and Servants*, p. 336; Headlam, 27 September 1933 (Ball, *Headlam Diaries*, pp. 279–80). See also his Christmas gift of coal to miners in 1933 (*The Times*, 18 December 1933). Londonderry's prominence in the industrial affairs of the region was recognised in 1932 when he was appointed president of the North Eastern Development Board (ibid., 19 December 1932).

54 See ibid., 26 October 1928; Londonderry to Baldwin, 5 March 1929 (CUL, Baldwin 85, ff. 144–6).

55 Lady Londonderry's comments in 1931 referred to an accusation made in 1929 by the Labour MP for Newcastle, Sir Charles Trevelyan (*The Times*, 27 October 1931). Lord Londonderry strongly disliked Trevelyan: 'I think the man must be literally mad because he talks of nothing but his riches, but takes no steps whatsoever to reduce them. I should have thought that there was nothing easier than for a rich man to become poor' (Londonderry to R. D. Blumenfeld, 4 November 1931 (HLRO, BLU/Lon/8)).

56 James, *Davidson*, p. 405.

57 *The Times*, 29 July 1927; Royal Commission on London Squares, Minutes and Papers (PRO, HLG/10/1).

58 *Hansard 5 (Lords)*, 72, 1022–3 (21 February 1929).

59 David Cannadine, *The Decline and Fall of the British Aristocracy* (rev. edn., London, 1992), p. 581.

60 Richard Kelly, 'The party conferences', in Anthony Seldon and Stuart Ball (eds), *Conservative Century: The Conservative Party Since 1900* (Oxford, 1994), p. 241.

61 Philip Williamson, *Stanley Baldwin: Conservative Leadership and National Values* (Cambridge, 1999), pp. 219–20.

62 Macmillan to Londonderry, 9 October 1927 (D/3099/2/13/A/4B).

63 *The Times*, 7 October 1927.

64 John W. Hills assured Londonderry that 'history will justify' his position and not the die-hards (Hills to Londonderry, 8 October 1927 (D/3099/2/13/A/3B)); Churchill to Londonderry, 22 October 1927 (D/3099/2/21/A/274).

65 Cannadine, *Decline and Fall*, p. 352.

66 Channon, diary, 8 June 1935 (Robert Rhodes James (ed.), *Chips: The Diaries of Sir Henry Channon* (London, 1967), p. 35).

67 Robert Vansittart, *The Mist Procession: The Autobiography of Lord Vansittart* (London, 1958), p. 452.

68 Ross McKibbin, *Class and Cultures: England, 1918–1951* (Oxford, 1998), p. 24.

69 Bernays, diary, 8 February 1934 (Nick Smart (ed.), *The Diaries and Letters of Robert Bernays, 1932–1939: An Insider's Account of the House of Commons* (Lampeter, 1996), p. 119).

70 MacDonald to Londonderry, 16 February 1926 (JRUL, RHD/1/14/68).

71 Malcolm Muggeridge, *The Thirties, 1930–1940 in Great Britain* (London, 1940), p. 49; David Marquand, *Ramsay MacDonald* (London, 1977), pp. 687–8; R. Bassett, *Nineteen Thirty-One: Political Crisis* (London, 1958), p. 320; Hugh Dalton, diary, 9 July 1930 (Ben Pimlott (ed.), *The Political Diary of Hugh Dalton: 1918–40, 1945–60* (London, 1986) pp. 116–17); Beatrice Webb, diary, 14 February 1928, 5 September 1930 (Margaret Cole (ed.), *Beatrice Webb's Diaries 1924–1932* (London, 1956), pp. 161–2, 249). See also Patrick Balfour, *Society Racket: A Critical Survey of Modern Social Life* (London, 1933), p. 125.

72 James, *Davidson*, p. 405; Bernays, diary, 22 November 1932 (Smart, *The Diaries and Letters of Robert Bernays*, p. 18).

73 Martin Green, *Children of the Sun: A Narrative of 'Decadence' in England after 1918* (rev. edn., London, 1977), pp. 241–305 and *passim.*

74 Headlam, 17 December 1930 (Ball, *Headlam Diaries*, p. 183).

75 Headlam, 20 November 1933 (ibid., p. 284).

76 Londonderry to Baldwin, 11 October 1930 (CUL, Baldwin 165, f. 209).

77 Patrick Gower to Baldwin (memorandum), 29 November 1930 (CUL, Baldwin 165, 170, ff. 136–7).

78 J. C. C. Davidson to Londonderry, 17 June 1931 (HLRO, DAV/191); Londonderry to Davidson, 19 June 1931 (ibid.).

79 The Londonderrys closely resemble the characters of Lord and Lady Anchorage of Anchorage House, London (Evelyn Waugh, *Vile Bodies* (rep. edn., London, 2000), pp. 106–7.

80 Beaverbrook to Londonderry, 3 January 1932 (HLRO, BBK/C/224); Londonderry to Beaverbrook, 5 January 1932 (ibid.); Beaverbrook to Londonderry, 12 January 1932 (ibid.). When Londonderry demanded to know why no society reports on Beaverbrook were printed he received a curt reply: 'I am not in Society. I spring from the working classes and belong to them. I don't go to parties. I never dine outside my own house or go to restaurants' (Beaverbrook to Londonderry, 12 January 1932 (ibid.)).

81 A. J. P. Taylor, *Beaverbrook* (London, 1972), p. 339.

82 Edith, Lady Londonderry to Beaverbrook, 11 February 1932 (HLRO, BBK/C/224); Londonderry to Beaverbrook, 22 February 1932 (ibid.). He commented to Baldwin that having 'the Beaver' against them would do the government more favours than if he were with them (Londonderry to Baldwin, 22 February 1932 (CUL, Baldwin 118, ff. 164–69)).

83 Headlam, 17 October 1928 (Ball, *Headlam Diaries*, p. 155).

84 Londonderry, *Wings of Destiny*, p. 35; *The Times*, 19 October 1928.

85 Ibid., 20 June 1928.

86 Londonderry to Craig, 17 October 1928 (PRONI, T/3775/23/2).

87 *The Times*, 3 March 1926; Churchill to Londonderry, 6 March 1928 (D/3099/2/5/17).

88 Churchill to Londonderry, 14 August 1927 (PRONI, D/3084/C/C/3/9A–B).

89 Churchill to Londonderry, 24 August 1927 (D/3099/2/5/20).

90 Lord Stamfordham to Londonderry, 20 October 1928 (D/3099/2/4).

91 Londonderry's Ministry oversaw repairs to Westminster Palace (Londonderry to Baldwin, 28 January 1929 (CUL, Baldwin 59, ff. 333–6)).

92 Londonderry to Baldwin, 13 February 1929 (ibid., 64, f. 103).

93 Londonderry, *Wings of Destiny*, p. 36; A. Hardinge (Buckingham Palace) to Sir E. E. Bridges (Cabinet Office), 11 June 1942 (PRO, CAB/21/2677).

94 For Cecil's bill see *Hansard 5 (Lords)*, 72, 562–71 (12 December 1928); Wilfred Ashley to Londonderry, 6 December 1928 (D/3099/2/4/45); Londonderry to Ashley, 7 December 1928 (D/3099/2/4/46); Londonderry to Ashley, 13 December 1928 (D/3099/2/4/49); Londonderry to Cecil, 7 January 1929 (D/3099/2/4/57); Cecil to Londonderry, 9 January 1929 (D/3099/2/4/60); *Hansard 5 (Lords)*, 72, 801–3 (29 January 1929); Ashley to Londonderry, 20 April 1929 (D/3099/2/4/71); Cecil to Londonderry, 23 April 1929 (D/3099/2/4/72). Londonderry was convicted of speeding in 1920 (*The Times*, 10 September 1920).

95 Londonderry to Baldwin, 1 February 1929 (H. Montgomery Hyde, *Baldwin: The Unexpected Prime Minister* (London, 1973), p. 297).

96 Stuart Ball, *The Conservative Party and British Politics, 1902–1951* (London, 1995), p. 82.

97 *The Times*, 3 January 1929); Headlam, diary, 24 January 1929 (Ball, *Headlam diaries*, p. 161); *The Times*, 22 March 1929, 15 April 1929, 30 April 1929.

98 Ibid., 8 March 1929; Benyon and Austrin, *Masters and Servants*, pp. 347–8. See Londonderry to MacDonald, 22 July 1929 (JRUL, RMD/1/14/69). Londonderry enclosed a copy of the communist paper of Dawdon *The Lamp* to MacDonald (Londonderry to MacDonald, 19 March 1930 (ibid.)). During the campaign Londonderry accused a local vicar of having socialist sympathies (Rev. Duncan to Londonderry, 29 May 1929 (D/3099/2/4/75)).

99 Neil Riddell, *Labour in Crisis: The Second Labour Government, 1929–1931* (Manchester, 1999), pp. 2–3.

100 *The Times*, 6 January 1930; ibid., 28 March 1930.

101 Salisbury to Londonderry, 19 March 1930 (D/3099/2/4/77).

102 *The Times*, 28 April 1930; *Hansard 5 (Lords)*, 77, 180–92 (29 April 1930).

103 Londonderry to Leo Amery, 6 June 1936 (DCRO, D/Lo/C/237 (3)). Baldwin arranged to stay at Mount Stewart at the end of 1929 (Londonderry to Baldwin, 18 November 1929 (CUL, Baldwin 164, f. 161)).

104 Londonderry to Beaverbrook, 16 December 1929 (HLRO, BBK/C/224); Beaverbrook to Londonderry, 19 December 1929 (ibid.).

105 *The Times*, 15 February 1930.

106 Ibid., 17 July 1930.

107 Londonderry to Beaverbrook, 19 July 1930 (HLRO, BBK/C/224).

108 *The Times*, 6 August 1930.

109 Londonderry to Baldwin, 11 October 1930 (CUL, Baldwin 165, f. 209).

110 Londonderry addressing Conservatives at Norwich (*The Times*, 11 November 1930).

111 Ibid., 1 March 1929.

112 *Hansard 5* (*Lords*), 83, 667–75 (29 February 1932); Buchan to Londonderry, 3 March 1932 (D/3099/2/16/4).

113 Londonderry to Baldwin, 31 October 1930 (CUL, Baldwin 165, f. 214).

114 *The Times*, 24 November 1930.

115 Londonderry to Beaverbrook, 5 March 1931 (HLRO, BBK/C/224); Beaverbrook to Londonderry, 9 March 1931 (ibid.).

116 *The Times*, 14 May 1931.

117 Board member of Sun Life Insurance Office Ltd., Sun Life Assurance Society, London and North-Eastern Railway Company (ibid., 10, 26 July 1929); received a DCL at Durham (ibid., 16 December 1929); voted Chancellor in 1930 and installed in 1931 (ibid., 21 November 1930, 21 May 1931).

118 Lord Stamfordham to Londonderry, 21 January 1931 (D/3099/2/4/80).

119 Londonderry to George V, January 1931 (Hyde, *Londonderrys*, pp. 186–7); George V to Londonderry, 25 January 1931 (D/3099/2/4/82); Robert Lynn to Londonderry, 3 October 1925 (D/3099/2/11/8).

120 *The Times*, 26 August 1931; Londonderry to Baldwin, 25 August 1931 (CUL, Baldwin 44, f. 2).

121 *Hansard 5* (*Lords*), 82, 3–4 (8 September 1931); ibid., 288–93 (7 October 1931); *The Times*, 19 September, 9, 20, 21 October 1931.

122 Churchill to Londonderry, 22 October 1931 (D/3099/2/5/25).

123 MacDonald campaigning at Seaham (*The Times*, 20 October 1931).

124 Headlam, diary, 24 August 1931 (Ball, *Headlam Diaries*, p. 214); Beatrice Webb to Women's Section of Seaham Labour Party, 14 October 1931 (Norman MacKenzie (ed.), *The Letters of Sidney and Beatrice Webb: vol. 3: Pilgrimage, 1912–1947* (3 vols, Cambridge, 1978), p. 369).

125 Marquand, *MacDonald*, p. 690.

126 Philip Williamson, *National Crisis and National Government: British Politics, the Economy and Empire, 1926–1932* (Cambridge, 1992), pp. 150–1.

127 *The Times*, 6 November 1931.

128 Londonderry, *Wings of Destiny*, p. 44. See also MacDonald to Londonderry, 28 February 1932 (D/3099/2/12/9).

6. Secretary of State for Air, 1931–1935

1 Piers Brendon, *The Dark Valley: A Panorama of the 1930s* (London, 2000), p. xiii.

2 Winston S. Churchill, *The Second World War: vol. 1: The Gathering Storm* (rep. edn., London, 1949), p. 113.

3 *The Times*, 10 November 1931; Correspondence file of congratulations to Londonderry, 5–8 November 1931 (D/3099/2/9/16–82).

4 *Hansard 5* (*Lords*), 83, 61– 4 (17 November 1931).

5 Ibid., 84, 842–8 (14 June 1932).

6 Ibid., 85, 961–6 (1 November 1932); ibid., 88, 993–8 (20 July 1933).

7 Ibid., 86, 413 (14 December 1932).

8 *Hansard 5 (Lords)*, 93, 856–9 (19 July 1934); ibid., 96, 600–3 (4 April 1935).

9 *The Times*, 8 November 1933. Londonderry defended the existence of a separate transport ministry (*Hansard 5 (Lords)*, 86, 742–51 (15 February 1933). Londonderry resigned his seat on the board of a railway company (Extract from minutes of London and North Eastern Railway Company, 28 January 1932 (PRO, RAIL/390/875); *The Times*, 30 January 1932).

10 *The Times*, 2 March 1933. During the Road and Rail Traffic bill debates Viscount Cecil attempted an amendment to compel vehicles to display an external speedometer; Londonderry dismissed it as impractical (*The Times*, 16 November 1933). He gave the same reason when asked why parachutes were not fitted on all commercial aeroplanes arguing that they were of little use when taking off or in most accidents (*Hansard 5 (Lords)*, 88, 1095–8 (25 July 1933); He had a flying accident the following year (*The Times*, 8 June, 9 June 1934).

11 *The Times*, 20 April 1934.

12 *Hansard 5 (Lords)*, 96, 301 (21 March 1935).

13 *The Times*, 22 October 1934.

14 *Hansard 5 (Lords)*, 92, 536 (30 May 1934).

15 Headlam, diary, 19 June 1934 (Stuart Ball (ed.), *Parliament and Politics in the Age of Baldwin and MacDonald: The Headlam Diaries, 1923–1935* (London, 1992), p. 306).

16 He argued that they ruled for all regardless of privilege and therefore the Liberal party had lost its *raison d'être* (Londonderry at Oxford University Carlton Club (*The Times*, 11 February 1933)).

17 Stuart Ball, *The Conservative Party and British Politics, 1902–1951* (London, 1995), p. 89.

18 Viscount Snowden, *An Autobiography, vol. 2: 1919–1934* (2 vols, London, 1934), p. 1016. The policy caused the cabinet resignations of Labour's Snowden and the Liberal Herbert Samuel. Londonderry regretted the former but thought the latter to MacDonald's advantage (Londonderry to MacDonald, 28 September 1932 (JRUL, RHD/1/13)).

19 *The Times*, 21 April, 9 November 1934; Neville Chamberlain to Londonderry, 21 March 1934 (D/3099/2/4/90); Londonderry to Beaverbrook, 20 October 1934 (HLRO, BBK/C/224); on Rothermere (*Hansard 5 (Lords)*, 95, 185 (11 December 1934).

20 Viscount Swinton, *I Remember* (London, 1948), p. 105. See *The Times*, 13 April 1933, 13 April 1934, 25 October 1934.

21 Londonderry at International Air Traffic Association meeting (*The Times*, 28, 29 September, 9 December 1933.

22 *The Times*, 5 October, 9 December 1933. Londonderry took exception to Birmingham's attempt to create it's own airline on the grounds of unfair competition (*The Times*, 3 April 1935); ibid., 9 January 1935.

23 Londonderry statement on British commercial transport, 8 February 1934 (PRO, AIR/5/1427); Londonderry to Sir Robert Hoare MP, 18 February 1935

(ibid., RAIL/257/55); Hoare to Londonderry, 26 February 1935 (ibid.). See also *The Times*, 14 May 1935.

24 *The Times*, 13 December 1933.

25 Ibid., 1 September 1934.

26 Ibid., 4 November 1932.

27 Ibid., 21 July 1934; Londonderry to David Margesson MP, 27 September 1934 (CUL, Baldwin 2, f. 362); *Hansard 5 (Lords)*, 95, 59–63 (21 November 1934).

28 Londonderry to C. W. Fisher, 8 December 1934 (ibid., 169, ff. 194–5); Londonderry to Baldwin, 10 December 1934 (ibid., f. 196); *The Times*, 19 December 1934. This row contributed to Bullock's dismissal from the civil service in 1936 (G. C. Peden, *British Rearmament and the Treasury, 1932–1939* (Edinburgh, 1979) p. 53).

29 See Londonderry to Baldwin, 19 May 1936 (Baldwin 171, ff. 166–7).

30 *The Times*, 13 November 1931.

31 *Hansard 5 (Commons)*, 259, 281–2 (12 November 1931).

32 Bernard Porter, *The Lion's Share: A Short History of British Imperialism* (3rd edn., London, 1993), *passim*; Paul Kennedy, *The Realities Behind Diplomacy: Background Influences on British External Policy, 1865–1980* (London, 1981), p. 21.

33 David Reynolds, *Britannia Overruled: British Policy and World Power in the 20th Century* (2nd edn., London, 2000), *passim*.

34 Correlli Barnett, *The Collapse of British Power* (London, 1972), p. 411.

35 Scot Robertson, *The Development of RAF Strategic Bombing Doctrine, 1919–1939* (London, 1995), p. 31; Anthony Clayton, 'Imperial defence and security, 1900–1968', in Judith M. Brown and Wm. Roger Louis (eds), *The Oxford History of the British Empire, vol. 4: The Twentieth Century* (Oxford, 1999), p. 287.

36 Taylor, *English History*, p. 363. Londonderry's paternalistic loyalty to his Ministry and the RAF was in some ways like that of a landlord, defending not just senior advisors, but also the entire Ministry. See Bullock to Londonderry, 15 June 1935 (PRO, AIR/2/223); Sir John Salmond to Londonderry, 12 July 193[?] (D/3099/2/16/68); Air Ministry Employees to Londonderry, March 1932 (PRO, AIR/20/6259); Londonderry to MacDonald, 3 May 1932 (ibid., PREM/1/114).

37 Uri Bialer, *The Shadow of the Bomber: The Fear of Air Attack and British Policies, 1932–1939* (London, 1980), pp. 42–3.

38 Londonderry to MacDonald, 19 July 1932 (D/3099/2/12/16).

39 H. Montgomery Hyde, *British Air Policy Between the Wars, 1918–1939* (London, 1976), p. 276.

40 *The Times*, 3 December 1931, 11 January 1932.

41 Robertson, *Development of RAF*, p. 41; *Hansard 5 (Lords)*, 91, 190 (14 March 1934). Londonderry complained to MacDonald about the schoolboy style of wording in official Foreign Office documents, the Prime Minister agreed (Londonderry to MacDonald, 11 August 1933 (PRO, PRO/30/69/706); MacDonald to Londonderry, 18 August 1933 (ibid.)); evidence does suggest

that the Foreign Office was relatively informal with a 'frat-house atmosphere' (see Paul W. Doerr, *British Foreign Policy 1919–1939: 'Hope for the Best, Prepare for the Worst'* (Manchester, 1998), p. 134). Simon informed Londonderry that it 'grieved' him to differ with Londonderry on policy (Simon to Londonderry, n.d. (D/3099/2/16/61)).

42 *The Times*, 6, 25 February 1932.

43 Sassoon to Londonderry, 20 January 1932 (D/3099/2/16/1).

44 David Marquand, *Ramsay MacDonald* (London, 1977), p. 693; *The Times*, 3 March 1932. The general committee had one member from each country (ibid., 9 March 1932).

45 Londonderry to Baldwin, 22 February 1932 (CUL, Baldwin 118, ff. 164–9).

46 MacDonald to Londonderry, 28 February 1932 (D/3099/2/12/9); Londonderry to Baldwin, 10 March 1932 (CUL, Baldwin 118, f. 170).

47 Londonderry to Baldwin, 22 February 1932 (ibid., ff. 164–9). There was a brief mention of his address (*The Times*, 20 February 1932).

48 *The Daily Express*, 17 February 1932.

49 R. Bassett, *Democracy and Foreign Policy, a Case History: The Sino-Japanese Dispute, 1931–33* (London, 1952), pp. 103–4.

50 Londonderry to Baldwin, 10 March 1932 (CUL, Baldwin 118, f. 170).

51 He added that he did not want to write too much in a letter 'as one is never sure under whose eyes they come' (MacDonald to Londonderry, 13 March 1932 (D/3099/2/12/10)).

52 Bassett, *Sino-Japanese Dispute*, p. 115.

53 Maurice Hankey to Londonderry, 20 April 1932 (D/3099/2/16/10).

54 *The Times*, 4 March 1932.

55 Press copy of air estimates memo from Ministry of Air (*The Times*, 4 March 1932).

56 Sassoon to Londonderry, 20 January 1932 (D/3099/2/16/1); *The Times*, 9 March 1932.

57 Hyde, *Air policy*, p. 279; Robert Paul Shay, *British Rearmament in the Thirties: Politics and Profits* (Princeton, 1977), p. 35.

58 Hyde, *Air Policy*, pp. 279–80.

59 Keith Middlemas and John Barnes, *Baldwin: A Biography* (London, 1969), pp. 731–2.

60 The lecture was announced weeks in advance (*The Times*, 19 April 1932); Londonderry, notes for a public lecture, 4 May 1932 (D/3099/2/16/22).

61 Hyde, *Air policy*, p. 280.

62 Simon to Londonderry, 1 June 1932 (D/3099/2/16/25).

63 Salmond to Londonderry, 8 June 1932 (D/3099/2/16/26).

64 Londonderry to MacDonald, 9 June 1932 (D/3099/2/12/13).

65 *The Times*, 7, 11 June 1932.

66 Londonderry to MacDonald, 10 June 1932 (D/3099/2/12/14); MacDonald to Londonderry, 29 June 1932 (D/3099/2/12/15).

67 Hyde, *Air Policy*, pp. 280–1; Londonderry to Sir Clive Wigram (Buckingham Palace), 21 July 1932 (D/3099/2/16/29A).

68 Londonderry, notes for a public lecture, 4 May 1932 (D/3099/2/16/22); Londonderry to Mrs Lees (Tonbridge Women's Adult School), 5 May 1932 (D/3099/2/16/24).

69 *The Times*, 7 July 1932; Salmond refers to their opponents as 'Anti-Christs' (Salmond to Londonderry, 12 July [1932] (D/3099/2/16/68)).

70 Londonderry to MacDonald, 19 July 1932 (D/3099/2/12/16).

71 Londonderry to Edith, Lady Londonderry, 17 July 1932 (Marquess of Londonderry, *Ourselves and Germany* (London, 1938), pp. 47–48); MacDonald to Londonderry, 23 July 1932 (D/3099/2/12/17).

72 Marquand, *MacDonald*, p. 717; Londonderry to Hankey, 24 July 1932 (D/3099/2/16/31).

73 MacDonald to Londonderry, 28 July 1932 (D/3099/2/12/18).

74 Londonderry to MacDonald, 19 July 1932 (D/3099/2/12/16); Londonderry to Hankey, 24 July 1932 (D/3099/2/16/31); Sir Alex Cadogan to Londonderry, 25 November 1933 (D/3099/2/16/41).

75 Londonderry to Sir Clive Wigram, 21 July 1932 (D/3099/2/16/29A).

76 Londonderry, notes for a public lecture, 4 May 1932 (D/3099/2/16/22).

77 *The Times*, 19 October 1932. See also ibid., 28 October 1933, *The Sunderland Echo*, 29 April 1941.

78 Simon to Londonderry, 7 November [1932] (D/3099/2/16/66).

79 Hyde, *Air Policy*, p. 284.

80 Salmond to Londonderry, 6 November 1932 (D/3099/2/16/32); Sir Christopher Bullock to Londonderry, 7 November 1932 (D/3099/2/16/33); MacDonald to Londonderry, 9 November 1932 (D/3099/2/12/20).

81 *Hansard 5* (*Commons*), 270, 630–8 (10 November 1932).

82 Salmond to Londonderry, 10 November [1932] (D/3099/2/16/67).

83 Hyde, *Air Policy*, pp. 286–7.

84 *The Times*, 3 February 1933.

85 Ibid., 31 January, 3 February 1933.

86 Eden, diary, 9 February 1932 (Robert Rhodes James, *Anthony Eden* (London, 1996), p. 124).

87 *The Times*, 21 February 1933.

88 Ibid., 28 February 1935.

89 Ibid., 9 March 1933.

90 Londonderry to Hailsham, 8 March 1933 (D/3099/2/16/40).

91 Londonderry to Churchill, 14 March 1933 (PRONI, D/3084/C/C/3/10A–B).

92 Londonderry, *Wings of Destiny*, p. 90.

93 Robert Rhodes James, *Churchill: A Study in Failure, 1900–1939* (Harmondsworth, 1973), pp. 286–7.

94 Londonderry to Baldwin, 29 May 1933 (CUL, Baldwin 121, ff. 35–7).

95 *The Times*, 31 May, 1 June 1933.

96 B. H. Liddell Hart, *Memoirs* (2 vols, London, 1965) vol. 1, p. 206.

97 *The Times*, 8 June 1933. Londonderry did briefly return to London probably to keep in touch with Cabinet developments (*The Times*, 5 June 1935).

98 *The Times*, 9, 10 June 1933; Londonderry, *Wings of Destiny*, pp. 78–9.

99 David Carlton, *Anthony Eden: A Biography* (London, 1981), p. 42.

100 Chamberlain to Hilda Chamberlain, 5 March 1932 (Robert C. Self (ed.), *The Austen Chamberlain Diary Letters: The Correspondence of Sir Austen Chamberlain with his Sisters Hilda and Ida, 1916–1937* (Cambridge, 1995), pp. 408–9).

101 Londonderry to Chamberlain, 24 June 1933 (D/3099/2/16/44); Chamberlain to Londonderry, 26 June 1933 (D/3099/2/16/45).

102 Carlton, *Anthony Eden*, p. 42.

103 *The Times*, 25 July 1933.

104 Clayton, 'Imperial defence', p. 292; Londonderry to MacDonald, 20 August 1933 (PRO, PRO/30/69/706).

105 *The Times*, 10 June; 11 July 1933. Londonderry House continued to be a venue for high profile meetings, for example between MacDonald and the French air minister (*The Times*, 5 April 1932) and the government and General Balbo (ibid., 29 June 1932).

106 Ibid., 4 November 1932, 3, 17 May, 2 August, 4 October 1933, 8, 18, 19 May, 5 June 1934. He was also made an Honorary Colonel of the Artists Rifles (ibid., 24 April 1934); ibid., 22 June 1934.

107 Londonderry to MacDonald, 16 August 1933 (PRO, PRO/30/69/706); *The Times*, 23 June 1933.

108 Ibid., 18 July 1933.

109 Ibid., 3 July 1933.

110 Ibid., 4 July 1933.

111 Ibid., 3, 17 July 1933.

112 Londonderry to editor of *The Times*, 8 July 1933 (D/3099/2/16/46).

113 *The Times*, 20 July 1933.

114 Londonderry to Baldwin, 20 November 1933 (CUL, Baldwin 55, f. 225).

115 *The Times*, 28 October 1933. Londonderry was appointed Chairman of the Committee for International Understanding (ibid., 15 February 1934).

116 Hailsham kept Londonderry in touch with government business (Hailsham to Londonderry, 28 December 1933 (D/3099/2/4/89)).

117 *The Times* gave coverage to the tour (*The Times*, 28 November, 14, 28, 29 December 1933, 2, 3, 8 January, 3 February 1934).

118 Ibid., 10, 13, 15, 16 January 1934.

119 Ibid., 24, 30, 31 January, 1, 2, 3 February 1934.

120 Nick Smart, *The National Government, 1931–40* (London, 1999), p. 91.

121 Martin Ceadel, *Pacifism in Britain 1914–1945: The Defining of a Faith* (Oxford, 1980), p. 134. It came days after Londonderry awarded Baldwin an honorary degree at Queen's University (*The Times*, 21 October 1933).

122 Ibid., 6 November 1933.

123 *Hansard 5 (Lords)*, 90, 178–86 (29 November 1933).

124 *The Times*, 6 November, 18 November 1933; *Hansard 5 (Lords)*, 90, 370–9 (7 December 1933).

125 *The Times*, 3 March, 10 November 1934.

126 Londonderry to Sir F. Humphrys (British Ambassador to Iraq), 13 March 1934 (D/3099/2/16/34).

127 Philip Williamson, *Stanley Baldwin: Conservative Leadership and National Values* (Cambridge, 1999), p. 306.

128 *The Times*, 25 May 1934.

129 Speaking at a garden party hosted by Lord Clydesdale MP at Lanarkshire (ibid., 18 June 1934); MacDonald to Londonderry, 15 June 1934 (D/3099/4/21).

130 *The Times*, 11 July 1934. He reiterated this belief the following month (ibid., 6 August 1934).

131 Londonderry to Baldwin, 17 July 1934 (CUL, Baldwin 1, f. 106); *Hansard 5 (Commons)*, 292, 1273–8 (19 July 1934).

132 *Hansard 5 (Lords)*, 93, 943–58 (23 July 1934).

133 Londonderry, *Wings of Destiny*, pp. 115–6; Ellington to Londonderry, 2 August 1934 (D/3099/2/16/50).

134 *The Times*, 23 October 1934.

135 Ibid., 10 November 1934.

136 Notes of a meeting between Göring and Mr and Mrs Oliver Stanley, 5 October 1934 (D/3099/2/19/3).

137 Londonderry to Hailsham, 22 November 1934 (D/3099/2/19/4A).

138 Londonderry to Hailsham, 23 November 1934 (D/3099/2/19/5A).

139 Londonderry to Hailsham, 22 November 1934 (D/3099/2/19/4A).

140 Hailsham to Londonderry 29 August 1939 (D/3099/2/17/52A).

141 Hailsham to Londonderry, 29 August 1939 (D/3099/2/17/52A); Middlemas and Barnes, *Baldwin*, pp. 790–5.

142 Londonderry to Simon, 11 December 1934 (D/3099/2/16/52).

143 Londonderry, memorandum, 26 November 1934 (PRO, PREM/1/155).

144 Londonderry to Baldwin, 30 November 1934 (CUL, Baldwin 1, f. 147).

145 Middlemas and Barnes, *Baldwin*, pp. 787–9.

146 Londonderry House continued to host diplomatic functions (*The Times*, 25 February 1935).

147 Londonderry to Simon, 11 December 1934 (D/3099/2/16/52).

148 Middlemas and Barnes, *Baldwin*, p. 790.

149 Lothian to Londonderry, 7 February 1935 (D/3099/2/17/56).

150 Londonderry, *Wings of Destiny*, p. 109.

151 *The Times*, 18 December 1934; Londonderry to Craigavon, 3 January 1935 (PRONI, T/3775/23/4); *The Times*, 18, 21, 23, 28 January 1935; Graham Stewart, *Burying Caesar: Churchill, Chamberlain and the Battle for the Tory Party* (London, 1999), p. 135.

152 *The Times*, 17 March 1933.

153 Ibid., 23 October 1934.

154 Ibid., 27 November 1934.

155 Londonderry addressing Conservatives at Seaham Harbour (ibid., 28 January 1935); ibid., 20 February 1935.

156 Ibid., 6 March 1935.

157 Ibid., 14 March 1935.

158 Londonderry to Baldwin, 14 March 1935 (CUL, Baldwin 1 ff. 152–4).

159 *The Times*, 28 March 1935.

160 See Viscount Rothermere, *My Fight to Rearm Britain* (London, 1939). Rothermere assured Londonderry he did not mean to attack him personally (Rothermere to Londonderry, 13 May 1935 (D/3099/2/21/A/274)).

161 Robert Rhodes James (ed.), *Memoirs of a Conservative: J. C. C. Davidson's Memoirs and Papers, 1910–37* (London, 1969), p. 404.

162 Wesley K. Wark, *The Ultimate Enemy: British Intelligence and Nazi Germany, 1933–1939* (London, 1985), p. 47.

163 Simon's memoirs barely mention Londonderry's opposition (Viscount Simon, *Retrospect: The Memoirs of the Rt. Hon. Viscount Simon G.C.S.I., G.C.V.O.* (London, 1952), p. 202).

164 Londonderry to MacDonald, 10 April 1935 (CUL, Baldwin 1, f. 165).

165 David Dilks, "The unnecessary war'? Military advice and foreign policy in Great Britain, 1931–1939', in Adrian Preston (ed.), *General Staffs and Diplomacy before the Second World War* (London, 1978), p. 110.

166 Churchill, *The Gathering Storm*, p. 114.

167 Middlemas and Barnes, *Baldwin*, pp. 814–5.

168 James, *Davidson*, p. 405. See also Vansittart to Londonderry, 12 July 1933 (D/3099/4/20).

169 Chamberlain to Ida Chamberlain, 12 January 1935 (Self, *Chamberlain Diary Letters*, p. 472); Londonderry to Baldwin, 14 March 1935 (CUL, Baldwin 1, ff. 152–4). See also Ronald W. Clark, *Tizard* (London, 1965), pp. 105–27

170 Londonderry, *Wings of Destiny*, pp. 134–5.

171 Londonderry to Lady Londonderry, 27 April 1935 (Hyde, *Londonderrys*, p. 212).

172 Londonderry to MacDonald, n.d. [1935] (JRUL, RMD/1/14/75); Londonderry to MacDonald, 2 May 1935 (ibid., RMD/1/13/4).

173 Londonderry to MacDonald, 6 May 1935 (ibid., RMD/1/13/5).

174 Londonderry to Cunliffe-Lister, 11 May 1935 (CUL, Baldwin 1, f. 182); Ellington to Cunliffe-Lister, 11 May 1935 (Hyde, *Air Policy*, p. 339).

175 Copy of Cabinet minutes from Hankey to Londonderry, 21 May 1935 (D/3099/2/15/8).

176 *Hansard 5 (Commons)*, 302, 359–82 (22 May 1935).

177 James, *Davidson*, p. 404.

178 Londonderry concluded with John Milton's *Aeropagitica*: 'Methinks I see in my mind a noble and puissant nation rousing herself like a strong man after

sleep and shaking her invincible locks. Methinks I see her as an eagle mewing her mighty youth and kindling her undazzled eyes in the midday beam.' (*Hansard 5 (Lords)*, 96, 1002– 9 (22 May 1935).

179 Londonderry, *Wings of Destiny*, p. 143. Around the same time as his speech an RAF aeroplane was shot down in Iraq, probably 'by disaffected tribesmen', and Londonderry was forced to detail Britain's controversial bombing role in the Middle East (*Hansard 5 (Lords)*, 96, 1094–6 (23 May 1935). He later wrote to Clement Attlee and Herbert Morrison regretting his Lords speech (Londonderry to Attlee/Morrison, 17 November 1937 (DCRO, D/Lo/C/237 (ii))). See also Londonderry to Lord Strabolgi, 23 November 1937 (D/3099/2/17/22).

180 His last days in office were spent performing ceremonial duties (*The Times*, 25 May, 28 May, 4 June 1935).

181 Marquand, *MacDonald*, p. 774.

182 Hailsham to Baldwin, 28 May 1935 (Cowling, *Impact of Hitler*, p. 60).

183 Channon, diary, 8 June 1935 (Robert Rhodes James, *Chips: The Diaries of Sir Henry Channon* (London, 1967), p. 35); Marquand, *MacDonald*, p. 783.

184 A. J. P. Taylor (ed.), *W. P. Crozier: Off the Record: Political Interviews, 1933–1943* (London, 1973), pp. 46–8.

185 Londonderry to Baldwin, 6 June 1935 (CUL, Baldwin 171, ff. 152–59).

186 Baldwin to Londonderry, 6 June 1935 (D/3099/2/17/4A).

187 Londonderry to Alexander Cadogan, 18 June 1935 (D/3099/2/17/5).

188 *The Times*, 8 June 1935; Air ministry memorandum, 17 June 1935 (PRO, AIR/2/223) published in the press (*The Times*, 21 June 1935). He received his letters patent as His Majesty's Keeper of the Privy Seal the same day (L. C. Ridley to Londonderry, 17 June 1935 (PRO, LCO/6/1240)).

189 Cowling, *Impact of Hitler*, p. 60.

190 He successfully sought to remain President of the Oil Board (Londonderry to Baldwin, 9 July 1935 (D/3099/2/17/6A)).

191 Hailsham to Londonderry, 17 September 1935 (D/3099/2/17/7B).

192 See Londonderry to Hailsham, 16 December 1935 (D/3099/2/15/6).

193 Cunliffe-Lister to Londonderry, 9 September 1935 (D/3099/6/11); *The Times*, 28 June 1935; Hendriks to Londonderry, 20 September 1935 (D/3099/2/4/91A). The Duke of Northumberland was Londonderry's parliamentary private secretary (*The Times*, 12 July 1935). Londonderry had Hendriks transferred with difficulty from the Northern Ireland civil service (Londonderry to MacDonald, 11 August 1933 (PRO, PRO/30/69/706)); Hendriks to Londonderry, n.d. (D/3099/5/14/3).

194 Londonderry to Craigavon, 16 October 1935 (D/3099/6/11).

195 Londonderry to Baldwin, 17 October 1935 (CUL, Baldwin 171, ff. 157–8).

196 *The Times*, 29 July 1935.

197 Kenneth Harris, *Attlee* (rep. edn., London, 1995), p. 118.

198 *The Times*, 31 July 1935.

199 *Hansard 5 (Lords)*, 98, 1090–1100 (22 October 1935).
200 F. W. S. Craig, *British General Election Manifestos, 1900–1974* (London, 1975), p. 108. Hendriks advised Londonderry that this was a libel as he had acted in Geneva for the government, but nothing, at least in the courts, was pursued (Memorandum from Hendriks to Londonderry, 29 October 1935 (D/3099/2/16/58)).
201 *The Times*, 6, 8, 13 November 1935.
202 Ibid., 14 November 1935.
203 Marquand, *MacDonald*, pp. 779–80. See also Londonderry to Derby, 14 November 1935 (D/3099/2/8/19).
204 Baldwin to Londonderry, 21 November 1935 (D/3099/2/17/11).
205 Hyde, *Londonderrys*, p. 226.
206 Chamberlain to Ida Chamberlain, 20 June 1936 (Self, *Chamberlain Diary Letters*, p. 509).
207 Marquess of Londonderry, 'Bombing from the air', *Nineteenth Century and After*, cxxv (March 1939). The depth and paranoia of Londonderry's concern led him to complain personally about press reports in a range of journals, from the *Rotheram Advertiser* (Londonderry to the editor, 20 July 1936 (DCRO, D/Lo/C/237 (4))) to the *Aeroplane* (editor to Londonderry, 21 October 1940 (D/3099/2/17/67A)).
208 Londonderry to Baldwin, 22 November 1935 (CUL, Baldwin 171, f. 162).
209 Londonderry to Baldwin, 18 May 1936 (ibid., f. 163).
210 *Hansard 5 (Lords)*, 99, 181–87 (11 December 1935); Londonderry to Beaverbrook, 26 December 1935 (HLRO, BBK/C/224); Beaverbrook to Londonderry, 30 December 1935 (ibid.).
211 James, *Davidson*, p. 405; Robert Vansittart, *The Mist Procession: The Autobiography of Lord Vansittart* (London, 1958), p. 445.
212 Londonderry to Beverly Baxter MP, 28 April 1947 (D/3099/2/21/A/264).
213 Hailsham to Londonderry, n.d. [November 1935] (D/3099/2/4/94).
214 Templemore to Londonderry, 23 November 1935 (D/3099/2/4/100).
215 Swinton, *I Remember*, pp. 104–5.
216 Salisbury to Londonderry, 26 November 1935 (D/3099/2/4/113A); Desborough to Londonderry, 23 November 1935 (D/3099/2/6/25). See also Archbishop D'Arcy of Armagh to Londonderry, 25 November 1935 (D/3099/2/4/108).
217 *The Times*, 28 November 1935; Kipling to Londonderry, 30 November 1935 (D/3099/2/4/119).
218 Churchill, *The Gathering Storm*, pp. 114–5.
219 Vansittart, *The Mist Procession*, p. 499.
220 *The Times*, 30 December 1935.
221 Cato, *Guilty Men* (rep. edn., London, 1998), p. 33; *The Times*, 15 March 1935.
222 Malcolm Muggeridge, *The Thirties, 1930–1940 in Great Britain* (London, 1940), p. 136.

223 John F. Kennedy, *Why England Slept* (New York, 1940), p. 109. Kennedy mentions Londonderry and uses his article in *Nineteenth Century and After*.
224 Taylor, *English History*, p. 365.
225 Liddell Hart, *Memoirs*, vol. 1, pp. 157–8.
226 Carlton, *Anthony Eden*, p. 35.
227 Shay, *British rearmament*, p. 38.
228 Martin Gilbert and Richard Gott, *The Appeasers* (rep. edn., London, 2000), p. 333.
229 Robert Rhodes James, *The British Revolution: British Politics, 1880–1939* (London, 1978), p. 554.
230 Londonderry to Cadogan, 18 June 1935 (D/3099/2/17/5).

7. Ourselves and Germany, 1936–1949

1 Oliver Harvey, diary, 1 March 1938 (John Harvey (ed.), *The Diplomatic Diaries of Oliver Harvey 1937–1940* (London, 1970), p. 118).
2 These comments do not refer to Ian Kershaw's *Making Friends with Hitler: Lord Londonderry and Britain's Road to War* (London, 2004), published as this book was in press.
3 R. A. C. Parker, *Chamberlain and Appeasement: British Policy and the Coming of the Second World War* (London, 1993), p. 1.
4 Paul W. Doerr, *British Foreign Policy 1919–1939: 'Hope for the Best, Prepare for the Worst'* (Manchester, 1998), 150–1.
5 David Cannadine, *The Decline and Fall of the British Aristocracy* (rev. edn., London, 1996), p. 547.
6 Peregrine Worsthorne, *In Defence of Aristocracy* (London, 2004), pp. 30–2.
7 Eric Hobsbawm, *Age of Extremes: The Short Twentieth Century, 1914–1991* (London, 1995), p. 123.
8 Richard Thurlow, *Fascism in Britain: From Oswald Mosley's Blackshirts to the National Front* (London, 1998), pp. 61–87.
9 Marquess of Londonderry, *Wings of Destiny* (London, 1943); Anon. to Londonderry, n.d. [1941/2] (PRONI, Londonderry papers hereafter cited as D/3099, D/3099/2/21/A/277).
10 Londonderry to Lady Milner, 11 March 1937 (DRCO, D/Lo/C/237 (8)).
11 Londonderry indicated that his voluminous correspondence might fend off unkind treatment by historians (Londonderry to Baldwin, 18 May 1936 (CUL, Baldwin, 171, f. 163); see *The Evening Standard*, 7 October 1936; Londonderry to Baldwin, 7 November 1939 (D/3099/2/17/55)).
12 Londonderry to Baldwin, 29 December 1938 (CUL, Baldwin 171, ff. 178–91). A possible opportunity for political revenge came at the end of 1936 when rumours abounded about the possibility of Churchill forming a 'King's Party' in support of Edward VIII and against Baldwin. However, neither the papers of Churchill or Londonderry indicate any such plan although both sympathized with Edward's position (Philip Zeigler, 'Churchill and the monarchy', in Robert Blake and Wm. Roger Louis (eds), *Churchill* (Oxford, 1996), pp. 193–5).

13 Richard Griffiths, *Fellow Travellers of the Right: British Enthusiasts for Nazi Germany, 1933–9* (London, 1980), p. 140. As noted above, such statements do not refer to Kershaw's *Making Friends with Hitler.*

14 At Hartlepool (*The Times*, 27 August 1923).

15 At Sunderland (ibid., 25 October 1923).

16 Typed copy of Londonderry's broadcast on the BBC, 7.35 p.m., 11 November 1924 (D/3099/5/13).

17 Addressing Birmingham conservatives (*The Times*, 1 March 1929).

18 Addressing Essex conservatives (ibid., 25 June 1931).

19 Ibid., 20 July 1931.

20 See Londonderry, *Wings of Destiny*, pp. 118–19.

21 Londonderry to Beaverbrook, 22 March 1936 (HLRO, BBK/C/224).

22 Londonderry, *Ourselves and Germany*, p. 147.

23 Londonderry to Halifax, 24 December 1936 (D/3099/2/18/18B).

24 Londonderry to Mr McKee (editor of *Belfast News-Letter*), 5 January 1938 (D/3099/2/21/A/4).

25 Londonderry to Dr Seton-Watson, 21 April 1938 (D/3099/2/21/A/36).

26 H. Montgomery Hyde, *Baldwin: The Unexpected Prime Minister* (London, 1973), p. 543.

27 See Wolfgang Michalka, 'Joachim von Ribbentrop: from wine merchant to foreign minister', in Ronald Smelser and Rainer Zitelmann (ed.), *The Nazi Elite* (London, 1993), pp. 166–7.

28 G. T. Waddington, "An idyllic and unruffled atmosphere of complete Anglo-German misunderstanding': aspects of the operations of the Dienststelle Ribbentrop in Great Britain, 1934–1938', *History*, 82 (1997), p. 46.

29 See Londonderry to Lady Milner, 11 March 1937 (DCRO, D/Lo/C/237 (8)).

30 Londonderry, *Wings of Destiny*, p. 171.

31 Londonderry, *Ourselves and Germany*, pp. 81–2.

32 *The Times*, 6 February 1936.

33 Michael Burleigh, *The Third Reich: A New History* (London, 2000), p. 245. For alternative view on Nazi-aristocratic relations see Manuel Sarkisyanz, *Hitler's English Inspirers* (Belfast, 2003), pp. 210–28.

34 Londonderry to Dr F. W. Pick, 26 November 1946, D/3099/2/21/A.

35 Crowson, *Facing Fascism*, p. 23.

36 Nicholson to Vita Sackville-West, 20 February 1936 (Nigel Nicholson (ed.) *Harold Nicholson: Diaries and Letters, 1930–1939* (London, 1966), p. 245).

37 Londonderry to Lady Londonderry, 30 March 1936 (D/3099/3).

38 Göring to Londonderry, 24 March 1937 (D/3099/2/19/34A).

39 Lady Londonderry to Ribbentrop, 9 May 1936 (D/3099/3/35/15); Ribbentrop to Lady Londonderry, 5 June, 1936 (D/3099/3/35/20). Ribbentrop had attended the Jubilee Ball at Londonderry in May 1935, but it did not lead to any communication with Londonderry who was still in the cabinet.

40 Ribbentrop to Lady Londonderry, 5 June, 1936 (D/3099/3/35/20); *The Times*, 16 November 1936; Henry Channon, diary, 29 May 1936 (Robert Rhodes James, (ed.) *Chips: The Diaries of Sir Henry Channon* (London, 1999), p. 62).

41 John Weitz, *Hitler's Diplomat: Joachim von Ribbentrop* (London, 1997), p. 15; Norton Medlicott, 'Britain and Germany: the search for agreement, 1930–37', in David Dilks (ed.), *Retreat from Power: Studies in Britain's Foreign Policy of the Twentieth Century* (London, 1981), pp. 78–101.

42 *The Times*, 12 March 1936.

43 Lady Londonderry's correspondence with leading German figures, 1936–39 (D/3099/3/35/1–42).

44 Beaverbrook to Londonderry, 19 March 1936 (HLRO, BBK/C/224).

45 Londonderry to Beaverbrook, 22 March 1936 (ibid.).

46 Beaverbrook to Londonderry, 29 March 1936 (ibid.).

47 *Hansard 5 (Lords)*, 100, 37–43 (17 March 1936).

48 Ibid., 540–6 (8 April 1936).

49 Londonderry to Churchill, 9 May 1936 (D/3099/2/5/29); Londonderry to Göring, 3 June 1936 (D/3099/2/19/28B); Göring to Lady Londonderry, 16 May 1936 (D/3099/3/35/16); Göring to Lady Londonderry, 3 July 1936 (D/3099/3/35/24B).

50 Londonderry to Baldwin, 19 May 1936 (CUL Baldwin 171, ff. 166–71).

51 Göring to Lady Londonderry, 16 May 1936 (D/3099/3/35/16); Londonderry to Baldwin, 21 May 1936 (CUL Baldwin 171, ff. 171–3).

52 *The Times*, 27 June 1936; *Hansard 5 (Commons)*, 314, 605–6 (2 July 1936).

53 Halifax to Londonderry, 1 July 1936 (D/3099/2/18/7).

54 Londonderry to Halifax, 4 July 1936 (D/3099/2/18/8).

55 Halifax to Londonderry, 16 July 1936 (D/3099/2/18/10).

56 Londonderry to Halifax, 17 July 1936 (D/3099/2/18/11).

57 Halifax to Londonderry, 25 August 1936 (D/3099/2/18/12).

58 *The Times*, 1 August 1936; Londonderry to Baldwin, 1 December 1936 (CUL Baldwin 171, ff. 175–7); Lloyd George to Londonderry, September 1936 (Londonderry, *Wings of Destiny*), p. 176.

59 Londonderry to Halifax, 16 September 1936 (D/3099/2/18/13).

60 Londonderry to Halifax, 19 December 1936 (D/3099/2/18/17); *The Times*, 16 December 1936.

61 Londonderry to Halifax, 24 December 1936 (D/3099/2/18/18B).

62 *The Times*, 31 October 1936.

63 Londonderry to Halifax, 19 December 1936 (D/3099/2/18/17); Londonderry to Halifax, 24 December 1936 (D/3099/2/18/18B).

64 Londonderry, notes, 22 September 1937 (D/3099/2/19/36).

65 Londonderry to Ribbentrop, 26 October 1937 (D/3099/4/44).

66 Londonderry to Göring, 29 September 1937 (D/3099/2/19/37A).

67 Ben Pimlott, *The Political Diary of Hugh Dalton, 1918–40, 1945–60* (London, 1986), p. 237.

68 Ribbentrop, 'Strictly Confidential and Personal Conclusions Concerning the Report 'German Embassy London A5522' on the future of Anglo-German relations', 2 January 1938 (Alan Bullock (ed), *The Ribbentrop Memoirs* (London, 1954), pp. 206–7).

69 Londonderry to Halifax, 7 October 1937 (D/3099/2/18/27); Baldwin to Londonderry, 11 November 1937 (D/3099/2/19/39).

70 Londonderry to Nevile Henderson, 7 October 1937 (DCRO, D/Lo/C/237 (9)).

71 *The Times*, 8 October 1937; Leo Amery to Londonderry, 9 October 1937 (D/Lo/C/237 (10) (iii–iv)).

72 Londonderry to Halifax, 2 November 1937 (D/3099/2/18/28); *The Evening Standard*, 13 November 1937.

73 Andrew Roberts, *'The Holy Fox': The Life of Lord Halifax* (London, 1991), p. 67.

74 *The Times*, 6 November 1937; Londonderry to Halifax, 2 November 1937 (D/3099/2/18/28); Halifax to Londonderry, 8 November 1937 (D/3099/2/18/29); Halifax to Londonderry, 12 November 1937 (D/3099/2/18/30).

75 Londonderry to Halifax, 13 November 1936 (D/3099/2/18/31).

76 Ribbentrop to Londonderry, 4 December 1937 (D/3099/2/19/40A); Londonderry to Ribbentrop, 8 December 1937 (D/3099/2/19/41); Londonderry to Ribbentrop, 20 January 1938 (D/3099/2/19/53).

77 Londonderry to J. L. Garvin, 5 February 1938 (D/3099/2/21/A/19).

78 Londonderry to Ribbentrop, 21 February 1936 (Londonderry, *Ourselves and Germany*, p. 97).

79 Rothschild to Londonderry, 8 April 1938 (D/3099/2/21/A/22A); Londonderry to Rothschild, 11 April 1938 (D/3099/2/21/A/24A); Rothschild to Londonderry, 12 April 1938 (D/3099/2/21/A/25A); Londonderry to de Rothschild, 13 April 1938 (D/3099/2/21/A/28A). For example of Londonderry's view of Jewish influence as synonymous with socialism see correspondence at the end of 1938 in which he complains of critical Jewish influence in the press to one correspondent and of a critical socialist press to another (Londonderry to F. C. Spenser-Davison, 14 November 1938 (D/3099/2/19/171); Londonderry to S. S. G. Parker, 29 December 1938 (D/3099/2/19/210)).

80 See N. J. Crowson, 'The British Conservative party and the Jews during the late 1930s', *Patterns of Prejudice*, 29, nos. 2 and 3 (1995), pp. 15–32; see also Annabel Goldsmith, *Annabel: An Unconventional Life* (London, 2004), p. 13.

81 Hobsbawm, *Age of Extremes*, p. 27.

82 Geoffrey Saviour to Londonderry, 18 January 1938 (D/3099/2/19/50); Londonderry to Hitler, 5 April 1938 (D/3099/2/19/73).

83 Londonderry to Ribbentrop, 17 February 1938 (D/3099/2/19/56); *Hansard 5 (Lords)*, 107, 901–6 (24 February 1938).

84 Londonderry to Countess de la Feld, 23 March 1938 (D/3099/2/19/70).

85 *Hansard 5 (Lords)*, 108, 139–44 (16 March 1938).

86 Londonderry to Ludwig Noe, 3 May 1938 (D/3099/2/21/A/42).

87 Lady Londonderry to Ribbentrop, 19 March 1938 (D/3099/3/35/33); Göring to Lady Londonderry, 22 March 1938 (D/3099/3/35/34B). The Londonderrys sheltered the Austrian refugee Baron Frankenstien (*The Daily Express*, 27 July 1938).

88 Londonderry to Hitler, 5 April 1938 (D/3099/2/19/73).

89 Hitler to Londonderry, 10 April 1938 (D/3099/2/19/77); Londonderry to Göring, 18 July 1938 (D/3099/2/19/115).

90 Londonderry to Beaverbrook, 24 May 1938 (HLRO, BBK/C/224); Beaverbrook to Londonderry, 26 May 1938 (ibid.).

91 Londonderry to Beaverbrook, 31 May 1938 (ibid.).

92 *The Daily Express*, 27 July 1938; Londonderry to Beaverbrook, 30 July 1938 (HLRO, BBK/C/224); Beaverbrook to Londonderry, 2 September 1938 (ibid.).

93 Oberführer Görnnert to Londonderry, 15 June 1938 (D/3099/2/19/95).

94 Londonderry to Kingsley Wood, 21 June 1938 (PRO, AIR/19/28).

95 Harvey, diary, 14 June 1938 (Harvey, *Diplomatic Diaries*, p. 153).

96 Londonderry to Halifax, 28 June 1938 (D/3099/2/18/38B).

97 Londonderry to Halifax, 20 July 1938 (D/3099/2/18/39).

98 Londonderry to Horace Wilson, 17 September 1938 (D/3099/2/19/124).

99 Churchill to Londonderry, 5 November 1938 (D/3099/2/5/33B).

100 *The Times*, 3, 7 October 1938.

101 Londonderry, *Wings of Destiny*, pp. 208–9.

102 *The Times*, 11 October 1938.

103 *The Times*, 12 October 1938.

104 Londonderry to Viscount Powerscourt, 26 October 1938 (D/3099/2/21/A/107); Londonderry to Churchill, 14 November 1938 (D/3099/2/5/37A).

105 Londonderry to Göring, 24 November 1938 (D/3099/2/19/184A).

106 *Hansard 5 (Lords)*, 111, 232–40 (30 November 1938); *The Times*, 14 December 1938; Londonderry to Marjorie D. Brooks, 14 December 1938 (D/3099/2/19/202).

107 Londonderry was later asked to join the Friends of National Spain but there is no evidence that he did (Lord Phillimore to Londonderry, 17 January 1938 (D/3099/2/19/49). The Londonderrys were close friends with the deposed King Alfonso XIII of Spain.

108 *The Times*, 13 March 1939.

109 Londonderry to Sven Hedin, 20 March 1939 (D/3099/2/21/A/191).

110 *The Times*, 20 April 1939.

111 Londonderry to Ward Price, 28 March 1939 (D/3099/2/19/271).

112 Londonderry to Göring, 23 May 1939 (D/3099/2/19/297).

113 Londonderry to Papen, 9 June 1939 (D/3099/2/19/306A).

114 Londonderry to Halifax, 12 June 1939 (D/3099/2/18/41A).

115 Londonderry to German ambassador, 17 June 1939 (D/3099/2/19/310); German ambassador to Londonderry, 21 June 1939 (D/3099/2/19/315).

116 *The Times*, 22 June 1939.

117 Conwell-Evans to Londonderry, 21 June 1939 (D/3099/2/19/316).

118 Londonderry to Halifax, 10 July 1939 (D/3099/2/18/43).

119 *The Times*, 22 June 1939; Londonderry to Halifax, 4 July 1939 (D/3099/2/18/42); Halifax to Londonderry, 11 July 1939 (D/3099/2/18/44).

120 Londonderry, *Wings of Destiny*, p. 224; Londonderry to Dr Silex, 29 July 1939 (D/3099/2/19/328); Londonderry to Count Deym, 13 July 1939 (D/3099/2/19/326). Winterton does not mention in his memoirs advising Londonderry to take such a course (Earl Winterton, *Orders of the Day* (London, 1953)).

121 Londonderry to Halifax, 2 August 1939 (D/3099/2/18/46).

122 Halifax to Londonderry, 2 August 1939 (D/3099/2/18/47).

123 Londonderry to Halifax, 12 August 1939 (D/3099/2/18/50); Halifax to Londonderry, 23 August 1939 (D/3099/2/18/51).

124 *The Times*, 16 August 1939.

125 Hailsham to Londonderry, 29 August 1939 (D/3099/2/17/52A); Londonderry to Chamberlain, 19 September 1939 (D/3099/2/17/53).

126 Chamberlain to Londonderry, 27 September 1939 (D/3099/2/17/54A); Edward Bridges to Chamberlain, 2 October 1939 (PRO, CAB/21/2676).

127 Londonderry to Chamberlain, 1 October 1939 (D/3099/4/52).

128 Sarkisyanz, *Hitler's English Inspirers*, p. 257.

129 *The Times*, 16 August, 20 September 1939.

130 Londonderry to Halifax, 25 December 1939 (D/3099/2/18/54). This included a concern that lord lieutenants were not being utilized (Londonderry to Halifax, 25 December 1939 (D/3099/2/18/54)).

131 Sir William Goode (secretary of A.-H. Society) to Londonderry, 6 December 1938 (D/3099/2/20/6); Goode to Londonderry, 13 December 1939 (D/3099/2/20/9); Londonderry to Goode, 27 August 1940 (D/3099/2/20/17).

132 See Peter Hadfield, *Hess: The Führer's Disciple* (rep. edn., London, 2001), p. 150.

133 *The Times*, 14 October 1939, 24 April 1940.

134 Londonderry to Wood, 21 October 1939 (PRO, AIR/19/27); Wood to Londonderry, 26 October 1939 (ibid.). He also asked that Trenchard be allowed a post in the RAF (Londonderry to Wood, 18 October 1939 (ibid.)).

135 *The Times*, 16 November 1939; Londonderry to Churchill, 17 November 1939 (D/3099/4/52).

136 Londonderry to Halifax, 27 November 1939 (D/3099/2/18/52); Londonderry to Halifax, 2 December 1939 (ibid.); Londonderry to Halifax, 25 December 1939 (D/3099/2/18/54).

137 Londonderry to Amery, 6 June 1936 (DCRO, D/Lo/C/237 (3)). They shared

a dislike of the 1938 Anglo-American Trade Agreement (Scott Newton, *Profits of Peace: The Political Economy of Anglo-German Appeasement* (Oxford, 1996) p. 120).

138 See Londonderry to Oliver Stanley (War Minister), 18 March 1940 (D/3099/4/56).

139 Londonderry to Swinton, 23 March 1940 (D/3099/4/56); see John Ramsden, *An Appetite for Power: A History of the Conservative Party since 1830* (London, 1999), p. 228.

140 Salisbury to Londonderry, 1 April 1940 (ibid.).

141 Larry L. Witherell, 'Lord Salisbury's 'watching committee' and the fall of Neville Chamberlain, May 1940', *English Historical Review*, cxvi, no. 469 (November 2001), p. 1149.

142 Londonderry to Salisbury, 11 April 1940 (D/3099/4/56). Londonderry was appointed Regional Commissioner and Commandant of the Air Training Corps (*The Times*, 29 April, 23 July 1942).

143 See Londonderry to Salisbury, 13 April 1940 (D/3099/4/56); Salisbury to Londonderry, 16 April 1940 (ibid.); Londonderry to Salisbury, 22 April 1940 (ibid.).

144 Londonderry to Salisbury, 11 April 1940 (ibid.); see Lady Londonderry to Swinton, 9 April 1938 (PRO, AIR/19/28).

145 Londonderry to MacDonald, 28 July 1932 (JRUL, RMD, 1/14/73); *The Irish News*, 9 August 1932; Paul Canning, *British Policy Towards Ireland, 1921–1941* (Oxford, 1985), pp. 142–3.

146 Londonderry to Prime Minister's Office, 26 October 1937 (D/3099/4/44).

147 Canning, *British Policy towards Ireland*, pp. 205–6.

148 Londonderry to Chamberlain, 21 January 1939 (D/3099/4/50); Chamberlain to Londonderry, 31 January 1939 (ibid.). Perhaps to reward Londonderry, Craigavon appointed him to a trade mission to North America (*The Times*, 8 July 1939).

149 *The Belfast News-Letter*, 10 July 1933; Gillian McIntosh, *The Force of Culture: Unionist Identities in Twentieth-Century Ireland* (Cork, 1999), p. 46.

150 Londonderry to Richard Dawson Bates, 8 September 1939 (D/3099/4/52); Bates to Londonderry, 13 September 1939 (ibid.); Brooke to Londonderry, 11 June 1940 (D/3099/4/57); see Brian Barton, *Brookeborough: The Making of a Prime Minister* (Belfast, 1988), pp. 158–9.

151 Londonderry to Wood, 12 July 1939 (PRO, AIR/19/27).

152 Londonderry to Eden, 16 May 1940 (D/3099/4/57); Eden to Londonderry, 21 May 1940 (ibid.).

153 Londonderry to Eden, 23 May 1940 (ibid.); Eden to Londonderry, 30 May 1940 (D/3099/4/50).

154 Londonderry to Eden, 11 June 1940 (D/3099/4/57). Londonderry wrote Craigavon's obituary notice (Lady Desborough to Londonderry, 29 November 1940 (D/3099/2/6/35)).

155 Londonderry to Churchill, 21 June 1940 (D/3099/4/57); Churchill to

Londonderry, 22 June 1940 (ibid.).

156 Salisbury to Londonderry, 8 July 1940 (ibid.). For Londonderry's more constructive criticism see *The Times*, 12 June 1940.

157 Londonderry to Salisbury, 19 July 1940 (D/3099/4/57).

158 See Lady Desborough to Londonderry, 30 June 1940 (D/3099/2/6/31); Eden to Londonderry, 14 August 1940 (D/3099/4/57). Chips Channon recorded in his diary that a celebratory service in St Paul's Cathedral on 19 May 1943 had to be moved from noon to six o'clock when Londonderry's butler telegraphed him the details from Mount Stewart. The censor had intercepted it and the authorities took the precaution of changing the time in case the Luftwaffe would target a building full of 'all the notabilities of England' (Channon, diary, 19 May 1943 (James, *Chips*, pp. 258–9)).

159 Wood to Londonderry, 7 December 1939 (PRO, AIR/19/27); Londonderry to Wood, 19 December 1937 (ibid.); Air Ministry to Londonderry, 11 May 1938 (ibid., AIR/19/28); Wood to Londonderry, 13 July 1938 (ibid.); Wood to Londonderry, 3 August 1938 (ibid.); Londonderry to Wood, 12 January 1939 (PRO, AIR/19/27). His appointment was renewed in 1939 (Wood to Londonderry, 4 August 1939 (ibid.)). Also appointed an Honorary Air Commodore (Air ministry to Londonderry, 2 August 1938 (PRO, AIR/19/28)).

160 Londonderry to Wood, 18 April 1939 (ibid., AIR/19/27); Wood to Londonderry, 24 April 1939 (ibid.); Londonderry to Sir Edward Campbell MP, 19 April 1939 (ibid.).

161 Londonderry to Wood, 20 August 1938 (PRO, AIR/19/28). Wood to Londonderry, 24 August 1939 (ibid.); Londonderry to Wood, 21 September 1939 (ibid.). Nor was Londonderry allowed to stop 'airliners' as he was once allowed to (Londonderry to Wood, 10 July 1939 (ibid.)).

162 Guy Warner, 'Civil aviation in Ulster - a brief survey', *Due North*, 1, no. 4 (Autumn/Winter, 2001) p. 18.

163 See Londonderry to Beaverbrook, 13 February 1942 (D/3099/4/64); Londonderry to Beaverbrook, 25 September 1943 (HLRO, BBK/D/139); Londonderry to Beaverbrook, 11 October 1943 (ibid.).

164 Londonderry to Beaverbrook, 3 December 1943 (ibid.); Beaverbrook to Londonderry, 24 January 1944 (ibid.); Beaverbrook to Londonderry, 31 March 1944 (ibid.). There is a file of documents among the Beaverbrook papers solely concerned with Londonderry and the Civil Aviation bill, May 1944 (HLRO, BBK/F/160).

165 When Beaverbrook left the job at the end of the year Londonderry commented that he would never take on the job because Churchill 'destroyed' him adding that he was too old (Londonderry to Beaverbrook, 13 October 1944 (ibid., BBK/D/139)).

166 See Londonderry to Sir Walford Selby, 7 July 1945 (D/3099/2/22/74).

167 Lynn to Londonderry, 15 March 1941 (D/3099/8/1).

261

168 Hyde, *Londonderrys*, p. 256.

169 Memorandum, n.d. [1941] (D/3099/2/21/A/277).

170 Londonderry to Hyde, 9 October 1938 (D/3099/2/21/A/85). Kershaw argues that Londonderry was not helped by Hyde and repeats the view of Sir Edward Bridges that it was written by a Fleet Street 'ghost' (Kershaw, *Making Friends with Hitler*, p. 448).

171 Londonderry to Beaverbrook, 26 June 1941 (HLRO, BBK/C/224); Londonderry to Sir Rupert Howarth, 5 July 1941 (PRO, CAB/21/2676).

172 Rather than approach the government directly, Londonderry preferred to rest his hopes on aristocratic influence by sending the first draft to the Prime Minister's wife (Londonderry to Clementine Churchill, 1 January 1942 (ibid., PREM/4/6/12)). Churchill's close associate Brendan Bracken warned Londonderry that the book was written in a bad temper (Bracken to Londonderry, 5 June 1942 (ibid., CAB/21/2677)). The senior civil servant Edward Bridges urged Churchill to prevent publication and the King object-ed to four passages (Bridges, memorandum for Churchill, 6 June 1942 (ibid., PREM/4/6/12); Sir Alexander Hardinge to Bridges, 1 June 1942 (ibid., CAB/21/2677)). See also David Reynolds, *In Command of History: Churchill Fighting and Writing the Second World War* (London, 2004), pp. 30–1.

173 Churchill to Bridges, 16 June 1942 (PRO, PREM/4/6/12).

174 Lord privy seal, memorandum, 14 November 1942 (ibid., PREM/4/6/12); Bridges to Londonderry, 19 November 1942 (ibid., CAB/21/2678).

175 Halifax to Londonderry, 12 December 1942 (D/3099/2/18/56).

176 *The Times*, 20 August 1941, 26 March 1942. In the aftermath of Maureen's death, her father-in-law, Lord Derby, wrote to Londonderry complaining that Churchill's position as head of the Conservatives would damage hopes of an election victory after the war (Derby to Londonderry, 18 August 1942 (Liverpool Record Office, 920/DER (17) 33)).

177 *The Times*, 27 February 1942.

178 Channon, diary, 4 December 1943 (James, *Chips*, p. 381).

179 Londonderry to Lady Desborough, n.d. [1943] (PRONI, T/3201/54).

180 *The Times*, 23 November 1945; Londonderry to Selby, 27 November 1945 (D/3099/2/22/84).

181 *The Times*, 23, 29 November 1945, 28 February 1946; Telford Taylor, *The Anatomy of the Nuremberg Trials: A Personal Memoir* (London, 1993), pp. 320, 351–3.

Conclusion

1 Harold Nicolson, diary, 8 May 1945 (Nigel Nicolson (ed.), *Harold Nicolson Diaries and Letters, 1939–45* (London, 1967), pp. 458–9).

2 Despite his difficulties with Baldwin Londonderry acted as his sponsor when the former was introduced to the House of Lords in 1937. Baldwin's son claimed that Londonderry and his father made-up when Londonderry was in

hospital 'not very long before the death of both of them' (A. W. Baldwin, *My Father: The True Story* (London, 1955), p. 324).

3 Londonderry to Lady Desborough, n.d. [1943] (PRONI, T/3201/54).

4 Londonderry to Selby, 19 February 1946 (PRONI, Londonderry papers hereafter cited as D/3099, D/3099/2/22/95).

5 Londonderry to Bridges, 11 March 1946 (PRO, CAB/21/2678).

6 Bridges to P. J. Dixon (Foreign Office), 14 March 1946 (ibid.); Bridges to Sir Thomas Barnes (Treasury Solicitor), 17 April 1946 (PRO, TS/27/529).

7 Londonderry to Dr Pick, 24 April 1946 (D/3099/2/21/A/253); Bridges to Londonderry, 29 April 1946 (PRO, CAB/21/2678); Londonderry to Bridges, 6 May 1946 (ibid.).

8 R. C. Chilver to E. A. Armstrong, 8 February 1947 (ibid.); Bridges to Chilver, 13 February 1947 (ibid.).

9 Baxter to Londonderry, 28 February 1947 (D/3099/2/21/A/260). This was confirmed by the Committee on the use of Official Information in Private Publications, April 1947 (PRO, CAB/21/2678).

10 Londonderry to Baxter, 7 March 1947 (D/3099/2/21/A/261).

11 Londonderry to Commander W. S. Mann (Northern Ireland Governor's Office), 1 May 1947 (D/3099/2/21/A/268).

12 Mount Stewart and Wynyard were retained by the family. Two properties at Seaham Harbour remained as hospitals after the war. Following the war the Royal Aero Club used Londonderry House as its headquarters rent free. The Welsh estate of Plâs Machynlleth was given after the war to the local people (H. Montgomery Hyde, *The Londonderrys: A Family Portrait* (London, 1979), pp. 258–61). The present Lord Londonderry lives in England and has avoided politics (Graham Turner, 'The stronghold of labour', in Martin Bulmer (ed.), *Mining and Social Change: Durham in the Twentieth Century* (London, 1978), p. 125).

13 *The Times*, 28 January 1946.

14 Londonderry to Desborough, 21 September 1947 (PRONI, T/3201/55). For a similar view about Churchill see Sebastian Haffner, *Churchill: Life and Times* (London, 2003).

15 *The Times*, 12 February 1949.

16 *The Times*, 17, 18 February 1949. Viscount Swinton commented on Londonderry's youthful qualities when he paid a tribute to him in the House of Lords, (ibid., 16 February 1949).

17 Ibid., 12 February 1949.

18 Ibid., 17 February 1949.

19 Kennedy, diary, 16 December 1938 (Gordon Martel, *The Times and Appeasement: The Journals of A. L. Kennedy, 1932–1939* (Cambridge, 2000), p. 282).

20 Ibid.; Headlam, diary, 1 July 1938 (Stuart Ball (ed.), *Parliament and Politics in the Age of Churchill and Attlee: The Headlam Diaries 1935–1951* (Cambridge, 1999), p. 132).

21 Ibid., 7 February 1939 (ibid., p. 285).

22 David Cannadine, *The Decline and Fall of the British Aristocracy* (rev. edn., London, 1992), p. 217.

23 Headlam, diary, 11 February 1939 (Ball, *Politics in the Age of Churchill and Attlee*, p. 573).

24 Channon, diary, 11 February 1949 (Robert Rhodes James (ed.), *'Chips': The Diaries of Sir Henry Channon* (rep. edn., London, 1999), p. 434).

25 Robert Boothby, *I Fight to Live* (London, 1947), p. 140.

26 Channon, diary, 17 February 1949 (ibid.).

27 Tom Paulin, *The Invasion Handbook* (London, 2002), pp. 62–3.

Bibliography

Primary Sources

1. Personal papers

Cambridge University Library (CUL)
Baldwin papers (Baldwin)

Churchill College Archives Centre, Cambridge
Churchill (Chartwell trust) papers (copies at PRONI, D/3084/C/C/3)

Durham County Record Office (DCRO)
Londonderry papers (D/Lo)

Hertfordshire County Record Office
Lady Desborough papers (copies at PRONI, T/3201)

House of Lords Record Office, London (HLRO)
Beaverbrook papers (BBK)
R.D. Blumenfeld papers (Blu/Lon)
Bonar Law papers (BL)
J.C.C. Davidson papers (DAV/191)
Lloyd George papers (LG/F)
J. St L. Strachey papers (STR)

John Rylands University Library, Manchester (JRUL)
Ramsay MacDonald papers (RMD/1)

Liverpool Record Office and Local History Department
Derby papers (920/DER)

Public Record Office of Northern Ireland (PRONI)
Carson papers (D/1507)
Craigavon papers (T/3775)
H.M. Hyde papers (D/3084)
Londonderry papers (D/3099)
R.J. Lynn papers (D/3480)

2. State and Institutional Records

National Archive, Kew (PRO)
Cabinet Office papers (CAB)
Domestic papers of Public Record Office (PRO)
Foreign Office papers (FO)
Home Office papers (HO)
Lord Chancellor's Office papers (LCO)
Ministry of Air and Royal Air Force papers (AIR)
Ministry of Housing and Local Government papers (HLG)
Ministry of Munitions papers (MUN)
Pre-Nationalization Railway Company papers (RAIL)
Treasury Solicitor and HM Procurator General's Department papers (TS)

Public Record Office of Northern Ireland (PRONI)
Cabinet (Northern Ireland) papers (CAB)
Ministry of Education (Northern Ireland) papers (ED)
Ulster Unionist Council papers (D/1327)

Trinity College Library, University of Dublin
Irish Convention papers

3. Newspapers and journals

Aeroplane
The Belfast News-Letter
The Colliery Guardian
The Daily Express
The Daily Mail
The Evening Standard
The Guardian
The Irish News
The Irish Independent
The Kent Times
The Lamp
Llandudno and North Wales Weekly News
The Morning Post
The New Statesman and Nation
News Chronicle
Nineteenth Century and After
The Northampton Mercury
The Rotherham Advertiser

The Spectator
The South Eastern Gazette
The Standard
The Sunday Chronicle
The Sunday Express
The Sunderland Echo
Surrey Herald
Teachers' World
The Times
T.P.'s & Cassell's Weekly
The Tribune
The Westminster Gazette
The World

4. Published autobiographies, letters, and diaries

Ball, Stuart (ed.), *Parliament and Politics in the Age of Baldwin and MacDonald: The Headlam Diaries 1923–1935* (London, 1992).

—— (ed.), *Parliament and Politics in the Age of Churchill and Attlee: The Headlam Diaries 1935–1951* (Cambridge, 1999).

Boothby, Robert, *I Fight to Live* (London, 1947).

Buckland, Patrick (ed.), *Irish Unionism 1885–1923: A Documentary History* (Belfast, 1973).

Buckmaster, Herbert, *Buck's Book: Ventures-Adventures and Misadventures* (London, 1933).

Bullock, Alan (ed.), *The Ribbentrop Memoirs* (London, 1954).

Callwell, C. E. (ed.), *Field Marshal Sir Henry Wilson: His Life and Diaries* (London, 1927).

Cole, Margaret (ed.), *Beatrice Webb's Diaries 1924–1932* (London, 1956).

Harvey, John (ed.), *The Diplomatic Diaries of Oliver Harvey 1937–1940* (London, 1970).

Goldsmith, Annabel, *Annabel, An Unconventional Life: The Memoirs of Lady Annabel Goldsmith* (London, 2004).

James, Robert Rhodes (ed.), *'Chips': The Diaries of Sir Henry Channon* (London, 1967).

—— (ed.), *Memoirs of a Conservative: J.C.C. Davidson's Memoirs and Papers, 1910–37* (London, 1969).

Liddell Hart, B. H., *Memoirs* (2 vols, London, 1965), vol. 1.

Lloyd George, David, *War Memoirs of David Lloyd George, vol. 2* (2 vols, London, 1938).

Londonderry, Marchioness of, *Retrospect* (London, 1938).

Londonderry, Marquess of, 'In the days of my youth', *T.P.'s & Cassell's Weekly*, 21 March 1925.

—— *Wings of Destiny* (London, 1943).

MacKenzie, Norman (ed.), *The Letters of Sidney and Beatrice Webb: vol. 3: Pilgrimage, 1912–1947* (3 vols, Cambridge, 1978).

Martel, Gordon (ed.), *The Times and Appeasement: The Journals of A.L. Kennedy, 1932–1939* (Cambridge, 2000).

Middlemas, Keith (ed.), *Thomas Jones Whitehall Diary, vol. 2: 1926–1930* (3 vols, London, 1969).

—— (ed.), *Thomas Jones Whitehall Diary, vol. 3: Ireland, 1918–1925* (London, 1971).

Midleton, Earl of, *Records and Reactions 1856–1939* (New York, 1939).

Nicolson, Nigel (ed.), *Harold Nicolson: Diaries and Letters 1930–1939* (London, 1966).

—— (ed.), *Harold Nicolson: Diaries and Letters 1939–45* (London, 1967).

Ó Bróin, Leon (ed.), *In Great Haste: The Letters of Michael Collins and Kitty Kiernan* (Dublin, 1996).

Petrie, Charles (ed.), *The Life and Letters of the Right Hon. Sir Austin Chamberlain K.G., P.C., M.P.* (London, 1939).

Pimlott, Ben (ed.), *The Political Diary of Hugh Dalton: 1918–40, 1945–60* (London, 1986).

Rothermere, Viscount, *My Fight to Rearm Britain* (London, 1939).

Self, Robert C. (ed.), *The Austen Chamberlain Diary Letters: The Correspondence of Sir Austen Chamberlain with his Sisters Hilda and Ida, 1916–1937* (Cambridge, 1995).

Simon, Viscount, *Retrospect: The Memoirs of the Rt. Hon. Viscount Simon G.C.S.I., G.C.V.O.* (London, 1952).

Smart, Nick (ed.), *The Diaries and Letters of Robert Bernays, 1932–1939: An Insider's Account of the House of Commons* (Lampeter, 1996).

Snowden, Viscount, *An Autobiography, vol. 2: 1919–1934* (2 vols, London, 1934).

Swinton, Viscount, *I Remember* (London, 1948).

Taylor, A. J. P. (ed.), *W. P. Crozier: Off the Record: Political Interviews, 1933–1943* (London, 1973).

Vansittart, Robert, *The Mist Procession: The Autobiography of Lord Vansittart* (London, 1958).

Williamson, Philip and Edward Baldwin, *Baldwin Papers: A Conservative Statesman, 1908–1947* (Cambridge, 2005).

Winterton, Earl, *Orders of the Day* (London, 1953).

5. Contemporary works and works by contemporaries

Baldwin, A. W., *My Father: The True Story* (London, 1955).

Balfour, Patrick, *Society Racket: A Critical Survey of Modern Social Life* (London, 1933).

Cato, *Guilty men* (rep. edn., London, 1998).

Churchill, Winston S., *The Second World War, vol. 1, The Gathering Storm* (rep. edn., 6 vols, London, 1949).

Colvin, Ian, *The Life of Lord Carson* (3 vols, London, 1934), vol. 2.

Kennedy, John F., *Why England Slept* (New York, 1940).

Londonderry, Marchioness of, *Henry Chaplin: A Memoir* (London, 1926).

—— *Character and Tradition* (London, 1934).

—— *Mount Stewart* (privately printed, 1956).

—— *Frances Anne. The Life and Times of Frances Anne, Marchioness of Londonderry and her Husband Charles, Third Marquess of Londonderry* (London, 1958).

Londonderry, Marquess of, *Ourselves and Germany* (London, 1938).

—— 'The Irish problem, 1922', *Nineteenth Century and After*, xcii (December 1922).

—— 'Bombing from the air', *Nineteenth Century and After*, cxxv (March 1939).

McNeill, Ronald, *Ulster's Stand for the Union* (London, 1922).

Marjoribanks, Edward, *The Life of Lord Carson* (3 vols, 3rd edn., London, 1932), vol. 1.

Muggeridge, Malcolm, *The Thirties, 1930–1940 in Great Britain* (London, 1940).

Nicolson, Harold, *George V: His Life and Reign* (London, 1952).

Oxford, Margot, *More Memories* (London, 1933).

Taylor, Telford, *The Anatomy of the Nuremberg Trials: A Personal Memoir* (London, 1993).

Townsend, Peter, *Duel of the Skies: The Struggle for the Skies from the First World War to the Battle of Britain* (rep. edn., London, 2000).

Ulster Unionist Council, *The Ulster Unionist Demonstration of 1912: In Royal Agricultural Show Grounds, Balmoral, Belfast* (Belfast, 1912).

6. Literature and fiction

Ishiguro, Kazuo, *The Remains of the Day* (London, 1989).

Paulin, Tom, *The Invasion Handbook* (London, 2002).

Sackville-West, Vita, *The Edwardians* (London, 1930).

Spring, Howard, *Fame is the Spur* (London, 1940).

Waugh, Evelyn, *Vile Bodies* (London, 1930).

7. Reference works

Butler, David and Gareth Butler, *Twentieth-Century British Political Facts, 1900–2000* (London, 2000).

Cahill, Kevin, *Who Owns Britain: The Hidden Facts behind Landownership in the UK and Ireland* (London, 2001).

Fleming, N. C., and Alan O'Day, *The Longman Handbook to Modern Irish History since 1800* (London, 2005).

Moody, T. W., F. X. Martin, F. J. Byrne (ed.), *A New History of Ireland: A Chronology of Irish History to 1976: A Companion to Irish History Part 1* (Oxford, 1982).

Walker, Brian M., *Parliamentary Election Results in Ireland, 1918–92* (Dublin and Belfast, 1992).

8. Official Papers

Coal Industry Commission: Report and Minutes of Evidence, vol. 2 (Cmd. 360), P.P. (1919), XII

Parliamentary Debates, House of Commons (Hansard), series 4 and 5.

Parliamentary Debates, House of Lords, (Hansard), series 5.

Parliamentary Debates, Northern Ireland House of Commons, (Hansard), series 1.

Parliamentary Debates, Northern Ireland Senate, (Hansard), series 1.

Plunkett, H. C., *The Irish Convention: Confidential Report to His Majesty the King by the Chairman* (Dublin, 1918).

—— *Report of the Proceedings of the Irish Convention* (Dublin, 1918).

Secondary Sources

9. Articles, biographies, and monographs

Adams, R. J. Q., *Bonar Law* (London, 1999).

Adonis, Andrew, *Making Aristocracy Work: The Peerage and the Political System in Britain, 1884–1914* (rep. edn., Oxford, 2002).

Akenson, D. H., *Education and Enmity: The Control of Schooling in Northern Ireland, 1920–50* (London, 1973).

Allen, Nicholas, 'National Reconstruction: George Russell (Æ) and the Irish Convention', in D. George Boyce and Alan O'Day (eds), *Ireland in Transition, 1867–1921* (London, 2004).

Aristotle, *The Politics* (trans. T.A. Sinclair) (rep. edn., London, 1992).

Balfour-Paul, Glen, 'Britain's informal empire in the Middle East', in Judith M. Brown and Wm. Roger Louis (eds), *The Oxford History of the British Empire, vol. 4 : The Twentieth Century* (5 vols, Oxford, 1999).

Ball, Stuart, 'The national and regional party structure', in Anthony Seldon and Stuart Ball (eds.), *Conservative Century: The Conservative Party Since 1900* (Oxford, 1994).

—— *The Conservative Party and British Politics, 1902–1951* (London, 1995).

Barnett, Correlli, *The Collapse of British Power* (London, 1972).

Barton, Brian, *Brookeborough: The Making of a Prime Minister* (Belfast, 1988).

Bassett, R., *Democracy and Foreign Policy, A Case History: The Sino-Japanese dispute, 1931–33* (London, 1952).

—— *Nineteen Thirty-One: Political Crisis* (London, 1958).

Beckett, J. V., *The Aristocracy in England, 1660–1914* (Oxford, 1988).

Bennett, G. H., *British Foreign Policy during the Curzon Period, 1919–24* (New York, 1995).

Benyon, Huw, and Terry Austrin, *Masters and Servants, Class Patronage in the Making of a Labour Organisation: The Durham Miners and the English Political Tradition* (London, 1994).

Bew, Paul, *Ideology and the Irish Question: Ulster Unionism and Irish Nationalism, 1912–1916* (Oxford, 1998).

——, Peter Gibbon and Henry Patterson, *Northern Ireland 1921/2001: Political Forces and Social Classes* (London, 2002).

Bialer, Uri, *The Shadow of the Bomber: The Fear of Air Attack and British Policies, 1932–1939* (London, 1980).

Blewett, Neal, *The Peers, the Parties and the People: The General Elections of 1910* (London, 1972).

Bond, Brian, *British Military Policy Between the Two World Wars* (Oxford, 1980).

Boyce, D. George, 'British conservative opinion, the Ulster question, and the partition of Ireland, 1912–21', *Irish Historical Studies*, xvii, no. 65 (March 1970).

—— *Nineteenth-century Ireland: The Search for Stability* (Dublin, 1990).

Brendon, Piers, *The Dark Valley: A Panorama of the 1930s* (London, 2000).

Bryan, Dominic, *Orange Parades: The Politics of Ritual, Tradition and Control* (London, 2000).

Buckland, Patrick, *Irish Unionism: One: The Anglo-Irish and the New Ireland 1885–1922* (Dublin, 1972).

—— *Irish Unionism: Two: Ulster Unionism and the Origins of Northern Ireland 1886–1922* (Dublin, 1973).

—— *The Factory of Grievances: Devolved Government in Northern Ireland 1921–39* (Dublin, 1979).

Burk, Kathleen, 'The Treasury: from impotence to power', in Kathleen Burk (ed.), *War and the State: The Transformation of Government, 1914–1919* (London, 1982).

Burleigh, Michael, *The Third Reich: A New History* (London, 2000).

Campbell, John, *F. E. Smith, First Earl of Birkenhead* (London, 1983).

Cannadine, David, *Aspects of Aristocracy: Grandeur and Decline in Modern Britain* (London, 1994).

—— *The Decline and Fall of the British Aristocracy* (rev. edn., London, 1996).

Canning, Paul, *British Policy Towards Ireland 1921–1941* (Oxford, 1985).

Carlton, David, *Anthony Eden: A Biography* (London, 1981).

Ceadel, Martin, *Pacifism in Britain 1914–1945: The Defining of a Faith* (Oxford, 1980).

Chilston, Viscount, *Chief Whip: The Political Life and Times of Aretas Akers-Douglas, 1st Viscount Chilston* (London, 1961).

Clark, Ronald W., *Tizard* (London, 1965).

Clayton, Anthony, 'Imperial defence and security, 1900–1968', in Judith M. Brown and Wm. Roger Louis (eds), *The Oxford History of the British Empire, vol. 4: The Twentieth Century* (5 vols, Oxford, 1999).

Colley, Linda, *Britons: Forging the Nation, 1707–1837* (London, 1992).

Cook, Chris, *The Age of Alignment: Electoral Politics in Britain, 1922–1929* (London, 1975).

Cowling, Maurice, *The Impact of Labour 1920–40: The Beginning of Modern British Politics* (Cambridge, 1971).

—— *The Impact of Hitler: British Politics and British Policy, 1933–1940* (Cambridge, 1975).

Craig, F. W. S., *British General Election Manifestos, 1900–1974* (rev. edn., London, 1975).

Craig, Gordon A., *The Politics of the Prussian Army, 1640–1945* (New York, 1964).

Crowson, N. J., 'The British conservative party and the Jews during the late 1930s', *Patterns of Prejudice*, 29, nos. 2 and 3 (1995).

—— *Facing Fascism: The Conservative Party and the European Dictators, 1935–1940* (London, 1997).

Dangerfield, George, *The Strange Death of Liberal England* (rep. edn., London, 1966).

De Courcy, Anne, *Circe: The Life of Edith, Marchioness of Londonderry* (London, 1993).

Dilks, David, '"The unnecessary war"? Military advice and foreign policy in Great Britain, 1931–1939', in Adrian Preston (ed.), *General Staffs and Diplomacy before the Second World War* (London, 1978).

Doerr, Paul W., *British Foreign Policy 1919–1939: 'Hope for the Best, Prepare for the Worst'* (Manchester, 1998).

Dugdale, Blanche E. C., *Arthur James Balfour, First Earl of Balfour, K.G., O.M., F.R.S., etc.* (2 vols, London, 1936), vol. 1.

Dutton, David, *Austen Chamberlain: Gentleman in Politics* (Bolton, 1985).

—— *'His Majesty's Loyal Opposition': The Unionist Party in Opposition, 1905–1915* (Liverpool, 1992).

Ervine, St John, *Craigavon: Ulsterman* (London, 1949).

Evans, Stephen, 'The conservatives and the redefinition of unionism, 1912–21', *Twentieth Century British History*, 9, no. 1 (1998).

Fair, John D., *British Interparty Conferences: A Study of the Procedure of Conciliation in British Politics, 1867–1921* (Oxford, 1980).

Farrell, Michael, *Northern Ireland: The Orange State* (rep. edn., London, 1992).

Farren, Sean, *The Politics of Irish Education, 1920–65* (Belfast, 1995).

Ferris, John Robert, *Men, Money, and Diplomacy: The Evolution of British Strategic Policy, 1919–26* (New York, 1989).

Fitzpatrick, David, 'Militarism in Ireland, 1900–1922', in Thomas Bartlett and Keith Jeffery (eds), *A Military History of Ireland* (Cambridge, 1996).

Fleming, N. C., 'Lord Londonderry and education reform in 1920s Northern Ireland', *History Ireland*, 9, no. 1 (Spring, 2001).

—— 'New Ireland, same old heroes', *Fortnight*, no. 405 (June 2002).

—— 'The Marquess of Londonderry: a political life', Ph.D. thesis (The Queen's University of Belfast, 2002).

—— 'Lord Londonderry and Ulster politics, 1921–6', in J. Augusteijn, M. A. Lyons and D. McMahon (eds), *Irish History: A Research Yearbook, no. 2* (Dublin, 2003).

—— 'Old and new unionism: The seventh Marquess of Londonderry,

1905–1921', in D. George Boyce and Alan O'Day (eds), *Ireland in Transition, 1867–1921* (London, 2004).

——'The landed elite, power and Ulster unionism', in D. George Boyce and Alan O'Day (eds), *The Ulster Crisis* (London, 2005).

Follis, Brian, *A State Under Siege: The Establishment of Northern Ireland, 1920–1925* (Oxford, 1995).

Foster, R. F., *Paddy and Mr Punch: Connections in Irish and English History* (rep. edn., London, 1995).

Fussell, Paul, *The Great War and Modern Memory* (London, 1977).

Gailey, Andrew, 'King Carson: an essay on the invention of leadership', *Irish Historical Studies*, xxx, no. 117 (May 1996).

—— 'The destructiveness of constructive unionism: theories and practice, 1890s–1960s', in D. George Boyce and Alan O'Day (eds), *Defenders of the Union: A Survey of British and Irish Unionism since 1801* (London, 2001).

Garside, W. R., *The Durham Miners, 1919–1960* (London, 1971).

Gilbert, Martin, and Richard Gott, *The Appeasers* (rep. edn., London, 2000).

Gilmour, David, *Curzon* (London, 1994).

Green, E. H. H., *The Crisis of Conservatism: The Politics, Economics and Ideology of the British Conservative Party, 1880–1914* (London, 1995).

Green, Martin, *Children of the Sun: A Narrative of 'Decadence' in England after 1918* (rev. edn., London, 1977).

Griffiths, Richard, *Fellow Travellers of the Right: British Enthusiasts for Nazi Germany, 1933–9* (London, 1980).

Grigg, John, 'Churchill and Lloyd George', in Robert Blake and Wm. Roger Louis (eds), *Churchill* (Oxford, 1996).

Hadfield, Peter, *Hess: The Führer's Disciple* (rep. edn., London, 2001).

Haffner, Sebastian, *Churchill: Life and Times* (London, 2003).

Harris, Jose, *Private Lives, Public Spirit: Britain 1870–1914* (London, 1994).

Harris, Kenneth, *Attlee* (rep. edn., London, 1995).

Harris, Mary, *The Catholic Church and the Foundation of the Northern Irish State* (Cork, 1993).

Harrison, Brian, *Separate Spheres: The Opposition to Women's Suffrage in Britain* (London, 1978).

Havighurst, Alfred F., *Britain in Transition: The Twentieth Century* (Chicago, 1979).

Hobsbawm, Eric, *Age of Extremes: The Short Twentieth Century 1914–1991* (London, 1995).

Howe, Anthony, *Free Trade and Liberal England 1846–1946* (Oxford, 1997).

Howson, Joyce, 'The general strike: a bluff which was called?', *Modern History Review*, 8, part 1 (September 1996).

Hutchinson, John, and Anthony D. Smith (eds), *Ethnicity* (Oxford, 1996).

Hyde, H. Montgomery, *Carson: The Life of Sir Edward Carson, Lord Carson of Duncairn* (London, 1953).

—— *Baldwin: The Unexpected Prime Minister* (London, 1973).

—— *British Air Policy Between the Wars, 1918–1939* (London, 1976).

—— *The Londonderrys: A Family Portrait* (London, 1979).

Jackson, Alvin, 'Unionist myths 1912–1985', *Past & Present*, no. 136 (1992).

—— 'Irish unionism, 1870–1922', in D. George Boyce and Alan O'Day (eds), *Defenders of the Union: A Survey of British and Irish Unionism since 1801* (London, 2001).

—— *Home Rule: An Irish History, 1800–2000* (London, 2003).

James, Robert Rhodes, *Churchill: A Study in Failure 1900–1939* (Harmondsworth, 1973).

—— *The British Revolution: British Politics, 1880–1939* (London, 1978).

—— *Anthony Eden* (London, 1996).

Kelly, Richard, 'The party conferences', in Anthony Seldon and Stuart Ball (eds), *Conservative Century: The Conservative Party since 1900* (Oxford, 1994).

Kendle, John, *Ireland and the Federal Solution: The Debate Over the United Kingdom Constitution, 1870–1921* (Kingston and Montreal, 1989).

Kennedy, Paul, *The Realities Behind Diplomacy: Background Influences on British External Policy, 1865–1980* (London, 1981).

Kershaw, Ian, *Hitler, 1936–45: Nemesis* (London, 2000).

—— *Making Friends with Hitler: Lord Londonderry and Britain's Road to War* (London, 2004).

King, Carla, 'Defenders of the union: Sir Horace Plunkett', in D. George Boyce and Alan O'Day (ed.), *Defenders of the Union: A Survey of British and Irish Unionism since 1801* (London, 2001).

Kirby, M. W., *The British Coalmining Industry, 1870–1946* (London, 1977).

Koss, Stephen, *Nonconformity in Modern British Politics* (London, 1975).

—— *The Rise and Fall of the Political Press in Britain* (London, 1990).

Lees-Milne, James, *Harold Nicolson: A Biography 1886–1929* (London, 1980).

Lyman, Richard W., *The First Labour Government, 1924* (London, 1957).

Lynn, Pauline, 'The impact of women. The shaping of political allegiance in County Durham, 1918–1945', *The Local Historian* (August, 1998).

Lyons, F. S. L., *Culture and Anarchy in Ireland, 1890–1939* (Oxford, 1979).

McCavery, Trevor, *Newtown: A History of Newtownards* (Belfast, 1994).

McCoole, Sinead, *Hazel: A Life of Lady Lavery 1880–1935* (Dublin, 1996).

McDowell, R. B., *Irish Convention, 1917–18* (London, 1970).

McGrath, Michael, *The Catholic Church and Catholic Schools in Northern Ireland: The Price of Faith* (Dublin, 2000).

McIntosh, Gillian, *The Force of Culture: Unionist Identities in Twentieth-Century Ireland* (Cork, 1999).

McKibbin, Ross, *The Ideologies of Class: Social Relations in Britain 1880–1950* (rep. edn., Oxford, 1991).

—— *Class and Cultures: England 1918–1951* (Oxford, 1998).

Mac Loughlin, Jim, *Reimagining the Nation-State: The Contested Terrains of Nation-Building* (London, 2001).

Malcomson, A. P. W., *The Pursuit of the Heiress: Aristocratic Marriage in Ireland, 1750–1820* (Belfast, 1982).

Mansergh, Nicholas, *The Unresolved Question: The Anglo-Irish Settlement and its Undoing 1912–72* (London, 1991).

Marquand, David, *Ramsay MacDonald* (London, 1977).

Marwick, Arthur, *The Deluge: British Society and the First World War* (rep. edn., London, 1978).

Matthews, Kevin, *Fatal Influence: The Impact of Ireland on British Politics, 1920–1925* (Dublin, 2004).

Medlicott, Norton, 'Britain and Germany: the search for agreement, 1930–37', in David Dilks (ed.), *Retreat from Power: Studies in Britain's Foreign Policy of the Twentieth Century* (London, 1981).

Michalka, Wolfgang, 'Joachim von Ribbentrop: from wine merchant to foreign minister', in Ronald Smelser and Rainer Zitelmann (eds), *The Nazi Elite* (London, 1993).

Middlemas, Keith, and John Barnes, *Baldwin: A Biography* (London, 1969).

Moody, T. W., and J. C. Beckett, *Queen's, Belfast 1845–1949: The History of a University* (2 vols, London, 1959), vol. 2.

Morgan, Austen, *Labour and Partition: The Belfast Working Class, 1905–23* (London, 1991).

Morgan, David R., *Suffragists and Liberals: The Politics of Woman Suffrage in England* (Oxford, 1975).

Morris, Margaret, *The General Strike* (Harmondsworth, 1976).

Mowat, Charles Loch, *Britain Between the Wars, 1918–1940* (rep. edn., London, 1966).

Murray, Bruce K., *The People's Budget 1909/10: Lloyd George and Liberal Politics* (Oxford, 1980).

Newton, Scott, *Profits of Peace: The Political Economy of Anglo-German Appeasement* (Oxford, 1996).

Nicholson, Colin, 'Edwardian England and the coming of the First World War', in Alan O'Day (ed.), *The Edwardian Age: Conflict and Stability 1900–1914* (London, 1979).

Nietzsche, Friedrich, *Untimely Meditations* (Cambridge, 1983).

O'Brien, Patrick, 'Is political biography a good thing', *Contemporary British History*, 10, no. 4 (winter, 1996).

O'Day, Alan, *Irish Home Rule 1867–1921* (Manchester, 1998).

O'Halpin, Eunan, *The Decline of the Union: British Government in Ireland 1892–1920* (Dublin, 1997).

Parker, R. A. C., *Chamberlain and Appeasement: British Policy and the Coming of the Second World War* (London, 1993).

Patterson, Henry, *Class Conflict and Sectarianism: The Protestant Working Class and the Belfast Labour Movement 1868–1920* (Belfast, 1980).

Pauley, J. A., 'The Social and political Roles of Edith, Marchioness of Londonderry, 1878–1959', Ph.D. thesis (University of Ulster, 1994).

Peden, G. C., *British Rearmament and the Treasury, 1932–1939* (Edinburgh, 1979).

Pelling, Henry, 'Churchill and the Labour Movement', in Robert Blake and Wm. Roger Louis (eds), *Churchill* (Oxford, 1996).

Porter, Bernard, *The Lion's Share: A Short History of British Imperialism* (3rd edn., London, 1993).

Powis, Jonathan, *Aristocracy* (Oxford, 1984).

Ramsden, John, *An Appetite for Power: A History of the Conservative Party since 1830* (London, 1999).

Rempel, Richard A., *Unionists Divided: Arthur Balfour, Joseph Chamberlain and the Unionist Free Traders* (Newton Abbot, 1972).

Reynolds, David, *Britannia Overruled: British Policy and World Power in the 20th Century* (2nd edn., London, 2000).

—— *In Command of History: Churchill Fighting and Writing the Second World War* (London, 2004).

Riddell, Neil, *Labour in Crisis: The Second Labour Government, 1929–1931* (Manchester, 1999).

Robbins, Keith, *Munich 1938* (London, 1968).

Roberts, Andrew, *'The Holy Fox': The Life of Lord Halifax* (London, 1997).

Roberts, J. M., *Europe, 1880–1945* (3rd edn., London, 2001).

Robertson, Scot, *The Development of RAF Strategic Bombing Doctrine, 1919–1939* (London, 1995).

Rubinstein, W. D., *Men of Property: The Very Wealthy in Britain Since the Industrial Revolution* (London, 1981).

Russell, A. K., *Liberal Landslide: The General Election of 1906* (Newton Abbot, 1973).

Sarkisyanz, Manuel, *Hitler's English Inspirers* (Belfast, 2003).

Shay, Robert Paul, *British Rearmament in the Thirties: Politics and Profits* (Princeton, 1977).

Smart, Nick, *The National Government, 1931–40* (London, 1999).

Stevenson, John, *British Society: 1914–45* (rep. edn., London, 1990).

Stewart, A. T. Q., *The Ulster Crisis: Resistance to Home Rule 1912–1914* (rep. edn., Belfast, 1999).

Stewart, Graham, *Burying Caesar: Churchill, Chamberlain and the Battle for the Tory Party* (London, 1999).

Supple, Barry, *The History of the British Coal Industry: vol. 4: 1913–1946: The Political Economy of Decline* (5 vols, Oxford, 1987).

Sykes, Alan, *Tariff Reform in British Politics 1903–1913* (Oxford, 1979).

Symons, Julian, *The General Strike: A Historical Portrait* (London, 1957).

Taylor, A. J. P., *Beaverbrook* (London, 1972).

—— *English History 1914–1945* (rep. edn., Oxford, 1990).

Taylor, Tony, *The Politics of Reaction: The Ideology of the Cecils and the Challenge of Secular Education, 1889–1902* (Leeds, 1997).

Thompson, F. M. L., *English Landed Society in the Nineteenth Century* (London, 1963).

—— 'Britain', in David Spring (ed.), *European Landed Elites in the Nineteenth Century* (London, 1977).

—— *Gentrification and the Enterprise Culture: Britain 1780–1980* (Oxford, 2001).

Thompson, J. Lee, *Northcliffe: Press Baron in Politics, 1865–1922* (London, 2000).

Thurlow, Richard, *Fascism in Britain: From Oswald Mosley's Blackshirts to the National Front* (London, 1998).

Todd, Jennifer, 'Unionist political thought, 1920–72', in D. George Boyce, Robert Eccleshall and Vincent Geoghegan (eds), *Political Thought in Ireland since the Seventeenth Century* (London, 1993).

Turner, Graham, 'The stronghold of labour', in Martin Bulmer (ed.), *Mining and Social Change: Durham in the Twentieth Century* (London, 1978).

Turner, John, *Lloyd George's Secretariat* (Cambridge, 1980).

—— *British Politics and the Great War: Coalition and Conflict 1915–1918* (New Haven, 1992).

Urquhart, Diane, 'Peeresses, patronage and power: The politics of ladies Frances Anne, Theresa and Edith Londonderry, 1800–1959', in Alan Hayes and Diane Urquhart (eds), *Irish Women's History* (Dublin, 2004).

Waddington, G. T., ''An Idyllic and Unruffled Atmosphere of Complete Anglo-German Misunderstanding': Aspects of the Operations of the Dienststelle Ribbentrop in Great Britain, 1934–1938', *History*, 82 (1997).

Wark, Wesley K., *The Ultimate Enemy: British Intelligence and Nazi Germany, 1933–1939* (London, 1985).

Warner, Guy, 'Civil aviation in Ulster – a brief survey', *Due North*, 1, no. 40 (Autumn/Winter, 2001).

Wasson, Ellis, *Born to Rule: British Political Elites* (London, 2000).

Weitz, John, *Hitler's Diplomat: Joachim von Ribbentrop* (London, 1997).

Williams, A. Susan, *Ladies of Influence: Women of the Elite in Interwar Britain* (London, 2000).

Williams, Gwylmor Prys, and George Thompson Brake, *Drink in Great Britain 1900–1979* (London, 1980).

Williamson, Philip, *National Crisis and National Government: British Politics, the Economy and Empire, 1926–1932* (Cambridge, 1992).

—— *Stanley Baldwin: Conservative Leadership and National Values* (Cambridge, 1999).

Witherell, Larry L., 'Lord Salisbury's 'watching committee' and the fall of Neville Chamberlain, May 1940', *English Historical Review*, cxvi, no. 469 (November 2001).

Worsthorne, Peregrine, *In Defence of Aristocracy* (London, 2004).

Zebel, Sydney H., *Balfour: A Political Biography* (Cambridge, 1973).

Zeigler, Philip, 'Churchill and the monarchy', in Robert Blake and Wm. Roger Louis (eds), *Churchill* (Oxford, 1996).

Zeman, Z. A. B., *Nazi Propaganda* (2nd edn., Oxford, 1973).

Index